ENTREPRENEURSHIP AND SME RESEARCH: ON ITS WAY TO THE NEXT MILLENNIUM

Entrepreneurship and SME Research: On its Way to the Next Millennium

Edited by
RIK DONCKELS
Small Business Research Institute, Brussels

ASKO MIETTINEN
University of Tampere

Routledge
Taylor & Francis Group

LONDON AND NEW YORK

First published 1997 by Ashgate Publishing

Reissued 2018 by Routledge
2 Park Square, Milton Park, Abingdon, Oxon, OX14 4RN
52 Vanderbilt Avenue, New York, NY 10017

Routledge is an imprint of the Taylor & Francis Group, an informa business

A Library of Congress record exists under LC control number:

ISBN 13: 978-1-138-39141-3 (hbk)
ISBN 13: 978-0-429-42272-0 (ebk)

Contents

List of Tables   vii

List of Figures   x

List of Contributors   xi

Acknowledgement   xii

Introduction: Rik Donckels and Asko Miettinen   xiii

PART I: ENTREPRENEURS AND ENTREPRENEURSHIP

1   Are Types of Business Owner-Managers Universal? A Cross Country Study of the UK,   3
    New Zealand and Finland
    Elizabeth Chell, Nina Hedberg-Jalonen and Asko Miettinen

2   How to Survive as the Small Fish in the Pond: The Case of Danish Independent Labels   19
    Per Darmer and Per V. Freytag

3   Personal Values and Identity Structures of Entrepreneurs: A Comparative Study of   33
    Malay and Chinese Entrepreneurs in Malaysia
    Habrizah Hussin

4   Telling Stories of Entrepreneurship - Towards a Narrative-Contextual Epistemology   47
    for Entrepreneurial Studies
    Chris Steyaert and René Bouwen

PART II: START-UPS

5   A Typology of Angels: A Better Way of Examining the Informal Investment   65
    Phenomena
    Patrick Coveney and Karl Moore

6   Sector-Related Opportunities and Threats for Small Business Starters in the Ukraine   81
    Nina Isakova

7   Growth Intentions and Expansion Plans of New Entrepreneurs in the Former Soviet   93
    Bloc
    David Pistrui, Harold P. Welsch and Joseph Roberts

8   Portfolio Entrepreneurs: Some Empirical Evidence on the Multiple Ownership or   113
    Control of SMEs, and its Implication for our Understanding of Start-Up and Growth
    Peter J. Rosa and Michael G. Scott

9   The Urban-Rural Dimension of New Firm Formation   127
    Olav R. Spilling

PART III: GROWTH AND INTERNATIONALISATION

10 Entrepreneurial Behaviour in the International Development of Small Firms   149
    Francesco Bifulco

11 The Impact of Size, Industry, and Nation on Internationalisation in Small and   163
    Medium-Sized Enterprises
    Håkan Boter and Carin Holmquist

12 The Internationalisation Process of Small and Medium Sized Enterprises: An   185
    Evaluation of the Stage Theory
    Harold G.J. Gankema, Henoch R. Snuif and Koos A. van Dijken

13 Measuring Growth: Methodological Considerations and Empirical Results   199
    Frédéric Delmar

14 Information Use as Counter-Proof for the Stochastic Growth Theories   217
    Nadine Lybaert

List of Tables

1.1	Scores and Ranking of Finland, Great Britain, Hong Kong and New Zealand According to Hofstede (1990)	8
1.2	The Incidence of Business Owner-Types from New Zealand and Finland Compared with the Original British Study	11
1.3	The Incidence of Stage of Development from New Zealand Businesses and Finland Compared with the Original British Study	12
1.4	The Incidence of Growth Orientation of New Zealand and Finnish Businesses Compared with the Original British Study	13
1.5	Business Owner-Type Tabulated with Growth Orientation for all Three Countries	14
1.6	Stage of Development of the Business Cross-Tabulated with Growth Orientation for all Three Countries	15
3.1	Mean Scores of SP Index on Personal Values of Malay Entrepreneurs	39
3.2	Mean Scores of SP Index on Personal Values of Chinese Entrepreneurs	40
3.3	Summary Findings of the Identity Structures of Malay and Chinese Entrepreneurs	43
5.1	The Source of Questionnaire Responses (N=437)	67
5.2	Analysis of Variance	69
5.3	Summary of the Different Characteristics and Preferences of Four Types of Active Angel Investor	71
5.4	Factors which would Encourage Virgin Angels to Increase their Investment Activity	76
6.1	Small Business in the Ukraine as of Mid 1995	82
6.2	Dynamics of Small Business Development in the Ukraine	83
6.3	Sectoral Structure of Small Business	83
6.4	Business Infrastructure Institutions in the Ukraine	84
6.5	Small Business Employment: Sectoral Structure	85
6.6	Three Sets of Key Business Success Factors	88
7.1	Implementable Attributes of Planned Growth	101
7.2	Factor Analysis of Expansion Plans	103
7.3	Demographics	106
7.4	Intensity	106
7.5	Sacrifice	107
7.6	Motivation	108
7.7	Obstacles	109
7.8	Regressions (R^2, N = 410)	109
8.1	Number of Associated Companies	116
8.2	Employment in Associated Companies	117
8.3	Average Employment for all Associated Companies	117
8.4	Number of Directors Associated with Base Company	117
8.5	Number of Other Current Businesses by Sex of Respondent (of those Owning Others)	118
8.6	Owning More than One Business by Number of Employees	119
8.7	Owning More than One Business by Type of Organisation	119
9.1	Total Sample of Firms and Response Rate	129
9.2	Annual Start-Up Rates 1988-1992 by Industry for the Investigated Areas	129

9.3	Industrial Structure of the Investigated Areas as of 1987 and Number of Recorded Start-Ups (Establishments) 1988-1993	131
9.4	Distributions of New Firms (%) According to Employment and Turnover by 1996	132
9.5	Characteristics of the New Firms	133
9.6	Background and Occupational Status of Founders Before Start-Up	134
9.7	Start-Up Motives of the Founders, Per Cent of Founders Claiming Factors to be Very Important or of Some Importance	135
9.8	Idea Development and Start-Up of New Firms	135
9.9	Locational Factors Claimed to be Very Important or of Some Importance	137
9.10	Use of Public Support Programs, Percentage of Start-Ups that have Taken Advantage of Different Types of Support Programs	137
9.11	Background and Occupational Status of Founders Before Start-Up	139
9.12	Start-Up Motives of the Founders, Per Cent of Founders Claiming Factors to be Very Important or of Some Importance	139
9.13	Idea Development and Start-Up of New Firms	140
9.14	Location Factors Claimed to be Very Important or of Some Importance	141
9.15	Use of Public Support Programs, Percentage of Start-Ups that have Taken Advantage of Different Types of Support Programs	141
9.16	The Urban-Rural Dimension of Factors Affecting New Firm Formation	142
10.1	Sample Characteristics	153
10.2	Firm Characteristics	155
10.3	Preferred Forms of Co-operation	157
11.1	The Original Database	168
11.2	The Final Database	169
11.3	Size: Turnover/Exports/Export Quota	170
11.4	Size: Percentage of Exporters, Importers and Companies with Subsidiaries Abroad for Distribution and Manufacturing	170
11.5	Industry: Turnover/Exports/Export Quota	171
11.6	Industry: Percentage of Exporters, Importers, and Companies with Subsidiaries Abroad for Distribution and Manufacturing	172
11.7	Nation: Turnover/Exports/Export Quota	172
11.8	Nation: Percentage of Exporters, Importers, and Companies with Subsidiaries Abroad for Distribution and Manufacturing	173
11.9	Size/Industry: Export Quota	174
11.10	Size/Nation: Export Quota	175
11.11	Industry/Nation: Export Quota	175
11.12	Size: Measures for Internationalisation, Bivariate Logistic Regression	176
11.13	Size/Industry/Nation: Exporting/Not Exporting Companies, Bivariate and Multivariate Logistic Regression, Analysis with Subcategories	177
11.14	Size/Industry/Nation: Importing/Not Importing Companies, Bivariate and Multivariate Logistic Regression, Analysis with Subcategories	178
11.15	Nine Independent Variables: Exporting/Not Exporting Companies, Bivariate and Multivariate Logistic Regression	179
11.16	Nine Independent Variables: Importing/Not Importing Companies, Bivariate and Multivariate Logistic Regression	180
12.1	Panel Background in 1991	189
12.2	Weighting Scheme	190
12.3	Stage Assignment Criteria and Firms Per Stage Per Year	191
12.4	Cross Tabulation of 1991 Versus 1993	192
12.5	Del Scores for a One Year Period	192
12.6	Mean Del Scores	193

13.1	Descriptive Statistics for the 55 Studies	201
13.2	Dimensions of Growth and their Frequencies	202
13.3	Calculations of Growth and their Frequencies	203
13.4	The Measurement Periods in Number of Years and their Frequencies	205
13.5	Correlation Matrix of the Investigated Twelve Growth Measures	208
13.6	Explained Variance for Different Growth Measures with the Same Model	209
13.7	Results from the Empirical Model with 95% Confidence Interval for B (N=378)	210
14.1	The Number of Firms in the Final Sample	227
14.2	The Results of the Regression, Presented in Equation (6)	229
14.3	The Chosen Manifest and Latent Variables	234
14.4	The Latent Variable Model	236

List of Figures

2.1	The Structure of the Danish Music Industry	21
2.2	Comparison of Independent and Multinational Labels	28
5.1	Variables Used to Develop a Typology of Active Angels Using a K-Means Cluster	70
5.2	Types of Active Angels and their Deal Activity	70
5.3	Matrix of Angel Investor Based on Funds Required and Number of Ventures	78
6.1	Business Related Factors: Profiles of Success	89
6.2	Personal Characteristics of Starter: Profiles of Business Success	89
10.1	Model of Analysis of Entrepreneurial Behaviour	153
14.1	The Variability of Growth in the Industrial Sectors, 1990	220
14.2	The Variability of Growth in the Industrial Sectors, 1989	220
14.3	The Variability of Growth in the Industrial Sectors, 1988	221

List of Contributors

Bifulco, Francesco	University of Naples "Frederico II", Italy
Bouwen, René	Catholic University of Leuven, Belgium
Boter, Håkan	Umeå University, Sweden
Chell, Elizabeth	University of Newcastle upon Tyne, UK
Coveney, Patrick	McKinsey & Company, UK
Darmer, Per	Southern Denmark Business School, Denmark
Delmar, Frédéric	Entrepreneurship & Small Business Research Institute (ESBRI), Sweden
Donckels, Rik	Small Business Research Institute, Catholic University of Brussels, Belgium
Freytag, Per V.	Southern Denmark Business School, Denmark
Gankema, Harold G. J.	University of Groningen, the Netherlands
Hedberg-Jalonen, Nina	Lappeenranta University of Technology, Finland
Holmquist, Carin	University of Umeå, Sweden
Hussin, Habrizah	University Pertanian Malaysia, Malaysia
Isakova, Nina	National Academy of Sciences of Ukraine, Ukraine
Lybaert, Nadine	University of Antwerp, Belgium
Miettinen, Asko	University of Tampere, Finland
Moore, Karl	Oxford University, UK
Pistrui, David	University of Bucharest, Romania
Roberts, Joseph	University of Chicago, USA
Rosa, Peter J.	University of Stirling, Scotland
Scott, Michael G.	University of Stirling, Scotland
Snuif, Henoch R.	University of Groningen, the Netherlands
Spilling, Olav R.	Norwegian School of Management, Norway
Steyaert, Chris	Copenhagen Business School, Denmark
van Dijken, Koos A.	EIM Small Business Research & Consultancy, the Netherlands
Welsch, Harold P.	DePaul University, USA

Acknowledgement

The editors wish to thank Foundation for Economic Education in Helsinki for its generous financial assistance which made this publication possible.

Introduction

Rik Donckels and Asko Miettinen

The next millenium is coming closer and closer. The whole society is looking for the magic year 2000. A number of phenomena bring us back to a kind of a 'fin du siècle' mentality, but here are also signs of hope. The continuing and even growing interest in entrepreneurship and SMEs undoubtedly is one of them. All over the world the role of entrepreneurship and SMEs for economic development, welfare and wellbeing is going to be emphasised more than ever before.

The same hold for research in these fascinating fields. In a recent survey publication (Landström, et.al., 1997) it has been shown how impressive the research efforts have been during the last decade. With the present book we want to give an idea of the state of the art for the time being. This implies that we also prepare the reader for the start of the next millenium.

The 14 contributors for the book have been severely selected from the 44 papers presented at the RENT X Conference on Research in Entrepreneurship and Small Business, organised in Brussels, 20-23 November, 1996. About 100 researchers coming from 20 different countries covering the five continents, attended the conference.

How does the structure of the book look like? The contributors are classified in three different parts:

Part I:	Entrepreneurs and Entrepreneurship
Part II:	Start-Ups
Part III:	Growth and Internationalisation

In Part I we have four papers:

E. CHELL, N. HEDBERG-JALONEN and A. MIETTINEN try to find an answer to the question *'Are Types of Business Owner-Managers Universal?'* Data for this study were gathered from three different countries: the UK, Finland and New Zealand. The study has demonstrated that there are indeed identifiable differences between business owners, with a distinct set of generic characteristics to be associated with those labelled 'entrepreneurs'.

P. DARMER and P.V. FREYTAG ask the question: *'How to Survive as the Small Fish in the Pond?'* Their contribution deals with the case of Danish independent labels, more particularly they want to find out how the independent labels differ from the multinational corporations in the music industry. The overall conclusion is that independent labels can survive in the pond of the industry, mainly because the multinationals let them. But they emphasise that an important phenomenon is the drive that makes the owners and entrepreneurs in the small independent companies stay in business. Once more the conclusion is that the starting point for the entrepreneur in the small business is the passion for doing what they want to do.

The third paper by H. HUSSIN comes from the other side of the world and deals with *'Personal Values and Identity Structures of Entrepreneurs: A Comparative Study of Malay and Chinese Entrepreneurs in Malaysia'.* The main conclusion of the author is to be summarised as follows: despite the differences if socio-cultural background, individuals may possess similar values. Furthermore, it is emphasised that different values are central in different individuals and that values can undergo changes when people become aware of contradictions within themselves.

The last paper by C. STEYAERT and R. BOUWEN on *'Telling Stories of Entrepreneurship. Towards a Narrative-Contextual Epistemology for Entrepreneurial Studies'* won the best paper award at the RENT X Conference. In this pioneering paper some epistemological reflections on

xiii

doing entrepreneurship research are elaborated, trying to show that a narrative approach to entrepreneurship can contribute in a constructive way to some of the epistemological and methodological problems this domain currently faces. In the second part of the paper the authors go into the domain of narrative epistemology, and they explore how it can guide us in telling stories of entrepreneurship. Finally they describe a framework in which 'telling' stories of entrepreneurship can be developed.

In Part II different aspects of start-ups are considered:

P. COVENEY and K. MOORE concentrate on '*A Typology of Angels: A Better Way of Examining the Informal Investment Phenomena*'. The authors were able to survey 437 Business Angel investors/potential investors. In addition they profiled 467 actual investment deals, involving a total level of funds of more than £50 million. They concluded that Business Angels constitute a diverse, heterogeneous group of active and inactive investors. By isolating a series of distinct types of Angel investor, the authors were able to develop a more powerful framework for the analysis of the characteristics and investment activity of informal investors. In all, six different types of Business Angels were identified.

N. ISAKOVA presents a number of interesting comments on '*Sector-Related Opportunities and Threats for Small Business Starters in the Ukraine*'. Apart from the difficulties of data collection, the author faces some methodological problems caused by a.o. the differences in classifying sectors by official statistic agencies in the country and in the world, the level of aggregation in sectors and the existence of a vast black and grey business which should not be ignored in the analysis. The general tendency is that retail, finance, insurance and services are easier to enter than manufacturing, innovation and construction. This seems to be similar to other transition countries.

The third paper by D. PISTRUI, H. P. WELSCH and J. ROBERTS also deals with Eastern Europe. More particularly they focus on '*Growth Intentions and Expansion Plans of New Entrepreneurs in the Former Soviet Bloc*'. One particular country, Romania, was examined. A series of predictor variables associated with ability, need and opportunity led to the development of a theoretical model. This theoretical model was empirically tested based on a sample of 410 entrepreneurs. The Romanian entrepreneurs seem to have definite, well-defined expansion plans for the future. They have already devised the mechanisms by which they plan to control their future and also appear to have the strength and motivation to carry them out. Similar entrepreneurial motivations seem to come into play both initiating and expanding the business.

P. ROSA and M. G. SCOTT deal with a totally different issue, namely the '*Portfolio Entrepreneurs: Some Empirical Evidence on the Multiple Ownership or Control of SMEs, and its Implication for Our Understanding for Start-Up and Growth*'. They agree that, although difficult to operationalise, units of analysis which go beyond the single firm may provide quite different insights into the way small businesses operate, and in particular the processes by which they are started and grow. Based on Scottish data the authors conclude that the importance of the portfolio entrepreneur may have been understated in earlier studies. It is their conviction that if control of different companies is vested in groups or clusters of such individuals, then analysis of firm start up and growth cannot be adequate if only based on the firm as the unit of analysis. They conclude that the policy implications of shifting the unit of analysis may be substantial.

In the fifth paper of Part II, O. SPILLING analyses '*The Urban-Rural Dimension of New Firm Formation*'. Data on a large sample of start-ups in Southern Norway reveal that, with the exception of the sectoral distribution of start-ups, there are small differences between start-ups in urban and rural areas. The founders have very much the same type of background in urban and rural areas, and the start-up processes seem to be very much the same. However, significant differences are revealed when environmental factors are examined: these factors, including public assistance programs, seem to be much more significant in rural areas than in urban ones.

In Part III, dealing with growth and internationalisation, we have again five papers:

The research by F. BIFULCO studies *'Entrepreneurial Behaviour in the International Development of Small Firms'*. After studying some theoretical models the author wants to find an answer to the following two questions:
- Does a culture of co-operation exist or, rather, should firms be regarded simply as territorial aggregates with individualised forms of behaviour?
- Can such firms give rise to local productive systems with models of development (traditional or evolved area-systems) comparable to those identified in other parts of Italy or abroad?

The answers are based on a sample of 181 industrial small businesses in the region of Campania (Southern Italy).

H. BOTER and C. HOLMQUIST in their paper want to discuss *'The Impact of Size, Industry, and Nation for Internationalisation in SMEs'*. Theoretical argument for this is that size reflects the market and resource base, industry reflects the technological base and nation reflects the cultural base for internationalisation. The empirical investigation is based on observations for 1758 companies, taken from the INTERSTRATOS research project in seven European countries. The results show that even if there are some differences between industries and nations, the impact of size on internationalisation is the strongest. This holds true also when other factors, such as level of education and company characteristics, are considered.

H. G. J. GANKEMA, H.R. SNUIF and K. A. VAN DIJKEN in their paper focus on *'The Internationalisation Process of SMEs'*. For their empirical investigation they use data from the INTERSTRATOS project. In general they clearly observe a growing degree of international involvement within SMEs. The variation of this increase in involvement, however, is enormous. Some SMEs are rocketing from one of the first stages into one of the last stages. Other SMEs seem to stop the process of internationalisation before they have reached the committed involvement stage. They somehow seem to limit themselves from being too dependent on foreign markets. The result suggests that stagnation is quite a common phenomenon for a substantial group of SMEs. Although the process of internationalisation proved to be irreversible and hardly any decline in stages was found, it isn't found to be a never ending process to all firms.

F. DELMAR deals with a very delicate problem, namely, *'Measuring Growth: Methodological Considerations and Empirical Results'*. His purpose is to show that the heterogeneity of different growth measures is problematic for theory and development in entrepreneurship research. For doing so 55 recent growth studies were reviewed, and data from a sample of 400 small businesses were used to examine the effects of different growth measures. The conclusion of the author is that apparently, there is little knowledge about the two choices made when designing the growth measure:
- How does the choice of indicator such as e.g. number of employees or sales affect the model?
- How does the choice of measurement period affect the model?

Some arguments are presented that suggest that these two factors may have a higher importance for our models than previously acknowledged.

The final paper by N. LYBAERT deals with *'Information Use as Counter-Proof for the Stochastic Growth Theories'*. The author formulates the central research question as follows: do SMEs which are better at gathering and analysing information have a competitive advantage over their rivals, or stated differently, do those SME owner-managers who are strongly information oriented, have a better chance of surviving and being successful? The empirical results, based on observations in Belgium, show that the more frequently entrepreneurs use information, the better results they made in the past years, and the more optimistic their view for the future. It is also demonstrated that there is a relation between success and the use of information concerning competitors and R&D activities. By way of conclusion the author emphasises that measures should be taken to convince the owner-managers of SMEs of the importance of information and to help them in their search for information and the development of sound information systems.

The above survey of the content of the book shows that a very wide range of research topics have been tackled. In addition it is to be emphasised that very diverging methodological approaches have been used. In our opinion there is only one right conclusion: entrepreneurship and SME research is ready for the next millenium. What a promising finding and a sign of hope!

References

Landström, H., Frank, H., Veciana, J. M. (Eds.), 1997, *Entrepreneurship and Small Business in Europe, An ECSB Survey*, Avebury, Aldershot.

PART I
ENTREPRENEURS
AND
ENTREPRENEURSHIP

1 Are Types of Business Owner-Managers Universal? A Cross Country Study of the UK, New Zealand and Finland

Elizabeth Chell, Nina Hedberg-Jalonen and Asko Miettinen

With the increasing internationalisation of business, a global cultural focus is critical to the success of international business ventures. Throughout the world, business and management communities are required to surrender an ethnocentric strategic focus for a multi-cultural one which recognises global cultural diversity and its multi-faceted implications for international business and management strategy. As such the pervasive influence of culture likewise impacts upon academic business and management research communities, requiring the adoption of a cross-cultural research perspective to generate informative research of global value to the business and management communities. Thus it is critical to refine further the methodology of exploring entrepreneurship by comparative research across cultures and thereby to ensure that the study may be replicated in other cultures and industrial sectors. In this context, defining what entrepreneurship *is* (or is not), and developing a model of the process, are necessary prerequisites.

Entrepreneurship is a management process which academicians continue to attempt to model. Such models have laid emphasis on different contexts (for example, founding) and different person variables (for example, demographic characteristics, motivational, intentional and personality). The place and the importance of *personality* in entrepreneuring has been the subject of considerable controversy; from the questioning of its theoretical underpinnings, methodology and general relevance. Yet in practice, the idea of 'personalities' leading and shaping organisations is firmly evidenced. Senior appointments of 'blue chip' corporations is a matter of public as well as business interest. In small businesses the role of 'personalities' and their influence upon the business is more immediate and readily captured (Minzberg, 1983). Yet much research which has attempted to capture the essence of such 'personalities' has been confounded, challenged, or ignored. In this paper we present further evidence of the importance of 'personality' based on cross cultural data. Moreover, the paradigm drawn upon is *not* the positivist paradigm of the psychometrician nor that of the interactionist (Pervin, 1990; Furnham, 1992), rather it is the paradigm of social constructionism which enables us to transcend the psychological discipline and present a Management Theory of entrepreneurship.

'Personality' and Business Owner 'Types'

There is a continued interest in identifying and profiling the 'entrepreneur'. The literature demonstrates the diversity of approaches used by different researchers. Some fundamental problems like a lack of agreed definitions, the measurement of different characteristics and the use of different statistical techniques leading to low comparability of findings, and the absence of an accepted research problematic, are still to be addressed after decades of effort (Chell and Haworth, 1992a&b).

One of the essential factors inherent in entrepreneurship is the impact of personality in stimulating, initiating and developing entrepreneurial business ventures (Brockhaus and Horwitz, 1986; Chell et al., 1991; McClelland, 1987; Timmons, 1989). Indeed, the entrepreneurial personality appears to have an enduring influence on entrepreneurship: prior to the creation of the new business venture, at the generation of business idea; through to the implementation of the business idea, on the establishment of the enterprise; and during the subsequent phases of business growth and development (Chell et al., 1991). However, the traditional trait approach towards developing an understanding of psycho-economic behaviour of entrepreneurs has been heavily criticised (Chell, 1985; Gartner, 1989, a&b). Further, within the positivist paradigm, psychologists have developed *Interactionism* as the way forward for Personality Theory (Pervin, 1990; Furnham, 1992). Interactionism enables the researcher to take account of context, and the interaction between context and personality in shaping behavioural outcomes. A clear problem within the field is being able to correctly identify the salient aspects of context and being able to measure them.

A further theoretical development in the psychology of personality was put forward by Sarah Hampson. She suggested a 'social construction theory' of personality (Hampson, 1988). This theoretical perspective was adopted by Chell, Haworth and Brearley when they investigated the possibility of generic entrepreneurial behaviours of small to medium sized business owner-managers (Chell et al., 1991). In this work, the issues addressed were: (1) the theoretical problem of the application of personality theory to the notion of the entrepreneurial personality; (2) the heterogeneity of business owner-managers and the over-attribution of the term 'entrepreneur' to certain types of business owner-manager; and (3) methodological issues ranging from definitional and conceptual problems, through to sampling and the use of research instruments (Chell et al., 1991; Chell and Haworth, 1992a&b; Chell and Adam; 1994).

There is still much work, particularly of a refining nature, to be carried out. Nevertheless, this initial study was able to demonstrate the heterogeneity of business owner-managers of small to medium sized enterprises in a four-fold typology of basic categories, which is itself only one level of a hierarchically ordered set of categorial types. Detailed 'trait' characteristics and the essential parameters of business contexts in which business owner-managers operate have been identified. The relationship of behaviour to trait and trait profile to personality-type has been explored. Further work has begun to examine the critical aspects of context which set the problems and the opportunities facing the business owner on the one hand, and the business outcomes (in terms of performance) on the other (Chell, 1997).

Thus, a primary objective of this work is to gain an understanding of business development. Briefly, it is argued that capital accumulation and wealth creation are 'external' criteria of what counts as entrepreneurial behaviour, business development being one important manifestation which indicates *sustained entrepreneurial performance* (Chell, 1996). Whilst the particularities of the critical decision contexts facing the business owner will vary, the question is whether, as it were, at a superordinate level, there is a profile of personality-type characteristics based on ways of being and ways of doing which is universal to entrepreneurs across the world. This would mean entrepreneurs in different countries exhibiting the same types of characteristics and behavioural tendencies.

It is envisaged that as further cross-cultural studies are undertaken, the ability to encapsulate critical aspects of the cultural and business contexts will be essential to gain a more detailed understanding of entrepreneurial and managerial behaviour across national boundaries. This is especially important in a world in which both the geographical boundaries between countries and the political allegiances within countries have changed considerably in recent years. It is also important in order to identify those aspects of management development which are needed now, and will be needed in the future, for successful business venturing and economic development (Chell and Adam, 1994).

A Paradigm for Understanding the Entrepreneurial Personality

When assuming traditional trait theory as a paradigm for investigating the entrepreneurial personality, three major problems emerge. One problem is the equivocal nature of the findings of researchers purporting to measure various traits assumed to be characteristic of entrepreneurs. A further problem is that trait theory itself has been the subject of considerable criticism because the trait, i.e. personality, is assumed to be the *sole* determinant of behaviour. There is a great deal of evidence about how aspects of business behaviour and the business context may shape entrepreneurial actions. This suggests the relevance of seeking to identify particular aspects of the entrepreneur's situation when attempting to distinguish entrepreneurial characteristics and to differentiate the entrepreneur as one type of business owner. That is, the entrepreneur must be explored in context. A third issue arising from both of these logically prior problems is whether it is useful (both theoretically and practically) to include personality at all; why not concentrate solely on behaviour? (Gartner, 1989a) However, the fact that behaviour and personality are related conceptually is evident. Rather, the problem is the theoretical paradigm which enables the connections to be made.

Gartner (1989b) has also argued that a rigorous psychometric approach to identifying personality traits of 'entrepreneurs' should involve the determination of a sample *prior to the act of founding*. This suggestion raises a number of issues: business founding is the one entrepreneurial act that researchers can be sure about, however, it confines investigations to pre-start-up situations; consequently, it is not possible to theorise about personality in relation to entrepreneurial behaviour of business owners post-start-up, nor can actions which are associated with sustained entrepreneurial performance be related to personality. Such a methodological constraint prevents the serious researcher of entrepreneurship from addressing issues which the business community might see as being of relevance.

A number of researchers have argued that different problems and opportunities face the business owner at different stages in the development of the business (Churchill and Lewis, 1983; Kazanjian, 1984; Flamholtz, 1986). There are both essential changes in the behaviour and management practices to enable the progression of the business from one stage to another, and awareness and ability to deal with the different problems encountered at each of the stages. The identification of such discrete stages is controversial. Indeed, so too is the idea that, with increased formality as the business grows in size, entrepreneurial behaviour gives way to increased managerialism. However, with such organic growth, there are likely to have been opportunities for innovation and business development, clearly indicating scope for entrepreneurship. 'Stage of development' thus serves to provide a way of conceptualising the context in which owner-managers carry out their business affairs and enables a deeper understanding of what is driving their behaviour.

Social construction assumes that social reality is negotiated and contested by means ultimately of language, that is, by the application of categories ('words') in order to place a construction (i.e. interpretation) on social interaction. Thus, based partially on their prior history and experience, a person develops ways of dealing with situations which reflect in part what they want to achieve and what impressions they wish to make. This behaviour may be perceived by 'the self' and regulated as such. Where it is also perceived by another, a construction will be placed on it. In everyday life, how behaviour is perceived and categorised *is* a matter of descriptive convenience. People are known through their interactions with others, usually witnessed in a narrow set of contexts. Conclusions are drawn based on the frequency and consistency with which they exhibit particular behaviours, although for the lay person the observation of one instance of a behaviour may be enough for conclusions to be drawn! Thus, people use language to label behaviours. It is not necessary to make assumptions about their 'thingness' or tangibility, they are a consequence of interpretation and in that sense are not 'real'. Indeed, according to Hampson, the 'trait term' is a relational construct which *exists* between the interacting couple. A behavioural act may thus be assumed to be a consequence of interaction in a context; the need to assume the existence of a *trait* which is hard, real, and tangible is not necessary.   Thus, people develop repertoires of behaviours which they learn and acquire in response to situations and circumstance. These behaviours are labelled and are used as shorthand ways of describing how a person usually behaves; what they are like. These characteristics may be called 'traits' but that does not mean that they are 'things' lodged somewhere in the person's psyche! However, whilst some psychologists would argue that this is *not personality it is merely* person perception the counter *is* that the combination of more than one source of evidence, from different observers, across a range of situations provides both objectivity and consistency by which means the social scientist can apply trait terms systematically and build up a profile of an individual's 'personality' (Chell et al., 1991; Hampson, 1984, 1988).

Hampson's (1988) basic idea was to use trait terms to categorise behaviours and nouns and noun phrases to develop typologies of people. In other words, her constructivist theory assumes that traits are based on actual behaviour which is perceived by observers and categorised in 'trait' terms.

The task of categorisation requires the identification of those personal characteristics that individuate the person. These are primarily grounded in the data, but the precise categorical terms were drawn from the relevant literature and previous research. The process of categorisation takes place at two different levels:

1) the categorisation of behaviour as being prototypical of a particular trait or characteristic of the individual;
2) the further categorisation of a set of traits as being prototypical of a category of business owner.

When applying this theory to the categorisation of the business owner, a set of key ingredients may be identified such that the blend of these ingredients determines the categorisation of the business owner into four basic level categories. These have been defined in this research study as entrepreneur, quasi-entrepreneur, administrator and caretaker. This approach enables the researcher to differentiate the entrepreneur from other business owners and allows him/her to relate types of business owner, stage of development of the business and growth orientation (Chell et al., 1991).

In brief, for the purposes of this study three stages of development were identified: post-start-up, established and professionally managed. In addition, four categories of growth were classified: declining, plateauing, rejuvenating and expanding. Subsets of attributes were arrived at by a grounded method - by means primarily of analysis of critical incident interview data - and as such they were categorised. However, it is important to be aware of the interactions of all the attributes in determining the categorisations on the three dimensions and that the attributes are not necessarily exclusively associated with a particular dimension.

Nature of Prototypical Categories: Dynamics and Fuzzy Boundaries

None of the three dimensions is static. For example, the behavioural characteristics of the business owner can change during the life course. In particular, a person who may have been categorised as an entrepreneur in earlier years may be classified as a caretaker or an administrator in later years as their energy levels, 'hunger', goals and motivations change. On the other hand, it is unlikely that a caretaker type will gain the characteristics that would re-classify them as entrepreneurs. Also, in the normal course of events one would not expect a caretaker to be managing a professionally-managed business. However, should one observe such a situation, one would suggest that this could have arisen through one or two incidents: either the business owner has inherited an already professionally-managed firm or the person has 'lapsed' to become a caretaker in later years (Chell et al., 1991).

The stage of development of the enterprise, by definition, may also change over time. The post start-up firm, provided it survives the problems and difficulties of the early years, will become an established business. But an established firm cannot regress and become post-start-up. However, there is no guarantee that an established enterprise will go through the transitional stage to become professionally managed for example by the next generation. This particular transition requires putting in place a professional manager or a management team. The speed with which firms can move between the stages can also vary from a very short period for a 'fast track' firm to time periods whose duration spans more than one generation. It may also happen that the demands of a market place or a turbulent business environment call for more adaptive capacity to survive (Chell et al., 1991).

The growth orientation dimension is more volatile than the other two as it is subject to external forces such as the prevailing economic climate and the type of industry or other types of 'tyranny of environment'. Since the 1991 study we have separated out the business owner's 'attitude to growth' (or 'intention to grow the business') and the actual growth behaviour of the business (see, especially, Chell and Baines, forthcoming). Thus, for example, the intention could be positive whilst the outcome (actual growth) negative.

Impact of Culture

Both interactionism and social constructionism suggest the importance of context in shaping behaviour. In a cross-country study taking account of possible cultural differences is important (Chell and Adam, 1994). In this study we draw primarily upon Hofstede's framework of 'national culture' which enables the comparative positioning of countries on four fundamental dimensions of cultural difference (Hofstede, 1980, 1990). Hofstede suggested that societies attempt to resolve four fundamental problems; how power should be distributed in society, to what extent an individual's needs take precedence over those of the collective, how ambiguity and uncertainty are resolved, and how the roles of male and female are played out. This yields four cultural dimensions which are based on the deep-seated values held within any given community.

Power Distance concerns the degree of inequalities in society; the distance both within and between groups, such as 'bosses' and subordinates. Put another way, it concerns the hierarchisation and stratification of the social structuring of society. *Individualism* describes the way people live together and the societal norms which shape the structure and functioning of social institutions. It juxtaposes the tendency towards individualism and self-interest or towards the subordination of individual needs in the interest of the collective. The *Masculinity* dimension concerns the extent to which the biological differences in the sexes should or should not have implications for social roles. The emphasis on strong differentiation suggests a highly masculine culture. *Uncertainty Avoidance* identifies the problem facing all societies in respect of how they deal with the uncertainty of the future and reveals the different degrees of tolerance in respect of this (Hofstede, 1980). Table 1.1 shows Hofstede's reported data on the four target countries - Great Britain, New Zealand, Finland, and Hong Kong.[1]

---

[1] The Hong Kong data are yet to be analysed and so are not reported in this paper.

Table 1.1   Scores and Ranking of Finland, Great Britain, Hong Kong and New Zealand According to Hofstede (1990)

	Great Britain		Finland		Hong Kong		New Zealand	
	Score	Rank	Score	Rank	Score	Rank	Score	Rank
Power Distance	35	42/44	33	46	68	15/16	22	50
Individuality	89	3	63	17	25	37	79	6
Masculinity	66	9/10	26	47	57	18/19	58	17
Uncertainty Avoidance	35	47/48	59	31/32	29	49/50	49	39/40

The scores for the four countries revealed that Great Britain and New Zealand are quite close in their espoused cultural values. They have a low Power Distance index, high Individualism, relatively high Masculinity score, and are shown to be low on Uncertainty Avoidance. Finland differs largely on its Masculinity score which is low (though rises to 51 when adjusted for sexual composition of the sample) and it has much the highest score on Uncertainty Avoidance. Although we are not dealing with the Hong Kong data it is worth noting that the scores for Hong Kong differ markedly. Here a high Power Distance is more greatly valued, society is Collectivist, and appears to have a high tolerance of uncertainty. Subsequent studies by Hofstede and others have revealed a fifth dimension - the so called Confucian Dynamism - which suggests that there is a philosophical divide between the East and the West, the former pursuing 'virtue' and the latter concerned with 'truth'. This suggests that Uncertainty Avoidance is probably 'a uniquely Western dimension' (The Chinese Cultural Connection, 1987; Hofstede and Bond, 1988).

The Hofstede framework was used to position countries at a national level. Interestingly, Hofstede has not sought to develop these dimensions at an organisational level. Instead he has suggested that the basis of organisational culture resides in organisational *practices* (Hofstede et al., 1990). The poles of these dimensions do suggest the possible differences between an entrepreneurial and a managerial culture. The dimensions are: process versus results orientation, employee versus job orientation, parochial versus professional interest, open versus closed system, loose versus tight control, and normative versus pragmatic orientation. We would suggest that both national cultural dimensions and organisational level cultural practices are cross cutting. Indeed, arguably, understanding the nature of internal culture could be further complicated, for example, by a consideration of the socio-political orientation inherent in an organisation's dynamic (Newman, 1995) and the potentiality for culture clashes through exchange and negotiated relationships between organisations from different cultures (Trompenaars, 1993).

Object of the Study

The purpose of the study is to test the universality of a three-dimensional categorisation system of British owner-managers that was developed by Chell, Haworth and Brearley (1991) in 'The Entrepreneurial Personality: Concepts, Cases and Categories'. Furthermore, this study seeks to glean further support for the social constructionist paradigm of the so-called 'entrepreneurial personality' and to examine the possibility of a universal profile which is independent of cultural influence.

What counts as entrepreneurship depends first and foremost on the economic framework in which countries satisfy their needs. Within the Capitalist system of the West the functions of the entrepreneur concern, by and large, the creation of new goods and services with the objective of wealth creation. At a behavioural level the question is how the entrepreneur achieves those ends. The hypothesis is that there is an entrepreneurial profile which is universal i.e. it is a profile of generic characteristics which is likely to typify any entrepreneur in a Western capitalist economy. This hypothesis is qualified as follows: (a) business owner-managership per se does not guarantee entrepreneurial behaviour or the label 'entrepreneur'; (b) specific behavioural acts for dealing with opportunities and threats will be exemplary of the basic level categories of entrepreneurship, for example, opportunism, innovativeness, adventurousness, etc. Their outward expression may reflect behaviours which are acceptable within a particular culture. This reflects the structuring of the capitalist system, and the scope of the categorical elements; 'opportunism' and 'innovativeness' for example, have greater breadth for inclusion of a wide variety of types of behavioural expression than has 'restlessness'.

Method

Two follow up studies to the project published in 1991 (Chell et al.,) were conducted in New Zealand and Finland in 1994 and 1995 respectively. In New Zealand a purposively selected sample of business owners in the catering, beverages (including viticulture), food processing and hotel industries in New Zealand[2] was taken (Chell and Adam, 1994). The research process for the identification of business owners comprised the use of contacts from the respective industrial sectors who possessed a broad knowledge of the sector, its structure and key players. The locations of the businesses were also a consideration and were spread between Auckland, Wellington, Christchurch and their environs. The contacts were asked to provide the research team with the names and addresses of business owners who were managing successful, growing businesses. Twenty four business owners were identified and contacted by telephone. They were interviewed at their business premises. The interview format was an unstructured, critical incident method in which they were asked to identify three incidents - two positive and one negative which had impacted the development of their business (Flanagan, 1954; Chell, 1997). The interviews, which were on average two hours in length, were transcribed and coded using grounded theory (Strauss and Corbin, 1990).

In Finland, the data collection was carried out by Nina Hedberg and Asko Miettinen from the University of Lappeenranta. A sample of 10 firms was taken from food manufacture (e.g. bakeries, meat industry, confectionery) and a further 10 firms from the service sector of the food industry (e.g. catering and restaurants). Firm size in terms of employment varied from 3 to 300 full time employees. None of the businesses were newly founded indeed the youngest business had operated for nine years and in several firms the owner manager was second or even third generation within the business. The locations of the businesses were within the sample were in various regions in Southern Finland.

Both sets of data - New Zealand and Finnish - were categorised according to the definitions and criteria of the original British study (Chell et al. 1991). In this study a three fold categorisation system was developed of *type of business owner*, *growth orientation* and *stage of development of the business*. They were defined as follows:

---

[2] We are indebted to Richard Higham, the Department of Management and Industrial relations, the University of Auckland, for his help and support in the fieldwork for the project. I would like to thank the University of Auckland for its offer of a Visiting Professorship, and to the then Head of Department, Professor Kerr Inkson, for his support in accommodating me within the Department. I would also like to acknowledge the assistance of Elaine Adam for her contribution to data collection and analysis in the initial stages of the project.

The three stages of business development identified were: *post-start-up, established,* and *professionally-managed.*

> A post-start-up firm has an under-developed infrastructure, low employment levels and has been trading for a relatively short period ...
> The prototypical established business is semi-formal in its management procedures and insufficiently resourced to have a professional management team ...
> The professionally managed business is relatively formal, of a size sufficient to support a professional management team, and has an owner-manager who has previous business performance and/or training. (Chell et al., 1991: 72).

There appeared to be four distinct stages of development: *expanding, rejuvenating, plateauing* and *declining.*

> In the prototypical expanding business the owner is not reluctant to change, intends to grow in terms of people employed, and has demonstrated growth over the past three years by increasing employment and floor space. In contrast, the declining business displays none of these attributes. (*op.cit.* 72-3).
> In the rejuvenating business the owner has shown some reluctance to change but changing circumstances ... result in some actual or desired growth ...
> In the prototypical plateauing business, the owner is reluctant to change and consequently the business has experienced a period of arrested growth, whilst in the short term some contraction may have occurred (*op.cit.*:73).

The four owner-types that were distinguished were the *entrepreneur, quasi-entrepreneur, administrator* and *caretaker.*

> The prototypical entrepreneur is alert to business opportunities which will be pursued if thought to have a moderate to high probability of success regardless of resources currently controlled. ...Entrepreneurs) are proactive, that is they take initiative, attempting to control events rather than simply reacting to them. Entrepreneurs are also highly innovative ... (they) utilise a variety of sources of finance ... they promote themselves by elaborate business networks, thus establishing the reputation of the company and creating a high profile. Entrepreneurs appear to become bored easily ... create situations which result in change ... In addition they see themselves as being adventurous in so far as they are often exploring new terrain. In all these attributes, the entrepreneur contrasts with the prototypical 'caretaker' who possesses none of these ...
> The quasi-entrepreneur has many, but not all, of these characteristics in common with the entrepreneur...
> The prototypical administrator is reactive rather than proactive; they are moderately innovative and they may take opportunities, but not regardless of current resources ... (*op. cit.* 71-2).

The more detailed information of the variables defining these three dimensions is presented in Chell et al., 1991: 76.

Findings

It was to be expected that a high proportion of the business owners whom we interviewed would be engaged a variety of business acts which could be labelled 'entrepreneurial'. The following table shows the initial overall finding.

Table 1.2 The Incidence of Business Owner-Types from New Zealand and Finland Compared with the Original British Study

Business Owner Classification	British Study (Chell et al.,1991) n = 20	New Zealand Study (Chell and Adam 1994) n = 20	Finnish Study (Chell, Hedberg and Miettinen, 1995) n = 20
Entrepreneur	9 (29%)	9 (37.5%)	5 (25%)
Quasi-Entrepreneur	6 (19%)	8 (33.3%)	4 (20%)
Administrator	7 (23%)	7 (29.2%)	6 (30%)
Caretaker	9 (29%)	0 (0%)	5 (25%)

All the distinct types of business owner were represented in the British and Finnish studies, but we found no evidence of the Caretaker-type in the New Zealand sample. This plus the greater proportion of entrepreneurs in the New Zealand study reflects the more focused purposive sampling which we were able to achieve. None of the samples were based on representation of a particular population so no inferences can be drawn about the incidence of entrepreneurial behaviour. An aim of the study was to examine the nature of entrepreneurial behaviour not its incidence.

It is worth noting that the British data were collected towards the end of an economic boom - the year being 1989 - when attitudes towards business venturing were still very positive. This was very apparent in the confident opportunism of a very high proportion of the sample. Two Administrators, for example, one who produced workwear and other clothing for the Health Service sector and the other a furniture manufacturer, both reacted to the 'enterprise culture'. The clothing manufacturer spun off a business by setting up a highly specialised business on a greenfield site:

> (He) acknowledged that such an entrepreneurial venture scared him, it was not his style. But the combination of circumstances - the threat to his existing business, the 'enterprise culture' which encouraged entrepreneurial activity of the kind proposed, and the fact that his son was in a position to manage the new venture - had tipped the scales in favour of going ahead. (Chell, Haworth and Brearley, 1991: 131).

The Caretaker is a business owner-manager who usually owns a small business in a niche market, over which he/she can exercise full control. Caretakers wish to maintain the business at the current level of activity and much prefer routine to change. The businesses they manage can be quite solid, lucrative businesses. The motives of the Caretaker for not pursuing business growth are complex, for example, as a result of social learning arising from past bad experiences such as having to manage downsizing or closing a factory; the desire for control and inability to let go; the inability to delegate where the business has been passed on to the next generation (Chell et al., op. cit.).

The New Zealand data were collected at a time of sustained economic recovery. There had been economic restructuring especially in the agriculture and dairy industries and the economy was moving out of a recession. No Caretaker business owner-managers were identified despite the fact that the private hotel industry which was still in the doldrums was sampled. Of the five hoteliers, one was prototypically entrepreneurial, three were led by Quasi-entrepreneurs and two appeared to be solid businesses managed by Administrators. In contrast, the wine and drinks industry showed a great deal of entrepreneurialism; only one business owner was categorised as being an Administrator.

The age profile of the New Zealand business owners revealed that about 40% of the sample were under 40 years of age: 10 (42%) founded or acquired the business in their early 20s, a further 8 (33%) founded or acquired in their 30s, 2 were in their 40s (8%) and the remainder 4 (17%) were in their 50s when they founded or acquired the business. Only one business (in the wine industry) was into a second generation of management (the wife of the deceased founder and their two sons). This youthfulness of the owners is also reflected in the 'stage of development of the business' as shown in Table 1.3 below. In respect of gender of the business owner, four were female, three being already in their fifties. They were distributed amongst the sectors, one being in wine, a second in hotels and two in catering.

From the Finnish data, the distribution across the different types of business owner was very similar to that of found in the British study. It appeared however, that there was a slightly higher proportion of 'Administrators'. A very striking difference was to be found in some of the demographics. For example, the Finnish firms were on the whole much older -certainly than the New Zealand businesses and they were more likely to be 'family-owned and managed' businesses. Five were run by women, one of whom had won the Finnish Business Woman of the Year award in 1994, two were husband and wife teams, one a father and daughter and another was a family business which included two sons. In the New Zealand sample, however, there were two 'family businesses', one 'husband and wife' owner-managed business and four businesses which were founded and managed by two brothers. The higher involvement of women in the Finnish sample is consonant with the national cultural differences between the three countries on this dimension.

Table 1.3   **The Incidence of Stage of Development from New Zealand Businesses and Finland Compared with the Original British Study**

Stage of Development	**British Study** (n = 31)	**New Zealand Study** (n = 24)	**Finnish Study** (n = 20)
Post Start-up	3 (10%)	2 (10%)	2 (10%)
Established	13 (42%)	12 (60%)	12 (60%)
Professionally managed	15 (48%)	6 (30%)	6 (30%)

It can be seen from Table 1.3 that there was a greater preponderance of younger businesses in the New Zealand sample; these businesses lacked much of the infrastructure of formal business management. However, the Finnish study revealed a high proportion of Established businesses (60%) with a moderate proportion of businesses which were Professionally-managed (30%). Given the age of these businesses it is at first sight surprising that there were not more with a well developed formal management structure. One possible explanation lies in the business sectoral differences and management style. Manufacturing businesses across all three countries tended to show greater management structure according to function - for example, production, marketing and sales, accounting, etc. - the larger the business, the greater the role differentiation. Thus, there was a high number of manufacturing businesses in the British sample, in particular clothing manufacturers. In the New Zealand sample, this was confined to food processing and wine/drinks manufacture. Whereas in Finland ten businesses were in food processing and comprised bakeries or smoked sausage manufacture. Event catering, whilst it required a great deal of organisational capability, especially in respect of very large events, tended to be much less formally structured. There was dependence on a small management team, with additional help being drafted in on a job by job basis. Both the New Zealand and Finnish samples included event caterers.

Table 1.4   **The Incidence of Growth Orientation of New Zealand and Finnish Businesses Compared with the Original British Study**

Growth Orientation	British Study (n = 31)	New Zealand Study (n = 24)	Finnish Study (n = 20)
Expanding	11 (35%)	15 (62%)	6 (30%)
Plateauing	12 (39%)	5 (21%)	10 (50%)
Rejuvenating	7 (23%)	4 (17%)	2 (10%)
Declining	1 (3%)	0 (0%)	2 (10%)

Table 1.4 shows quite starkly the differences in growth orientation between and within each sample of businesses. The evidence seems to point to the fact of a more cautious approach by the Finnish business owners; an attitude, it is suggested, shaped by five years of recession in the early 1990s. It is clear that this sample of business owners did not on the whole favour rapid expansion.

When to go for growth is certainly a matter of judgement. For instance, one British business owner held growth until a deal was done and the time was right to proceed to the next phase of growth. But what is possible is also shaped by the constraints of the situation. An unfavourable external economic climate depresses an economy by engendering more cautious attitudes towards business development. However, there are also internal constraints and these were apparent for example, in the British sample. They included; the size of the premises, lack of role definition, poor co-ordination, absence of systems and procedures, an ageing workforce, absence of fresh ideas or the means to implement them. Growth in the larger professionally managed business can be planned; it was found to be both proactive and thought through. Decline, however, can also be planned. Indeed, one of our Finnish business owners describes graphically the downsizing of her business as a planned response to the effects of the recession.

Table 1.5   Business Owner-Type Tabulated with Growth Orientation for all Three Countries

Business Owner-Type	Country[1]	Growth Orientation									
		Expanding		Rejuvenating		Plateauing		Declining		Sub-Totals[2]	
		no.	%	no.	%	no.	%	no.	%	no.	%
Entrepreneur	NZ	6	25	1	4	2	8	0	0	9	37.5
	BR	4	13	0	0	5	16	0	0	9	29
	FIN	3	15	0	0	2	10	0	0	5	25
	Total	13	17	1	2	9	12	0	0	23	31
Quasi-Entrepreneur	NZ	6	25	1	4	1	4	0	0	8	33
	BR	5	16	1	3	0	0	0	0	6	19
	FIN	2	10	1	5	1	5	0	0	4	20
	Total	13	17	3	4	2	2	0	0	18	24
Administrator	NZ	3	12.5	2	8	2	8	0	0	7	29
	BR	2	6	2	6	3	10	0	0	7	22
	FIN	1	5	1	5	4	20	0	0	6	30
	Total	6	8	5	6	9	12	0	0	20	27
Caretaker	NZ	0	0	0	0	0	0	0	0	0	0
	BR	0	0	4	13	4	13	1	3	9	29
	FIN	0	0	0	0	3	15	2	10	5	25
	Total	0	0	4	5	7	9	3	4	14	19
Totals	NZ	15	62.5	4	17	5	21	0	0	24	32
	BR	11	35	7	23	12	29	1	3	31	41
	FIN	6	30	2	10	10	45	2	10	20	27
		32	*43*	*13*	*17*	*27*	*31*	*3*	*4*	*75*	*101[3]*

[1] NZ - New Zealand, BR - England, FIN - Finland
[2] Row totals and percentage by country
[3] Error due to rounding

As argued above, entrepreneurship concerns capital accumulation and wealth creation therefore it should not surprise us that the Entrepreneurs were found to be managing Expanding businesses on the whole (as shown in Table 1.5). However, growth intention (of the business owner) and actual growth of a business concern are not an identity so it should not surprise us either that nine of the Entrepreneurs (12% of the overall sample) were managing Plateaued businesses. Similarly a dominant pattern for the Quasi-entrepreneurs was that they were either managing Expanding businesses (13 or 17% of the overall sample) or Rejuvenating businesses (3 or 4% of the overall sample). The pattern for the Administrators contrasted, they were just as likely to be managing Expanding, Rejuvenating or Plateauing businesses. (The dominant GO category is Plateauing due to the predominance of this growth form amongst the Finnish Administrator Owner types). The pattern changed again for the Caretakers. Here we identified no Caretakers within the New Zealand sample, but for the British and Finnish samples there was a tendency for the Caretakers to manage Plateaued businesses. There was also some evidence of businesses which were undergoing rejuvenation, whilst the few examples of businesses in Decline were led by the Caretaker Owner-managers.

Table 1.6   Stage of Development of the Business Cross-Tabulated with Growth Orientation for all Three Countries

Stage of Development	Country[1]	Growth Orientation								
		Expanding no. %		Rejuvenating no. %		Plateauing no. %		Declining no. %		Sub-Totals[2] no. %	
Professionally-Managed	NZ	1	4	3	13	1	4	0	0	5	21
	BR	8	26	4	13	3	10	0	0	15	48
	FIN	5	25	1	5	0	0	0	0	6	30
	Total	14	19	8	11	4	5	0	0	26	35
Established	NZ	6	25	1	4	3	13	0	0	10	42
	BR	2	6	3	10	7	23	1	3	13	42
	FIN	1	5	1	5	9	45	1	5	12	60
	Total	9	12	5	7	19	25	2	3	35	47
Post-Start-Up	NZ	8	33	0	0	1	4	0	0	9	37
	BR	1	3	0	0	2	6	0	0	3	10
	FIN	0	0	0	0	1	5	1	5	2	10
	Total	9	12	0	0	4	5	1	1	14	19
Totals	NZ	15	63	4	17	5	21	0	0	24	100
	BR	11	42	7	23	12	39	1	3	31	100
	FIN	6	30	2	10	10	50	2	10	20	100
		32	*43*	*13*	*17*	*27*	*31*	*3*	*4*	*75*	*101[3]*

[1] NZ - New Zealand, BR - England, FIN - Finland
[2] Row totals and percentage by country
[3] Error due to rounding

As shown in Table 1.6 stage of development is essentially in this study a proxy for formality of operations and nature and extent of management development. It summarises important contextual differences between the businesses falling into the different categories. The Professionally managed businesses in all three countries tended to be expanding or rejuvenating. Apart from the fact that the businesses tended to be younger, we are hypothesising that the less formal, more easy-going style may mark a cultural difference between New Zealand and the rest. All countries had a relatively high proportion of Established businesses. The dominant pattern was Established-Plateaued, though there were again some cross country differences. For example, a high proportion of New Zealand businesses were Expanding. The most likely explanation is the age structure of the business in this sample; many of the businesses which were growth oriented had not reached the stage where it was felt important or appropriate to put in place a professional team of senior managers, to hold formal regular meetings or to operationalise written business plans. Indeed such measures would have dramatically changed the organisational culture. In one example, an eleven year old business led by an Entrepreneur and his brother operated very flexibly and informally. Another entrepreneurially led business, also in food processing, had developed rapidly and was now negotiating the sale of the business to a large producer which would impose a Professional Management team on operations. In contrast, the Finnish business owners wished to keep the firm small enough for them to be able to exercise control over all functional areas:

> Well, I don't harbour ideas of expanding much, I want to keep the firm suitably sized so that I know what happens and how things are done since I have experience in my previous job where I had 100 subordinates - and you cannot keep that in hand as well. (Translated from the Finnish).

The category Post Start Up also revealed some differences between countries. A high proportion of the New Zealand sample were managed informally, with a small group of managers who had grown up with the business. Few of the British businesses had this characteristic. Here both age and business sector were important factors. Two small businesses in Information Technology and one in the production of greetings cards fell into this category. The IT businesses were managed by 'boffins' who recognised the need to grow in order to survive but had no real interest in its pursuit. Whereas, the greetings card business was owned by someone who was more interested in the product from an artistic point of view than the administrative systems necessary to ensure the firm establishment of the business (see, Chell et al., 1991: 92-9).

Conclusions

The original study of the 'entrepreneurial personality' set out to demonstrate the heterogeneity of business owners of SMEs and to show that only a proportion of such business owner-managers were truly entrepreneurial. The present comparative study has sought to investigate a further question: whether there is a universal profile of characteristics of the 'entrepreneur'. Data for this study were gathered from three countries: the UK, Finland and New Zealand. The countries show sufficient variance in terms of the four Hofstede dimensions of culture to make valid comparisons between them.

The study has demonstrated that there are indeed identifiable differences between business owners, with a distinct set of generic characteristics to be associated with those labelled 'entrepreneurs'. This perhaps should not surprise us. The wider economic context of Western Capitalism defines entrepreneurship as the pursuit of wealth and capital accumulation. Thus, by definition (as economists might argue) the economic function of the entrepreneur is to create conditions of disequilibrium through the processes of innovation and change. However, economists on the whole have not concerned themselves primarily with the behavioural or psychological aspects of entrepreneurial processes. The study has sought to investigate the possibility of the association of a set of generic behaviours and personality characteristics with the role played and the economic function being performed.

The study used as a proxy for wealth creation and capital accumulation 'business development' and sought to investigate the extent to which, and the ways and means by which, business owners pursued this primary economic goal. The assessment of the goal - business development - was made by a detailed analysis (sometimes longer) in order to further such a goal. The assessment was made on the basis of the intentions of the business owner, the performance of the business (actual changes in numbers employed, turnover and premises) and the way critical incidents were handled.

This method enables the researcher to differentiate between business owners. Further work using the Critical Incident Technique is used to determine the profile of person characteristics. The CRIT enables the researcher to identify discrete behavioural response patterns. Conducting such qualitative interview methods require considerable skill. Minimally, the interview must reveal what the incident was, how it was handled and what the outcome or consequences were (Chell, 1997).

Further work is underway on both the Finnish and the New Zealand data sets. In the former case, this includes inter-coder reliability tests and feedback and further investigation with the companies to assure the validity of the analysis. Additionally, the data are to be processed further using NUD-IST (Numerical Data Indexing, Searching and Theorising) software. This will add further rigour to the analysis. From this work we intend to analyse the cultural dimension. From the initial analysis there appears to be some cultural differences, notably in the style of operating (e.g. New Zealand showing greater informality in the management process), age, stage of development, extent of family involvement in the business and growth orientation (for example, the Finnish sample were older companies whose development tended to arrest at the 'established stage'; they were more likely to have family involved and more likely to maintain the business at a size over which they could exert control). Such cultural differences, should their existence receive further verification appear to influence the extent of entrepreneurship and the propensity towards entrepreneurship within a country or region. They do not appear to change the generic characteristics of the entrepreneur or the other types of business owner.

It is legitimate still to question why this particular set of personal characteristics. The research has found that they are clear differentiators. Innovation and opportunism require energy; they are dynamic forces of change. Combined with the transforming characteristics of a 'change agent' they represent a distinctive management (or more specifically entrepreneurial) style. Concern with the profile and image of the business, adopting whatever means to raise that profile, also differentiate the entrepreneur from the business owner who relies on word-of-mouth. This is not to suggest that one method of promotion is better than the other, just that they are different, and tend to be associated with different styles and ways of working in a 'holistic' sense.

Stage of development of the business is intended as a short hand description of the context in which the business is operating. The sense in which it is used in this research is to denote the degree of formality of operation and procedures. The idea that it has primarily to do with the age of the business is misleading. It is more likely perhaps that a young SME say under five years of age will operate informally, with ad hoc, unminuted meetings, etc. However, much older companies may operate in this post start up manner. Moreover such aspects as these help define the internal organisational culture. It appears therefore that this presents a fruitful avenue for further research.

Finally, very little has been reported in this chapter about other country-wide studies. Work on the Hong Kong data set is still undergoing analysis. The intention remains to sample countries according to contrasts in their national cultures and to add further validity to the theory. What the business owner does is important, but also crucially important in this increasingly global economy, is *how* it is done. Such behaviours influence judgements about what kind of person one is dealing with, what they are like, and whether at the end of the day one wants to do business with them. In this way, the entrepreneurial personality and the personality types of other business owners are socially constructed.

References

Brockhaus, R.H. and Horwitz, P.S. (1986) The psychology of the entrepreneur, in D.L. Sexton and R.W. Smilor (eds.) *The Art and Science of Entrepreneurship*, Cambridge, Mass.: Ballinger: 25-48.

Chell, E. (1985) The entrepreneurial personality: a few ghosts laid to rest? *International Small Business Journal*, 3,3: 43-54.

Chell, E. (1996) The Social Construction of the Entrepreneurial Personality. *Working Paper: Centre for Entrepreneurship, University of Newcastle*: Newcastle, England.

Chell, E. (1997) The Critical Incident Technique, in Cassell, C. and Symon, G. (eds.) *Qualitative Research In Organisations*. London: Sage (forthcoming).

Chell, E. and Adam, E. (1994) Researching Entrepreneurship and Culture: A Qualitative Approach, School of Business Management, University of Newcastle upon Tyne, *Discussion Paper No. 94-9.*

Chell, E. and Baines, S. (1997) Gender and Small Business Performance: Some Fresh Evidence, *Entrepreneurship and Regional Development*, (under review).

Chell, E. and Haworth, J.M. (1992a) A typology of business owners and their orientation towards growth, in Caley, K., Chell, E., Chittenden, F. and Mason, C. (eds.) *Enterprise Development: Policy and Practice in Action*, London: Paul Chapman.

Chell, E. and Haworth, J.M. (1992b) The development of a research paradigm for the investigation of entrepreneurship; some methodological issues, in Hills, G.E., LaForge, R.W. and Muzyka D.F. (eds.) *Research at the Marketing/Entrepreneuship Interface*, Chicago: University of Illinois at Chicago: 13-26.

Chell, E., Haworth, J. and Brearley, S. (1991) *The Entrepreneurial Personality: Cases, Concepts and Categories*. London: Routledge.

Chell, E., Hedberg, N. and Miettinen, A. (1996) Are types of business owner-managers universal: a validation study in the U.K. and Finland. Paper presented at RENT X (Research in Entrepreneurship), Katholieke Universiteit Brussel (KUB), Brussels, 21-22 November.

The Chinese Culture Connection (1987) Chinese Values and the Search for Culture-free Dimensions of Culture, *Journal of Cross Cultural Psychology*, 18, 2: 143-64.

Churchill, N.C. and Lewis, V.L. (1983) The five stages of small business growth, *Harvard Business Review*, 6, 3, 43-54.

Flamholtz, E.G. (1986) *How to make the Transition from an Entrepreneurship to a Professionally Managed Firm*. San Francisco: Jossey-Bass.

Flanagan, J.C. (1954) The Critical Incident Technique, *Psychological Bulletin*, 15: 327-58.

Furnham, A. (1992) *Personality at Work*. London: Routledge.

Gartner, W.B. (1989a) 'Who is an Entrepreneur?' is the wrong question, *Entrepreneurship Theory and Practice*, 13, Summer: 47-68.

Gartner, W.B. (1989b) Some Suggestions for Research on Entrepreneurial Traits and Characteristics. *Entrepreneurship Theory and Practice*, 14, Fall: 27-37.

Glaser, B.G. and Strauss, A.L. (1967) *The Discovery of Grounded Theory: Strategies for Qualitative Analysis*. New York: Aldine.

Hampson, S, (1984) Personality traits: in the eye of the beholder or the personality of the perceived? in M. Cook (ed.) *Psychology in Progress: Issues in Person Perception*, London: Methuen.

Hampson, S. (1988) *The Construction of Personality 2nd edn*, London: Routledge.

Hofstede, G. (1980) *Culture's Consequences: International Differences in Work-related Values*. London: Sage.

Hofstede, G. (1990) *Cultures and Organisations: Software of the Mind*. New York: McGraw-Hill.

Hofstede, G. and Bond, M.H. (1988) The Confucius Connection: From Cultural Roots to Economic Performance, *Organisational Dynamics*, 16, Spring: 4-21.

Kazanjian, R.K. (1984) Operationalising stage of growth: an empirical assessment of dominant problems, in J.A. Hornaday, F.Tarpley, J.A. Timmons and K.H. Vesper (eds.) *Frontiers of Entreprneeurship Research*, Wellesley, Mass.: Babson College, Center for Entrepreneurial Studies: 144-58.

McClelland, D.C. (1987) Characteristics of successful of entrepreneurs, *Journal of Creative Behavior*, 21, 3: 219-33.

Mintzberg, H. (1983) *Structure in Fives: Designing Effective Organizations*. Englewood-Cliffs, N.J.: Prentice-Hall.

Newman, J. (1995) Gender and Cultural Change, in C. Itzin and J. Newman (eds) *Gender, Culture and Organizational Change*. London and New York: Routledge: 11-29.

Pervin, L.A. (1990) A brief history of modern personality theory, in L.A. Pervin (ed.) *Handbook of Personality Theory and Research*. New York/London: The Guildford Press.

Strauss, A.L. and Corbin, J. (1990) *Basics of Qualitative Research: Grounded Theory Procedures and Techniques*. London: Sage.

Timmons, J.A. (1989) *The Entrepreneurial Mind*, Andover, Mass.: Brick House Publishing.

Trompenaars, F. (1993) *Riding the Waves of Culture*. London: Nicholas Brealey.

2 How to Survive as the Small Fish in the Pond: The Case of Danish Independent Labels

Per Darmer and Per V. Freytag

Introduction

The idea of this paper emerged from an interest for the music business in general and how the independent labels in this business manage to survive in particular. To a certain degree it could be said that the independent labels do not actually survive, since a lot of them pop up and disappear all the time, and very few of them stay alive for very long as independent labels. They either do not make it, or if they do, they end up being 'swallowed' by the multinational corporations that are dominating the music industry all over the world (Darmer, 1994).

Even though it seems that very few of the independent labels are blessed with a long and prosperous life, they still seem to be an immanent part of the industry. Several explanations can be used to explain this phenomenon, Drucker (1985), Storey (1994). This paper finds it interesting to look at it from the perspective of the independent labels themselves, since that angle has not been predominant in the scientific research so far and might give a new understanding of the business.

The paper will not look at independent labels all over the world, but limit itself to Danish experiences. This, of course, is done out of convenience and familiarity, as the authors are Danish and know a little about the business in Denmark. Furthermore they have the opportunity to get the data. The paper will be based on data from two Danish independent labels, and the results can first of all be applied to the music business in Denmark. One of the main reasons for looking at the independent labels was that the music industry was considered especially challenging for the small independent labels, as they are up against several well-established multinationals with a firm grip of the business.

Faced with such tough competition it is interesting to find out how the small fish (the independent labels) manage to stay alive and prosper (if they do so) in the pond of the multinationals. In our opinion a meaningful way to acquire such knowledge was to go to the source itself - the independent labels.

Purpose and Structure

The purpose of the paper is to find out how and why the independent labels survive in the fierce competition with the multinationals of the music industry in Denmark.

The how and the why of the independent labels may very well be interwined. It is, however, not a necessity since the single independent label may not be able to survive the competition for very long, but independent labels as a population may be an integrated part of the Danish music business.

The purpose of the paper is to get an understanding of the independent labels' role in the Danish music industry - an understanding of how they function and survive.

The paper fulfils the purpose of understanding by collecting data from the independent labels, since they ought to be the main source for revealing how they go about their business and keep alive (if they do). The authors have not interviewed all the independent labels in Denmark, and neither did we try to do so. Two independent labels (Cloudland and AGM) were interviewed. They have both existed for a while and established themselves as independent labels, and it is not too much of an overestimation to say that these two independent labels have served as role-models for many of the small independent labels. By sharing their own experiences Cloudland and AGM,[1] therefore, should be able to shed some light on how independent labels function and survive.

Today Cloudland and AGM stand out as major Danish independent rock labels, since the industry in the beginning of 1990 experienced a wave of takeovers, where several major independent labels were taken over by the multinational corporations. None of the other independent labels in Denmark are now as experienced and well-established in the rock business as Cloudland and AGM (although Kick Music and Crunchy Frog are both well on their way).

An overview of the music business in Denmark is sketched in the next part of the paper, which also contains a theory about the rock career process developed by Frith, 1978, and called 'the rock' (Shuker, 1994).

It is essential to point out that the description of both the Danish music industry and the theory of 'the rock' has to be verified by data. This is a consequence of the phenomenological approach adopted in this paper. The perspective of the independent labels is applied, and therefore our results have to be grounded on our interviews with Cloudland and AGM. Put in another way: Due to our scientific (and we deliberately call it that) approach we have to rely foremost on our data, as they reflect the view of the independent labels. The phenomenological approach has the effect that we are not looking for the objective truth of the music business (if it exists), but for the subjective reality of the independent labels, and to get that reality our results have to be verified by data - paralleling Grounded Theory (Corbin & Strauss, 1990).

The methodological approach to the paper, the way in which it is applied in the interviews with Cloudland and AGM as well as the problems related to it is discussed in part four of the paper.

Part five is the main part of the paper. Here the results of the interviews are put forward and interpreted to see how the independent labels actually manage to survive. The interpretation of the data is an unavoidable part of reflecting the reality of the independent labels with its similarities and differences, and drawing the overall picture of that reality.

The results of how and why the independent labels survive are discussed in the conclusion, and these results are put into perspective by considering and discussing small independent labels as a special kind of small enterprises or if and to what extent they have similar features as other entrepreneurial enterprises.

The Danish Music Business and 'the Rock'

The Danish music industry is dominated by the multinationals - 'The five sisters and a Virgin' (see also Figure 2.1). The five sisters are the five big multinationals, while Virgin is the smallest of the multinationals, too small yet to be a real member of the multinational family. (This may very well change, as Virgin has been very successful all over the world during the last decades and is growing stronger).

The next level consists of the national labels - the 'big' Danish labels that regard the whole country as their turf. The 'big' ones are only big when they are compared to the lower levels of independent labels. They turn out to be pretty small compared to the multinational labels. These labels

[1] We would like to thank Cloudland and AGM for their willingness to participate and share their knowledge of the business with us. Even though the paper uses the information from Cloudland and AGM it should be emphasized that the authors alone are responsible for the interpretations put forward in the paper.

are mostly independent labels that have gone national, or they are backed by a larger corporation (e.g. Replay which is owned by Metronome - a movie corporation).

The third level consists of the established independent labels that actually exist as such and have produced more than one or two records - this level is the focus of the paper, and here both Cloudland and AGM are located. The labels of this level are locally based, foremost around the big cities, where a club and underground stage exists. In Denmark there are approximately 15 of these labels at the moment, and some of them have the same owners, who use different labels for different types of music (one label for Techno, one for Heavy Metal, and a third for Rap Music and so forth). Some of the independent labels only produce records of a certain type of music, but it does not apply to all of them (Cloudland does, but AGM does not).

The fourth level is the undergrowth of small independent labels that are formed to produce one or maybe two records. Then they are out of business again. Many of these independent labels are formed by artists / bands that cannot get a contract with the labels on the other three levels. So if they want to get their music produced, they have to form a label and do it themselves (see also Souder (1987)). If they stay in business and begin to produce more records and records with music of other artists, they become established independent labels (level three). But most of these labels stay non-established. They come and go all the time. The levels of the music industry are illustrated in Figure 2.1.

Figure 2.1   The Structure of the Danish Music Industry

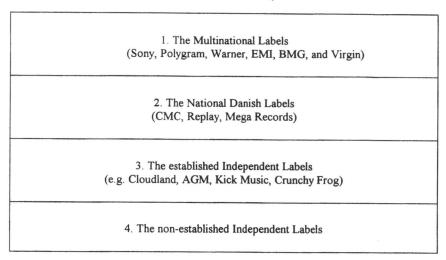

1. The Multinational Labels
(Sony, Polygram, Warner, EMI, BMG, and Virgin)

2. The National Danish Labels
(CMC, Replay, Mega Records)

3. The established Independent Labels
(e.g. Cloudland, AGM, Kick Music, Crunchy Frog)

4. The non-established Independent Labels

Source: Constructed by the authors

Like the rock industry the evolution may be divided into phases. 'The Rock', Frith, 1978, has called this the evolution of the rock artist. 'The Rock' can be illustrated by the four different stages that the successful rock artist passes through. It should be stated that only the successful artists go through all four stages. Many of the artists on the rock stage do not get further than stage one and two (and a great undergrowth of rock bands is not even making it to stage one).

Stage one: The rock artist plays in the small local clubs to build up a reputation.

Stage two: The rock artist gets regional reputation and builds up a following. The following and the local 'fame' lead the artist to recording at small independent labels.

Stage three: The rock artist gets nation wide recognition, leading to a major recording contract with national exposure, hits, and touring.

Stage four: The last step to fame and stardom is international recognition with the record and tour contracts that this brings along.

The four stages of 'The Rock' illustrate that the rock artist has to make it at the local level and get recognition there in order to get the attention of the major record labels for to sign with them and become a superstar.

'Success at the local and regional level, or nationally on a smaller scale, with a niche or cult audience, on 'independent' labels and via college radio and the club stage, is still necessary to attract the attention of the major record companies.' (Shuker, 1994, p. 103).

Of course everyone that signs with the major labels, does not become a superstar (few artists are that fortunate). Certain artists do not make it the hard way by playing on the club stages - making themselves a name before they move on (these artists start at stage three or four in 'The Rock'). To some extent the multinationals of the music industry create stars out of nowhere through promotion. The independent labels are unable to do so as they do not have the necessary economical means.

Method and Choice of Cases

The approach of a scientific inquiry is very much influencing the result of the research. Different approaches will show different perspectives of reality and the way in which knowledge subsequently can be acquired. Here the intention is to obtain an understanding of a certain industry, how certain actors within this industry perceive themselves, the industry as a whole, and the interaction within the industry. The goal is not to tell the 'truth' about how small independent labels 'really' act within their industry, and how they for instance try to distribute and promote their products. Instead we try to express the small independent labels' own perception of their importance and their way to distribute and promote products.

Description and understanding of actors are problematic. In connection with gathering information a central question concerns the way in which such information can in fact be collected. A preconceived form as to how certain relations appear and must be interpreted will be problematic, as it might easily stand in the way of or maybe even supersede the actors' perceptions and experiences. Instead we only risk a 'confirmation' of the preconceived form, and it will be a problem that it may be more than doubtful how well the part of reality, which we want to describe, has really been 'caught'. Inversely, one must not be blind to the fact that the researcher, who is collecting information, cannot do so impartially, but that his questions will i.a. be influenced by the professional socialisation and the dominating theories and models within the field. (Enderud 1982).

Therefore, the task is to try to discover the conceptions, myths, events a.s.o., to which the actors within this specific industry attach importance, but at the same time be as aware as possible of the preconditions and limitations by which the researcher himself is influenced when studying the phenomena, events a.s.o. in question. (Hunt 1976).

Which actors are to be selected as informant in such a kind of research is a difficult problem. When looking at the single company, we find two extremes. In principle, we can either try to interview all the persons who may be said to be part of the company and who are in some way in touch with the problem that we want to illustrate, or we can choose one or a few informants. Here we have chosen the last option. Firstly, because it is a question of very small companies with few employees, and secondly because small companies with few employees, as is the case here, are often identical with the owner or the entrepreneur.

Thus the entrepreneur (the owner) is the central key informant whose perception of the company, the industry and the interaction within the industry controls the development of the company.

Another more superior question concerns the number of companies within a certain industry that one has to include in order to reach an understanding. The central question is what kinds of understanding you are interested in. Here the aim is not representativity but to a higher degree an achievement of overview, understanding and depth. An overview touches representativity, but the aim is not to be able to say that this and this factor have such and such great importance - measured on percent or the like. The aim is to identify the factors which are important seen from the actors' perspectives. Understanding concerns the question of the importance that is attached to the identified factors, and, finally, depth concerns the question as to why certain factors have been attached certain importance.

On this basis the choice of companies with the described aim does not become less important, although the procedure is as for static analysis, in which it must be ensured that the choice can be randomised. In this case, however, it is a question of making a deliberate and appropriate choice of a case-company which in a meaningful way can illustrate the relevant aspects of the problem.

Here we have chosen two companies within an industry which - depending on the way of statement - has together 12 to 15 companies within the category: small independent labels, i.e. companies with less than 10 employees / voluntary assistants. As described in the introduction, in the early 1990s Denmark saw a number of new, small labels. The two chosen companies belong to this group. One of the labels - Cloudland - is probably the first that established itself during the mentioned period. Cloudland is known for a deliberate quality strategy within a self-elected, relatively well defined kind of music. The other producer - AGM - has fewer years of experience as music producer and represents a wider opinion with regard to what kinds of music it wants to produce.

However, the choice of the two music producers was not as deliberate as we might have wanted. The choice of the two independent labels was a mix of knowledge and availability, meaning that we were aware of the two labels and their position among the independent labels and were able to get them to participate. We were aware of the names of a few other independent labels, but for various reasons it was impossible to get hold of them. In principle, one should prefer to have a relatively good overview of an industry and the companies that act inside this industry, before the choice of case-companies takes place. In this case this was not possible. The music business, and especially the part which is interesting to us, is characterised by a relatively poor transparency. Thus, new producers establish themselves all the time - often with the purpose of bringing out their own production, as it has not been possible getting the product brought out through one of the already established music producers. Furthermore, it is often rather difficult to detect, what hides behind a certain company name etc. Therefore, the two chosen companies are partly a function of the limited possibilities of mapping the industry before the choice of company. Thus, the estimation as to whether the chosen case-companies in an appropriate way form the basis of a good overview, an appropriate understanding of the industry and a sufficient depth could primarily take place in connection with the collection of data. This is not quite satisfactory, but inversely it has proved that both companies can meet the demands for validity. Thus, the two companies reflect in a meaningful way the industry that we want to describe and understand.

It will be suitable to give a brief account of the specific collection and interpretation of data before we will subsequently discuss the knowledge that we have obtained through our case-studies. Common for both cases is that the data collection is based on personal interviews of 1½ to 2 hours duration in the companies. The basis of the interviews was a guide of questions which was primarily elaborated as a kind of superior theme frame. The interviews proceeded as a narrative dialogue, in which the interviewed person very much himself was able to control the concrete content of the dialogue. The guide of questions was only used as a kind of memory support, starting basis in connection with the beginning of the interview, and support in case the dialogue was interrupted or stopped. The dialogue was not subject to an attempted control. Therefore, it was to a large extent left to the interviewed person to continue the dialogue. The way, in which we used the guide of questions, therefore only made it function as a kind of superior frame of reference for securing the ground that was examined in different directions and levels. The extent, to which the single levels and directions were examined, was very much controlled by the importance that the actors attached to them.

The weakness of this approach is that the actors can deliberately withhold information or try to promote certain attitudes, points of view, perspectives, etc. The advantage is that one does not as interviewer try to press the actors into certain preconceived forms. A few items/questions were, however, also treated explicitly by us in order to elucidate the connections and the importance. The impression of the actors' answers was, however, a confirmation of great sincerity and interest in a contribution to a varied description of the situation and their perception of it. On the other hand the approach is necessary, as it is the reality of the independent labels we are aiming at, and we need to give the respondents a certain amount of leeway, if they are to express that reality.

At Cloudland the interview was carried out as a group interview by two respondents and two interviewers at the same time. At AGM the interview was carried out by two interviewers and one respondent. Cloudland is owned by four persons, and we interviewed two of these persons. At AGM we interviewed the owner. The interviews were tape-recorded, and the subsequent interpretation of the result was sent to the two companies which, however, only resulted in comments of less importance. Both the tapes and the two interviewers may be said to have acted as measuring and recording instruments in connection with the case elaboration, as we have not only leaned on the tape-recording; we have also included our perception of the situation and the importance of the spoken word in the given situation. Thus, the described results may be said to express a kind of double interpretation - first by the actors themselves and then by us and the importance that we have chosen to attach to them in our description. The subjects/categories, around which we have chosen to build our description, thus express our interpretation, and the attachment of importance does likewise express our interpretation of the collected data.

Analysis and Results

Cloudland Records was founded in 1991 by four young people, who shared an interest for music in general and for a certain band (Trains, Boats, and Plains) in particular. Cloudland was primarily founded in order to produce Trains, Boats, and Plains, and to make that possible the four founders each invested 15.000 DKK in the company. The four founders are still running the company, and all important decisions (which records to produce etc.) are taken by the founders as a team (collective management).

Cloudland produces pop music, but they only make records for the bands / artists they like and consider being quality within the kind of music, they produce. In that way the label becomes a brand name for quality products. The founders of Cloudland have produced records with other types of music than pop (e.g. Techno and Heavy Metal), but under other labels (each type of music has its own separate label). So far Cloudland has produced 15 records with seven different bands.

AGM was founded in 1992 by Anders Eigen, who is still manager of AGM. Anders Eigen was interested in realising 'the total concept', in which AGM both produced records, was in charge of the booking and management, owned rehearsal rooms and a club where the artists could perform live. It did not work out, so AGM had to drop the total concept. The rehearsal rooms and the club were abandoned, and AGM now concentrates on production of records, booking, and management.

AGM produces all kinds of music as long as it is music of a certain quality within its own field. Today AGM has made 44 productions (albums and EPs) with various bands, and at the moment about 10 bands are members of the AGM family.

The settings for the establishment of the two case companies are very much alike. Both companies felt that there was a need for producing new music and promoting new artists. Obviously, a weakness of the established music industry was its interest in going on promoting the well-known artists in order to obtain relatively high sales figures. At the beginning of the 1990s, however, the distributive trade began to show great interest in new (Danish) artists. In connection with Cloudland's first records many distributors in retail trade were willing to try to sell the new products.

This response almost became a provoking factor for other actors connected with the music industry. The fact that it was really possible to get new Danish produced music distributed without using the established channels made the industry prosper.

The fact that for a long period (from the middle of the 1980s till the beginning of the 1990s) the established and multinational part of the music industry had neglected new artists resulted in a growing interest for renewal in other links of the distribution-sales-chain. Today however, this effect has disappeared concurrently with the great prosperity of the new small independent labels, that try to promote new and, as a rule, quite inexperienced artists, and last but not least the fact that the multinationals rode the wave too, by purchasing several of the independent labels and made them manage this part of the multinational companies (Sanjek & Sanjek, 1991).

The independent labels have an important function in the Danish music industry. The strength of the big labels is obviously their ability to carry through a heavy promotion of artists whose creations appeal more broadly to an audience. Inversely, the strength of the small independent labels is to trace, test, and train new artists. Thus, the small label becomes a kind of product development mechanism.

The two independent labels have the same 'drive' for getting into and staying in the business. They want to produce good music, and for both Cloudland and AGM good music is what they like and consider being quality music. None of the labels could imagine themselves producing records from artists they did not like, because that would make the enthusiasm disappear, and this would be a catastrophe, as the enthusiasm is the fuel on which these two independent labels are running.

Neither Cloudland nor AGM makes money. They never really have, and they probably never will. They both hope and dream that one (or more) of their records 'breaks' and makes the label big. Naturally because it would be nice to taste that kind of success, but foremost because it would provide the economic foundation to continue (and expand) what they enjoy doing.

Even though none of the labels make money, they behave quite differently. Cloudland is built up in such a way that it cannot go bankrupt, as Cloudland only produces what it can afford. AGM, on the other hand, is running up a considerable debt by producing almost everything, they like and believe in. Some of the debts are covered by management and booking operations, and some of them are covered by the earnings that the manager of AGM (Anders Eigen) makes in his civil occupation as an entrepreneur in the building industry. A job he performs at the same time as he runs AGM.

Carrying out other functions than the producer function is a way of trying to make the labels (or connected business) profitable. Both case companies are also publishing businesses, i.e. they own the rights of the produced music. The royalty fee typically varies from 1/6 to 1/3 of the net profit.

Distribution may also provide a certain profit. Cloudland does not have a distribution of its own, but in connection with the company two of the four owners have established a distribution company. This distribution company is used to make the necessary profit for Cloudland to keep in business through indirect support in the shape of free premises. Add to this that by means of a network co-operation that was established with other independent labels there are increased possibilities of selling Cloudland's music in Denmark, Europe, and the rest of the world. Even a small number of records (50 to 100) can be sold to the other network partners. The network co-operation has an important effect on Cloudland's profits.

AGM has not like Cloudland taken over the distribution function. However, the owner of AGM considers the established distribution network in Denmark and especially the wholesale function as an obstacle to increased sales. There is one wholesale company in Denmark, owned by the big multinational record companies, which in principle distributes all the music. It is, however, a problem that the sellers in the wholesale company are not necessarily much interested in selling AGM's products. Small unknown artists do not sell very well, whereas well-known foreign and Danish artists represent opportunities of quick and relatively good sales. Therefore, AGM considers skipping the wholesale link in order to sell directly to the shops.

A third way of making profit is booking and management, and AGM has both booking and management. Booking is presentation of artists at different stages. Managing takes care that the administrative work in connection with contracts and the performance on stage so that this takes place in a meaningful way. However, neither booking nor managing is very lucrative, and, therefore, AGM's owner must continue financing production, distribution, booking, and managing by means of other sources of income.

Even though Cloudland and AGM pretty much want their records and artists to break, they realise that if the artists do so, they are better off going to one of the major (multinational) labels, as neither Cloudland nor AGM has the resources and capabilities of handling a big artist. This demands several full-time employees. It also demands another kind of knowledge than that of the independent labels. It seems that the independent labels are aware of 'The Rock' (see part 3), and that they both consider it healthy that the artists, who make it, leave them and sign up with one of the multinationals, if they are to further their career in the music business.

The independent labels hope that the stardom of their former artist will make them sell more of the records that they have already produced with him, as these records are now of historical value and interesting to his new audience. At the same time the independent labels hope that they will get a 'piece of the action', when their artist signs up with one of the major labels (e.g. a share of sales of the first record on the new label).

In a way both Cloudland and AGM stand in the situation that the band, which the label was formed around, to a certain degree has made it and signed up with one of the multinationals.

AGM started out by producing Hotel Hunger, which has now signed up with EMI. AGM and EMI have made the deal that AGM continues doing booking and management for the group, and that Anders Eigen is the sixth member of Hotel Hunger (besides the five musicians of the band). In that way AGM (or Anders Eigen who in economical terms seems to be pretty much the same) gets one sixth of everything that Hotel Hunger makes.

Cloudland started out by producing Trains, Boats, and Plains featuring Nikolaj Nørlund. When Trains, Boats, and Plains split up, Cloudland produced the next band that Nikolaj Nørlund formed - Rhonda Harris. Recently Nikolaj Nørlund has made a solo record putting music to the words of the late Danish poet Michael Strunge. Cloudland did not produce this record. Cloudland realises that if Nicolaj Nørlund gets the audience that his talent indicates, he is bound to move to the major labels. So at the moment Cloudland is in a transition period concerning the artist that it was built around in the first place.

Cloudland and AGM both mention flexibility, their sense of and closeness to the rock stage, independence, and artistic freedom as their advantages compared to the multinational labels.

One may say that in the music industry there is a division of labour between the independent label and the multinational company, where the former spots the talents, builds up a following, makes their first record(s) and makes them ready. Then the multinational company takes over and uses its resources to make the artists well-known to a wider audience.

If the independent labels were to put all their money on one artist, they would have to be sure that both the artist and the labels themselves made it big. Because, if not, they would be out of business and the independent labels are too fond of their independence to risk everything, especially as they realise that they are not quite tuned for this kind of task.

Of course the independent labels do whatever they can to 'break' their artist, but they do it 'the independent way', meaning that they get airplay for their artist on national radio. This is not that hard, as the productions of Cloudland and AGM are mostly considered to be quality by the rock-critics (they get good reviews in the press). The reviews stir up the curiosity and interest of the DJs on national radio and television. It is harder for the artists from the independent labels to get airplay on the local radio, because the local radios play hit music. This is due to the fact that they are commercial radio, which the national radio is not.

The possibilities for the low-budget videos, that the independent labels make, of getting airplay in Denmark are, indeed, very limited. Danish television has only few programmes showing rock videos. The independent labels can only afford low-budget videos, which makes it hard to get airplay on the international video channels (foremost MTV). The reason is that the low-budget videos have to compete with the professional high-budget videos from the multinational labels, and the independent labels are bound to lose that competition.

The good reviews in the press (mostly newspapers since Denmark has only few rock magazines) make the audience aware that the artist has made a new record. This is important, but the good reviews as such are not considered very important by the independent labels.

The independent labels make posters to tell the audience that they have produced a new album. They send CD's to the press and radio, and they also distribute them to trendsetters, as they influence the taste of the rock audience and can raise sales of the record.

Other important features in promoting artists and their records are the artists themselves as live acts. The independent labels are close to the rock stage, and the bands they represent have their base as live-bands. A good live performance is considered of the utmost importance, as this is what builds up the band's following (the fans), who buy the records and promote the band by word-of-mouth.

The independent labels get their music distributed to the record stores, but it is not very visible here, as the record stores are mostly music supermarket chains. They promote and display the famous artists from the multinational labels, which can afford the displays and the promotion. The records from the independent labels are competing with the famous artists in the music stores, and they very easily get defeated in this competition.

The independent labels miss the old-fashioned music stores in general and the old-fashioned salesmen in particular. They could and would promote music that they liked, to the customers when they discussed the music with them. This stands in contrast to the new music store (music supermarkets), where customers buy their music at the cash register. The local supermarkets also sell CD's, so that customers can buy music together with their groceries. The local supermarket sells the hit record and some 'special-price' records. The productions of the independent labels are not available at the local supermarket.

So it is not sheer nostalgia, when the independent labels talk about the devoted music salesman at the music store. It is a realistic interpretation that he or she was their opportunity to get their productions promoted in the music stores.

Nostalgia should not be considered a prominent feature among the independent labels. Both Cloudland and AGM are aware of the development of the Internet, and the possibilities of displaying and buying music here. Cloudland and AGM expect a change in the business to the effect that the publishing rights become important together with marketing. Marketing, because there will be a huge amount of music on the Internet, and it will be so easy to put it there. Cloudland and AGM expect the Internet to be benefiting the independent labels, because the access to their artists will be easier, and people only have to pay for the music they hear. In this way they can easily get familiar with the artist. It will also be cheap (they do not have to buy a CD). The two independent labels are preparing for the development and expecting it to better their position. Here the problem (which was only slightly touched in the interviews) is that the independent labels have no chance of matching the multinationals regarding marketing. They will still have to rely on the local rock and underground stage to get the attention of the audience in order to make them listen to the productions of the independent labels.

The strengths and weaknesses of the independent labels are illustrated and related to the multinational labels in Figure 2.2.

Figure 2.2   Comparison of Independent and Multinational Labels

Type of label	Role	Strengths	Weaknesses
The established Independent	Innovator	'Drive' (love of products) Flexibility Closeness to the local rock stages Independence Artistic freedom	Economy Limited capacity: - marketing and promotion Limited markets
The multinationals	Market leader	Resources (economic and other) Economies of scale Worldwide markets	Inflexibility Limited knowledge of the local rockstage Limited artistic freedom

Source: Constructed by the authors

The biggest difference between the independent labels and the multinationals can primarily be found in the role that they play in the music market. To a certain extent the economic capacity of the multinationals enables them to make the agenda for the mass market. This is done by a massive marketing effort and by a certain uniformity of the artists. The last mentioned creates a fertile soil for really new development trends and the appearance of new artists. Here the small independent labels have their strong point: Because they are near the market they are good at picking up the signals from the underground stage. In this way many artistic music innovations are initiated by the small independent labels.

Conclusion and the Implications seen from Certain Perspectives

The Overall Conclusion

The independent labels survive in the pond of the music industry mainly because the multinationals let them. The independent label has primarily had a serving function that the multinationals benefit from. The independent labels search the club and underground stages for talents and develop the talents into artists. If they grow big enough, the multinationals take over the artists and try to make them big nation wide or even all over the world. Doing this the multinationals do not have to use lots of resources engaging the club and underground stage, as the really big fish (bands and artists) will eventually swim into their net anyway.

The More Specific Conclusions at Different Levels

First of all the music industry does not differ very much from other industries. It is a very internationally oriented industry where few multinationals define the conditions for the independent labels. Using the independent labels mainly as a screening mechanism, the multinationals can concentrate on the internal rivalisation within the multinational group of music companies. Secondly the independent labels are aware of their role within the industry and to some extent they see it as a natural division of labour. In one way this has something to do with the independent labels' reasons for being in this industry. The overall goal of the multinationals is to generate as much profit as possible. The means for this is marketing, where promotion is especially important. The independent labels also try to generate turnover and profit, but liquidity is more important. Their main problem is to stay alive and avoid liquidation. Therefore, cash management is a central function even though they may never have heard the term. Most important for the labels is the opportunity to promote music of new artists who would not have had the possibility of getting their music published elsewhere. As the owner of AGM puts it, 'It could be nice to have a lot of money to invest in new artists and then earn it back so that you could still promote other new artists'.
   Thirdly, to be able to promote new artists it may be necessary to co-operate with other companies - foremost the multinationals. The independent labels realise that there are limitations as to how close they can get to the multinationals without losing their independence. If they lose their independence, it may become a problem to promote the music and artists, that the company would like to promote. It is also a risk that the owner (entrepreneur) may lose his identity and passion for his work. To create music and artists, who would not otherwise have been promoted, is the most important task seen from the small independent companies' perspective. Of course, it is important to be able to live on the work you are doing, but the wish to get rich is not behind the interest for music and artists.

Theoretical Conclusion

A phenomenon, which is of importance, is the drive that makes the owners or entrepreneurs in the small independent companies stay in business. The starting point for the entrepreneurs in the small business is the passion for doing what they want to do. The whole idea behind what the entrepreneurs in the music business are doing, is to be innovative by creating new products in the form of new records and artists. The similarities between the entrepreneurs in the music business and other businesses are striking (Shan, Walker & Kogut (1994), Sexton & Kasarda (1992)). The aim is to create, and the means is to use all the possible resources. The entrepreneurs believe so strongly in their own ideas that it does not matter very much, whether the realisation of the ideas means losing money or maybe even going into debt.

The similarity between the independent labels and entrepreneurs in general is striking. This is surprising when you take into consideration that the independent labels are in a special industry dominated by the multinationals, and that the independent labels, as shown in the paper, fill their place in the division of labour within this industry.

What makes the independent labels almost classic examples of entrepreneurs are the visibility and speed. Every CD or artist that the independent labels produce is a new product (an innovation). Most entrepreneurs have one or two innovations (ideas or products) in a lifetime. The established independent labels have a string of these, as it is an immanent part of their business to produce CDs and artists, and as every single CD / artist gives them the feeling and spirit of being entrepreneurs, and this feeling, spirit and love for the product is the very stuff that they thrive on.

So what makes the independent labels differ from the average entrepreneur (to the extent that you can talk about this) is neither the aim to create, nor their love for or belief in the product, but the sheer amount of innovations, which is generally much higher for the independent labels than for other entrepreneurs.

In the innovation theory there is made a distinction between technology push and demand pull (Christensen 1992) approaches. Seen from this perspective the small independent record companies may be said to have a technology push approach by trying to create new artists and music so to say from scratch. The multinationals may be said to have a more demand pull oriented approach in which they try to find out what the market wants and then try to distribute and promote it in the most effective ways. Seen from an economic viewpoint the demand pull approach, which the multinationals use, seems to be the most effective.

References

Christen, Jens Frøslev (1992) *Produktinnovation - proces og strategi* (Product Innovation - Process and Strategy). Handelshøjskolens Forlag.

Corbin, Juliet & Anselm Strauss (1990) *Basics of Qualitative Research*. Sage Publications, Newbury Park.

Darmer, Per (1994) *The Business of Rock is Rolling - Organizing Rock Music*. Paper presented at the 12th International SCOS Conference 'Organizing the Past'. Calgary, Alberta, Canada, 10 - 13 July.

Drucker, P. (1985) Innovation and Entrepreneurship. Publishers Harper & Row, New York.

Enderud, H. (1982) *Metodeovervejelser i organisationsforskningen. Artikler.* (Method considerations in organizational research. Articles). Nyt fra Samfundsvidenskaberne. København.

Frith, Simon (1978) *The Sociology of Rock*. Constable, London.

Hunt, Shelley (1976) 'The Nature and Scope of Marketing'. *Journal of Marketing*, vol. 40.

Sanjek, Russell & David Sanjek (1991) *American Popular Music Business in the 20th Century.* Oxford University Press, New York.

Sexton, D.L. & J.D. Kasarda (eds.) (1992) *The State of the Art of Entrepreneurship*, PWS-Kent, Publ. Comp. Boston.

Shan, W. & G. Walker & B. Kogut (1994) 'Interfirm Cooperation and Start-Up Innovation in Biotechnology Industry'. *Strategic Management Journal, 3.*

Shuker, Roy (1994) *Understanding Popular Music*. Routledge, London.

Souder, William E. (1987) *'Managing New Product Innovations'*, Lexington Books. Lexington MA.

Storey, D.J. (1994) *'Understanding the Small Business Sector'*. Routledge, London.

Appendix 1   Interview Guide for Independent Labels

1. The company (background data)
    - Name:
    - History (establishment and development)
    - Number of employees
    - Turnover / number of records per year
    - Number of connected artists

2. The industry and its place within this industry
    - How is the industry in general?
    - And how is the development within the industry?
    - What is the role of the independent labels within the industry?

3. The independent labels' way of operation
    - What characterises the independent labels?
    - And how do they operate?
    - How do the independent labels hold their own in the competition with the big multinational corporations?
    - What can and what are the independent labels doing in order to attract and keep 'the stars'?
    - How are they operating when trying to find new musicians?

4. Marketing (communication)
    - How and to which extent do the independent labels promote their artists/records?
    - How are the new musicians launched (if this differs from the ordinary promotion)?
    - How is the label itself promoted (if it is promoted at all)?
    - The role of the critics in the promotion?

5. Co-operation
    - Do the independent labels in Denmark co-operate or do they look at each other as competitors?
    - Do the Danish independent labels try to become international (on their own)?
    - Or do they co-operate with independent labels in other countries (are they in touch with them at all)?

3 Personal Values and Identity Structures of Entrepreneurs: A Comparative Study of Malay and Chinese Entrepreneurs in Malaysia

Habrizah Hussin

Introduction

Personal values provide a potentially powerful explanation of human behaviour, serves as standards or criteria of conduct (William, 1965), tend to be limited in number (Rokeach, 1973), and tend to be remarkably stable over time (Inglehart, 1985; Rokeach, 1973). Although personal values are stable, they do undergo changes over time, or the mix of values may shift (Tropman, 1984). England (1968) states that a person's value system is considered to be relatively permanent perceptual framework, likely to shape and influence the general nature of an individual's behaviour. Because personal values are presumed to be a determinant of social behaviour (Rokeach, 1973), the study of values has been important in all major social science disciplines (Feather, 1975; Kilman, 1977) People behave in accordance with their personal values far more than not, despite variations in situations.

It is difficult for one to deny that entrepreneurship is a matter of individuals, *'the entrepreneurs'*, whose personal values, beliefs, and ideologies, along with their product, service, market, technology and management form the strategic template for the emerging business. Because the founder of the enterprise is the main decisionmaker, his or her personal values inform and underlie much of what the entrepreneur intends. These personal values help him or her to link the past to the present, and the future, and are fundamental to the process of alignment and attainment that define intentional action (Bird, 1989).

Much entrepreneurial study from behavioural science perspective typically has focused on the psychological make-up or personality traits of entrepreneurs and upon how others perceive entrepreneurs or on comparisons between entrepreneurs and others in their society who are not entrepreneurs (Brockhaus, 1982; Sexton and Bowman, 1985; Schere, 1982). Brockhaus and Horwitz (1986) note that the overall results of the psychological studies of entrepreneurs have been disappointing. Carsrud and Johnson (1989) state that most theories have traditionally focused on stable characteristics of entrepreneurs, and stable groups or organisations that were neither new, nor in the flux of change. However, entrepreneurial behaviour is a dynamic ever-changing process that is usually evidenced in situations of instability and changes. They further argue that researchers in entrepreneurship often have made naive and simplistic assumptions about relationships between personality and social behaviours. The conclusion made by McClelland (1961) based on his early work that achievement motivation drives people to become entrepreneurs is an example of such simplistic assumptions.

Research has found that not only entrepreneurs are high achievers, successful executives are high achievers, too. Motivation alone does not seem to be effective differential variable between entrepreneurs and non-entrepreneurs. To conclude that achievement motivation drives people to become entrepreneurs would be a naive assumption. A more reasonable interpretation is that achievement motivation has a general causal effect on any type of performance success (Carsrud and Johnson, 1989). Rokeach (1973) emphasises that trait approach can be regarded as rather limiting in that '*it carries with it a connotation of human characteristics that are highly fixed and not amendable to modification by experimental or situational variations*'. He further stated that a major advantage in thinking about a person as a system of values rather than a cluster of traits is that it becomes possible to conceive the individual undergoing change as a result of changes in social conditions. The trait concept has established into it a characterological bias that forecloses the possibilities for change. This study adopts a different approach. It avoids from the search for a single set of characteristics that explain entrepreneurial behaviour.

In this research, 'cognitive content' refers to the personal values of the entrepreneur towards various aspects of his or her life and business environment which are important for the dynamic functioning of their enterprises. The personal values acquired by entrepreneurs are a composite of personal values derived from the entrepreneurial role in business, and his roles in life. The entrepreneur acquires personal values as part of the process of personal and social development. Social factors influence both cognitions and information processing related to role enactment (Aldrich and Zimmer, 1986). The entrepreneurial role is embedded in a social context. Fulfilling this role and other roles is facilitated or constrained by people's positions in social networks, role expectations, and social pressures to conform (Moscovici, 1985).

Knowledge and enactment of appropriate roles are important for entrepreneurial success. Personal values are internalised and some of them are associated with the person's life and others with the person's multiple roles, one of which is the entrepreneurial role. Since personal values hold a pivotal place in both the conceptualisation of the parameters of identity structure (Weinreich, 1980; 1986), this study also investigates the identity structure of the Malay and Chinese entrepreneurs. Individuals develop their personal values, notions of their identities and characteristic ways of thinking about themselves through complex social and development processes. Such processes include those of forming identifications with significant others, internalising ascriptions of self to others, comparing self with others in relation to various skills and competencies and assessing self in terms of one's personal value system.

Research on identity development may also be useful in the study of the changes that occur during life phases of the entrepreneurs. For example, entrepreneurs may experience identity conflict due to role transition as a part of achieving company growth (Sexton and Bowman, 1985; Stevenson, et al., 1985). Identity conflict may exist resulting from contradictory personal values associated with multiple roles. The entrepreneur is affected not only by his multiple roles but also by members of his social network. Role partners such as spouse, clients, and business, associates help shape role expectations and behaviours (Hirsch and Rapkin, 1986). The role partners may provide or withhold emotional support and/or material goods that can assist the fulfilment of role tasks and help reduce conflict experienced. Identities give direction and purpose to the person's behaviour (Stryker and Statham, 1985). In assuming the multiple identities of entrepreneurs, they must be able to adapt to the set of personal values and behaviour that are associated with the multiple identities.

The entrepreneur is first of all a human being. As a human being he shares the universal values wanting to be certain that his life has a meaning and purpose. But the nature of his role as an entrepreneur places him contiguously in a position of conflict. It forces him constantly to choose between alternative courses of action reflecting differing priorities of personal values. In his analysis of these alternatives, and in consideration of the personal values they represent, the entrepreneur inevitably finds himself in a state of inner conflict. He wants to do the right thing, but does not always find it easy to know what the right thing is. Efforts to deny the existence of such conflict, however persistently pursued, offer only temporary and superficial relief. Like all human beings, the entrepreneur inevitably returns to the question of ultimate personal values and to the question of whether his total life is serving those personal values in the way he would wish. In analysing personal values and applying personal identification theory to entrepreneurship, this research seeks to link intrapsychic and sociocultural processes and show how both are necessary for the working of identity development among entrepreneurs.

Therefore, the argument of this study is that the way in which an entrepreneur functions is partly conditioned by the requirements of the environment in which he operates and is partly dependent on the cognitive contents in terms of personal values of the individual entrepreneur.

An Overview of Malaysia

Since this study focuses on two ethnic groups that are Malays and Chinese entrepreneurs in Malaysia, it is appropriate to give a brief description of their social and cultural background. The perspective can enhance a better understanding of the cultural diversity of Malaysia and one can begin to appreciate the importance of the research. Malaysia is a multi-cultural society with a population estimated at eighteen million, of which 82% are in Peninsular Malaysia, 10% in Sarawak and 8% in Sabah. Under the colonial rule the term *'Malay'* was formalised by the British to distinguish the Malay-speaking Muslims residing on the Peninsular Malaysia and offshore islands from large immigrant groups of Indians and Chinese. The colonial government categorisation of Malay was retained until the granting of independence to Malaysia in 1957. The constitution formalised colonial practice by defining *'Malay'* as *'one who speaks the Malay language, professes Islam and habitually follows Malay customs'*. The non-Malay denotes Malaysians descended from Chinese, Indian, European, Eurasian and other non-indigenous races. Some 58% of Malaysia's total population are Malays and other indigenous groups, 31% are Chinese and 10% are Indians while other races account for the remaining 1%.

Despite Malaysia's rapid rate of economic growth in the years of independence, two fundamental problems persist; widespread poverty and serious racial imbalance. The present Malaysian government acknowledges the economic imbalance among the ethnic groups as the main cause for the problems besetting the country today. In response to these problems government developed a strategy which emphasises eradication of poverty among all Malaysians and to restructure Malaysia's society so that identification of race with economic function and geographic location is reduced and eventually eliminated. While there are plentiful supply of Chinese and Indian entrepreneurs, the government feels there is a shortage of Malay entrepreneurs. In order to reduce this imbalance, the government estimated it would have to create at least 20,000 new entrepreneurs by the year 1990. The government has spent more than US$100 million since 1975 on entrepreneurship development programmes. Malaysia's efforts in developing its indigenous people is neither unique nor different. All over the world may countries are trying to ensure that indigenous people play a more active role in their respective economies. In East Africa, for example, there is an attempt to replace Asian with African businessmen and industrialists (Marris and Somerset, 1971), whereas in Indonesia there is the *'Pribumi'* policy of favouring indigenous businessmen (Y. Hamzah, 1979).

A race is distinct not only because of its physiognomy, language and usual habitat, but also because of its culture. Culture is deeply interwoven in the value systems of a given ethnic group or race. Values and value systems affect development and progress of human communities (Ayal, 1963; Begum, 1988). In a multi-racial society like Malaysia, entrepreneurs bring with them differing systems of values. Extremely heterogeneous value profiles may result in conflict that threaten nation's stability, harmony and growth. An understanding of Malay entrepreneur's beliefs and values is therefore a pre-requisite for planning their future. The goal of development is, in fact, the well-being of individuals. Development viewed in this perspective lays great importance on the values of the individuals involved in the process. All these people are thinking-feeling human beings and share the culture and heritage of the society in which they have been brought up. They have their own belief, values, prejudices, and attitudes that influence their actions while playing their respective roles.

The nature of values, attitudes and lifestyle of the Malays has been regarded as the main reason for their relatively depressed economic position. Lack of capital and international contacts as the Chinese and Indian entrepreneurs have established for centuries, and opposition from them were some of the difficulties encountered by Malay entrepreneurs. It can be argued that the colonial policy of 'protection' of Malays has not only reinforced the values, attitudes and lifestyle that make them less attracted to commerce, but has also made it difficult for them to enter commerce as the non-Malays have become well established in the field. The Malaysian Chinese are predominantly urban and conspicuous in the business sector. The Chinese's success in Malaysia has been acknowledged by many writers. The Chinese in Malaysia formed the team of *'Overseas Chinese'* who migrated from China for economic or political reasons. In fact, the *'Overseas Chinese'* all over the world are noted for their success.

Research Objective

This is a study of the entrepreneurial value systems and identity structures of Malay and Chinese entrepreneurs in Malaysia. The study seeks to:
1. Identify the personal values of Malay and Chinese entrepreneurs
2. Identify the differences and similarities between the personal values of Malay and Chinese entrepreneurs
3. To investigate the identity structure of Malay and Chinese entrepreneurs

Methodology

This study is based on a sample of 40 Malay and 40 Chinese entrepreneurs operating in Kuala Lumpur, the capital city of Malaysia and within its radius of 40 miles. The sample of Malay and Chinese entrepreneurs was carefully chosen from the lists supplied by the Malay Chamber of Commerce and Industry of Malaysia and the Associated Chinese Chamber of Commerce and Industry Malaysia. For the purpose of this study, the definition of an entrepreneur is proposed to be: *'someone who perceives a business opportunity, assumes a significant amount of risk associated with it, undertakes the entire co-ordinating functions in bringing together factors of production to create a new business venture for the purpose of profit and growth, which has been established for at least five years, and which is continuously managed by himself or herself'*.

This definition includes, but is not limited to entrepreneurs responsible for new products, or production processes. This study focuses on personal values and identity development of the individual entrepreneur. Therefore, the main interest is the individual entrepreneur's values and what they tell us about his behaviour. The study is not about business organisation or industries although each entrepreneur studied certainly can be placed within these broader frames of reference. In addition, the emphasis is on 'owner-founder' of the enterprise and at the same time continuously managing his business. This is to avoid people who provide capital without managing the venture. The justification for choosing the minimum number of years in business as five years is solely to ensure that the business is not in the pre-start-up or start-up but at least in the establishment, that is, completion of successful start-up phase. Although, the establishment of a business stage may take more or less than five years, it is assumed that the minimum five years used in the proposed definition would suggest that the business has undergone some form of growth.

The entrepreneurs were selected with the following criteria:
1. Owner and founder of the business organisation and continuously managing and co-ordinating the affairs of his business at the time of the study
2. Must have been in business for at least 5 years

The study focuses on Malay and Chinese, and male entrepreneurs only. The decision to focus on male entrepreneurs only is not based on any elements of sexism but more to limit the number of research variables to a manageable size. The research design is based on the research objectives mentioned earlier. The research is divided into four stages. Stages one covers the literature search on the subject, and stages 2-4 cover the field work. The objective of stage 2 is to identify the personal values of Malay and Chinese entrepreneurs. These personal values become the foundation to the construction of the Identity Structure Analysis Instrument (ISA) for Stage 4. In addition to that the demographic data of the Malay and Chinese entrepreneurs was collected using a standard questionnaire. The personal values mentioned in the literature were developed in the Western culture and there is a possibility that those personal values are not suitable to be applied to both groups. The in-depth interviews with 10 Malay and 10 Chinese entrepreneurs were designed to elicit personal values and to generate a wide-ranging survey of the entrepreneur's past experiences in life, their current views of themselves and other people, their views about how they had changed over the years, their aspirations and fears about the future. Thought and feelings were thereby invoked about people who had been influential in their lives. The techniques of data collection used were semi-structured in-depth interviews. In this analysis, the unit of analysis is *'the whole of the entrepreneur's reply which is treated as a single entry under one category, regardless of number of sentences'*. Given that this investigation seeks to identify the entrepreneurs' personal values, it is important to ensure the transcribed statements are related to their personal values. Each verbatim extracted was coded according to the value categories (refer to Appendix 1) and tabulated for frequency count.

Stage 3 involved feedback sessions with respondents. The data which was content analysed was cross-checked with all the twenty entrepreneurs and the feedback sessions with them helped to ensure that the personal values were meaningful to them, and that claims and assertions are not derived from a misrepresentation of transcribed data from the in-depth interviews. Stage 4 focuses on administering the Identity Structure Analysis (ISA) instrument. The data collected in Stage 2 which was content analysed qualitatively and quantitatively was used at this stage. The data collected from ISA instrument was analysed using Identity Exploration software (IDEX). The Statistical Package for Social Sciences (SPSS) was used to analyse the biographical data of entrepreneurs.

Most of the value instruments such as Rokeach Value Survey (RVS) (Rokeach, 1973), Personal Values Questionnaire (PVQ) (England, 1967), Allport-Vernon-Lindzey Study of Values (SV) (Allport, Vernon and Lindzey, 1970) were developed in the western culture, this research ruled out using these value instruments to studying Malay and Chinese entrepreneurs. There was a possibility of employing Chinese Values Survey (CVS) (Chinese Culture Connection, 1987) as it was developed in an eastern culture and is considered suitable for studying Chinese entrepreneurs' values. However, CVS was not appropriate to study Malay entrepreneurs' values. The decision to use CVS would have favoured one group over the other. Moreover, the nature of the CVS is that it was developed according to the Chinese world view and definitely does not represent the Malay world view and culture. Within one culture, there will be a degree of consensus over many basic beliefs and values, although there will be areas of disagreement, and standard psychometric scales may be appropriate to establish such variation expressed within overall consensus. But, it is inappropriate to assume that people from different ethnicity with an alternative world view will evaluate self and others in terms of the values and beliefs of the first, so that the psychometric scale of one culture often becomes irrelevant to the other.

Identity Structure Analysis (ISA), a metatheoretical framework devised by Weinreich (1980), provides a means of investigating people's value systems and their identifications with others. ISA allows for the complexity of the individual entrepreneurs, allowing entrepreneurship to be viewed as a developmental process rather than an end in itself. It acknowledges that entrepreneurs are a heterogeneous group and allows for the fact that individual characteristics may change over time. A very important and probably unique feature of ISA is that it anchors the analysis in the value system of and individual, the latter being determined from the data almost entirely provided by the individual himself (Weinreich, 1980). Since the value system of the individual is first ascertained, the techniques may be applied in any language or dialect without translation (Weinreich, 1983). The theoretical orientations that underpin ISA are:

1. The psychodynamic approach to identity development (Erikson, 1968; Hauser, 1971; Marcia, 1966, 1980)
2. Theories of cognitive affective consistency (Festinger, 1957; Rosenberg and Abelson, 1960; Weinreich, 1969)
3. Symbolic interactionist views of self and society (self as process and situated self) (Mead, 1934; Weigert, 1969)
4. Personal construct theory (Kelly, 1965; Fransella and Bannister, 1977)

The ISA instrument is a kin to the repertory grid in that it consists of a series of scales and bipolar constructs made up of contrasting words and statements. In this study the entities used are *'successful entrepreneurs'*, *'unsuccessful entrepreneurs'*, *'mother' 'father'*, *'wife'*, *'most Malay entrepreneurs'*, *and 'most Chinese entrepreneurs'*. There are in addition, certain entities which are mandatory. These are facets of self-concept, that is *'ideal self-image'* (*Me as I would like to be*), the *'current self-image'* (*Me as an entrepreneur, Me as Malay / Chinese, and Me as a husband*), the *'past-self image'* (*Me as I was when I left school, and Me as I was when I worked for someone*), and *'admired person'*, and a *'disliked person'*. The second type of data is a set of bipolar constructs. The constructs used in this identity instrument are personal values of Malay and Chinese entrepreneurs previously elicited from a sample of 10 Malay and 10 Chinese entrepreneurs, representative of the general sample of both groups of entrepreneurs. Each pole of a construct is placed at the left and right hand side at the top of a page. The list of entities are arranged down the left-hand margin of each page below a construct. To complete the instrument the entrepreneur is required to rate each of the entity against the personal value at the top of the sheet. A nine-point, rather than seven, five or three point scale was selected to allow for maximum discrimination in the ratings.

A person's indentity structure is analysed idiographically within the conceptual framework of ISA with the aid of the Identity Exploration (IDEX) system of computer software, in particular here, IDEXPC software (Weinreich et al., 1989). The IDEX-IDIO software for mainframe computers also provides idiographic analysis and can be used in conjunction with IDEX-NOMO for nomothetic analysis. IDEXPC and IDEX-IDIO encapsulate the ISA theoretical definitions of pertinent psychological concepts, the algebraic translations of which can be found in the *'Manual for Identity Exploration Using Personal Constructs'* (Weinreich, 1980/86/88). Analysis of variance is available for use in INDEX-NOMO, and was used to investigate variance between a maximum of three independent factors. Before presenting the results of ANOVA tests, it is to be noted that degrees of freedom associated with F-ratios concerning identification may vary with particular target entities. These variations are due to the fact that not all respondents rate all entities.

Findings

The statistical analysis of the demographic data for both groups of entrepreneurs did not reveal any significant differences between Malay and Chinese entrepreneurs with respect to age, educational background of entrepreneur and entrepreneurs' fathers. Moreover, marital status, and gender was held constant, and they must have been in business for at least five years. Therefore, the samples of Malay and Chinese entrepreneurs used in this study were reasonably matched. The findings of this research revealed sixteen personal values of Malay entrepreneurs and seventeen personal values for Chinese entrepreneurs. It is important to clarify that the difference in the total number of personal values identified for each group does not have any significant meaning to it neither does it reflect the exact number of personal values that each group might possess. The total number of personal values were derived from the analysis of the data gathered from in-depth interviews and the Identity Structure Analysis.

The nature of ISA indices makes it possible to perform comparisons between individuals. The cut-off points for ISA indices used in this study is as suggested by Weinreich (1992). It is stressed that the cut-off points are by their nature somewhat arbitrary. The indices themselves should be regarded as *'estimates'* of the underlying parameters. *'Structural Pressure'* (SP) is a technical term in ISA measuring the evaluative consistency with which a person uses a construct to evaluate self and others (Scale -100 to +100). Constructs with measures of (>50) are a person's core evaluative dimensions, figures around '0' indicate *'unclear'* personal values or non-evaluative dimension and *'large negative'* figures indicate *'consistently incompatible'* evaluative dimensions. *'Core personal values'* are thought of as stable and impervious to change, whereas personal values with large negative index values are assumed to be subject to *'pressure'* towards change that is re-evaluation. In this study, only personal values with index values (>70) were considered as *'core personal values'* due to the fact that the overall level of index values in the two samples were high. For comparison across groups, the SP requires 'normalisation' whereby the IDEX-NOMO computes the total magnitude of 'pressure' irrespective of sign, for each construct. The personal values for both groups of entrepreneurs are listed according to their relative importance based on the analysis on their ratings. It is important to note that the negative sign assigned to certain personal values is only on the basis of inconsistent use of that particular value in the evaluative process of self and others. Table 3.1 and Table 3.2 show the findings on personal values of Malay and Chinese entrepreneurs respectively.

Table 3.1   **Mean Scores of SP Index on Personal Values of Malay Entrepreneurs**

	Personal Values of Malay Entrepreneurs (N=40)	Mean Scores SP Index
1	High Achievement	93.24
2	Religious Piety	91.57
3	A Comfortable Life	86.85
4	Personal Independence	84.88
5	Perseverance	79.61
6	Mutual Obligation and Reciprocity to Family and Kinship	77.42
7	Self-Discipline	76.98
8	Trustworthiness	73.53
9	Frugality	70.1
10	Benevolence	68.1
11	Hard Work	-64.1
12	Create and Utilise Opportunities	63.37
13	Versatility	62.68
14	Innovativeness	58.23
15	Risk Taking	53.81
16	Fatalism	48.68

Table 3.2   Mean Scores of SP Index on Personal Values of Chinese Entrepreneurs

	Personal Values of Chinese Entrepreneurs (N=40)	Mean Scores SP Index
1	Sustaining Growth and Continuity as Family Business	94.23
2	High Achievement	92.23
3	Personal Independence	87.51
4	A Comfortable Life	86.05
5	Trustworthiness	83.77
6	Harmonious Relationship with Others	81.76
7	Perseverance	80.36
8	Mutual Obligation and Reciprocity to Family and Friends	79.11
9	Self-Discipline	75.99
10	Frugality	74.23
11	Benevolence	72.65
12	Hard Work	-67.01
13	Risk Taking	65.9
14	Versatility	63.21
15	Create and Utilise Opportunities	60.45
16	Innovativeness	55.88
17	Fatalism	46.15

The following discussions were based on the comparison made between the findings of this study with the other findings found in the literature. Despite the fact that the techniques and samples used in this study were different from those used by other researchers, the findings showed some similarity. The findings from De Carlo and Lyons (1979) revealed that non-minority female entrepreneurs placed high on the scale of *'achievement'*, *'support'*, *'recognition'*, and *'independence'*. Minority female entrepreneurs scored higher on *'conformity'* and *'benevolence'*. The personal values such as *'high-achievement'*, *'independent'*, *'benevolence'* are found to be similar with those possessed by Malay and Chinese entrepreneurs sampled in this study. However, Malay and Chinese entrepreneurs put greater emphasis on *'high achievement'*, *'personal independence'* than *'benevolence'*.

Rezaian's (1984) study focuses on the personal value systems of immigrant Iranian entrepreneurs operating in the United States. Rezaian uses the Allport-Vernon-Lindzey study of values and found that Iranian entrepreneurs score high on the *'theoretical'*, *'economic'*, and *'political'* values. If Rezaian's findings were compared with the findings of this study, the *'economic'* value can be considered as similar to personal value *'a comfortable life'* which was emphasised as equally important by both Malay and Chinese entrepreneurs sampled in the study. The list of personal values revealed in this study was compared with the list of values listed in *'Chinese Values Survey'* (CVS) developed by the Chinese Culture Connection (1987). The personal values listed in CVS such as *'filial piety'* (obedience to parents, respect for parents, honouring of ancestors, financial support of parents), *'industry'* (working hard), *'benevolent authority'*, *'having few desires'*, *'thrift'*, *'persistence'*, *'trustworthiness'*, *'harmony with others'*, and *'wealth'* were considered as similar to *'mutual obligations and reciprocity to family and kinship'*, *'hard work'*, *'harmonious relationships with others'* and *'a comfortable life'* found in the study. Those personal values not found under CVS were *'high achievement'*, *'personal independence'*, *'create and utilise opportunities'*, *'risk taking'*, *'fatalism'*, and *'innovativeness'*.

The personal values of Malay and Chinese entrepreneurs sampled in this study such as *'high achievement', 'personal independence', 'risk taking', 'create and utilise opportunities', 'innovativeness', 'versatility', 'self-discipline',* and *'hard work'* were compared with those reported in past entrepreneurship research (McClelland, 1967; Gasse, 1977; Sexton and Bowman, 1984; Brockhaus, 1976; De Carlo and Lyons, 1979). It was found that these personal values do not differ from those reported by those researchers. On the other hand, there is a difference in relation to the personal value *'fatalism'*. Western researchers concluded that entrepreneurs have *'internal locus of control'*, referring to a belief that the individual entrepreneurs actually control their own world. The findings of this research revealed that Malay and Chinese entrepreneurs sampled in this study believe in *'fate'*. This finding contradicts with the findings of Western researchers. It is important to consider that entrepreneurs are not homogeneous groups and there are many factors affecting the psychological make-up of the person. The SP indices for *'fatalism'* for Malay and Chinese entrepreneurs were 48.86 and 46.15 respectively. This indicated that *'fatalism'* is not considered of high importance to them as compared with other personal values. It is true that both groups of entrepreneurs believe in *'fate'* and *'luck'*; they also believe in importance of human effort in bringing positive outcomes. Theirs was a unique blend of *'fatalism'* which did not exclude human efforts and involvement. Malay and Chinese entrepreneurs seemed to believe in an intrinsic connection between effort and outcome. Once they have done their best, they have discharged their basic duty as a human, the rest is left to destiny, so to speak.

This empirical evidence supports the assertions of Pederson (1979) that there are differences between Western psychologies and non-Western psychologies, based on the value differences in both societies. Therefore, it is suggested that the cross-cultural differences of non-Western and Western should be acknowledged before any form of generalisation is made. The findings also revealed that there are similarities and differences between the personal values of Malay and Chinese entrepreneurs. Despite the diversity of the socio-cultural background, the findings of this study suggest the Malay and Chinese entrepreneurs sampled in this study have many common personal values. These common personal values are *'high achievement', 'personal independence', 'a comfortable life', 'perseverance', 'mutual obligation and reciprocity to family and kinship', 'self-discipline', 'trustworthiness', 'frugality', 'benevolence', 'hard work', 'create and utilise opportunities', 'versatility', 'innovativeness', 'risk taking'* and *'fatalism'*. The single value found to be specific to Malay entrepreneur is *'religious piety'*. On the other hand the personal values revealed to be specific Chinese entrepreneurs are *'sustaining growth and continuity as family business'* and *'harmonious relationship with others'*.

This study also investigated the identity development of Malay and Chinese entrepreneurs. The importance of significant others has been cited in the entrepreneurship literature but traditional approaches have found it difficult to measure and understand the extend of identifications. ISA draws on the psychodynamic theories of identity which argue that individuals interpret personal values in relation to other influential people and their expectations. The summary of the findings is presented in Table 3.3. The findings from this study show that there are similarities and differences in the identity structures between both groups of entrepreneurs. Most Malay and Chinese entrepreneurs have a high level of *'idealistic identification'* with *'admired person', 'successful entrepreneur'* and *'most Chinese entrepreneurs'*. Malay entrepreneurs perceived Chinese entrepreneurs as having qualities that they wish to emulate especially in relation to their success in business. Furthermore, in the in-depth interviews, Malay entrepreneurs claimed that there are not many Malay entrepreneurs that can be considered their role models. On the other hand, Chinese entrepreneurs sampled in this study have a *'moderate'* level of *'idealistic'* identification with Malay entrepreneurs. It is not a problem on the part of Chinese entrepreneurs to role model their successful counterparts as there are an abundance of them in their society. Malay entrepreneurs have a *'moderate'* level of *'idealistic identification'* with their *'father'*, whereas Chinese entrepreneurs identification can be considered *'high'*. However, there is no one single explanation to support such differences. The possible explanation is that most entrepreneurs evaluate these significant people based on their personal values which they perceived as either non-existent or in conflict with their present personal values.

It is important to note that the *'global'* (and crude) descriptions of entrepreneur's identity variants in relation to the *'current self'* and *'past self'* should be interpreted with caution. Both groups of entrepreneurs show a high degree of confidence with respect to their achieved and scribed role. The degree of confidence attained by them would give them greater advantage in achieving success in business. Although there are many factors that contribute to personal growth and development, it is assumed that responsibility for multiple roles also opens the doors to interrole conflicts, involving potentially incompatible demands of individuals across domain. However, the findings of this study show both groups of entrepreneurs have a high self-confidence with regards to their roles as *'an entrepreneur'*, *'as a husband'*, and *'as a Malay / Chinese*.

Conclusion

As mentioned in the earlier part of this paper, past research in entrepreneurship has made many attempts to identify single 'traits' of entrepreneurs and to predict factors which influence business success, but for the most part the results have been inconclusive, unfruitful and often conflicting. This empirical research into personal values of entrepreneurs in general and in particular linking it with entrepreneur's identity and role expectation broadened the socio-psychological perspective of entrepreneurs. The empirical findings of this research provide a new insight into the existing personal values and identity structures of Malay and Chinese entrepreneurs. This study has found that despite the differences in socio-cultural background, individuals may possess similar values; that different values are central in different individuals and that values can undergo changes when people become aware of contradictions within themselves. The personal values and identity study can be used as a diagnostic tool to identify the needs, goals, aspirations, and conflicts within and between individuals and groups.

It is hoped that this study accomplishes its objectives. Such a goal by itself is not an end, but rather a means by which the accomplishment of an end can be achieved. Such an end is, of course, and ever-widening wealth of information concerning entrepreneurial personal value systems and identity development.

Table 3.3   **Summary Findings of the Identity Structures of Malay and Chinese Entrepreneurs**

	Malay Entrepreneurs (n=40)	Chinese Entrepreneurs (n=40)	Malay Entrepreneurs (n=40)	Chinese Entrepreneurs (n=40)	Malay Entrepreneurs (n=40)	Chinese Entrepreneurs (n=40)	Malay Entrepreneurs (n=40)	Chinese Entrepreneurs (n=40)
Entity	Idealistic Identification	Idealistic Identification	Contra Identification	Contra Identification	Ego Involvement	Ego Involvement	Evaluation of Self & Others	Evaluation of Self & Others
Admired Person	0.9 (High)	0.91 (High)	0.09 (Low)	0.07 (Low)	4.53 (High)	4.81 (High)	0.85 Very High	0.95 Very High
Disliked Person	0.08 (Low)	0.07 (Low)	0.91 (High)	0.88 (High)	4.67 (High)	3.82 Moderate	-0.87 Very Low	-0.77 Very Low
Successful Entrepreneur	0.91 (High)	0.91 (High)	0.09 (Low)	0.07 (Low)	4.63 (High)	4.56 (High)	0.86 Very High	0.9 Very High
Unsuccessful Entrepreneur	0.08 (Low)	0.06 (Low)	0.84 (High)	0.75 (High)	3.72 Moderate	2.66 Moderate	-0.73 Very Low	-0.62 Very Low
Most Malay Entrepreneurs	0.65 (High)	0.64 (Moderate)	0.28 Moderate	0.26 (Low)	2.05 Moderate	2.08 Moderate	0.25 Low	0.27 Low
Most Chinese Entrepreneurs	0.76 (High)	0.87 (High)	0.18 (Low)	0.1 (Low)	3.79 (High)	3.95 (High)	0.64 Moderate	0.76 Very High
Father	0.65 (High)	0.76 (High)	0.3 Moderate	0.18 (Low)	3.08 Moderate	3.17 Moderate	0.41 Moderate	0.55 Moderate
Mother	0.62 (Moderate)	0.61 Moderate	0.31 Moderate	0.25 Moderate	3.05 Moderate	2.57 Moderate	0.39 Moderate	0.35 Moderate
Wife	0.32 (Low)	0.26 (Low)	0.24 (Low)	0.31 Moderate	1.32 (Low)	1.41 (Low)	0.1 (Low)	-0.66 Very Low
Past Self					1.88 (Low)	1.51 (Low)	-0.36 Very Low	-0.3 Very Low
Ideal Self					4.32 (High)	4.17 (High)	0.98 Very High	0.96 Very High
Current Self					4.5 (High)	4.4 (High)	0.83 Very High	0.87 Very High

Note: The criteria in this table were based on the Identity indices for each identification mode

References

Aldrich, H., and Zimmer, C. (1986), Entrepreneurship Through Social Networks, In D. L., Sexton and R. W. Smilor (Ed.), *The Art and Science of Entrepreneurship*, Cambridge: Ballinger.

Allport, G. W., Vernon P. E. and Lindzey, G. (1931), *The Study of Values*, Boston: Houghton-Mifflin Co. (1960 edition).

Aya, E. B. (1963), Value Systems and Economic Development in Japan and Thailand, *Journal of Social Issues*, 19 (1), pp. 35-51.

Begum, H. A. (1988), Attitudes, Values and Concept of Development: An analysis in the Context of Bangladesh, in Sinha, D. and Kao, H. S. R. (Ed.), *Social Values and Development*, Sage Publications.

Bird, B. J. (1989), *Entrepreneurial Behaviour*, Scott, Forresman and Company.

Bobbit, H. R. and Ford, J. D. (1980), Decision Maker Choice as a Determinant of Organisational Structure, *Academy of Management Review*, 5, pp. 13-23.

Brockhaus, R. H. (1982), The Psychology of Entrepreneur, in Kent, C. A., Sexton, D. L., and Vesper, K. H. (Ed.), *Encyclopedia of Entrepreneurship*, Englewoods-Cliffs, W. J., Prentice-Hall.

Brockhaus, R. H. (1975), I-E Locus of Control Scores as Predictors of Entrepreurial Intentions, Proceedings of Academy of Management, pp. 433-445.

Brockhaus, R. H., and Horwitz, P. S., (1986), The Psychology of Entrepreneur, in Sexton, D. L., and Smilor, R. W. (Ed.), *The Art and Science of Entrepreneurship*, Cambridge: Ballinger.

Carsrud, A. L., and Johnson, R. W. (1989), Entrepreneurship: A Social Psychological Perspective, *Entrepreneurship and Regional Development*, 1, pp. 21-32.

Chinese Culture Connection (1987), Chinese Values and Research for a Culture Free Dimension of Culture, *Journal of Cross-Cultural Psychology*, 18, pp. 143-174.

De Carlo, F., and Lyons, R. F. (1979), A Comparison of Selected Personal Characteristics and Non-Minority Female Entrepreneurs, Journal of Cusiness Management, Vol. 7, No. 4, pp. 22-29.

England, G. W. (1967), Organisational Goals and Expected Behaviour of American Managers, Academy of Management Journal, Vol. 10, No. 2, pp. 107-117.

Erikson, E. H. (1968), *Identity, Youth and Crisis*, New York: Norton.

Feather, N. T. (1975), *Values in Education and Society*, New York: Free Press.

Festinger, L. A. (1957), *A Theory of Cognitive Dissonance*, Stanford University Press.

Fransella, F., and Bannister, D. (1977), A Manual of Repertory Technique, London: American Press.

Gasse, Y. (1977), *Entrepreneurial Characteristics and Practices: A Study of the Dynamics of Small Business Organisations and Their Effectiveness in Different Environments*, Sherbrooke, Canada: Rine Prince Imprimaeur.

Hauser, S. T. (1971), *Black and White Identity Formation*, New York, Wiley.

Hamzah, Y. (1979), *Small Industry Development Strategy in Indonesia*, Ministry of Industry, Jakarta, Indonesia (mimeo).

Hirch, B. J., and Rapkin, B. D. (1986), Multiple Roles, Social Networks, and Women's Well Being, *Journal of Personality and Social Psychology*, 51(6), pp. 1237-1247.

Inglehart, R. (1985), *The Silent Revolution: Changing Values and Political Styles Among Western Publics*, Priceton University Press.

Kelly, G. A. (1965), *The Psychology of Personal Constructs*, 2 Vols, New York, Norton.

Kilman, R. H. (1977), *Social Systems Design: Normative Theory and MAPS Design Technology*, New York: Elsevier.

Marcia, J. (1966), *Identity in Adolescence*, in Adelson, J. (Ed.) Handbook of Adolescent Psychology, New York, Wiley.

Marcia, J. (1980), *Identity in Adolescence*, in Adelson, J. (Ed.), Handbook of Adolescent Psychology, New York, Wiley.

Marris, D. and Somerset, A. (1971), *African Businessmen*, Routledge and Kegan Paul, London.

McClelland, D. C. (1961), Achievement Motivation Can Be Development, *Harvard Business Review*, November-December.

Mead, G. H. (1934), *Mind, Self and Society: From the Standpoint of a Social Behaviourist*, Chicago: University of Chicago Press.

Mitzberg, H. and Waters, J. A. (1982), Tracking Strategy in an Entrepreneurial Fism, *Academy of Management Journal*, 25, pp. 456-499.

Pederson, P. (1979), Non-Western Psychology: The Search for Alternative, In A. J. Marsella, R. G. Tharp, and T. J., Civordwski (Ed.), *Perspectives on Cross-Cultural Psychology*, New York, Academic Press.

Rezaian, Y. H. (1984), *A Study of Personal Value Systems of Iranian Entrepreneurs Operating in United States*: Unpublished Thesis, Nova University.

Rokeach, M. (1973), *The Nature of Human Values*, London, Free Press.

Rosenberg, M. J. and Abelson, R. P. (1960), An Analysis of Cognitive Balancing in Rosenberg, M., and Turner, R. H. (Ed.), *Social Psychology: Sociological Perspectives*, New York, Basic Books.

Schere, J. L. (1982), Tolerance and Ambiguity as Discriminating Variable Between Entrepreneurs and Managers, *Proceedings of Academy of Management*, pp. 404-408.

Sexton, D. L. and Bowman, N. (1985), The Entrepreneur: A Capable Executive and More, *Journal of Business Venturing*, 1(1), pp. 129-140.

Stevenson, H. H., Roberts, M. J., and Grousbeck, H. I. (1985), *New Business Vetures and the Entrepreneur*, Homewood, III:Irwin.

Stryker, S. and Statham, A. (1985), Symbolic Interaction and Role Theory, in G. Lindzey and E. Aronson (Ed.), *The Handbook of Social Psychology*, New York: Random House.

Tropman, J. E. (1984), Value Conflicts and Policy Decision Making: Analysis and Resolution, *Human Systems Management*, 4, pp. 214-219.

Weigert, A. J. (1983), Identity: Its Emergence Within Sociological Psychology, Symbolic Interaction. No. 6, pp. 183-206.

Weinreich, P. (1986) *A Manual of Identity Exploration Using Personal Constructs*, Reprint, Coventry: University of Warwick, Economics and Social Science Research Council, Centre for Research in Ethnic Relations.

Weinreich, P. (1980), *Manual of Identity Exploration Using Personal Constructs*, London: Social Science Research Council.

Weinreich, P. (1969), *Theoretical and Experimental Evaluation of Dissonance Process*, Unpublished Ph. D. Thesis, Univesity of London.

Weinreich, P. (1983), Emerging from Threatened Identities: Ethnicity and Gender in Redefinitions of Ethnic Identity, Breakwell, G. (Ed.), *Threatened Identities*, Chichester: Wiley.

William, A. S. (1965), *Values and Organisations, A Study of Fraternities and Sororities*, Chicago, Rand McNally.

4 Telling Stories of Entrepreneurship - Towards a Narrative-Contextual Epistemology for Entrepreneurial Studies

Chris Steyaert and René Bouwen

> The Master gave his teaching in parables and stories which his disciples listened to with pleasure - and occasional frustration, for they longed for something deeper. The master was unmoved. To all their objections he would say, 'You have yet to understand, my dears, that the shortest distance between a human being and Truth is a story'
>
> Anthony de Mello, 1985

Stories: Second Hand Study or Creative Science?

Entrepreneurial studies consist many times of portraits, cases, stories, and biographies of (un)successful entrepreneurs and (un)fortunate entrepreneurial companies. Stories and biographies of entrepreneurs and their companies are registered either in a scientific or more popular version as founders' stories, life stories, autobiographies, success stories, quasi-hagiographies, or as painful accounts of failure, loss, and bankruptcy. Such 'entrepreneurs' stories often show a strong resemblance to fiction in which the heroine skims the highest peaks or the hero plumbs the depths, or they form the basis of characters in films or plays. Tsoukas (1994, p. 768) points out that such publications are so popular because they are more accessible to practitioners: 'Narratives, being loose flexible frameworks, are close to the activities of practitioners, are richer in content, and have a higher mnemonic value'. Such a story captures the attention and the imagination of the reader who identifies with the vicissitudes of the main characters and recognises partly one's own experiences. The story allows the experiences of others to be linked to one's own story or to view the latter in a new light.

However, the positioning towards narratives takes extreme forms or causes at least 'mixed feelings'. For some, stories are obvious while for others, they are out of the question. On the one hand, there is a group of researchers, who plea in favour of writing and publishing stories. For instance, Dyer & Wilkins (1991) argue that in order to generate better theory through case studies, 'better stories' are needed instead of better constructs. The idea of case study work is to write a thick description of a field experience which can stimulate understanding and theoretical insight, and not to control the research process according to the principles of hypothesis-testing research.[1] Some scholars go one step further and see already *fiction* stories as a way to develop imagination and creativity in the daily enactment of the organising process (Alvarez & Merchan, 1992, Czarniawska-Joerges & Guillet de Monthoux, 1994). On the other hand, researchers are rather sceptical concerning the use of this genre in scientific research, reducing stories into second hand research or only valid as a first exploration. For instance, the many (early) attempts to describe entrepreneurial endeavours in journalistic essays or case studies have been received very critically from those researchers who wanted to see the entrepreneurship field to turn to 'normal science' as

---

[1] Dyer & Wilkins (1991) react here against a scenario developed by Eisenhardt (1989) which describes the process of inducting theory using case studies, partly based on the principles of hypothesis-testing research.

soon as possible, claiming that entrepreneurship should develop itself through quantitative oriented inquiry and that it should not after all stick to case studies. [2]

We think we should not throw away the child with the bathwater. The value of stories for entrepreneurship research depends very much on the paradigmatic, epistemological and methodological position one takes and on how stories are constructed and used. Although entrepreneurship has seldom been conceived of as narrative, this text wants to see how a narrative study of entrepreneurship can come onto the horizon. It will be claimed that stories can be useful outcomes of qualitative research which are directly accessible fragments, open for the sense making of the reader and user of the study. More strongly, it will be claimed that storytelling becomes appealing if science (and practice) wants to be imaginative (Chia, 1996).

First, we will elaborate some epistemological reflections on doing entrepreneurship research, trying to show that a narrative approach to entrepreneurship can contribute in a constructive way to some of the epistemological and methodological problems this domain currently faces. Second, we will go into the domain of narrative epistemology, and explore how it can guide us in telling stories of entrepreneurship. Third, we will describe a framework in which 'telling' stories of entrepreneurship can be developed.

Epistemological Reflections on Entrepreneurship Research

Writing and telling stories brings research close to literary activities. Although some might appreciate stories for their entertaining potential and their 'telling' qualities, they would be reluctant to accept this as 'good' or valuable science. This scientific resistance to the art of telling stories will be situated in a broader epistemological context as the different reactions to stories are linked with different paradigmatic conceptions. With regard to entrepreneurship studies, we see currently three epistemological problems which are the heart of the knowledge production process of entrepreneurship, and in which a narrative approach can take a stimulating stand.

Entrepreneurship Studies as Reconstructing a World out there or a Creative Activity?

The development of entrepreneurship as an academic discipline is very much a boundary activity, where new ways of theorising, new methods and new questions can emerge (Steyaert, 1995). Although entrepreneurship scholars have not been afraid of exploring alternative modes of inquiry (Stevenson & Harmeling, 1990; MacMillan & Katz, 1992), they have mainly followed a logo-scientific mode of knowing (Steyaert, 1995). The research on entrepreneurial companies is there to represent in an objective and accurate way the (entrepreneurial) reality out there, which dictates on itself the accounts we make of the world. The resulting ambition is to explain and to predict entrepreneurial action. But many scholars experience that the entrepreneurial reality itself does not tolerate such a rigorous and especially stabilising and reifying intervention formed by this kind of objectivist and positivist research. This 'feeling' has been expressed among others by Hisrich (1988) who does not see a possible solution in the choice for predictive cause and effect relationships: 'By its very nature, success in the field of entrepreneurship reflects changing internal and external environments. It is doubtful, therefore, that a formal predictive scientific theory of entrepreneurship will ever emerge.'

The alternative is to engage in studies which approach entrepreneurship as a creative process in which it is accepted that entrepreneurs are creators of new realities walking on the boundary between destabilising existing situations and actualising implicit possibilities into new contexts. This requires research that engages in entrepreneurship as a process instead of a fixed entity, and implies a constructionist view of reality by researchers who are as much creators as

---

[2] For an example see, Wortman (1986), for a critical discussion, see Aldrich (1992).

representators of the reality they study. The step towards creativity as an important research criterion comes hardly as a surprise, since it is the process-philosopher Whitehead who stressed creativity as the heart of academic work: 'the university imparts information but it imparts it imaginatively... A university which fails in this respect has no reason for existence. This atmosphere of excitement, arising from imaginative consideration, transforms knowledge. A fact is no longer a bare fact. It is invested with all its possibilities. It is no longer a burden on the memory: it is energising as the poet of our dreams, and as the architect of our purposes.' Chia (1996), quoting Whitehead, recently advocated that academic research most of all requires entrepreneurial imagination. We claim here that if there is one discipline to take this advice literally it is the discipline of entrepreneurship itself, studying one of the most inventive human activities, that one of 'entrepreneuring'.

Entrepreneurship Theory as a One-Truth Science or Multi-Perspectivistic Reality?

In accordance with the first point, the universality principle of research, aiming at formulating an encompassing version of entrepreneurial reality, might be reconsidered. The principle that research is there to formulate general theories and universal insights has started to be questioned by entrepreneurial scholars. For instance, Churchill (1992, p. 593) notices that reports of non-homogenous populations are written 'as if the principles or generalisations were universal and could be safely applied to any industry'. However, how to generalise is not only a question of sample selection but goes back to paradigmatical positions. Only recently, a paradigmatical awareness has entered discussions on entrepreneurship research (Bouwen & Steyaert, 1992; Aldrich, 1992). Aldrich suggests that entrepreneurship is more than one all-encompassing science, and that there are in fact at least three approaches present: 'a unitary, normal science view; a multiple paradigms view; and a totally pragmatic antipositivist view' (1992, p. 208). These are different pathways entrepreneurship as an academic discipline is following. But it is difficult to find many supporters of views two and three in the entrepreneurship field, and it should be noted that the whole suggestion comes from Aldrich, a sociologist brought in for the occasion of a handbook on entrepreneurship, who only superficially outlines here what he describes in detail elsewhere (Reed & Hughes, 1992), in the context of organisational theory, *nota bene*. Taking the framework of Burrell & Morgan (1979) as point of departure, it becomes obvious that many problem formulations and research themes in the entrepreneurship literature are mainly approached in functionalist terms, while the possibilities of a more interpretive, radical humanist or radical structuralist orientation remain unused (Johannisson 1991; Bouwen & Steyaert, 1992). The needed diversity of paradigmatic perspectives to study such a complex and multi-layered phenomenon as entrepreneurship is thus far from being reached.

 Not only on the level of research perspectives, but (as a consequence) also with regard to the different parties studied, one can claim the same line of argument. Many times, studies on entrepreneurship are like a one-truth-study, namely giving the perspective of the entrepreneur (who filled in the questionnaire, or who has been interviewed) while many other perspectives (from the other key actors and employees to the clients and competitors) are not heard or studied apart in another study, actually neglecting the interaction between the different actors at play in an entrepreneurial endeavour.

Fragmentation or Fragments of Entrepreneurship?

The one-truth strategy of science has not lead to a grand theory but to a state of fragmentation. Scientific thinking is fragmented, and has accused itself many times of being disconnected, despite the cohesion-directed intentions, despite the quest for unity, the belief that all the separate pieces of the puzzle will someday fit together. This is so for management and organisational studies (Whitley, 1984) not differing much from other disciplines, which do not fare much better and often do worse. One example is psychology, of which Bruner has written: 'Psychology has become fragmented as never before in its history'.[3] Even a young discipline like entrepreneurship already threatens to capsize under the lack of conceptual ties, and can only meagerly attempt what its big sister disciplines themselves have never been able to accomplish, and what has landed them in a jam for some years now. The drive towards unification and coherence is very great, like expressed by MacMillan and Katz (1992) who see theory building as one of the most pressing issues for this young science, and they see enough studies 'to begin to piece together' them. The question is if entrepreneurship can save itself by aiming at an overall theory of entrepreneurship or if it should radically choose for a situation which aims at producing only locally 'valid' accounts. The latter option implies holistic studies which focus on local knowledge and create 'fragments' of entrepreneurial reality which are understood in their processual complexity without claiming any transfer to other contexts.

Towards a Narrative-Contextual Epistemology for Entrepreneurial Studies

In raising these three current epistemological choices of entrepreneurship research, we claim that a narrative approach and the narrative form in specific are appropriate to engage in entrepreneurship as a process-oriented, multiperspectivistic and contextual reality and science. In a narrative, the story teller tries to capture the sequences of events and the process of how 'things' are evolving, the different actors get a place on the scenery whenever their perspective is seen as adding to the dramatic course, and the story get its unique character as the context emerges in the line of narrating. Entrepreneurship research, engaging in story telling, might look a little bit more modest in its ambitions, but it comes closest to the creative contribution writers can make, according to Lyotard (1979, p. 64), 'the little narrative remains the quintessential form of imaginative invention'. Stories can form an epistemology of fragments as mentioned above. For the most part, the narrative - not the grand stories, but the *petites histoires* - comes down to a fragment, as Erich Fried has noted: 'The truth is that stories are in fact always fragments, even if their narrators and writers are not aware of it, and the listeners and readers even less so. The most complete stories are those that there, right where they leave off in the middle of a sentence, leave behind a fissure in the brain'.[4] De Kuyper[5] establishes that 'we live only by the grace of stories. La vie est un roman.... What has here taken place must remain an incident, and as a story, it remains a "fragment".' The story is thus a suitable epistemological category for the local and contextualised knowledge entrepreneurship research can aim for.

A paradigmatic anchoring which combines the idea of entrepreneurship research as process-oriented, multiperspectivist and contextual may be found in contextualism,[6] one of Pepper's four 'World Hypotheses', and closely related to Burrell and Morgan's 'interpretivism'. The contextualistic approach picks up the thread using the flux metaphor, where change and novelty are endemic qualities of every social system, where the event is the central focus, and the story is the

---

[3] See *Acts of Meaning* (1990).

[4] 'Es ist so, dass Geschichten eigentlich immer Fragmente sind, auch wenn ihre Erzähler und Schreiber das nicht wissen, und die Zuhörer und Leser erst recht nicht. Die vollständigste Geschichten sind die, die dort, wo sie mitten im Satz aufhören, einen Riss im Hirn hinterlassen.', as cited by Eric de Kuyper, 1994, p. 131.

[5] De Kuyper is a Flemish fiction writer who in this novel attempts to forget a love story, and as he writes, concludes his story with the quoted fragment.

[6] Contextualism is one of Pepper's four 'World Hypotheses'. For a recent discussion, see Tsoukas (1994). It was, however, earlier brought to the attention of organizational psychology by Payne (1975/ 1976, 1982).

interpretative construction of this unique episode. 'Contextualism is synthetic: it takes a pattern, a gestalt, as the object of study, rather than a set of discrete facts. (...) [it] is dispersive: the multitudes of facts it seeks to register are assumed to be loosely structured, not systematically connected by virtue of a lawful relationship. There is no search for underlying structures, and the distinction between appearances and an underlying reality is not accepted. Its root metaphor is the historic event, continuously changing over time.' Through the event, a researcher sets his or her sights on the present. This event, embedded in history is characterised by a certain quality and texture. Quality is the intuited wholeness while texture refers to the details and relations, the two being different sides of the same coin (Tsoukas, 1994). The event is oriented towards the present: 'In an actual event the present is the whole texture which directly contributes to the quality of the event. The present therefore spreads over the whole texture of the quality, and for any given event, can only be determined by intuiting the quality of the event' (Pepper, 1942, p. 242; cited in Tsoukas, 1994).

In further elaborating a narrative-contextual approach, we will take two steps. First, we will take a look at narrativity as it is practised in other disciplines than entrepreneurship. Second, we will discuss how a narrative approach can be practised in methodological terms.

Narrativity and the Art of Telling Stories

In developing a narrative approach to entrepreneurship, we can learn from experiences with narrativity in such disciplines as literary sciences, psychology, educational sciences, organization studies..., which can 'guide' us in elaborating a narrative approach to entrepreneurship. Firstly, we will explore some general principles of narrative reality construction which we will, secondly, more closely examine for how persons 'construct' narratives and tell stories.

Understanding Narrative Reality Construction

Narrativity is a specific form of reality construction, the process of which can be described more precisely as a manner of framing, feeling and identity formation, interactive actualisation, and language use.

In the first place, narrativity organises our experiences and interactions by framing them (Bruner, 1990, p.56). 'Framing provides a means of 'constructing' a world, of characterising its flow, of segmenting events within that world.' The story is a typical form for framing, structuring and remembering our experience such that the story and the knowledge contained in it coincide: 'One can better understand thoughts if one does not consider them as successive or co-existent properties per se, a permanent mental substance, but rather as moments in a narrative of which the author is himself the subject' (Harré, 1989, p. 137).[7] The story provides unity to a person's experiences, and experiences which are not organised narratively have little chance of being remembered (Mandler, 1984). Stories are constitutive for the memory and not merely derived from it: 'It is not that these reflexive narrations in themselves reflect a mentally pre-existent organization: their structure is the organization of the mind' (Harré, p. 138).[8] If stories are a re-presentation of an event experienced in the past, then we are here dealing not with a re-production, a re-flection, a story that corresponds with and about this event, but with a production, a performance in the

---

[7] 'On comprend mieux les pensées si on ne les considère pas comme des propriétés successives ou coexistentes du soi, substance mentale permanente, mais comme des moments d'une narration dont l'auteur est le sujet lui-même.'

[8] 'Non que ces narrations réflexives de soi reflètent une organisation mentale préexistente : leur structure est l'organisation de l'esprit.'

theatrical sense, by which the story is conjured up so that we may save it for later and perform it again in other contexts and in other performances.

The story that is told by framing is not only a form of experience and memory organization, it leads, in the second place, also to 'affect regulation' (Bruner, 1990)[9] and 'identity construction' (Gergen, 1994, chp. 8; Harré, 1989). Bruner makes a direct link between the activity of framing and the way stories incorporate emotional experiences and are in fact crucial for memory. There is here no question of a split between cognitive and affective processes. Often it is the emotional state that offers the key to reconstructing a particular set of circumstances in terms of a scheme. One recalls a certain feeling ('that was a nasty customer') around which the story is further recounted as it takes on the form of an account.[10] We tell the story in such a way that it can convince the listener about our feelings around the event ('Now do you see what a nasty customer that was?'). Through stories we show and account for our feelings and can also regulate and partially control those feelings by the same token: as people tell their stories, they 'come around' and can 'cool off', they can get a little distance and through making an account respect their feelings. When someone says 'Was I ever angry!', that person can master the feeling and do justice to it at the same time. Furthermore, this story, that links event and feeling, is told *to* someone[11] and is thus a part of a consequent social event with its own feelings around which 'new' stories can be told. The 'narratives' that we exchange with one another account not only for a person's emotional world, but more broadly for their self-image, self-definition, and identity (Bruner, 1990; Gergen & Davis, 1984; Gergen, 1994, ch. 9). The stories that we tell about ourselves and that others tell about us give meaning to my actions and to my existence. My life is ultimately my life-story, that grants an identity to myself and those whom I include or exclude from my stories.

Narrative sense making, which entails a form of experience, memory, feeling, and identity organization, demands thirdly an interactive process of actualisation. In communities, in families, and in high tech firms individuals agree upon or negotiate meanings by mediating narrative interpretations. One story is followed by another which partly mimics the first one and partly develops it. By 'narrating', meanings are actualised, which means that they become public and community property and thus negotiable. In this way a culture creates meanings which in turn actualise that culture and further give it shape. Culture is a process that exists in the present between previously negotiated meanings and future-directed intentions. Sense making never gets dull, because people do not simply 'repeat' the past, nor do they invent the future out of thin air. They are involved in their present sense making, in the tension between 'what has been' and 'what it all must become'. Individuals become involved with one another through the stories that they tell one another - in fact, they together write a local story in which each takes the other's story a step further, to be taken up by yet another person, and so on, and so on... In this way life is full of consecutive stories, from the great family-stories in which the lives of grandfather, father, and grandson are coupled together, to the little shop-stories over the customers who pass through the scene throughout the day.

This interactive character of narratives can be made clear with a metaphor from the theater. Just as we enter a drama at the moment that we are born, when we move to a new city, or get a new job - in fact, every time we find ourselves in a new situation, and begin to play our new role opposite the other players, all the while trying to figure out what the play or the scene is actually about but in the process shaping it and even changing it - so too do we end up in other people's

---

[9]   Gergen (1994) also sees an important mediating role for 'narratives' in the way emotions can be dealt with in relationships: 'emotions are not possessions of individual minds but constituents of relational patterns or lived narratives'.

[10]   Bartlett writes: 'The recall is then a construction made largely on the basis of this attitude (read affect), and its general effect is that of a justification of the attitude' (Bartlett, 1932 cited in Bruner, 1990, p. 58).

[11]   It is usually easier to tell a story to a third person than to the other person involved with the emotional experience.

stories and they in ours: 'When we enter human life, it is as if we walk on stage into a play whose enactment is already in progress - a play whose somewhat open plot determines what parts we may play and toward what denouements we may be heading. Others on stage already have a sense of what the play is about, enough of a sense to make negotiation with a newcomer possible' (Bruner, 1990, p. 34). A company is nothing but a quest for the point of the play that at the same time you are in the process of writing, and that you try to streamline through (the exchange of) stories. Having just made an exit, there is no longer any other way to play a meaningful part than by conferring about the course of the action which has just taken place. The alternative is to start your own play, as may often be seen in companies where apparently differing scenarios cross one another, or in ruined relationships, heart-rending family dramas, or foundering friendships, where each person starts to go their own way without much further regard for anyone else.

Narrative actualisation assumes that individuals can (further) interpret the meaning of these stories. This is possible through their participation in the symbolic systems within a culture by which people take language, forms of discourse, and ways of making experiences explicit through narrative, and make them their 'own'. This brings us to a fourth characteristic; namely, that narrative sense making employs a specific form of language use. The strength of a story for the sense-making process lies in a specific use of language. A story is a literary form, and whether one is recounting a 'true story' or fiction, there is a great deal riding on the language one employs, on the literary qualities of the narrator, and on the narrative genre itself. Narrative language use[12] is concrete, metaphorical, allusive, and context sensitive (Bruner, 1990). A story does not deal with abstraction, as is often the case with scientific language use, but seeks to be concrete, detailed, specific. It transcends the abstract further by using metaphors and other tropes.[13] It thus seeks comparison with other concrete worlds and is as a result suggestive, allusive, open to the reader's meaning. Finally, the story surpasses abstraction because the meanings it creates are extremely context sensitive and meaningful only within the contours that it delineates itself. Furthermore, there is in my opinion no universal (narrative) language use: communities, as well as businesses, develop their own way of storytelling and employ their own story forms which are part of their own language games and different language repertoires.

How do we tell Stories? - Constructing Narratives

According to Bruner, narrative sense making may be characterised in four dimensions: sequential,[14] 'indifferent' to facts, canonical, and dramatic. Inherent in a narrative is, firstly, its sequential character: 'a narrative is composed of a unique sequence of events, mental states, happenings involving human beings or actors' (1990, p. 43). We are dealing here with more than just chronology, however. The meaning of partial units such as 'events' is formed as part of the larger configuration to which they belong; that is, the plot or *fabula*. Here we can see the double task of every interpretation: meaning arises from the tension between part and whole. In order to grasp the meaning of a section it must be seen in terms of the whole, and it is only through the parts that one can track down the whole. The point here is thus not pure sequentiality, but also how the

---

[12] To explore the specificities of language use, Bruner has observed the way young children enter into a system of meaning and how they learn by speaking in stories. Developing this skill is for Bruner not so much a mental achievement as 'an achievement of social practice that lends stability to the child's social life' (Bruner, 1990, p. 68).

[13] Tropes includes such figurative expressions as simile, metaphor, and metonymy.

[14] A more elaborated vision on how somebody tells and structures a well-formed story, based on theories from such diverse disciplines as literary theory, semiotics, historiography, and certain sectors of social science, can be found in Gergen (1994, p. 189-193). Besides the ordering and sequencing of events, he discusses the following characteristics : establishing a valued endpoint, using stable identities, providing explanations and suggesting causal linkages, and employing demarcation signs as beginnings, endings, and so on.

progression of events fits into a broader configuration. The idea of a temporal ordering - 'an event chain operating through time' (Chatman, 1981, p. 808) - is only a minimal condition for being able to speak of a story. There is also a non-chronological dimension which in general terms accords with the configuration of the story, according to Ricoeur[15] (1981, p. 278-279): 'Any narrative combines, in varying proportions, two dimensions: a chronological dimension and a non-chronological dimension... the activity of narrating does not consist simply in adding episodes to one another; it also constructs meaningful totalities out of scattered events. The art of narrating, as well as the corresponding art of following a story, therefore require that we are able to extract a configuration from a succession... This complex structure implies that the most humble narrative is always more than a chronological series of events.'

Secondly, a story is indifferent to facts. Sequentiality, mentioned above, exists *per se*, and not on the basis of a true or a false representation of an extra-linguistic truth. A story can be both real or imaginary; its strength as story lies in its own chronology and internal structure, with the result that it is a form suitable to both fact and fiction and that there can be no difference claimed between the ways of recounting a historical story and a fictional story, ultimately no difference between 'history' and 'story'. The explanation for this 'co-incidence' has in the course of history been the source of many suppositions - stories, you could say - but Ricoeur's idea, that 'the form of life to which narrative discourse belongs is our historical condition itself',[16] would seem to us quite plausible. Our involvement in history makes us tend towards a historical form, allowing us to begin a story 'Once upon a time...'. The same is true of the 'story' in a scientific report which reads like a piece of fiction. It seems to us unlikely that pieces of fiction should be of a different order from the stories told by interviewees, or that these should be different again from the interviewer's story which re-tells them.

Thirdly, a story is canonical,[17] aimed at the expected and the habitual, while at the same time calculated to surpass these limits. Or better still, it attempts to make a connection between the ordinary and the extraordinary, between the canonical and the exceptional. Stories can make differences within a culture explicit, deal with conflicts, and re-examine community meanings. Here we get an answer to the question of how a 'folk psychology' can escape from the trivial and incorporate the new. Bruner believes that stories are capable of allowing for deviations from the norm, managing to accommodate impossible logic in an acceptable way. Many actions and meanings are self-explanatory and require no further comment, like a kiss from your mother or a handshake from your colleague. Unusual actions and meanings, like refusing to kiss your mother but bussing your colleague, can become transparent through stories, since the story provides the reasons for a particular action, thus giving it meaning. In this way you can get the action and its accompanying story 'across', and they become credible. All the same, this remains for us an insufficient explanation, since new meaning and change always generally involve an adjustment to the existing framework, and it is not (yet) clear how new frameworks arise out of cultural developments.

Finally, narrativity is dramatic. The story is dramatic because the event and the person involved in it can move, transport, or sweep along the listener or the reader. In this process the audience draws in its breath or is touched in its deepest feelings and morally humbled or, conversely, inspired to a renewed integrity. Bruner introduces Burke's 'pentad' (1962) in order to systematise the dramatic character of a story. For Burke, more or less the founder of dramaturgical sociology,[18] every dramatic event consists of an actor, an action, a goal, a scene, and an instrument,

---

15 For a general overview on Ricoeur's thinking on narrativity, see De Visscher (1994).
16 Ricoeur (1981) on 'the narrative function'. Also cited by Bruner (1990).
17 'Canonical' means 'that what has become the norm, the point of reference'.
18 Burke had his successors (Mangham & Overington, 1987). On the one hand he was a strong inspiration for one of his students, Duncan (1968), who equally puts the accent on interactionism and sees society as 'communication of significant symbols'. He developed and redeveloped completely Burke's dramatic impulses into a dramatic method, 'meant to serve as a methodological guide for

and of how these five elements relate to one another (Steyaert, 1992). Using this pentad, one can undertake a dramatic analysis of motivated action: 'In any rounded statement about motives, you must have some word that names the act (names what took place, in thought or deed), and another that names the scene (the background of the act, the situation in which it occurred); also, you must indicate what person or kind of person (agent) performed the act, what means or instruments he used (agency), and the purpose' (Burke, 1962; Mangham & Overington, 1983). A situation becomes dramatic when the pentad becomes unbalanced, for example when an instrument cannot or may not reach its goal, when the actor performs an action which does not fit the scene, or when there are multiple goals in play. The dramatic plays precisely on the balance between the conventional and the deviant, between the canonical and the new, between the known and the unknown. A story, played or told, makes use of this lack of balance, provides a commentary, considers the consequences on the level of values, norms and responsibilities, and possibly offers a new balance, by which values and norms are 're-thought': they are brought back into memory, are applied to themselves, and become reframed, morally charged, and emotionally celebrated.

Using these four characteristics, we have been able to indicate how the form of a story relates to the construction of reality: the story proceeds sequentially, as events are brought together in a chronological and non-chronological (part/whole relation) order, always linked to the point of view of the narrator rather than that of an external reality, in tension with the normal world it attempts to surpass, and dramatically born by the actions of actors who use various means to achieve their goal in a specific scene.

Telling Stories of Entrepreneurship: Narratives in a Methodological Frame

In order to discuss a narrative approach more concretely, we will focus on story telling both in the stages of data generation and data interpretation and presentation.

Collecting Stories and the Story Telling Interview

Interviews in an Epistemological Framework. Traditionally, the data-collecting phase is a period of fieldwork in which the researcher collects the planned data from such and such companies and subjects, using these questions, in this or that period of time. It is the most practical phase, and the art consists of allowing it to transpire in the most standardised way possible. It is an active phase with passive thought-work. Researchers involved with fieldwork often have the flair of those conducting experiments, that repetitive ritual in which one subject after another is offered the same stimulus. It does not particularly matter, nor is it allowed to matter, who the subject is. All subjects are the same. And the researcher acts as if he or she knows what wants to be known. In field research, time is also spent collecting 'passive' data, as if data were like so many Easter eggs just waiting to be found, as if reality were an orchard ripe for the picking.

In my view, the researcher intervenes and generates rather than collects the data. In fact, the data generating phase determines the contours of the researcher's understanding, mapping out the territory for further interpretation. This is not a neutral activity, but a crucial step which can never receive enough attention. The kind of experimental logic described above is thus not transferable to field research into 'phenomena-on-the-move' like entrepreneurship is. Here the researcher is in

---

investigators undertaking a substantive study of the enactment of social orders' (Mangham & Overington, 1987). He studied 'role playing' in various contexts where social order exists: family, religion, economy, art. On the other hand, many traces of Burke may be found in Goffman (1969), the most popular author of the dramatic school who has had the most further influence (on Harré, and also on others; see Zeegers & Jansz (1988)). For an example of how Burke's pentad is used in a literary analysis of employee involvement, see O'Connor (1995).

search of what he or she wishes to understand, and every subject represents a new step on this path. The researcher is caught up in the flow of the organization being studied, even at the risk of being dragged along willy nilly. From experimental logic we can retain the process of repetition, since it helps the systematic dimension necessary for every study. However, the fact that interviews need to be repeated does not mean that they are subject to repetition as standardised actions. The qualitative, interviewing researcher sets out and travels along with the object in question. This is by no means a passive ride, but rather, the researcher experiences the company, in the two senses of sharing its experiences and in helping to construct it.

This distinction between data collection and data generation goes back to the ontological and epistemological distinctions between a positivist and a constructionist model. It is about the choice between 'the made as the given' and 'the given as made'. This second position is presented in an extreme version by Harré (1981, p. 17): 'There are no data, and *a fortiori* to attempt to formulate the descriptions of regularities in the sequence of human action as data, is a folly.' The researcher enters into an interaction with the environment, with others, and this interaction is constitutive for what may be seen as 'data'. Data are not so much 'givens', but are 'mades', arrived at by mutual agreement. As a researcher in a field situation you must often explicitly negotiate about this: how many interviews, with whom, how long, about what? Individuals ask, 'Can I say this?' or 'Are you going to use this too?', and thereby express the notion that they are not only providing 'information' to an interviewer, but are actually saying something that they have never said before and will never say again. However, once something has been said, it has been said, so that whatever we have made becomes nonetheless a given, a 'datum'. It should here become clear that we are not making this distinction in order to preserve two irreconcilable positions the second of which we support. This distinction is important for us in order to indicate that there is more to this than merely 'given givens'; it is relative for us because we want to indicate that as a researcher one must move back and forth between the constructed and the constructed-as-made. We want in no way to make this distinction absolute. This is equally true in practice, where it is also a question of dealing with both positions. Generating data, but repeating too - that is what a researcher does. The issue then becomes how interviews can be seen as a way of 'generating data'. For this we will present the idea of the 'story telling interview'.

Questioning the Questioning Process. Although interviews are classically seen as a situation of 'asking questions', in a narrative approach, interviewing can be seen as a situation where the researcher is eliciting stories from the organisational members. This can be called a kind of 'storytelling' interview.[19] Interviewing is then not going through a checklist of questions but proposing interviewees to tell their story 'from their first contact with the organization, or even earlier, if they find it relevant, until now, and also to relate how they see the future for themselves and their organization'. Regular research means asking direct questions in order to get direct answers. This situation keeps interviewees from bringing in their own experience and the 'data' they work with. Storytelling gives interviewees the chance to frame their own, relevant experiences. This guarantees furthermore the possibility of discovering new things which are at the same time relevant. Although 'asking' for stories can look unnatural to classically trained interviewers, many interviewees seem to be very natural storytellers,[20] who enact the research situation as a way to (re)frame their past, present, and future within the firm and to frame their liaison with the firm. Often, interviewees told us that it was the first time they had given such an extensive account of

---

[19] The storytelling interview is receiving more and more attention in organizational research (Reason & Rowan, 1981) and in the social sciences (Denzin & Lincoln, 1994), in particular in pedagogical research (Carter, 1993; Kelchtermans, 1993).

[20] In the Ph research of Steyaert (1995), persons telling stories from two to four hours were not exceptional. With a kind of ease and natural elegance they told of their organizational 'career'. Furthermore, sometimes people seemed to feel 'interrupted' when they were asked a question (instead of feeling stimulated).

their experience in that firm, and found the interview experience clarifying to themselves. Storytelling opens the research relation between interviewee and interviewer, and both roles must change as a result. Finally, it should be stressed that an interview cannot be seen on its own, but rather in relation with the stories of other interviews. A researcher cannot assume *tabula rasa* when doing a new interview, which means that the same questions cannot be asked in the same order. On the contrary, the interviewer should be curious about the sequence of the larger organisational story, which is formed by all of these individual stories. These ideas on storytelling come close to Mishler's (1986a, p. 69) description and motivation:

> Telling stories is far from unusual in everyday conversation and it is apparently no more unusual for interviewees to respond to questions with narratives if they are given some room to speak. [...] In general, researchers in the mainstream tradition either have not recognised the pervasiveness of stories because, as I have already remarked, the standard survey interview 'suppresses' them, or have treated stories as a problem because they are difficult to code or to quantify. We are more likely to find stories reported in studies using relatively unstructured interviews where respondents are invited to speak in their own voices, allowed to control the introduction and flow of topics, and encouraged to extend their responses. Nonetheless respondents may also tell stories in response to direct, specific questions if they are not interrupted by interviewers trying to keep them to the 'point'.

Research Analysis and Presentation as Writing Stories

Not only generating data, but also data interpretation, representation and communication, briefly reporting data can be regarded as a form of storytelling. Here the boundary between 'data' analysis (which traditionally gets a lot of attention) and 'result' presentation (which is mostly seen as merely 'writing up') blurs and both 'activities' become closely interwoven: the way one writes and the forms one uses, guide the process of understanding and interpreting the data (Steyaert, 1996).

If human reality comes into existence in story form, then there is no reason why it should be any different for the researcher. The use of narrative and writing the text as a story may be seen as one possible rhetorical approach to the scholarly publication of research experience. The experience and the story are inextricable. Not only is it the case that 'human experience can be considered qua experience only when it is told as a story', in the words of Peters and Rothenbuhler (1989, p. 19), but, referring to the philosophy of Arendt (1958) and MacIntyre (1984), the experience does not in fact take precedence over the story. The relationship between experience and meaning, as formulated by Eliot's 'we had the experience, but missed the meaning', is not dictated by antecedence or consequence, but rather by coincidence. There is no primary experience followed by a secondary, told experience. Peters and Rothenbuhler voice this view (1989, p. 19): 'Experience is not something raw and dumb that gives our words their meaning; rather, our words give meaning to our experiences. (...) Experience of the world is always already symbolic.' Conversely, meaning may not be seen as inseparable from experience, nor truth from experience. Czarniawska-Joerges (1992) observes this in reference to Lakoff and Johnson (1980) and their experiential conception of truth, another attempt to reconcile objectivism and subjectivism, in which meaning is seen as metaphorically structured experience which has been interactively negotiated. Our understanding of an utterance or of a metaphor, and our addition of the predicate 'this is true' to that utterance, to that concrete story, comes into existence because it is linked to our understanding of a particular situation; it is linked to our way of experiencing. In order to illustrate how truth and story, experience and metaphor are inseparable - they are two sides of the same coin - two sources have been coupled here; namely, a rhetorical approach to communication (Peters & Rothenbuhler) and an anthropological view of culture (Czarniawska-Joerges). Czarniawska-Joerges adds that both sides - in her analysis, that means symbolic realism and experientialism - may be seen as the two sides, a reflective and active side, of the same *pragmatic* solution.

Qualitative research on the basis of a case study is usually reported in story or narrative form. The interpretations which we as researchers have made (often separate bits, not yet hanging together) call for continuity and melt into the form of a text with line, a narrative text. As researching authors we make a new intervention and thus attempt to make our insights as clear, but above all as lively, as possible. This is no caprice. Such a narrative approach is not a stylistic choice in order to make the report more attractive, but is rather 'inherent in the purpose of case studies and the nature of their inquiry' (Ely, 1991, p. 169). In this way the scholarly text attains the status of a literary truth.

Various authors have suggested ways to report research 'differently', with, as we see it, an increasing degree of extremity. We shall now consider the proposals made by Van Maanen (1988), Rose (1990), and Richardson (1994).

Van Maanen (1988, p. 7) distinguishes three forms in which a story may be written: realist tales, 'confessional' tales, and impressionistic tales.[21] He describes them as follows: 'Realist tales... provide a rather direct, matter-of-fact portrait of a studied culture, unclouded much by much concern for how the fieldworker produced such a portrait... Confessional tales focus far more in the fieldworker than on the cultures studied... Impressionist tales are personalised accounts of fleeting moments of fieldwork cast in dramatic form; they therefore carry elements of both realist and confessional writing.' The realist tale is the most prevalent form, while there are numerous objections to confessional or autobiographical tales (Burgess, 1984; Van Maanen, 1988). The autobiographical report answers the researchers' need to look back over their path, to make it known, to learn from it themselves, and to free themselves from it to some extent. It also becomes possible for others to learn from their experience, and through autobiographies we may gain a more systematic view of qualitative research. The realist and autobiographical versions by no means exclude one another, and can, in my opinion, be complementary: the meaning of the research tale can be strengthened against the background of the researchers' own tale. An autobiographical story picks up on the idea of the log-book in which the researcher makes lifelike yet careful notes on his or her experiences. The impressionist version, which combines both of the preceding versions, draws on the storytelling qualities of the researching writer in search of a good tale or a gripping yarn.

A story is one literary genre, but there are many others. In Rose (1990) we find a radical plea - perhaps too extreme for some - for the written forms of scholarly publications to be torn asunder. We are dealing here with more than a change in our writing style, the insertion of a quotation, a comparison or an allusion to art, or playing around with the table of contents; Rose aims for a sea-change, an ethnography of 'intimacy, not distance; of stories, not modes; of possibilities, not stabilities; and of contingent understandings, not detachable conclusions' (Van Maanen, Manning & Miller, 1990). This demands an examination of the relationship between text and (entrepreneurial) life, out of which a future authorship of many new forms can grow, 'a polyphonic, heteroglossic, multigenre construction' (Rosen, 1990, p. 56). What has Rosen got in mind? He himself provides examples of ethnographic poetry, but the spectrum of forms is much wider: novellas, visual material, mini-essays, critiques, personal and emotional impressions by the author,[22] but also letters, postcards, performances, dialogues, recordings... The main idea is not that one chooses an alternative form, but that one allows different forms, voices, and genres to co-exist within one text or volume.[23]

In its most extreme form, writing becomes in itself a research method. Laurel Richardson (1994) defends this point of view when she says that writing is always a manner of 'knowing', and not simply of 'telling what is already known'. Writing is a manner of discovering, both in the sense

---

[21] He also mentions the critical, formal, literary, and jointly-told story.

[22] See Rosen (1990, p. 57).

[23] Such statements may seem extreme, but Katriel and Sanders (1989) note that, for example, the use of epigraphs, those clever little quotations placed at the beginning of scholarly texts, at first glance appearing to be nothing more than pleasantries, is already outside the conventions of scholarly writing, and can be seen as an example of Bakhtin's multivoicedness.

of exploring and revealing, and of inventing, in the sense of giving meaning to one's experience. The relationship is turned around: not writing what you know, but knowing what you are writing. Crucial in this 'knowing' are the written forms which the author applies. The format of the scientific publication is to a large extent pre-scribed, in terms of structure, length, language use, style, manner of reference. Such conventions - in fact, literary conventions - exercise a strong influence over content, and even more over how the text will be read and by whom. In this sense, we are speaking of a limitation to the essence of the author's work, and the expression of his or her discoveries. As a result, some researchers are in search of new writing formats, which Richardson (1994) brings together under the name of 'experimental representations'. Common to these formats is that they run roughshod over the prescribed rules of writing, and seriously exceed the usual frontiers of socio-scientific documentation. Scholarly writing becomes no longer a habit or ritual. Richardson distinguishes five alternative forms of evocative writing. A first form is 'the narrative of the self', comparable to Van Maanen's confessional tale. Here, the researcher narrates his or her research experience, writing not so much about the other, as about himself or herself in relation to the other. In this way the writer in fact becomes the other, writing more under his or her own name than in the name of others. Through ethnographical, fictional representation, writers describe their work as fiction, as a product of their imagination. Building further on the narrative of the self, the writer begins to make use of more stylistic means, in order to evoke the cultural situation being examined. This is not a true-to-life representation, but a form of fiction in which some elements are emphasised and placed in a particular time sequence, and where persons and viewpoints are sharply characterised, perhaps to the point of caricature. Although we are here considering a form of fiction, the question remains how this form relates to the 'real' or to what is normally called fiction. The poetic representation is a third form of evocation, and above all plays on the emotional connection between reader and writer. The poem is marked in its constructedness, and as such makes us aware of the constructedness of each text. It is one of the most powerful forms for seeing the world and social realities in a new light, and calling up a deepened, more direct understanding. Fourthly, in the ethnographic drama, various points of view and perceptions appear simultaneously, as their mutual relationships are revealed. Furthermore, drama is a direct form which crosses the borderline between the written and the spoken text. A last form of expression, which comprises a number of possibilities, consists of a hybrid of scientific and literary genres. The hybrid is for Richardson a deconstructionist critique of triangulation, so highly praised in traditional circles. In short, the repertoire from which the scholarly writer may choose becomes markedly larger: tale, ethnographic fiction, poetry, drama, or a hybrid form. In all of these forms, the voice and the sensibility of the researcher becomes more pronounced. This is in contrast to the situation where the researcher is taught to write 'scientifically', and thus not from himself or herself. The traditional approach leads to texts which resemble one another, and scientific scholarship which arises from a movement of homogenisation.

The Entrepreneurial Audience

The last 'stage' concerns when we as researchers try to tell our stories to different research publics. We all know that writing a good paper and giving an interesting talk are two different things, and that research output is re-created whenever communicated. The question is how we can relate to the entrepreneurial audience and through what forms of dialogue the audience can play its own active role. Recently, in literature theory, the role of the reader, next to the role of the writer and the text, has been strongly emphasised, as there is no dialogue without readers. The creative and aesthetic role of the reader has been argued in the work of, among others, Eco (1989) and Barthes (1986), and it has gradually been transmitted from literary texts to other kinds of texts, such as translations, publications produced by business firms or scientific dissertations. Eco's notion of 'opera aperta' and Barthes' notion of 'textes scriptibles' indicates that the stories we can tell about entrepreneurial endeavour should be open, and leave the space for the interpretation and imaginative power of the reader. Many times, case writing has ended up in a kind of 'closed' story with a fixed story morale and with didactic questions on what to learn for user of the case. The case stories we envision are not supposed to be the exemplary one's or the so-called best practices cases, but consist of the narrative that departs from the here-and-now, everyday entrepreneurial events which come to life when they are brought in a specific dialogue between a narrating researcher and an audience interested and captured by the stories of others as these make them think about their own telling story.

Once Upon a Time: How to Get a Narrative Approach on the Rails in Entrepreneurship Research?

Our claim is that in the field of entrepreneurship, there is often implicitly a narrative approach present. In attending workshops and conferences on entrepreneurship, one can remark many times how presenters bring in examples to make their point or just to keep the attention of their audience. These examples are little narratives while the principles of narration are seldom made explicit. Also researchers presenting the results of a quantitative study refer to a short story to give some of the context of their 'data'. And conference organisers are always glad when they are able to programme some entrepreneurs who come to tell 'life' from their experience. In the class room, these same entrepreneurship scholars tell stories to their students based on their frequent contacts with entrepreneurs, but these stories are 'of the record', self-evidently not part of the exam requirements. Although, many more examples can be given, it is still a question if and how a more explicit narrative approach can be put on the rails. For this, the challenge is learning to tell 'telling' stories.

    In this text, we have tried to sketch a scenario towards a narrative approach which contains conceptual, epistemological and methodological reflections. First, the different positions towards a narrative approach have been identified somewhere in between 'stories as second hand research' and 'as a very appropriate way to creative science'. Second, a narrative approach has been situated within some actual epistemological issues of entrepreneurship research which is a need of conceiving its studies as constructionist, multi-voiced and contextualized. Third, we have explored principles at play in a narrative construction of reality in general and in storytelling in specific. Finally, we have in concrete explored how a narrative study of entrepreneurship can be conceived with regard to data generation, data interpretation and presentation and research communication.

    However, the reader might have missed a 'good story' in this text, which illustrates the issues and principles at stake. If the shortest way between the entrepreneur and the Truth is a story, this paper may look like a roundabout. Still, this is less easy as it looks. Telling a story, which takes maybe only a couple of minutes, is always embedded in a specific context, which needs some more time if to be addressed. Writing a story goes many times beyond the scope of academic publishing standards. For example, in the PhD dissertation of Steyaert, two narratives of two high techs companies are published, one counting 25 pages (p. 392-416), the other counting 12 pages (p. 416-427). It is hard to see how a journal editor or a workshop organiser would accept such a lengthy paper. From anthropology, we know that ethnographers prefer to publish via monographs instead of articles. In entrepreneurship, the well known cases of entrepreneurs and innovative companies have not been described by academic scholars in scientific journals but have been written in book-format by the entrepreneur self, by ghostwriters or journalists, seldom by an academic researcher. Performing a story, either by theatre, video, film, or multi-media, engages the scientific 'author' in developing experience and competence in genres, which is for most academics out of the question in the light of their busy schedule and booked agendas. The challenges of developing a narrative approach of entrepreneurship we have been enumerating throughout this text come here sharp in focus in: it is here no different as elsewhere that the proof of the pudding is in eating it.

And the audience stood up and yelled, 'tell a story, now!'. The light flipped off, the researcher, now narrator, cleared his throat, 'once upon a time there was an entrepreneur...'. Once upon a time, there was still time for telling a story.

References

Aldrich, H.E. (1992). Methods in our madness? Trends in entrepreneurship research. In: Sexton, D.L. & Kasarda, J.D. (Eds.) *The State of the Art of Entrepreneurship*. Boston: PWS-Kent Publishing Company.

Alvarez, J.L. & Merchan, C. (1992) The role of narrative fiction in the development of imagination for action, *International Studies of Management and Organization*, 22, 3, 27-45.

Arendt, H. (1958). *The Human Condition*. Chicago: University of Chicago Press.

Bartlett, C.A. (1932). *Remembering: A study in Experimental and Social Psychology*. Cambridge: Cambridge University Press.

Bouwen, R. & Steyaert, C. (1992). *Opening the domain of entrepreneurship: A social constructionist perspective*. Paper presented at the sixth RENT-workshop, Barcelona, Spain.

Bruner, J. (1990). *Acts of Meaning*. Cambridge, Mass.: Harvard University Press.

Burgess, R. (Ed.) (1984). *The Research Process in Educational Settings: Ten Case Studies*. London: Falmer Press.

Burke, K. (1962). *A Grammar of Motives and a Rhetoric of Motives*. Cleveland, OH: Meridian.

Burrell, G. & Morgan, G. (1979). *Sociological Paradigms and Organizational Analysis*. London: Heinemann.

Carter, K. (1993). The place of story in the study of teaching and teacher education. *Educational Researcher*, 22, 5-12.

Chatman, S. (1981). Critical Response: Reply to Barbara Herrnstein Smith. *Critical Inquiry*, 7, 121-140.

Chia, R. (1996). Teaching paradigm shifting in management education: university business schools and the entrepreneurial imagination. *Journal of Management Studies*, 33, 4, 409-428.

Churchill, N.C. (1992). Research issues in entrepreneurship. In: Sexton, D.L. & Kasarda, J.D. (Eds.) *The State of the Art of Entrepreneurship*. Boston, Mass.: PWS-Kent Publishing Company.

Czarniaska-Joerges, B. (1995). Narration or Science? Collapsing the Division in Organization Studies. *Organization*, 2, 1, 11-33.

Czarniawska-Joerges & Guillet de Monthoux, P. (1994) *Good Novels, Better Management: Reading Organizational Realities in Fiction*. Switzerland, Harwood Academic Publishers.

Czarniawska-Joerges, B. (1992). *Exploring Complex Organizations*. Newbury Park, CA: Sage Publications.

de Kuyper, E. (1994). *Te Vroeg ... Te laat. Een Liefdesgeschiedenis*. Nijmegen: SUN.[Too soon... Too late. A Love story]

De Visscher, J. (1994). Paul Ricoeur: Narrativiteit en wereldlijkheid. In: Berghs, H. (Ed.) *Denkwijzen*. Leuven: Acco. [Paul Ricoeur: Narrativity and secularity]

Denzin, N.K. & Lincoln, Y.S. (Eds.) (1994). *Handbook of Qualitative Research*. Thousand Oaks, CA: Sage Publications.

Duncan, H. (1968). *Symbols and Social Theory*. New York: Oxford University Press.

Dyer, W.G., Jr. & Wilkins, A.L. (1991). Better stories, not better constructs to generate better theory: a rejoinder to Eisenhardt. *Academy of Management Review*, 16, 3, 613-619.

Eisenhardt, K.M. (1989). Building theories from case study research. *Academy of Management Review*, 14, 4, 532-550.

Ely, M. (1991). *Doing Qualitative Research: Circles within Circles*. London: The Falmer Press.

Gergen, K.J. (1994). *Realities and Relationships. Soundings in Social Construction*. Cambridge, Mass.: Harvard University Press.

Gergen, K.J. & Davis, K.E. (Eds.) (1984). *The Social Construction of the Person*. New York: Springer-Verlag.

Goffman, E. (1969). *Strategic Interaction*. Philadelphia: University of Pennsylvania Press.

Harré, R. (1981). The positivist-empiricist approach and its alternative. In: Reason, P. & Rowan, J. (Eds.) *Human Inquiry: A Sourcebook of New Paradigm Research*. Chichester: John Wiley & Sons.

Harré, R. (1989). Grammaire et lexiques, vecteurs des représentations sociales. In: Jodelet, D. (Ed.) *Les Représentations Sociales*. Paris: Presses Universitaires de France.

Hisrich, R.D. (1988). Entrepreneurship: Past, present and future. *Journal of Small Business Management*, October, 1-4.

Johannisson, B. (1991). *Entrepreneurship - The Management of Ambiguity*. Paper prepared as a contribution to a volume dedicated to Sten Jönsson, Växjo University.

Katriel, T. & Sanders, R.E. (1989). The meta-communicative role of epigraphs in scientific text construction. In: Simons, H.W. (Ed.) *Rhetoric in the Human Sciences*. London: Sage Publications.

Kelchtermans, G. (1993). *De Professionele Ontwikkeling van Leerkrachten Basisonderwijs vanuit het Biografisch Perspectief*. Unpublished doctoral dissertation, Leuven: Katholieke Universiteit Leuven.

Lakoff, G. & Johnson, M. (1980). *Metaphors We Live By*. Chicago: University of Chicago Press.

Lyotard, J.-F. (1979). *Het Postmoderne Weten*. Kampen: Kok Agora.

MacIntyre, A. (1984). *After Virtue: A Study in Moral Theory*. Notre Dame: University of Notre Dame Press.

MacMillan, I.C. & Katz, J.A. (1992). Idiosyncratic milieus of entrepreneurial research: the need for comprehensive theories. *Journal of Business Venturing*, 7, 1-8.

Mangham, I.L. & Overington, M.A. (1987). *Organization as Theatre: A social psychology of dramatic appearances*. Chichester: John Wiley & Sons.

Mangham, I.L. & Overington, M.A. (1983). Dramatism and the theatrical metaphor. In: Morgan, G. (Ed.) *Beyond Method*. Beverly Hills, CA: Sage Publications.

Mishler, E.G. (1986). *Research Interviewing: Context and Narrative*. Cambridge, Mass.: Harvard University Press.

O'Connor, E.S. (1995). Paradoxes of participation: A literary analysis of case studies on employee involvement. *Organization Studies*, 16, 5, 769-803.

Payne, R. (1982). The nature of knowledge and organisational psychology. In Nicholson, N. & Wall, T. (Eds.) Theory and Method in Organizational Psychology. New York: Academic Press.

Payne, (1975/76). Truisms in organisational behaviour. *Interpersonal Development*, 6, 203-220.

Pepper, S.C. (1942). *World Hypotheses*. Berkeley: University of California Press.

Peters, J.D. & Rothenbuhler, E.W. (1989). The reality of construction. In: Simons, H.W. (Ed.) *Rhetoric in the Human Sciences*. London: Sage Publications.

Reason, P. & Rowan, J. (1981). Issues of validity in new paradigm research. In: Reason, P. & Rowan, J. (Eds.) *Human Inquiry*. London: John Wiley & Sons.

Reed, M. & Hughes, M. (1992). *Rethinking Organization*. London: Sage Publications.

Richardson, L. (1994). Writing. A method of inquiry. In: Denzin, H.K. & Lincoln, Y.S. (Eds.) *Handbook of Qualitative Research*. Thousand Oaks, CA: Sage Publications.

Ricoeur, P. (1981). *Hermeneutics and the Human Sciences*. Cambridge: Cambridge University Press.

Rose, D. (1990). *Living the Ethnographic Life*. Newbury Park, CA: Sage Publications.

Stevenson, H.H. & Harmeling, S. (1990). Entrepreneurial management's need for a more 'chaotic' theory. *Journal of Business Venturing*, 5, 1-14.

Steyaert, C. (1996). Ceci n'est pas un high tech. On Writing about high techs: Only a form-ality? Paper presented at the Seminar 'Approaches to the Study of High Tech Firms', Verteillac, France.

Steyaert, C. (1995). *Perpetuating Entrepreneurship through Dialogue. A social constructoinist view*. Leuven, Unpublished doctoral dissertation.

Steyaert, C. (1992). *Organisatie als theater: de toekomst van een oude metafoor*. Working paper, Leuven : Katholieke Universiteit Leuven. [Organizations as Theatre: the Future of a Classic Metaphor]

Tsoukas, H. (1994). Refining common sense: Types of knowledge in management studies. *Journal of Management Studies*, 31, 6, 761-780.

Van Maanen, J. (1988). *Tales of the Field. On Writing Ethnography*. Chicago: University of Chicago Press.

Whitley, (1984). The fragmented state of management studies: reasons and consequences. *Journal of Management Studies*, 21, 331-348.

Wortman, M.S., Jr. (1986). A unified framework, research typologies, and research prospectuses for the interface between entrepreneurship and small business. In: Sexton, D.L. & Smilor, R.W. (Eds.) *The Art and Science of Entrepreneurship*. Cambridge, Mass.: Ballinger Publishing Company.

Zeegers, W. & Jansz, J. (1988). Betekenisgeving als sociaal proces. *Psychologie en Maatschappij*, 12, 376-387.

PART II
START-UPS

5 A Typology of Angels: A Better Way of Examining the Informal Investment Phenomena

Patrick Coveney and Karl Moore

Introduction

A critical issue for vibrant young firms seeking to start and grow their business is finding sufficient funding. Most entrepreneurs first look to the formal sector: banks, the stock market and venture capitalists. However, for a variety of reasons the formal sector has moved away from providing the small-scale, high risk, equity packages which entrepreneurs require. This financing gap has been well documented. The MacMillan Committee (1931), The Bolton Report (1971), and more recently the Confederation of British Industry (1993) have consistently argued that small and growing firms have great difficulty locating loan and equity capital in the £50,000 to £500,000 range from Banks or venture capital companies. However many of these start-up ventures are able to locate funds to finance their expansion, but they find them in an area of the economy which is less well known, the informal venture capital sector.

The academic study of informal investors, or Business Angels as they have come to be known, is generally accepted to have begun with the work of William Wetzel (1981) in the United States. However in general most of the existing research has tended to treat Business Angels as a single homogeneous group of investors. In recent years some researchers have suggested that there might be a variety of different types of investor encompassed within the umbrella term Business Angel (Wetzel and Freear 1993; Mason and Harrison 1993). In fact Nat West's (1993) research suggests there may be three different types of Angel investor.

In our research we studied 437 Business Angel investors/potential investors and separately profiled 467 actual investment deals, involving a total level of funds of more than £50 million. We found considerable variation in the level of investment activity of the active Business Angels we studied. For example, while the mean number of informal investments made by this group during the past three years is 2.4, 38% of them had backed only one business and 31% had provided finance for 3 or more such businesses. Furthermore the level of funds invested by this group varied enormously. More than a third (36%) had invested less than £50,000 in their ventures, but almost a quarter (23%) had invested in excess of £200,000 in the businesses they support. In terms of the specific deals entered into by the Business Angels who participated in this study, the amounts invested per deal ranged from less than £10,000 to more than £1 million.

The financial and business backgrounds of these Business Angels were also very varied. Approximately a quarter (26%) had a net worth of less than £200,000, while more than a third of them were at least millionaires. Similarly there were large differences in the entrepreneurial backgrounds of these Angels. Nearly a quarter (22%) had founded three or more substantial new businesses during their own business careers, whereas almost a third (31%) had not started any substantial new businesses. Active Business Angels also cited different reasons for making informal investments. While half made this form of investment predominantly for financial gain, significant numbers indicated that they chose to back unquoted ventures to create a job or regular income for themselves (33%), or because of the fun and satisfaction of making these types of investment (29%).

Based on our results we saw the need to develop a typology of active Angel investors so that distinct groups of investors can be isolated, and their very different levels of investment activity examined. In this regard this study echoes the work of Mason and Harrison (1995) who suggested that informal investors are a heterogeneous group of different types of investors.

However, although Nat West (1993) pointed to the likely existence of three kinds of Angel investor, no major British academic study has statistically distinguished different types of Angel investors. In the US Gaston (1989) and Postma and Sullivan (1990) have tried to isolate different types of Angels. Using a variety of techniques Gaston (1989) identified ten distinct types of Business Angel. However it is conceptually difficult to distinguish between such a large number of Angel types. Postma and Sullivan (1990) focused purely on investment motive to distinguish three different types of Angel investor. Our research which draws on a large number of Business Angels, and a large number of actual investment deals uses multivariate analysis to isolate four distinct types of active Angel investors. We feel that employing this approach has enabled us to make a substantial contribution to this research area.

Research Approach

Despite the importance of informal investors, known as Business Angels, as a source of capital to entrepreneurs, very little large-scale research has been carried out on them. This dearth of academic research, particularly in Britain, has stemmed in part from difficulties in the identification of significant numbers of Angels, and also from the desire of many Angels to protect their privacy. These problems have had serious implications for the approaches used by previous researchers. In fact, the most influential British researchers in this area, Mason and Harrison et al. (1991, 1992, 1993, 1994a, 1994b, 1995) base their conclusions around a series of small-scale surveys (each of less than 100 investors) and a set of focused case studies. We felt that the biggest contribution which we could make to research in this field would be to generate a large pool of predominantly quantitative data and seek to examine the investment activities and characteristics of Business Angels using this data. For this reason we chose to use a large-scale mail questionnaire as our principal research instrument.

There are a number of methods of identifying target Angel populations available to the researcher. Ideally we would have sought to conduct a survey of a large-scale random sample of Business Angels. Conducting survey research on such a representative sample would have made it possible to generalise from the survey results and more accurately characterise the overall population of British Business Angels. However it would be almost impossible to develop a large-scale truly random sample of Business Angels. To construct a truly random sample the researcher would have to survey a sample of the population at large and it is likely that response rates from that sample would be extremely low. Such a project would be hugely demanding in terms of time and resources and even then would probably produce a response rate which would render the results difficult to interpret.

Instead we chose to develop a sample population of potential Angels through the help of a number of Business Introduction Services who granted the research access to a significant number of their current, former or likely subscribers. The majority of these actual or potential subscribers are likely to be interested potential Angel investors. The British Venture Capital Association (1993) has identified seventeen Business Introduction Services currently operating in Britain, and divides them into the categories of For-Profit, Not-For-Profit and Government sponsored organisations. In developing a convenience sample of possible Angel investors, this research project gained access to subscribers to each of these types of organisation.

From the beginning this research was supported by the privately operated Business Introduction Service, Venture Capital Report. They made their database of over 5,000 active and potential Angels available to this research. Their support has given this work access to a significantly larger pool of Business Angels than that which has been available to previous researchers. Support for this research was also received from three other British Business Introduction Services.

Level and Representativeness of the Survey Response

Table 5.1 summarises the level of response from each of the separate sources of Angel investors, the response rate from each of the sources, and the breakdown of the overall sample. A total of 437 completed questionnaires were returned from the target population of 4,373. This represents an overall response rate of 10%. The returned questionnaires contained responses from each of the sources of Angels which made up the target population. The questionnaires were colour coded so it was possible to determine the source of each of the respondents. However it is clear that the bulk of the responses (381, comprising 87% of the sample) came from Angels who either currently subscribe, formerly subscribed, or have considered using Venture Capital Report as a Business Introduction Service.

Table 5.1   The Source of Questionnaire Responses (N=437)

Target Angel Population	Number in Total Sample	Number of Total Responses	Percentage Response Rate	Percentage of Overall Sample
Current VCR subscribers	583	117	20%	27%
Former VCR subscribers	2500	174	7%	40%
VCR subscriber enquiries	1000	90	9%	20%
LINC subscribers	200	48	24%	11%
TEChINVEST subscribers	50	7	14%	2%
Bed. Inv. Ex. subscribers	40	1	3%	0%
Total	4373	437		100%

While an overall response rate of 10% is quite low it may well reflect both the desire of Angel investors for secrecy, and the speculative nature of some components of the convenience sample. Previous research projects in both Britain and the US have struggled to access large numbers of Business Angels. This problem is due in part to the invisibility of Business Angels and the fragmented nature of the market-place (Wetzel 1983). However it may also reflect the reluctance of Angels to respond to research surveys on account of the sensitive nature of the information being sought, and their fear of being deluged with subsequent investment proposals (Haar et al. 1988).

The leading British researchers Mason and Harrison have drawn most of their findings from a series of small-scale surveys of Business Angels. Most of these studies were either actively, or tacitly, supported by LINC and had much smaller target populations. Perhaps the study of Angels and Non-Angels carried out by Freear, Sohl and Wetzel (1994) in the US provides a more realistic comparison. They conducted a survey of 3,700 randomly selected high net worth individuals in Connecticut and Massachusetts and received a response rate of 5%. While our research draws on a convenience sample, rather than a random sample, the fact that Freear, Sohl and Wetzel (1994) attempted to survey a similar number of Angels makes comparing the response rates more appropriate.

It was extremely important to determine whether the respondents who returned the questionnaires were representative of the overall target population. We employed two techniques to analyse the non-response bias. First of all we compared our findings with those of an in-house database of Business Angels at Venture Capital Report. We found that the characteristics of the Angels on that database were very similar to those of the Angels who responded to our survey. VCR's database and our survey respondents are drawn from similar overall target populations and in effect the two studies represent two independent attempts to survey a roughly similar target group of Angels. The fact that the findings are similar for both studies suggests that our findings are likely to representative of those of the overall target population.

We also analysed the late respondents to our survey to check for non-response bias. Researchers such as Freear, Sohl and Wetzel (1994), Armstrong and Overton (1977), and Pace (1939) have argued that late respondents to a survey are more likely to represent the characteristics of the non-respondents than early respondents. We compared the completed responses of 37 late respondents with those of the overall group and found no statistical differences between the two groups. Given that the late respondents represent the non-respondents and that there were no differences between the late respondents and the overall group, it is possible to deduce that the Angels who responded to the survey are representative of the initial target population.

It is more difficult to draw firm conclusions on the larger issue of how representative the sample is of Business Angels in general. Mason, Harrison and Chaloner (1991a) have suggested that Angels who subscribe to Business Introduction Services tend to be younger, earn higher annual incomes, and invest greater levels of funds than other Business Angels. This research supports the finding of Mason, Harrison and Chaloner (1991a), in that it certainly does find that the Business Angels who participated in this study earn higher incomes, and are more active investors than indicated by previous research projects in the UK. However while the convenience sample is made up of investors who have either subscribed, or considered subscribing, to Business Introduction Services, the actual influence of these organisations on the investment activity of the Angels appears to be extremely limited. This study gained detailed information on 467 separate investment deals, involving more than £50 million, and found that only 13% of them were sourced through Business Introduction Services. In other words this research examined 406 different deals, totalling £46 million, which were sourced independently of Business Introduction Services. We found that the fact that Business Introduction Services were used to construct the convenience population of active and potential investors, does not imply that they represent a major source of investment opportunities for that population. As a result while it certainly must be acknowledged that the target sample did not draw from a random population of potential Angel investors, it is likely that the findings of this research have implications beyond the confines of Angels registered with Business Introduction Services.

Method Used to Develop the Typology

Punj and Stewart (1983) argue that cluster analysis has become a common tool for academic researchers who want to develop empirical groupings of persons, products or occasions which may serve as a basis for further analysis. Churchill (1987) suggests that where a number of different variables are likely to contribute to the overall characteristics of a group of objects then cluster analysis is an appropriate method of identifying natural groupings of those objects.

A number of variables were used to cluster the overall sample of active investors into four distinct sub-groups. First of all, private individual investors and company investors were separated. The 34 companies who were found to make informal investments were drawn from the general pool of active Angels, and are categorised as 'Corporate Angels'. The private individual Angels were then analysed using the K-means, iterative relocation, clustering procedure.

Punj and Stewart (1983) carried out empirical research on clustering techniques employed by a large number of researchers. They found that non-hierarchical techniques (referred to as iterative partitioning methods) are superior to hierarchical methods, particularly where non-random starting points are used. Churchill (1987) suggest that where the initial solution is known, a non-hierarchical approach which makes several passes through the data may be superior to the hierarchical approach which makes only one pass through the data. This research used non-random starting points to form the clusters and as a result chose to use a non-hierarchical clustering technique. There are various non-hierarchical methods available to the researcher and this project chose to use the K-Means iterative partitioning procedure which is particularly appropriate for large sample sizes (200 or more) (Punj and Stewart 1983). This method is based on Anderberg's (1973) nearest centroid sorting approach. Cases are reassigned by moving them to the cluster whose centroid is closest to that case. Reassignment continues until every case is assigned to the cluster with the nearest centroid.

A major issue with all clustering procedures is how to select the number of clusters (Hair, Anderson and Tatham 1987; Punj and Stewart 1983). Unfortunately, no standard, objective selection procedure exists. Hair, Anderson and Tatham (1987) contend that under these circumstances the researcher may have to use an intuitive conceptual or theoretical relationship to suggest a number of clusters. This research drew from the work of Stevenson and Coveney (1994) and Coveney (1994) which suggested the possible existence of three clusters of individual Angel investors. Nat West (1993) also used a series of interviews with Business Angels to identify three different types of active British Angels. However in themselves these studies were not sufficiently strong for the researchers to be certain that only three clusters should be sought. For this reason the researchers generated a series of K-Means clusters with an output of two, three and four clusters in each case. The researchers generated Cluster Mean Squares (Cluster MS) for examining differences between the clusters and Error Mean Squares (Error MS) for examining differences within the clusters. It was then possible to use an F ratio to test for the significance of these differences. These statistics were examined for each of the cluster processes. It was found that the two cluster process did not adequately characterise the range of different types of Angel investors. The four cluster process produced lower F values than the three cluster process, for the variables which detailed the frequency of investment, the level of funds invested, and the financial and business background of Angel investors. For these reasons it was decided to proceed with a three cluster analysis. The Cluster MS, Error MS, F values and tests of significance for this three cluster analysis may be seen in Table 5.2.

Table 5.2   Analysis of Variance

Variable	Cluster MS	DF	Error MS	DF	F value	Prob
Number of new business founded	135.0568	2	1.081	169	124.9012	.000
Number of informal investments made	35.4489	2	1.600	169	22.1461	.000
Level of funds invested in informal investments	100.8107	2	1.056	169	95.4265	.000
Expected Financial Returns	0.9067	2	1.236	169	0.7330	.482
To create a job/income for themselves	7.4837	2	1.241	169	6.0285	.003
Fun and satisfaction of investing in informal ventures	3.2691	2	1.353	169	2.4149	.092
Net worth of Angels	128.2143	2	0.902	169	142.0418	.000

Figure 5.1 highlights the variables which were used in generating this cluster. In all seven variables were used representing the investment activity, business and financial backgrounds, and the reasons for making informal investments, of these Business Angels.

Figure 5.1   Variables Used to Develop a Typology of Active Angels Using a K-Means Cluster

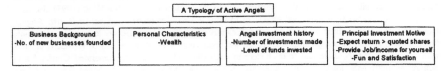

This procedure produced three types of individual Angels which we characterised as; 'Entrepreneur Angels', 'Wealth Maximising Angels' and 'Income Seeking Angels'. Together with 'Corporate Angels', they represent the four types of active Angel investors identified in this study. Exhibit 2 summarises this breakdown, highlights the number of Angels in each category and details the number of actual investments made by each type of Angel.

Figure 5.2   Types of Active Angels and their Deal Activity

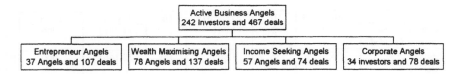

Six Types of Angel

It is important to recognise that Angels are extremely diverse. In fact this research has found that a number of distinct types of Angel investor exist. These types stem from the personal, business and investment characteristics of individual Business Angels, and significantly affect their investment activity. The six angel types can be broadly placed into two major categories, active and inactive angels. Active angels are angels which have made investments, in the case of this research in the last three years. Inactive angels include two types, Latent Angels which are inactive Angels who have made one or more informal investments in the past, but who have remained inactive for at least the past three years and Virgin Angels, which are inactive investors who have not yet made an investment in an unquoted venture and have the desire to do so. Exhibit Three outlines some of the key characteristics of the active Angels. The next sections will discuss each of the six types of angels in turn.

Table 5.3 **Summary of the Different Characteristics and Preferences of Four Types of Active Angel Investor**

Characteristic	Entrepreneur Angel	Wealth Maxing Angel	Income Seeking Angel	Corporate Angel
Number of Angels	37	78	57	34
Total Funds invested	£590,000	£131,000	£ 35,000	£540,000
No. of investments	3.4	2.1	1.5	3.0
Personal Net Worth	74% > £1m	43% > £1m	75% < £0.2m	-
No. of Businesses ounded	4.0	1.3	0.4	-
Reason for investing	Returns/Fun	Returns	Job/Income	Returns/SOSR *
Venture location	Unimportant	Unimportant	Some Concern	Some Concern

*SOSR is a Sense of Social Responsibility

Entrepreneur Angels

Entrepreneur Angels are the most active and experienced individual investors and represent a particularly and knowledge appealing source of finance for the first-time entrepreneur. Entrepreneur Angels are extremely wealthy. Almost three-quarters of this group were worth more than £1 million (after excluding their principal residence) and the majority continue to earn in excess of £100,000 a year. As with all Business Angels, these investors tend to be almost entirely self-made.

  They are more active investors both in terms of the total level of funds which they invest, and the number of separate ventures which they back. Almost half of Entrepreneur Angels had invested more than £500,000 in unquoted ventures over the past three years, while the average amount invested was £590,000. Entrepreneur Angels appear to be primarily interested in larger opportunities and are not limited to just one or two investments.

  An encouraging piece of news for entrepreneurs is that almost two-thirds of Entrepreneur Angels hope that their investment activity will increase in the next five years. In fact almost two-thirds of Entrepreneur Angels have more than £100,000 available for further informal investment, and more than half have more than £500,000 available.

  Entrepreneur Angels take large stakes in the ventures which they back. Almost half of these Angels had a preference for a majority stake, while the average size of their stakeholding was almost 40%. Typically these deals did not involve large numbers of co-investors. An average of 2.3 additional investors (including the founder/venture manager) participated with the Entrepreneur Angel in each deal.

  Entrepreneur Angels typically invest at the start-up stage. In fact almost two-thirds of the investments made by these Angels were made at this stage. Generally they prefer to 'get in' on the bottom floor of a budding business, they do not want to be part of a firm which is well on the road to maturity. This represents a slightly higher level of start-up investment than that for the other Angel types.

  Entrepreneur Angels invest in unquoted ventures for fun and satisfaction as well as for financial returns, and that they consider the personality of the venture founder to be the most important criteria when deciding who to invest with. It is interesting to note that in over 85% of their deal, Entrepreneur Angels had enjoyed making investments in start-ups - the highest level of satisfaction among all the Angel types.

  The most important criteria for Entrepreneur Angels in allocating their resources to particular ventures is the personality of the founder/manager of the venture. Over half of Entrepreneur Angels highlight this as their most important investment criteria. In fact almost a third of Entrepreneur Angels believed that their current investment activity is restricted by a lack of faith in the prospective founders/managers who approach them for funding. In our experience Entrepreneur Angels will relatively quickly decide whether they feel comfortable with the founder/manager of an opportunity they are investigating - we suggest that neither side invest too much time if the chemistry is negative from the start. However, Entrepreneur Angels appear to be successful in appraising their prospective managers because for 90% of the ventures, they indicated that they were satisfied with their relationship with the management.

Their own experience in the industry sector was the most important investment criteria for only one-fifth of Entrepreneur Angels. They are the most open of the Angel types to investing in ventures outside their own field of experience. With Entrepreneur Angels do not be afraid of proposing ventures outside their previous activities.

Fewer Entrepreneur Angels than other types of Angels felt that a formal management role was their most important contribution. This suggests that Entrepreneur Angels play a less active day-to-day role in the management of their informal investments than the other types. Nevertheless in the vast majority of the cases Entrepreneur Angels felt that they provide more than just capital to the ventures which they finance. Over 60% feel that experience or expertise is the most important non-financial benefit which they bring to a venture.

On average Entrepreneur Angels had started four substantial new businesses (businesses that had more than five staff or a turnover of more than £1 million) during the course of their own business careers. It is clear that these Angels have considerable first-hand experience in establishing and growing new businesses.

For a new entrepreneur without a great deal of experience in a particular industry of in start-ups in general Angels can potentially provide a valuable source of advice.

Income Seeking Angels

Income Seeking Angels are active investors who have made one or two low level investments over the past three years, investing less than £50,000 in total during that period. It is clear that the investment activity of Income Seeking Angels is dramatically lower than that of the other Angel types, both in number of ventures backed and total level of funds invested. In fact only 42% of Income Seeking Angels had made more than one investment, and only 27% had invested more than £50,000 in that period. However, almost three-quarters (73%) of Income Seeking Angels feel that their investment activity is likely to increase in the next five years. Nevertheless, Income Seeking Angels were found to earn very high average rates of return. The study found that they earned average annual returns of 50% from the ventures which they financed. This rate of return greatly exceeds their expected rate of 20%. Indeed of all the Angel deals only those of the Entrepreneur Angels, which earn average returns of 61% outperform them. They are very different from the other individual Angel types in terms of their financial and business backgrounds. Only one quarter of them have a net worth (excluding principal residence) in excess of £200,000, and 35% of them are worth less than £100,000. Income Seeking Angels were also significantly less entrepreneurial than both of the other Angel types during their own business career. On average they had founded only 0.4 substantial new businesses (businesses employing more than 5 people, or with a turnover of more than £1,000,000). In fact nearly two-thirds of these Angels had not founded any substantial new businesses.

A significantly lower proportion of Income Seeking Angels invest for fun or satisfaction compared to other Angels, suggesting that for these Angels investing is a very serious business. This is hardly surprising given the dramatically lower levels of funds which they have available for investing. Yet, even though this groups does not choose to invest for fun, more than three-quarters of them (77%) indicated that they had enjoyed making their informal investments.

For more than a third (35%) of Income Seeking Angels the most important factor was that they had experience in the industry sector in which the venture was located. This value is higher than for the other individual Angel types and may well reflect the desire of these Angels to take on a formal management position in the ventures. In fact Income Seeking Angels feel the greatest non-financial contribution that they can make to the ventures they finance is to take up formal management positions in them.

In general British Business Angels do not see venture location as being a particularly important investment criteria. However, a substantial minority segment (20%) of Income Seeking Angels indicated that they would only consider investment proposals located within 50 miles of their place of work, while another 24% felt restricted to investing within 100 miles. The fact that this number wish to invest in their locality may well stem from a desire of these Angels to be actively involved in the day-to-day running of the ventures which they finance.

This research examined 71 separate deals involving 48 different Income Seeking Angels. In two-thirds of the cases these Angels provided only one round of financing. Almost a third of these deals involved five or more co-investors. Only 27% of Income Seeking Angels had a preference for taking majority stakeholdings in the ventures which they financed. The average shareholding value of 20% reflects this and is lower than those taken by the other Angel types.

Wealth Maximising Angels

Wealth Maximising Angels are a contradictory bunch. Individuals with funds to spare, they invest mainly for financial gain but often end up getting involved in the running of the companies they fund. Richer but less focused than Income Seeking Angels and poorer but less experienced than Entrepreneur Angels, they end up doing less well than either group in returns of their investments. Defined largely in terms of negatives, they have an overall contribution, however, which is undeniably positive. The table opposite summarises the financial and business backgrounds of Wealth Maximising Angels. More than 80% of the group are worth more than £500,000 (excluding principal residences), with half that number again being worth over £1 million. Almost 40% continue to earn more than £100,000 a year. Although as with all Business Angels, their wealth was predominantly self-made, more of these Angels earned their wealth through inheritance than was the case for any of the other types. Wealth Maximising Angels are similar to Entrepreneur Angels in terms of wealth, but very different in entrepreneurial background. On average Wealth Maximising Angels had founded only 1.3 substantial new businesses during the course of their own business careers compared to 4.0 for Entrepreneur Angels.

Like Income Seeking Angels, Wealth Maximising Angels are primarily but not solely interested in financial return. They also invest to create a job or income for themselves. More than a quarter (26%) of these Angels look to invest in industries in which they have some personal experience. The importance which these Angel groups place on their own sector experience, allied to their greater desire to create a job for themselves, suggests that they are more likely to take on a day-to-day management role in their ventures than Entrepreneur Angels. Indeed when the actual non-financial contribution of Wealth Maximising Angels is examined for the 137 deals in which they participated, a substantially larger number were found to have taken on a formal, or full-time position, than was the case for Entrepreneur Angels.

This study examined 137 separate investment deals involving 68 different Wealth Maximising Angels. On average Wealth Maximising Angels were found to have invested £54,000 in each deal. Typically only about 40% of this sum was provided in the initial round of investment. Wealth Maximising Angels tend to acquire substantial minority shareholdings in the ventures which they back. The average size of the stakeholding for these investors was 31%. Only 29% of these Angels have a preference for majority holdings. 60% of these Angels had a preference for co-investment and on average their deals involved 2.5 other investors (including the venture founder/manager).

More than three-quarters of Wealth Maximising Angels felt that their current investment activity was being restricted by a lack of suitable business proposals. Business Introduction Services account for only 16% of the current deals for this group of Angels. It is clear that the investment activity of all the

Angel types could be increased by improving the quality of the deal flow between entrepreneurs and investors. It is also interesting to note that a significantly lower percentage (17%) of Wealth Maximising Angels cite a lack of available funds as restricting their investment than was the case for Entrepreneur Angels. This suggests that Wealth Maximising Angels have the funds available for further investment and would do so if the deal flow problems can be overcome. In fact 82% of Wealth Maximising Angels would like to increase their investment activity over the next five years. Exactly half of these Angels have more than £100,000 available for further informal investment.

Wealth Maximising Angels differ from other Angel types in that nearly three-quarters of them (73%) would be encouraged to increase their investment activity if they could either invest jointly with more experienced investors, or have access to the knowledge of these investors.

Corporate Angels

Corporate Angels are companies which make Angel-type investments investing large amounts in unquoted ventures. Corporate Angels make frequent investments in unquoted ventures and invest high levels of funds. Almost 40% of this group had invested more than £500,000 in new and growing businesses and on average these Angels supported about three ventures each. They are able to sustain this higher level of investment activity because they have significantly greater levels of funds at their disposal than the individual Angel types. For example more than a third (34%) of Corporate Angels had more than £1 million available for investing. Only 26% of Entrepreneur Angels, 17% of Wealth Maximising Angels, and none of the Income Seeking Angels had portfolios of this size.

The components of a typical Corporate Angel deal are summarised in the table opposite. These Angels provide extremely high levels of finance, usually take majority shareholdings in their ventures, and rarely co-invest. The biggest contribution which they make is to bring the experience or expertise of the company (51%) to the venture. More than a third (37%) of Corporate Angels also point to the formal role which one or more people from the company take up in the venture, as representing their biggest non-financial contribution. Perhaps the hands-on entrepreneurial experience of individual Angel types is a greater contributor to the success of small businesses than the specific resources of Corporate Angels.

Other factors distinguish the investment activity of this group. Almost a quarter (24%) indicated that they choose to make informal investments out of a sense of social responsibility. This compared to only 5% of Entrepreneur Angels, 4% of Wealth Maximising Angels, and none of the Income Seeking Angels. A substantial number (27%) of Corporate Angels consider it very important that prospective ventures be located in an industry sector in which they have experience. Corporate Angels also tend to invest more closely to their principal place of work than any of the other Angel types. On average the ventures which Corporate Angels backed were 54 miles away from their workplace.

However, only 15% of Corporate Angels feel restricted to solely investing within 50 miles of their workplace and 50% are willing to invest in prospective ventures located more than 200 miles away. It is clear that Corporate Angels, like other Angels, invest locally because they receive more proposals from local rather than national sources. In fact 66% of the ventures backed by this group of investors were sourced either through friends, family or business associates, and it is likely that the majority of these sources are locally based. All Angels feel that their current investment activity is restricted by inefficiencies in the informal venture capital market. A national network which provided Angels with a range of business proposals, regardless of their location, would clearly be one way to help overcome these.

Almost two-thirds (65%) of Corporate Angels expect that their investment activity will increase over the next five years. However, the current investment activity of Corporate Angels is restricted by a number of factors. The two principal restrictors are a lack of suitable business proposals, and a lack of faith in the venture founder or manager. In fact almost three-quarters (74%) of Corporate Angels stated that better access to suitable proposals during the past three years would have increased their investment activity. Corporate Angels were also found to have a greater concern with the trustworthiness of venture founders than any of the other Angel types. This concern may well reflect the constraints of making investments on behalf of a company rather than as an individual. A large number of Corporate Angels (56%) also expressed a desire to see improved tax incentives.

Latent Angels

Latent Angels are Angels who have made one or more informal investments in the past, but who have been inactive for at least the past three years. However, Latent Angels are very interested in making informal investments again. 63% of them expected to make one or more investments over the next five years, while only 14% of them thought it unlikely that they would invest in unquoted ventures during that period. Furthermore Latent Angels have substantial funds at their disposal for this form of investment. 72% of this group have more than £50,000 available for informal investments.

As a group Latent Angels tend to be very wealthy, highly educated men who are slightly older than the typical active Angel. In many respects their financial and business backgrounds resemble those of the Wealth Maximising Angels. More than half (53%) of the Latent Angels were worth over £500,000 after excluding their principal residence, while 42% of them were worth more than £1 million. As with most of the Angel types the wealth of Latent Angels is predominantly self-made. Indeed only 8% of them cite inheritance as their principal source of wealth. Almost three quarters (74%) of them continue to have annual incomes in excess of £50,000. It is therefore very unlikely that the current investment activity of Latent Angels has been curtailed by a lack of financial resources. Only a quarter of these Angels attributed their inactivity to a lack of available funds. One important factor inhibiting Latent Angels is that they are significantly more concerned with the proximity of the venture to their home or place of work than the active Angel types. The majority of Latent Angels will not consider proposals for ventures located more than 100 miles away, and about a quarter restrict themselves to proposals for ventures located within 50 miles of their place of work. Undoubtedly this desire to restrict their investment to local ventures reduces the pool of quality proposals available to Latent Angels.

The most common factor restricting the current investment activity of Latent Angels is again the lack of suitable business proposals. 78% of these Angels point to a shortage of quality investment proposals as being the principal reason behind their decision not to invest. In fact 77% of Latent Angels explicitly stated that they would have invested in one or more ventures over the past three years if there had been more suitable proposals available to them. These problems of information transfer in the informal venture market appear to effect all Business Angels. But it appears that this problem impacts particularly severely on Latent Angels because their level of concern (78%) is higher than for those for the other Angel types.

Virgin Angels

Virgin Angels are investors who have not yet taken the plunge. Research suggests that there are many more Virgin Angels than active Angels (Riding et al. 1993, Mason and Harrison 1995) It has been claimed that if only half of the Virgin Angels became active the total informal venture capital market in the UK would grow to ten times the size of formal venture capital market (Mason and Harrison 1995). In Britain very little research has been done on the characteristics of Virgin Angels. This survey found that Virgin Angels embraced people of very varied levels of wealth and income. But in general Virgin Angels are very well-off. After excluding the value of their principal residence, 59% of them were worth more than £200,000, while over a third (36%) were worth more than £500,000, and a quarter more than £1 million. In addition, the majority of these potential Angel investors continue to earn in excess of £50,000 a year. While Virgin Angels are significantly less wealthy than active Angels, they have large financial resources at their disposal and that they are willing to invest in the informal venture capital market. One important distinction between Virgin Angels and active Angels emerges when their entrepreneurial backgrounds are examined. On average Virgin Angels have started only 0.8 substantial new businesses (businesses employing more than 5 people or with a turnover of more than £1 million), with 57% of them never founding one. This represents a significantly lower level of entrepreneurship than that of active Business Angels, who founded an average of 1.6 substantial businesses during their business careers. The fact that active Business Angels clearly have a greater degree of experience in founding new businesses, particularly in terms of practical hands-on knowledge of how to effectively finance these deals, may well contribute to their greater investment activity in the informal venture capital market.

However, Virgin Angels have a very strong desire to invest in unquoted ventures. In fact 86% of this group indicated that they expected to make one or more informal investments over the next five years. Although the Business Angels and potential Angels who participated in this research were drawn from a convenience sample of likely informal investors, the fact that the pool of active investors is likely to increase by almost a third suggests that the economic potential of this source of small business finance is very large indeed. Furthermore Virgin Angels have substantial resources available for informal investment. Our research found that although Virgin Angels have significantly less funds available than active Angel investors, they still have considerable resources at their disposal. The majority (62%) have more than £50,000 available, while almost a third (31%) have in excess of £100,000 available to invest in unquoted ventures. This suggests that the investment activity of Virgin Angels is not generally curtailed by a lack of available funds. In fact only 15% of this group ascribe their inactivity to this cause. As with other Angels, difficulty in locating suitable business proposals, rather than a shortage of funds, was the principal reason for the inactivity of Virgin Angels. Almost two thirds (65%) of them highlighted a lack of quality proposals as the principal factor which prevented them from making direct investments in unquoted ventures. 69% of Virgin Angels indicated that they would have made one or more informal investments during the past three years if they had had access to suitable business proposals. It is clear that these problems of information transfer represent the biggest hindrance to the further expansion of the informal venture capital market.

However, there were a series of other issues which Virgin Angels feel could encourage their investment activity, please see Exhibit 4. As well as better knowledge of founders or managers many would like to see more clearly available exit routes such as unlisted stock market.

Table 5.4   Factors which would Encourage Virgin Angels to Increase their Investment Activity

Better knowledge of/trust in founder/manager	52%
Available exit routes, such as unlisted stock market	45%
Opportunity to co-invest with experienced investors	42%
Better tax incentives	36%
Corporate financing advice on making/structuring investments	33 %
Knowledge of other Angels' successful investment	24%
Other	20%

A high proportion would also be encouraged to invest by the opportunity to co-invest with other more experienced investors. The incidence of co-investment remains low in Britain. The establishment of mechanisms such as the successful Oxford Trust, which brings large groups of potential investors together with entrepreneurs seeking finance, represents one way of increasing the level of co-investment amongst British Business Angels. Almost a quarter of Virgin Angels would welcome the opportunity to gain a detailed knowledge of the successful investments of other Business Angels. Mechanisms which bring Angels of different types together would undoubtedly provide a forum for the transfer of such information. In addition to these slightly informal mechanisms by which Virgin Angels could gain an understanding of how to make direct investments, a significant number of them (33%) would like to be able to receive detailed, professional advice on making and structuring their Angel deals.

The criteria which Virgin Angels would consider applying when assessing investment proposals are similar to those indicated by active Business Angels. Their impression of the founder or manager of a venture, (39%) is significantly less important than for the 57% of active Angels who highlighted this factor. Virgin Angels appear to be willing to invest across most industry sectors. In fact only 28% of them indicated that their own experience in, or understanding of, the industry sector in which the venture was located was the most important factor when assessing business proposals. It is interesting to note that more than a fifth (21%) of Virgin Angels consider the content and presentation of the business plans which they receive to be the most important investment criteria. This is significantly higher than was the case for active Angels and probably stems from the fact that Virgin Angels have less experience in making this form of investment than active Angels. As a result they may rely more on a formal, detailed investment proposal, rather than make an ad-hoc judgement on the personality of the venture founder, when making their decision.

Virgin Angels are significantly more concerned than active Angels with the proximity of a venture to their place of work. 58% of Virgin Angels would not make an investment more than 100 miles from their place of work, which compares with only 40% of active Angels who feel restricted to investing locally. Furthermore over twice as many active Angels as Virgin Angels (44% compared to 21%) would back an otherwise suitable venture which was located more than 200 miles away. This is an extremely important finding because it suggests that Virgin Angels have the concern with venture location which previous researchers have attributed to active Business Angels.

Implications for Entrepreneurs

Business Angels have proven to be a considerable source of funding for many entrepreneurs. Thus a better understanding of business angels may help guide an entrepreneur in their search for funding. For example, Exhibit Five may help provide direction on how to match a entrepreneur's venture and business background with the six types of Angels to help provide the best potential match. The bottom axis in Exhibit Five represents the entrepreneur's experience, in this case, the number of ventures that they have previous been involved in. If they have worked for a large firm in the same industry and they are thinking of stating their new venture in then they may wish to add one to the number of ventures on bottom axis. The vertical axis is the amount of funds that they are seeking to find. The cut-offs are approximate but provide a useful rule of thumb which help an entrepreneur locate their venture on the exhibit.

Figure 5.3   Matrix of Angel Investor Based on Funds Required and Number of Ventures

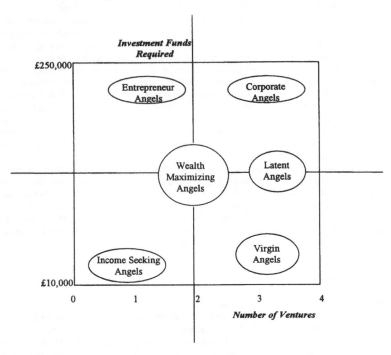

Directions for Future Research

The scope of this research has been confined to British Angels located with the help of Business Introduction Services. Future inquiry might be broadened in several directions, first by examining Angels from other countries and secondly by overcoming the considerable problem of conducting a representative random sample of Angels.

One criticism of current international business literature has been its tendency to be too episodic, in effect presenting its analysis in terms of a 'snapshot' of a single location at a single time (Schollhammer 1994). Consequently, a third means of broadening the inquiry would be to examine the phenomena in a longitudinal fashion, i.e., examining the evolution of Business Angels from the time they were first examined to a specified future date to see if they change type over time.

Conclusion

Business Angel investors do not constitute a homogenous group of similar investors, but rather encompass a variety of different types of investor, with distinct characteristics and exhibiting very different levels of investment activity. This study has recognised this and has used cluster analysis to develop a typology of active Angels comprising four types of investor, as well as two types of inactive investors, Virgin and Inactive Angels. Each of these types have very different characteristics and approaches to investment.

References

Anderberg, M. (1973) *Cluster analysis for applications*. New York: Academic Press.

Armstrong, J., and Overton, T. (1977) Estimating Non-response bias in Mail Surveys. *Journal of Marketing Research* XIV:396-402.

Bolton Report.(1971) reported in Coutarelli, S. (1977) *Venture Capital in Europe*, Praeger: London.

British Venture Capital Association (1993) A Directory of Business Introduction Services. *British Venture Capital Association*, London.

Churchill, G. (1987) *Marketing Research: Methodological Foundations*. Fourth edition, USA: Dryden.

Coveney, P. (1994) Informal Investment in Britain: An examination of the behaviours, characteristics, motives and preferences of British Business Angels. *Thesis submitted in partial fulfilment of the requirements for the degree of Master of Philosophy in Management Studies*, Templeton College, Oxford.

Confederation of British Industry (1993) Finance for Growth: Meeting the financing needs of small and medium enterprises. *A Report of the Confederation of British Industry (CBI) Smaller Firms Council*. CBI: London.

Freear, J., Sohl, J. and Wetzel, W. (1994) Angels and Non-Angels: Are there differences? *Journal of Business Venturing* 9:109-123.

Gaston, R. (1989) *Finding Private Venture Capital For Your Firm: A Complete Guide*. New York: Wiley.

Haar, N., Starr, J. and MacMillan I. (1988) Informal risk capital investors: Investment patterns on the east coast of the USA. *Journal of Business Venturing* 3 :11-19.

Hair, J., Anderson, R., and Tatham, R. (1987) Multivariate Data Analysis. Second Edition, London: Collier Macmillan Publishers.

Harrison, R., and Mason, C. (1992a) The roles of investors in entrepreneurial companies: A comparison of informal investors and venture capitalists *Venture Finance Research Project Working Paper No 5*, University of Southampton/University of Ulster.

Harrison, R. and Mason, C. (1992b) International perspectives on the supply of informal venture capital. *Journal of Business Venturing* 7: 459-475.

Harrison, R. and Mason, C. (1993) Finance for the growing business: The role of informal investment. *National Westminster Bank Quarterly Review* May 1993: 17-29.

Mason, C. and Harrison, R. (1991) A strategy for closing the small firm equity gap. *Venture Finance Research Working Paper No 3*. University of Southampton/University of Ulster.

Mason, C. and Harrison, R. (1992) Promoting informal investment activity: Some operational considerations for Business Introduction Services. *Venture Finance Research Project Working Paper No. 4*. University of Southampton/University of Ulster.

Mason, C. and Harrison, R. (1993) Strategies for expanding the informal venture capital market. *International Small Business Journal* II: pp 23-38.

Mason, C. and Harrison, R. (1994a) The informal venture capital market in the UK in Hughes, A. and Storey, D. (eds) *Financing Small Firms*. Routledge: London: 64-111.

Mason, C. and Harrison, R. (1994b) Why 'Business Angels' say no: a case study of opportunities rejected by an informal investor syndicate. *Venture Finance Research Project Working Paper No. 7* University of Southampton/University of Ulster.

Mason, C. and Harrison, R. (1995) Informal Venture Capital and the Financing of Small and Medium-Sized Enterprises. *Small Enterprise Research-The Journal of SEAANZ* 3, 1,2:33-56.

Mason, C., Harrison, R. and Allen, P. (1995) Informal Venture Capital: A study of the Investment Process, the Post-investment Experience and Investment Performance. Venture Finance research Project, *Working Paper No. 12*.

Mason, C., Harrison, R. and Chaloner, J. (1991a) The operation and effectiveness of LINC, Part 1: A survey of investors. *Urban Policy Research Unit Working Paper*, University of Southampton.

Mason, C., Harrison, R. and Chaloner, J. (1991b) The informal risk capital market in the UK: A study of the investor characteristics, investment preferences and investment decision-making. *Venture Finance Working Paper No. 2*, University of Southampton/University of Southampton.

National Westminster Bank (1993) Extracts from a study into private investor networks. *Research commissioned by National Westminster Bank PLC Technology Unit and carried out by The Innovation Partnership, Manchester.*

Pace, R. (1939) Factors influencing questionnaire returns from former university students. *Journal of Applied Psychology* 23:388- 397.

Postma, P. and Sullivan, M. (1990). *Informal risk capital in the Knoxville region*. Centre of Excellence for New Venture Analysis, College of Business Administration, University of Tennessee: Knoxville, Tn.

Punj, G., and Stewart, D. (1983) Cluster Analysis in Marketing Research: Review and Suggestions for Applications. *Journal of Marketing Research* 20:134-148.

Riding, A., Dal Cin, P., Duxbury, L., Haines, G. and Safrata, R. (1993) *Informal investors in Canada: the identification of salient characteristics*. Ottawa: Carleton University.

Schollhammer, H. (1994) Strategies and Methodologies in International Business and Comparative Management Research. *Management International Review* 34, no.1: 5-20.

Stevenson, H. and Coveney, P. (1994) *Survey of Business Angels: Fallacies corrected and six distinct types of Angel identified*. Venture Capital Report: Henley-on-Thames.

Wetzel, W. (1981) Informal risk capital in New England. In Vesper (ed) *Frontiers of Entrepreneurship Research*. Wellesley, MA: Babson College:217-245.

Wetzel, W. (1983) Angels and informal risk capital. *Sloan Management Review* Summer: 23-34.

Wetzel, W. and Freear, J. Promoting informal venture capital in the United States: Reflections on the history of VCN. In Harrison, R., and Mason, C., (eds), *Informal venture capital: Information, networks and public policy*. Hemel Hempstead, Woodhead-Faulkner, forthcoming.

6 Sector-Related Opportunities and Threats for Small Business Starters in the Ukraine

Nina Isakova

Introduction: An Overview of Economic Reforms

Despite a certain social tension, the Ukrainian internal political situation in 1995 and the first half of 1996 allowed to proceed with the economic reforms. Nevertheless the country's leadership did not take the chance and this was proved by the new strikes in coal industry regions. The official sources of information mention the following positive shifts in the economy of the country: a decrease in the rate of the fall of a number of macroeconomic indicators, an increase in exports, an increase in the dollar equivalent wages. Unfortunately, no conditions have been formed in the national economy to move over from a transformational recession to structural change. The discrepancy between the legal and illegal sectors of economy certainly is among the greatest constraints: actually almost 60% of GDP is produced in the 'shadow'.

As a result, the government has to operate with and formulate policy on the basis of false statistics. The sociological data on the economic 'progress' in 1995 conflict with the official statistics and are a great deal less optimistic. According to the report by the Social Monitoring Centre and the Ukrainian Centre of Economic and Political Research, 69% of the managers of enterprises, both state-owned and private, consider year 1995 less successful and 79% consider the economic situation worse compared to 1994.

By the present time the Ukrainian government assisted by the Western advisers has accumulated certain knowledge of the tactics and strategy of reforms, but they are fragmentary and need to be merged into a holistic conception of a stage-by-stage stabilisation and exit from the crisis, the way it was done in the Czech Republic case, for instance. Following the advice of the principal creditors to the Ukraine (International Monetary Fund, International Bank of Reconstruction and Development and European Bank of the Reconstruction and Development), the Ukrainian government pays too much attention to the inflation rate somewhat ignoring other macroeconomic indicators. The financial stabilisation is known to be gained not just through the money supply restraint, but through an enlargement of the internal commodity supply at the market, an increase in the internal investments, followed by growth of foreign direct investment. This may be the shortcut to the growth of competition and hence to a healthy market economy. The Ukrainian monetarism leads to a situation in which microeconomics cannot adapt itself to the new macroeconomic conditions and loses a lot of enterprises, sometimes perspective technology-based firms.

In these strained economic circumstances, the development of the small business sector in the Ukraine is believed to be central to economic reforms, to the creation of wealth and employment. The inherent instability and general weakness of the economy entails a number of obstacles to small business development, both external and internal; nevertheless the newcomers are eager to join the small business force, with the belief and hope that they will be more successful than their forerunners.

One more remark to end the introduction. The theme of the starters in small business is of great theoretical interest irrespective of the country, still for the Ukraine it is of a special significance: the country now needs a sharp increase in the number of small firms, that is why, in author's opinion, more attention should be paid both in research and in policy to the issue of successful starts.

Sectoral Structure and Trends in the Development of Small Business

The state of the national statistics does not satisfy researchers and policy makers in the Ukraine, and certain efforts are taken to reach the desirable quality of information supply by way of co-operating with European and international statistical agencies and adjusting the system to the international standards (e.g. OECD). Meanwhile, we shall analyse the data available. Due to the change occurred in the procedures of gathering information and indicators on small business activities, the data of 1995 are not presented in the tables. But with a great degree of certainty it can be acknowledged that there was no significant change in the general tendencies of small business development last year and the beginning of 1996.

Scholars on the former Soviet Union republics know very well that in our countries there are two main types of small business entities: small enterprises and co-operatives. Co-operatives in their contemporary meaning were allowed to be established at the early stage of perestroika (1986-1987), and they had some significant privileges which allowed them to operate quite successfully within the framework of the Soviet economy before its collapse in 1991. The boom of small business had started in 1990 after the resolution of the Soviet of Ministers of the Ukrainian SSR on the development of small enterprises. According to this resolution small enterprises during the first two years of operation were not supposed to pay any taxes. In 1991 the Ukraine had experienced a 20 fold increase in the number of SEs. The managers of large state-owned enterprises were very active in launching small enterprises because it was extremely profitable for them. Later in 1992 it was no longer legal and the number of small businesses began to increase on the account of private capital after the introduction of the law on private property. Small enterprises began to replace co-operatives. At the present time both types are operating and statistics are provided separately for each, but co-operatives tend to change their statute to that of small enterprises. The situation with the small enterprises had worsened in 1994 with the introduction of the law on enterprise and the profit tax of the enterprise (30%). The number of new small enterprises has sharply diminished. Now they have to pay 13 different taxes which amount to 70 to 90 % of the profit, so there are two alternatives: bankruptcy or shadow market. The absence of a special law on small enterprises partly explains the low rate on small business development in the country in comparison with others. This year, for instance, 90,000 SE have been registered but only 45,000 have reported as operating.

Table 6.1 below presents data based on expert evaluations of the gap in the development of SME sector in the Ukraine, Central and Eastern European countries and developed economies. These evaluations should be regarded as a qualitative, not quantitative representation of the situation. It follows from Table 6.1 that the Ukraine is far behind not only the developed countries, but also other transition economies by all indicators of the level of small business development.

Table 6.1   Small Business in the Ukraine as of Mid 1995

Indicator	Ukraine	Transition economies	Developed countries
Share of SE , %	20	50-60	80-90
Share of SE employment, %	10	30	50-70
Number of SE per 1,000 people	2	20	50-60
Share of SE in GNP, %	10	30	40-60

Sources: Official data of the Ministry of Statistics of the Ukraine; Piasecki, 1992

Table 6.2   **Dynamics of Small Business Development in the Ukraine**

Indicator	1990	1991	1992	1993	1994
Number of small enterprises	1,000	20,000	50,000	74,000	79,800
Number of co-operatives	30,000	27,000	17,000	11,000	6,000
Total number of SEs and co-operatives	31,000	47,000	67,000	85,000	85,800
Change to previous year, %		52	43	27	0.8

Source: Official data of the Ministry of Statistics of the Ukraine

The data in Table 6.2 show dynamics of small business development at the beginning of the process and the stagnation, which is characteristic of the last three years.

Table 6.3 presents data on operating small enterprises and co-operatives across sectors reported to the Ministry of Statistics. In the table there is no information on finance and insurance companies because they are not included in the small enterprises sectors and are in the category of business infrastructure entities registered regardless of the size of organisation. It is impossible to just add the information on the financial and insurance companies to the above table because not all of them are from the small business category.

Thus the information is provided separately in Table 6.4 to give a general idea of the dynamics of this sector of small business, it cannot be neglected as it is a leader among other categories of businesses and accounts for approximately 60% of GDP.

Table 6.3   **Sectoral Structure of Small Business**

Branch of economy	Small enterprises				Co-operatives			
	1993, #	1993, %	1994, #	1994, %	1993, #	1993, %	1994, #	1994, %
Industry	13599	18	12947	16.2	2687	27.4	1569	26.27
Transport	1628	2.2	1711	2.1	388	3.96	293	4.9
Communication	213	0.3	202	0.25	38	0.38	24	0.4
Construction	12283	16.3	11665	14.6	3707	37.9	2238	37.47
Retail trade & catering	28093	37.4	33840	42.39	853	8.72	595	9.96
Delivery & selling	1108	1.5	963	1.2	19	0.19	5	0.08
Agriculture	900	1.2	738	0.92	253	2.58	130	2.17
Purchases by the state	162	0.2	131	0.16	32	0.32	14	0.23
Total	75003	100	79827	100	9777	100	5972	100

Source: Official data of the Ministry of Statistics of the Ukraine

Table 6.4   **Business Infrastructure Institutions in the Ukraine**

	1993	1994
Commodity goods exchange	73	90
Stock exchange	1	1
Commercial banks	210	228
Investment companies & funds	-	650
Trusts	-	500
Insurance companies	156	570
Audit companies	-	250

Source: Official data of the Ministry of Statistics of the Ukraine

The largest number of small enterprises operate in retail and catering (42.39%) followed by industry (16.2%) and construction. The leading sectors in the co-operatives category are construction (37.47%), industry (26.27%), retail and catering (9.96%) and transport (4.9%). Although a certain decrease in number of small enterprises in industry and construction was observed, it was not significant; and retail, catering, and transport are responsible for the increase in the total number of small enterprises. The above mentioned tendency for co-operatives to be replaced by small enterprises accounts for the decrease in number of co-operatives across every sector with the sectoral shares almost the same. The business infrastructure institutions demonstrate a sharp increase in number: especially this concerns trusts, investment companies, audit companies, and to a lesser extent commodity goods exchange and commercial banks. Judging from the number of employees in these companies they may be referred to as small to medium-sized firms, and the expansion of this sector manifests a positive shift in economic reforms.

Small business employment (Table 6.5) in the Ukraine manifests a significant decrease for every sector, with the only exception of the 'services to population'. Although the absolute values for 'industry', 'construction' and 'retail' are lower in 1994, their shares in the total small business employment became larger on the account of a decrease in the percentage of 'research and development' firms (from 6.2% to 4.2 %), 'housing' (from 0.8% to 0.7%) and 'agriculture' (from 1.2% to 1%). Thus by the small business employment indicator, 'service to population' is the most fortunate and 'research and development' is the least fortunate among the sectors.

Table 6.5   Small Business Employment: Sectoral Structure

Branch of Economy	1993 #	1993 %	1994 #	1994 %
Industry	260,900	25.1	220,400	25.3
Agriculture	12,700	1.2	8,900	1
Transport	20,900	2.0	17,500	2
Construction	265,100	25.5	223,300	25.6
Retail, catering, delivery, supply, purchase by state	252,600	24.3	225,400	25.9
Other manufacturing	36,300	3.5	19,400	2.3
Housing/communal services	7,900	0.8	6,500	0.7
Services to population	48,300	4.7	50,500	5.8
Professional services	36,600	3.5	30,700	3.5
Research & development	63,400	6.2	36,900	4.2
Other	33,500	3.2	31,500	3.7
Total	1,038,200	100	871,000	100

Source: Official data of the Ministry of Statistics of the Ukraine

These data accord with the anecdotal information and survey results which state that 'retail and catering' and 'services to population' are the easiest for start-up and 'research and development' sector (in other words high technology firms) is at the top of the list of 'entry resistant' sectors. The Ukraine benefits from a highly qualified research potential which has recently undergone a sharp decrease due to the reduction of the R&D's share in state budget, and some other factors related to the transformation of science. Now at the time, when the Ukraine witnesses deep changes in the national economy and the research system, the demand for intellectual products is smaller than the supply; that is why the technology based enterprises face more constraints to their development than enterprises in other spheres of activities.

Although there is no reliable data on the sectors in the 'shadow', some Ukrainian experts evaluate the 'legal to illegal' small business ratio as follows: retail trade -- 30:70 %; services -- 40:60 %; manufacturing -- 50:50 %.

The Main Opportunities and Threats for Ukrainian Starters

Research studies on small business in transition are usually focused on a variety of macroeconomic and microeconomic factors and conditions for its development, with the focus on the challenges, and less attention is paid to the opportunities. (Lane, 1995; Klochko, Isakova, 1996; Arendarski, Mroczkowski, Sood, 1994; Piasecki, 1992) The economic literature on start ups provides a variety of research purposes, programmes and approaches: some authors investigate differences between firms that have ceased operations and those that continue to operate, by examining particular characteristics of the companies and/or their owners; e.g. awareness, use and assessment of small business support programmes (Good, 1993); others highlight the motivational and environmental influences (Dubini, 1987), for focus on public policy aspect (Mokry, 1988, Storey, 1993). This study has identified the main opportunities and threats for people who start firms pertaining to different sectors with the idea to comprehend in what way and degree do they influence the small business development.

Despite all the difficulties of transition economy, the business environment does provide certain opportunities for small businesses; otherwise the Ukraine would not have a single small firm. The following factors are referred to by the author as the opportunities for small business:
- legitimisation of private small business
- shortage on the market of consumer goods, foodstuffs and services
- great demand in particular professional services
- surplus of labour force
- high qualification of labour force
- low competition and niches in production sphere and services
- comparative independence on the former Soviet Union market
- availability of natural and technological resources

If we apply the list of opportunities to the small business sectors, we shall notice that the strength of their influence does not differ much across sectors, with one or two exceptions. For instance, the legislative environment (the quality of the legislation system is not regarded here) has equal importance for sectors, similar to surplus of labour forces, shortage of goods and services and comparatively low competition. But such factors as high qualification of labour force and technological resources have a narrow sphere of impact and are more important for technology based companies than the firms in other sectors. The 'independence on the former Soviet Union market' is a factor worth mentioning, because those sectors and individual businesses that had and have production and trade links within the Ukraine, have greater opportunities in comparison with the sectors integrated into the former all Union supply-demand system.

Unlike the opportunities, the threats for small businesses are more numerous and manifest a greater diversity of impact across sectors. The list of threats for Ukrainian small business people, compiled on the base of secondary and primary research of the author (Klochko, Isakova, 1996; Bernardini et al., 1996), looks the following way:
- absence of the law on SE, constantly changing laws and regulations
- currency controls
- burdensome taxes
- equity and loan capital, scarcity in sources of capital, inadequate banking system
- poverty of population
- commercial space/premises and equipment; raw materials, shortages of necessary suppliers
- underdeveloped infrastructure
- crime, corruption, racket, bribes
- relationship with large state enterprises
- lack of SME support programmes

In order to facilitate comprehension of the sector-related threats, the sectors have been arranged by *levels of entry difficulties* in the order of increasing number of threats and the value of the impact. This procedure has resulted in the series:
1st level: 'retail'; 'finance/insurance'; 'services/professional services'
2nd level: 'construction'
3rd level: 'industry'
4th level: 'research and development'.

Some sectors are not present, because there was not sufficient evidence on the threats and opportunities for the starters. (e.g. agriculture, transport, communications).

The results of the surveys and anecdotal data testify that starters in the 1st level group, *retail, finance/insurance, services,* encounter not all the threats from the list above: they do not need expensive equipment, network of suppliers, good relationship with large enterprises, long-term loans or access to industrial information. Although the threats of unsatisfactory legislation, taxation, infrastructure, bribing and racket are present, these sectors have been the easiest to enter during the last three years. The tendency may change with the saturation of this market and the increase in competition. For the time being, the 1st level group of sectors is comparatively easy for entry.

Construction small firms have demonstrated independence on the general economic recession in the country. In the beginning the construction co-operatives and then small construction firms have been very successful with both private and state contracts. Construction enterprises have solvent customers among private companies, joint ventures, state organisations and new financial institutions. They do not depend on production links with the former Soviet Union republics and benefit shorter production cycles in comparison with industry.

Industrial small enterprises are victims of the recession of the economy and the collapse of the USSR. There is no need to go into details on the topic of the integration of the Ukrainian economy and industry with the Soviet system. The most influential threats for industrial SE are the poverty of the state and population; broken links with suppliers and customers; mutual non-payment; stagnation in industrial sphere; absence of long-term loans; high prices on premises and equipment; raw materials; inadequate relationship with large state enterprises; monopoly in most branches of industry.

Research and development sphere suffers the greatest threats of all the sectors, although it is an important potential facility to overcome the crisis. One of the possible ways to facilitate the long and burdensome transition to market and to restore economic health is to turn to high technology, which is known to create value-added jobs, foster world-wide exports, generate the required rate of innovation and diffusion of new technologies. Emphasis on the emergence and development of technology based enterprises would significantly contribute to surmounting the existing crisis in research and development sphere and bridging the gap between research and industry. This gap was one of the most painful phenomena in the Soviet Ukraine and now the situation has worsened owing to the economic recession. The main threats for innovation in small firms are the absence of customers; absence of long-term loans; inadequate banking system and business infrastructure, absence of angels and venture capitalists in the country. The main constraints to innovation business development in the Ukraine are caused by the fact that the demand for intellectual products is smaller than the supply. As it has been already mentioned, in the country there are no institutions, big companies or charity foundations interested and responsible for survival of innovation business. The situation is still more aggravated by the fact that the legislation on intellectual property is not perfect. The high prices for getting patents on discoveries and inventions is another threat for entrepreneurs.

An Approach to Evaluate the Probability of Success or Failure

A research into the opportunities and threats for small business starters across sectors has been inspired by the novelty of the subject for a transition country more accustomed to broader areas of study. At the same time the progress, no matter how little, towards market requests for investigations of the issues associated with the success of not only the small business as part of the economy or its particular sectors, but individual small firms. Evaluation of the probability of success or failure for a starter has great practical implications for policymakers and individual entrepreneurs.

Theory and practice of small business management provide a vast field of information on key success factors, which can be classified into the following three groups: environment-related factors; business-related factors; personal characteristics. Table 6.6 presents lists of the three sets of factors identified.

Table 6.6   Three Sets of Key Business Success Factors

Environment-related factors	*Business-related factors*	*Personal characteristics*
Political system	Quality	Professional skills
Legislation	Price	Business skills
Taxation	Suppliers	Family support
Banking	Capital	Commitment
Insurance	Technology	Experience
Business associations/unions	Location	Financial resources
Business infrastructure	Distribution	Physical and emotional strengths
Socio-psychological issues	Markets	
	Advertising	

How do the factors differ (if they do) across sectors? The environment-related factors have similar effect (either positive or negative) on entering business in all sectors, but the second and the third sets of prerequisites can vary across sectors by the level of their importance for a successful start-up. Some of them may be more significant for a particular sector, some of them less. For instance, the weight of the 'personal commitment' cannot be compared to that of the 'suppliers', which is not critical for many sectors, especially in services or professional services.

The results of the study suggest that successful small business people usually rely on their background, professional skills, former professional links and knowledge even in cases when they do change the sphere of activities. For instance, a former economist starting a business training school, or a computer scientist entering computer trade and/or services make use of their previous experiences and knowledge transmitting the skills to new spheres of application and diversifying activities. But there are also numerous cases when small business starters enter quite a new sphere of activities, retail trade in most cases. In this situation we deal with the great attraction of the sector which provides opportunities for success even to the inexperienced newcomers.

A starter before going into business has to make a decision on what kind of business to start. As a rule, no thorough analysis is made and this increases the risk of failure. The following technique might facilitate the decision making and reduce the number of mistakes. Using the classification of Table 6.6 a starter must build a contrasting scale to evaluate the success profile of the business choice. To illustrate this let us take a case of a computer scientist who is forced to leave a scientific research institute and decides between several options of self-employment: research and development (technology based small firm); computer training services; translation of manuals on software; retail trade. The case is very typical for the Ukraine with a great number of researchers pushed out from research institutes by a sharp cut of R&D financing and general deterioration of conditions for research activities.

The first step to take is to compile a list of business options; the second -- to evaluate business-related factors and personal characteristics with regard to the options and the third -- to make the choice considering the two profiles of business success. Environment-related factors are ignored in the procedure because they are the same for all the options or the difference is insignificant. Figures 6.1 and 6.2 illustrate the case with a computer scientist who is to evaluate his chances in starting a technology based firm focused on research and development (activities very similar to what he has been doing in the research institute); in computer training services (also a high correlation with the background and education); in translation services (medium correlation with the previous experience; low professional interest); or in retailing (no connection at all with the previous experience and overqualified for the job).

Figure 6.1   Business Related Factors: Profiles of Success

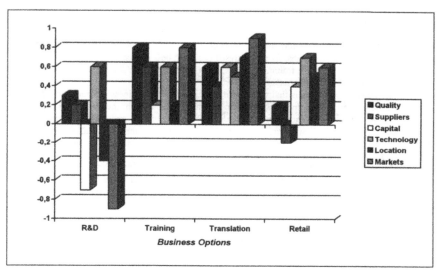

Figure 6.2   Personal Characteristics of Starter: Profiles of Business Success

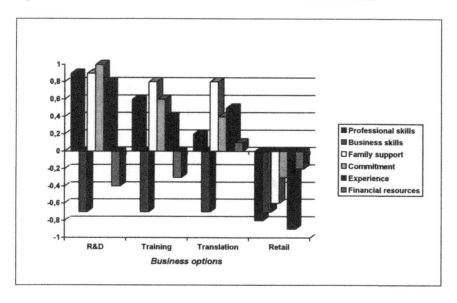

From Figure 6.1 it follows that the profile of the translation service small firm is the best and promises more success for the starter: although the quality of service is not high, it does not require much money to start and the market is great. But the decision is not to be made until the personal characteristics with regard to the options have been evaluated. A starter should thoroughly evaluate the business-related factors and personal characteristics, to compensate for the absence of the favourable external conditions. In the analysed case, the best choice is the translation services which is closely followed by the training services. Both options promise a relative business success, even under the unfavourable external environment.

The general conclusion is that with the improvement of the business environment the weight of the business-related factors and personal characteristics will diminish; meanwhile, as it has been already pointed out, starters should count on their personal abilities and courage more than on government business support programmes or incentives. And if we compare a small business starter in a developed market economy and in transition, the latter has to be twice as smart, brave and entrepreneurial as a businessman from the West.

On the other hand, the policymakers and business policy providers should focus on the first group of factors with the idea to facilitate business entry for ordinary people, not just 'business stars' or criminals. Small business should be an occupation for millions, otherwise it would not fulfil its social and economic functions. The special emphasis for the Ukraine, similar to other transition countries, should be made on the sectors with a larger list of threats, but a greater potential for economic stabilisation, that is, industrial production and high technology firms. In our opinion, the small business sector formation is a two-way process, with the leading role of the policy makers in the long run.

The results of this study did not allow for a strict model with quantitative characteristics, still the above technique may be helpful and successfully used by professional business advisers; employment centres officials and individual small business starters.

Conclusion

The analysis in this paper showed that even the unfavourable business environment of the Ukrainian slow transition to market allows for new small companies to emerge in selected sectors, like services, retail trade, catering, and finance. The survey of those who would like to start a small business clearly indicate their awareness of the threats and opportunities of different sectors and the intention to rely more on their own previous experience than on government support programmes.

The results of the current study must be interpreted with caution due to the drawbacks of the official statistics and the absence of data on the shadow economy. However, it does suggest some valuable directions for future research.

Acknowledgement

The author is grateful to the Research Support Scheme of the Open Society Institute (grant number 547/1996) for funding at the final stage of paper preparation and presentation. The author also thanks Dr. Yuri Klochko for his constructive comments.

References

Arendarski, A., Mroczkowski, T., Sood, J. (July 1994). 'A Study of the Redevelopment of Private Enterprise in Poland: Conditions and Policies for Continuing Growth'. *Journal of Small Business Management*, pp. 40-51.

Bernardini, P., Feletig, S., O'Neill, J., Pavlovskaya, T. Skorbun, I. (February-March 1996). 'New Entrepreneurs in Kiev'. *Unpublished report by the Agency for the Development of Enterprise*, Kiev.

Blanchflower, D.G., Meyer, B.D. (1994). 'A Longitudinal Analysis of the Young Self-Employed in Australia and the United States', *Small Business Economics* 6, 1-19.

Dubini, P. (October 1987). 'Motivational and Environmental Influences on Business Start-ups: Some Hints for Public Policy'. Working Paper Series, Wharton School of the University of Pennsylvania, Snider Entrepreneurial Center.

Good, W.S. and Graves, J. R. (January-March 1993). 'Small-Business Support Programs: The Views of Failed versus Surviving Firms'. *Journal of Small Business and Entrepreneurship*, vol. 10, N 2.

Klochko, Yu., Isakova, N. (1996). 'Small Business Sector in the Ukrainian Transition Economy: Achievements to Date'. *Entrepreneurship & Regional Development*, No. 8, pp. 127-140.

Lane, S. J. (May 1995) 'Business Starts during the Transition in Hungary', *Journal of Business Venturing*, Vol. 10, No. 3, pp. 181-194.

Lussier, R. (January 1995). 'A Nonfinancial Business Success versus Failure Prediction Model for Young Firms'. *Journal of Small Business Management*, Vol. 33, No. 1, pp. 8-20.

Mokry, B. W. (1988). 'Entrepreneurship and Public Policy. Can Government Stimulate Business Startsups?' Quorum books, N.Y.

Piasecki, B. (ed., 1992). 'Policy on Small and Medium-sized Enterprises in Central and Eastern European Countries', 19th International Small Business Congress, October 11 - 14, Lodz, 1992.

Shane, S., Kolvereid, L., Westhead, P. (1991). 'An Explanatory Examination of the Reasons Leading to New Firm Formation across Country and Gender'. *Journal of Business Venturing* 6, 431-446.

The State of Small Business. (1992). A Report of the President, US Government printing office, Washington.

Storey, D. J. (1993). 'Should We Abondon the Support to Start-up Businesses ?' The Warwick Business School, SME Centre, Working Paper No. 11.

Wickramanayake, E., Ming, W. (1995). 'Problems Facing Individual Industries in Jinning County, China'. *Small Enterprise Development*, Vol. 6, No 4, December, pp. 49-54.

Williams, M. L. (1993). 'Measuring Business Starts, Success and Survival: Some Database Considerations', *Journal of Business Venturing*, 8, p. 295-299.

7 Growth Intentions and Expansion Plans of New Entrepreneurs in the Former Soviet Bloc

David Pistrui, Harold P. Welsch and Joseph Roberts

Introduction

Entrepreneurship, and the development of new business continues to be at the forefront of socio-economic development in virtually all economies today. The collapse of the Soviet empire and subsequent liberation of the East Central European countries has created an opportunity for the rebirth of entrepreneurship, and private enterprise development. For example, in Romania, the entrepreneurial drive shown in recent years, including the expansion of thousands of small, private businesses has clearly been the stabilizing economic force (Carothers 1996).

In fact, Romania's private sector is the shining star in the country's struggle to transform it's crippled economy. The private sector is playing an increasing role in improving everyday life. Estimates by the Economist Intelligence Unit (1995) indicated that the private sector represented 35% of Romania's Gross Domestic Product, 56% of the retail trade and 50% of the services sector. Considering that over half the population of Europe's ninth largest nation live below the poverty level, private enterprise development is vital to sustained growth and improved living standards.

With entrepreneurship taking root, small and medium sized enterprises can greatly contribute to Romania's economic growth (United Nations Report, 1992). Amidst the sporadic economic reforms taking place, there is a need to gain an understanding as to the development of entrepreneurship and SME growth in transforming economies like Romania. As Davidsson (1991) points out 'when a firm operates above a mere subsistence level in a less than perfect market, the entrepreneur is free to choose whether to pursue expansion or not'. Thus the research question posed is *What are the levels, and specific types of expansion plans found among new entrepreneurs in a transforming economy of the former Soviet Bloc, specifically Romania, and what are predictors that can be examined that are related to expansion plans?*

The study operationalizes entrepreneurial growth intentions based on three types of expansion activities, 1) market expansion and development, 2) operations/production development, and 3) technological advancement. Drawing from the work of Gibb and Davies (1990); Kruger and Carsrud (1993); Davidsson (1989, 1991); Ward (1993); Kolveried (1990); Carland, Hoy, Boulton, and Carland (1984); and Greening, Barringer, and Macy (1996); two categories of predictor variables are established based on environmental and individual factors. Environmental predictors include demographics and infrastructure obstacles confronting entrepreneurs. Individual predictor variables include entrepreneurial intensity, individual motivation and personal sacrifice.

As a focused method of investigation one country from the former Soviet Bloc, Romania, was examined. A theoretical model composed of multi-level predictors was developed. The model was empirically tested with a sample of 410 entrepreneurs from various parts of Romania. Data were collected via the Entrepreneurial Profile Questionnaire (EPQ) which has been validated in Eastern Europe, Russia, South Africa, Mexico, and the United States. The sample includes a rich cross section of new business ventures across a variety of areas. The investigation is also designed to factor in the influence of external environmental conditions present during the economic transformation process in Romania.

Theoretical Background

General market based microeconomic theory contends that a firm grows until it has reached an optimal size. Under assumed perfect competition, a firm grows until it has reached the size where long run marginal cost equals price (Davidsson 1989; Kovereid et al. (1990); Mansfield 1979). Microeconomic theory grounded in deductive based assumptions of profit maximization most often ignores the entrepreneurial process. Economists in a general sense tend to view entrepreneurship as an independent variable. Consequently economists have usually played down the significance of entrepreneurship and have emphasized the economic conditions promoting its emergence, and concomitantly, with the occurrence of economic growth and development (Wilken 1979).

Schumpeter (1934) is considered one of the first economists to argue that the entrepreneur, as an individual, is fundamental to economic development. Schumpeter visualized the entrepreneur as the key figure behind economic development because of his other role in introducing innovation. Penrose (1959) presented the theory that growth is limited by a firm's 'productive opportunity'. She argued that the quality of entrepreneurial services including entrepreneurial versatility, fundraising integrity, entrepreneurial ambition, and entrepreneurial judgment impact growth. Today there continues to be an implicit assumption that the entrepreneur contributes disproportionately to economic development, yet little has been done to isolate the individual entrepreneur's contribution (Carland, Hoy, Boulton and Carland, 1984).

The applicability of general microeconomic and methamoric growth models across different socio-economic cultures must be widely questioned. The major shortcoming of these models has been the failure to consider differences in motivational patterns within the entrepreneurial population of a particular cultural environment (Davidsson 1989). Ginn and Sexton (1989) contended that if the decision to start a business is a choice of the founder, it can also be assumed that the decision to *grow* the business is a choice taken by the same entrepreneur. Understanding the concepts associated with small business success, growth, and failure are presently in their infancy. To date most of the attention has been focused on rapidly growing new ventures. Surprisingly little theoretical quantitative, and rigorous literature focuses on decisions of entrepreneurs to develop their firms (Ward, 1993). Conversely, given the complexity of the issues at hand, in combination with the importance of the economic policy implications, there is a call for research to incorporate a multidimensional approach. Plaschka and Welsch (1990) theorize that the development of entrepreneurship and subsequently the SME sector is a product of both external (policy, and infrastructure) and the internal components (characteristics of the entrepreneur and firm) of an economic system.

Frameworks for the Development of Growth Models

Researchers Gibb and Davies (1990) introduced a categorical series of frameworks aimed at the development of possible growth models. The Gibb and Davies framework was based on four categories; 1) Personality dominated approaches; 2) Organization development approaches; 3) Business management approaches; 4) Sectorial and broader market led approaches to growth. These approaches are further developed here.

Personality Dominated Approaches

The personality dominated approaches focus on the entrepreneur's personality traits, and psychological characteristics as the primary success factors impacting venture development. The achievement models proposed by McClelland and Atkinson, as well as the locus of control, and need for independence fall under this category.

Research associated with Need for Achievement (n Ach) models has been controversial. Hornaday and Aboud (1971) confirmed that entrepreneurs show a tendency to exhibit higher n Ach. By the same token, researchers Miller and Toulouse (1986) contend that n Ach does not correlate with the innovative success of a firm. Yasin (1996), in a study of Middle Eastern entrepreneurs, found no linkages between religious background and n Ach. He ties the social context rather than religious background alone to possibly explain differences in the level of n Ach.

Personality based research associated with locus of control suffers from a similar dilemma. For example, Brockhaus (1980), Begley and Boyd (1986), and Ward (1993) have produced contrasting results as to locus of control and growth factors. The major problem lies in the use of a small number of variables, often a single variable, within a simple model as a means of predicting failure or success, while often ignoring more complex phenomena such as growth intentions.

Innovation, ability, need for independence and tolerance of ambiguity fill out the remainder of personality dominated research.

Two general Shortcomings can be associated with this type of research. First, there is no unified agreed-upon definition of exactly what an entrepreneur is. This makes consistent measurement difficult. Second, much of the personality dominated research has produced conflicting results.

Organizational Development Approaches

Organizational development approaches tend to be focused on research dealing with stages of growth models and networking approaches. Churchill and Lewis (1983) argued that small businesses go through five stages of growth. Drawing from this model, Scott and Bruce (1987) integrated the Greiner Model (1978) of the five stages of growth to develop a hi-bred model. They argued that transition from one stage to another requires change, which is accompanied by some form of crises.

Dodge and Robbins (1992) further advanced the stages of growth concept by developing an organizational life cycle model for small firms. They discovered that the external environment impacted firms more in the early stages, and that planning was the primary problem confronting small firms as they grow. The stages of growth research also identified issues related to entrepreneurship and the transition to management during the various stages.

The use of entrepreneurial networks has recently received attention as a possible explanation for small firm growth. Johannisson (1992, 1995) suggested that entrepreneurs are more dependent upon their family and friends networks than on business plans to launch their ventures. Research concerning growth factors of Swedish high tech firms (Johannisson 1992) confirmed the importance of commercial and social networks and growth. Zhao and Aram (1995) in a study of young technology ventures in China found that networking bore a powerful association with firm development.

Gibb and Davies (1990) identified two significant shortcomings related to organizational development approaches. First, the majority of the growth stages based research is normative and lacks empirical evidence to support the theories. To a large extent this is the result of only a small body of relatively new research. Thus, there is a need to develop some empirically based longitudinal investigations. Second, although networking and the growth process is a rich and valuable approach to the small business growth process, only a minimal amount of research has been conducted to date. Consequently more research is essential to broaden the understanding of networking and small business growth.

Business Management Approaches

Three primary themes can be found in the business management approaches to small business growth; 1) management aspects; 2) environmental considerations; and 3) financial aspects. Gibb and Davies (1990) point out that strategic management approaches (primarily Ansoff's product-market typology) have been widely incorporated. Controversy surrounds the empirical findings of both product and market based strategies. For example Sandberg and Hofer (1987) argue that product based strategies performed better than focused strategies.

In contrast Cooper (1993) found the opposite, namely that focused strategies outperformed differentiated product strategies. Mullins (1996) has provided a bit of clarity. In a study employing Ansoff's (1975) typology of responses (include direct action, flexibility, and awareness responses) under changing market conditions, some explanations for conflicting predictions of different theoretical perspectives were identified. According to Mullins (1996), it was found that under changing market conditions, swift and vigorous responses (growth) occurred more often when: 1) a firm had a high level of competence combined with poor performance; or 2) when a firm had a low level of competence in combination with a good prior performance.

Research which studies environmental factors usually incorporates this aspect into a broader perspective. Plaschanka (1986) contends that behavior is a function of life space which includes both the person and his or her psychological environment. Dubini (1988) in her study of Italian firms relates motivational traits of individuals to the environmental conditions within which entrepreneurs find themselves. She identifies three broad groups of environmental aspects; 1) infrastructure (including information and technology); 2) capital structure (availability of private financial resources); and 3) governmental involvement (opportunity costs associated with start-up and capital availability).

Hay, Verdin, and Williamson (1993) took a different approach looking at the impact of product market environments. Generally they took a marketing based approach looking at push versus pull marketing strategies and their relationships to business growth and survival.

Financial performance represents the third Business Management approach under the Gibb and Davies framework. Norton (1991) looked at how capital structure was influenced by beliefs, behaviors, and motivations. Small firms appeared to follow a 'pecking order', using internal cash as much as possible, debt financing when necessary, and equity financing solely as a last result (Norton 1991). Much of the financial based research relies on financial ratios such as debt-to-equity, interest-to-earnings, and return on equity.

Research in the Business Management approaches to date has not truly made a significant impact to the fields of entrepreneurship and small business development. The major shortcoming being that most of this research has not been able to clearly explain how contrary approaches to product and market development have influenced growth (Herbeck 1994). Perhaps the greatest contribution comes from inclusion of environmental issues in relation to growth and development. However, more in-depth considerations need to be explored concerning both the external environment and internal environment associated with entrepreneurship and small business growth. With respect to financial analysis Gibb and Davies (1990) argue that simple financial ratios offer little true evidence as determinants of firm growth.

Sectorial and Broader Market Led Approaches

This aspect of research can largely be found in macroeconomic based approaches. Mainly focusing on external factors and constraints there are a great variety of studies which have marginal application to the focus of this paper. Gibb and Davies (1990) point out that most policymakers do not view these studies as confirmation that formal assistance, including training and consulting, have any significant impact on firm growth. Another point of contention has been that they lack empirical validation and that bureaucratic barriers such as taxation, legal constraints, or lagging technology conditions inhibit growth potential of small business.

For example, US Federal Reserve Bank Economist James A. Schmitz, Jr. (1993) stated 'the neoclassical theory of economic growth, that relies on differences in physical capital per person across countries to explain the wide disparity in per-capita output, cannot explain the observed inequality in the world'. He goes further to stress that newer theories of economic development which compare differences in human capital and education suffer from similar shortcomings. Schmitz (1993) argued that the key question is how to measure the true impact of bureaucratic legal constraints, or how tax structure and rates impact entrepreneurship, and SME development.

An example serves to illustrate this point. Researcher Bohdanowicz (1993) conducted a study of Polish entrepreneurs during transition. She found that as transition occurred and new markets emerged that a completely new set of barriers prevailed. Schmitz (1993) argued that these types of barriers are often created by groups in society with vested interests in the status quo. From a research perspective the problem lies in the fact that there are to date, no predictive models which provide specific guidelines to effectively arrange market conditions to stimulate growth.

Gnyawali and Fogel (1994) have identified a series of shortcomings which suggest how external factors and constraints could be better understood. First, they suggest that researchers need to consider the explicit links between what entrepreneur's needs are within the dimensions of their environments. Secondly, the needs of the policymakers must be taken into consideration. What type of information do they need? Are they supportive or threatened by entrepreneurship and SME growth? Only with these factors in mind can attention be given to the interrelationships between entrepreneurship, small business growth and economic development, especially in societies going through socio-economic transition.

Multidimensional Approach

The Gibb and Davies framework provides a sound starting point and should be considered as a directional mechanism toward understanding growth models in small firms. However, given the consistent contrasts in research findings associated with continued entrepreneurship, models of growth intentions need to advance to a higher level. Drawing from the work of Landstom and Huse (1995) concerning trends in entrepreneurship and small business research in Europe and the US, this paper strives to advance the field of growth and expansion understanding by addressing the following points:

1) Move away from an atheoretical stage to a more theoretically based empirical research aiming at building more rigorous concepts and models by exploring interlinks beyond the surface of present empirical knowledge.
2) Adopt a multidimensional research approach drawing from concepts and models within economics and the social sciences.
3) Employ the basic theories developed in earlier studies as a foundational starting point.
4) Seek to identify how cultural diversity relates to existing theories and models by incorporating a socio-cultural sensitivity as it relates to entrepreneurship and SME development.
5) Develop a conceptual framework providing direction toward the development of a multidimensional approach of scientific investigation.

As a method of achieving these objectives three theoretical perspectives are developed and combined to further advance the theoretical model: growth aspirations, growth willingness, and planned behavior. Each perspective provides a segment of theoretical and empirical consideration from which to build a multidimensional approach.

What is Planned Growth?

One of the fundamental problems at hand is how growth is defined. Aspirations, willingness, intentions, motives, and expansion are all common terms used in existing literature to describe growth. In order to add some clarity to the confusion a review of some of the most current research is used to construct a multidimensional framework. The following perspectives have been identified as noteworthy to the objectives of this study: Kovereid 1990; Davidsson 1989; Krueger and Carsrud 1993; Ward 1993; Carland, Hoy, Boulton, and Carland 1984; and Greening, Barringer, and Macy 1996.

Growth Aspirations

If the decision to start a business is a choice made by the founder, it may also be assumed that the decision to grow the business is a choice made by the same entrepreneur (Kolvereid 1991). In his study of Norwegian entrepreneurs Kolvereid adopted a multilevel approach looking at the relationships between the entrepreneur's motives to start the business, education, experience, industry, localization, characteristics of the organization and its environment, the firm's history of growth, and the entrepreneur's growth aspirations.

Drawing from a sample of 250 Norwegian entrepreneurs from four different regions of the country, the study developed a series of hypotheses which were empirically tested. The sample of businesses started in 1986 skews heavy toward services (67.5%). Although the relationships were not found to be very strong, the entrepreneur's motives to start their business were found to be related to their growth aspirations.

The dependent variable chosen for the analysis was a combination of revenue growth and employment aspirations. Four groups of entrepreneurs were identified 1) entrepreneurs who did not want to grow and did not intend to hire; 2) entrepreneurs who wanted to grow but did not plan to hire; 3) entrepreneurs who wanted to grow and intended to hire; 4) entrepreneurs who did not want to grow, but intended to hire. Following the methodology of Scheinberg and MacMillan (1988); Dubini (1989); and Blais et al. (1990); variables in the analysis were factor analyzed using the Varimax rotation method.

Kolvereid (1991, p. 213) found that 60.9% of entrepreneurs sampled answered that they wanted their firms to grow, and 35.6.% replied that they intended to hire new employees within the next two years. To the surprise of Kovereid almost 40% of the entrepreneurs did not aspire to grow their firms. This calls in to question as to whether revenue growth and hiring employees are perceived as measures of growth for Norwegian entrepreneurs. Some directional findings can be gleaned from this study, however:

1) Significant relationships were found between education and industry as well as a number of organizational variables, including past growth in both revenue and number of employees, in relation to an entrepreneur's aspirations to grow their firm.
2) No significant relationships were found between growth aspirations of entrepreneurs and experience, sex, location, or size of business as measured by employee count.
3) Higher growth aspiration levels tended to be related to entrepreneurs who desired personal achievement.
4) Entrepreneurs with the strongest growth aspirations were found in the manufacturing sector as opposed to services. Manufacturing firms were found to have smaller, and distant customer bases, often with more competitors.
5) When comparing like samples in Great Britain and New Zealand, a significantly larger percent of Norwegian entrepreneurs did not aspire to grow their firms.

As Kolvereid pointed out, this study was intended to explore and provide direction for future research. Perhaps the study's most pressing shortcoming was that many of the independent variables chosen were interrelated. For example, experience and industry clearly have the potential to overlap. Another question for future research can be found in the relationships between the perceptions of growth opportunity and the actual desire for growth which this study did not address.

It was also puzzling that the author did not go into greater detail regarding the large (40 %) of Norwegian entrepreneurs who did not aspire to grow, although Kolvereid (1991, p. 221) suggested that growth aspirations may be related to cultural factors such as legislation and the incentives, as well as deterring forces that are present in a country. Consequently, it becomes clear that a multidimensional approach should be incorporated into the study of entrepreneurship and small business growth.

Growth Willingness

According to Davidsson (1989; 1991) firm growth is an indication of continued entrepreneurship. One study in particular (Davidsson 1989) focused on the relationship between the expected outcomes and growth willingness. The study, like Kolvereid's (1991), incorporated a multidimensional approach, yet the Davidsson study relied heavily on psychological theories of motivation. Specifically the study strove to identify factors which either enhanced or reduced the willingness to grow.

Drawing a random sample of over 400 Swedish entrepreneurs, most firms were found to have between 2 and 20 employees. Enterprises of this size were routinely labeled micro-businesses. From the sample, four distinct categories of enterprises emerged: Manufacturing, High-Tech, Repair Servives, and Retailing. Three size categories were also created, 2-4, 5-9, and 10-19 employees. Davidsson (1989 p. 215) also identified a potential cultural peculiarity in the fact that Swedish legislation is restrictive in terms of the owner-manager's right to lay off personnel.

The author pointed out that the focus of the investigation was to try to answer the following questions: 1) Can differences in growth willingness be explained by differences in expected outcomes; 2) What expected outcomes are important growth motivators or deterrents; 3) Do different levels of achievement motivation affect growth willingness; 4) How does growth willingness, and its determinants differ among different classes of trade? The dependent variable, growth willingness, was developed as the logarithm of the percentage difference between present size and ideal size (five years later) based on the number of employees, and turnover (Davidsson, 1989, p. 215).

The results suggested that a significant relationship was found between expected outcomes and growth willingness. Davidsson (1989 pp. 222-223) summarized the key findings:

1) Certain expected outcomes seem to affect growth willingness in the predicted direction. Yet, money which often has been found to be the central motivating force in most economic theories was not found to have an important role.

2) Most firms favored growth, 62% favored moderate growth in the number of employees, and 87% favored growth in turnover.

3) Control and independence variables were found to have an asymmetric relationship. Each played a separate and distinct role in the relationship between growth and autonomy; their impact changed with firm size.

4) Growth was conditional on more than individual desire. External conditions and entrepreneurial ability were important, not just willingness. The perception of what growth will bring over time impacted growth.

5) The results suggest flat n Ach does affect growth. The concept that individuals with high n Ach perceive money as a measure of success was suggested.

As Kolvereid (1991) pointed out, significant relationships were found between growth willingness and expectations concerning employee wellbeing, control, independence, workload, and achievement motivation. This study certainly provided valuable insights, however, as Davidsson (1991 p. 223) pointed out himself: 'There will be a lot of situational influences unique to each firm, blurring relations'.

One possible solution could have been to reduce the number of micro variables and create stronger macro variables. Perhaps some correlation analysis could have provided directional insights between variables. Another shortcoming lies in the fact that the author hinted at cultural peculiarities yet failed to properly address any details. It seem that many scholars mention culture in passing yet do very little to build on the understanding of its roles and impact. The study should also be considered foundational in nature. The regression model provided valuable insight, yet as the author himself points out, the major share of growth willingness remained unexplained.

Planned Behavior

Researchers Krueger and Carsrud (1993) developed a theory driven model of intentions building on existing models for psychology and entrepreneurship. According to Krueger and Carsrud (1993 p. 315) theory-driven models are necessary due to the complex perception-based process underlying intentional planned behaviors such as new venture initiation. They grounded their study in the work of the social psychology, specifically Icek Ajzen's intentions based 'theory of planned behavior'. This approach was based on two contentions; 1) Intentions are the single best predictor of behavior, both conceptually and empirically; 2) Intentions based models of entrepreneurial behavior are comparable with existing research results, and open new approaches to studying venture intuition. Some of Ajzen's (1991) most recent empirical investigations have been found to explain approximately 30 % of future behavior (Krueger and Carsrud 1993).

Research has also shown that entrepreneurial intentions are critical to understanding the overall process of organizational emergence (Bird 1988, Boeker 1989, Schoonhoven and Eienhardt et al. 1990, Krueger and Carsrud 1993). Drawing from the Ajzen-Fishbein framework which has empirically confirmed that intentions successfully predict behavior and that attitudes successfully predict intentions, Krueger and Carsrud (1993) strive to integrate studies focused on entrepreneurial intentions. Shapero's model of the entrepreneurial event served as the main linkage.

The Shapero model theorized that the perceptions of the entrepreneur impacted actual intentions. Exogenous influences such as unemployment, divorce and other external events operated indirectly through attitudes of perceived desirability and feasibility (Krueger and Carsrud 1993 p. 322). The Shapero model considered the attractiveness, social perceptions, along with the entrepreneurs' perceived power to produce the desired results (Self-Efficacy).

The authors found support for the relationship between the Ajzen-Fishbein, and Shapero frameworks based on tests of the Shapero model which showed that perceived feasibility, perceived desirability, and the propensity to act should be considered as significant qualifications of entrepreneurial behavior. Krueger (1993) suggested that exogenous factors such as prior exposure to entrepreneurial activity influenced the various types of perception.

Krueger and Carsrud contended that theory-based intentional models which incorporate perception-driven considerations offer three key implications for researchers:

1) Intentions are the best predictors of planned behavior. Attitudes, behavior, and intentions are inter-linked to the situation (environment) and person (entrepreneur).
2) The strength of the intentions based models from social-psychology should encourage entrepreneurship to adopt more process based research.
3) An important distinction needs to be considered between situational and individual variables due to the fact they are exogenous factors which can influence entrepreneurial intentions indirectly.

Theory based intention models, especially the hi-bred type proposed by Krueger and Carsrud provide some valuable guidance to understanding the process of entrepreneurship. However, the approach has some shortcomings. First, an understanding of how intentions are formed, particularly across different socio-economic environments, is missing. The exogenous mechanisms tend to be an area recognized yet the understanding of their impact on perception, desirability, and feasibility are grossly underdeveloped. For example in the case of economies in transition, like those found in the former Soviet Bloc, self-efficacy, government, family, infrastructure and other exogenous variables must be mixed with person-based variables in order to provide a strong multidimensional predictive model.

Dependent Variable - Expansion Plans

Growth intentions and plans can take on various forms. In many cases growth is measured by increases in the number of employees, profits and sales. Whereas these measures may be 'final outcomes', it is necessary to ask the question about how those final objectives are achieved. A set of 'implementable attributes' which are 'intentions based' was called for.

Studying a variety of countries in the Soviet Bloc, Hungary, Estonia, Czech Republic, Russia, Poland and Lithuania, the authors observed how privatization and private enterprise initiatives are implemented in a number of transforming economies. Through a series of interviews and Entrepreneurial Questionnaire (EPQ) surveys incorporating the concept of 'planned growth', a variety of items (Table 7.1) were designed to measure the extent of this phenomenon. Planned growth is often seen as the variable which distinguishes small business owners from 'real entrepreneurs'. Carland, et al. (1984), suggested that this concept is an important method of categorizing types of entrepreneurs which may lead us through the maze discovering the essence of entrepreneurship. Karl Vesper (1996) has recently focused on 'high growth' entrepreneurship as a specialization within the field and has published a monograph of various universities offering courses on fast growing firms.

Table 7.1   Implementable Attributes of Planned Growth

1. Adding a new product or service
2. Selling to a new market
3. Adding operating space
4. Expanding distribution channels
5. Expanding advertising and promotion

6. Acquiring new equipment
7. Computerizing current operations
8. Upgrading computer systems
9. Replace present equipment
10. Expand current facilities

11. Adding specialized employees
12. Redesigning layout
13. Offsite training of employees
14. Redesigning operating methods

15. Seeking additional financing
16. Seeking professional advice
17. Researching new markets
18. Expanding scope of operating activities

Eighteen expansion plan items were factor-analyzed to determine if they fell into natural theoretical groupings. The extraction method was utilized via a principal components (pc) analysis. Three factors were identified (Table 7.2) which yielded separate identities with acceptable levels of reliability (Chronbach's alpha .76, .68, and .73 respectively).

Factor 1 was labeled 'Market Expansion' since it focused on researching new markets and expanding the scope of activities via additional financing, and by professional advice, etc.

Factor 2 was termed 'Operation/Production Expansion' since it involved adding a new product line or service, adding operating space and expanding output channels.

Factor 3 was based on technological factors such as upgraded equipment, computerizing operations and upgrading computer systems. This factor was called 'Technological Upgrade/Expansion'.

Table 7.2   Factor Analysis of Expansion Plans

Pattern Matrix:

	Factor 1	*Factor 2*	*Factor 3*
1	-.32953	.91782	-.04096
2	.07263	.86505	-.30598
3	-.19360	.78497	.00072
4	.03261	.90842	-.17516
5	.09392	.68649	-.02919
6	-.05363	-.08758	.84919
7	.73001	-.14960	.22949
8	.86479	-.20705	.15109
9	.34955	-.46065	.74650
10	-.34581	.22726	.88325
11	.41108	.05935	.38346
12	.84453	-.11695	-.02880
13	.70778	-.02319	.09115
14	.97052	-.20901	-.06369
15	.88841	.02860	-.36818
16	.89272	-.01455	-.22703
17	.51404	.45067	-.25633
18	.48471	-.07506	.27417
Chronbach's alpha:	.76	.68	.73

Predictors of Expansion Plans Based on the earlier literature review combined with empirical observations, a series of relationships were hypothesized to be related to expansion plans based on a series of exogenous and individually based variables, including demographic, entrepreneurial intensity, sacrifices willing to be made, strength of motivation and infrastructure obstacles confronting the entrepreneur.

Hypothesis 1:   Expansion plans will be positively related to family support and education while being negatively related to age and years of establishment.

Since younger entrepreneurs had less invested in the outmoded socialistic economic system than their older counterparts, they would be more willing to 'let go' of communism and invest their lives into expansion opportunities. They would also have established their businesses earlier, given a chance to cast their lot with private enterprise expansion. Their education and family support would serve as critical resources in their expansion plans.

Hypothesis 2:   Entrepreneurial intensity will be positively related to expansion plans.

Very intense entrepreneurs (high commitment to their profession) would seek to expand their business and take advantage of all possible opportunities. The growth of their business would be a very high (or highest) priority for them.

Hypothesis 3:   Entrepreneurial sacrifices would be positively related to expansion plans.

Individuals making major investments in the growth of their business would be willing to make substantial sacrifices in the course of their business. Short-term sacrifices would be made in order to provide for long-term business success.

Hypothesis 4:   Entrepreneurial motivation would be positively related to expansion plans.

This hypothesis would test Kolvereid's (1991) Norwegian prediction that higher growth aspiration levels would be related to entrepreneurs who desired personal achievement. In the research conducted in the current study, we would expand Kolvereid's achievement predictor and include other additional entrepreneurial motivations such as need for independence, freedom and financial reward, and also test the hypothesis in a different culture.

Hypothesis 5:   Infrastructure obstacles would be negatively related to expansion plans.

Romania is a country that is not yet fully operational to support entrepreneurial endeavors, much less encourage expansion plans. Therefore, it is predicted that the frequency of these types of problems would hinder the progress and growth of entrepreneurs. The post-Ceausescu government in particular has remained largely socialistic and has resisted privatization attempts almost at every turn.

Methodology

Four hundred and ten (410) entrepreneurs were surveyed, 75% in Bucharest and 25% in the remainder of the country. Cities included were Brosov, Timisoara, Cluj-Napoca, Constanta, Arad, Craiova and Galati. In order to gather data on expansion plans, demography, entrepreneurial intensity, sacrifices, motivations and infrastructure obstacles, the Entrepreneurial Profile Questionnaire (EPQ) was utilized. The EPQ has been administered and validated successfully in Russia, Poland, the Czech Republic, Hungary, Lithuania, Estonia, South Africa, Mexico, and the United States. The coefficients of the variables were statistically analyzed using the Chronbach alpha measure which resulted in an average $\alpha = .75$.

The EPQ was professionally translated and edited into Romanian, pretested, and then revised to clear up ambiguities or idiosyncratic terminology. Utilizing information regarding private enterprise formation from local chambers of commerce in combination with the Small Business Development Centers at the Polytechnic Institute of Bucharest and the Academy of Economic Studies Bucharest, an extended series of survey interviews with entrepreneurs occurred. The sample had no gender bias. To qualify, the enterprise was required to be legally operational.

The Entrepreneurial Profile Questionnaire (EPQ) was administered to 292 males and 118 females with a combined average age of 38.83 years. In terms of nationality, 95% were Romanian, the remaining 5% were primarily Hungarian. Only 19.5% of their fathers and 10.7% of their mothers were entrepreneurs. Yet today 33% have two family members working in the business full time, while 41% have a family member working part time. A five point Likert Scale ranging from strongly disagree (1) to strongly agree (5) was provided as response categories.

The data were analyzed for reliability and the items were tested for construct validity with satisfactory results. The enter method of the linear regression analysis was used to test the models and the R^2 are listed in the tables for each of the predictor variables. A bivariate Pearson correlation (1-tailed significance test) analysis was performed to determine the directional flow of the operationalization of the variables.

Results

Hypotheses were essentially confirmed with the surprising result of Hypothesis 5 being confirmed in the opposite direction. Taken in order, the hypotheses were tested via correlation analysis (Tables 7.3 to 7.7) and regressions (Table 7.8).

The education level and family support (as measured by the number of family members in the business) served the entrepreneur quite well in terms of expansion plans. Both were related significantly as valuable resources. Age and years of establishment were negatively related suggesting that younger entrepreneurs took to expansion planning earlier by starting their business sooner. R^2 was highest for Technological Upgrade (.248) as it was for every predictor category.

Hypothesis 2 was also confirmed showing evidence of high entrepreneurial intensity/commitment being positively associated with more expansion plans. Entrepreneurs were convinced that their business enterprise was a significant factor in their lives which had to be nurtured and grown for the future.

Similar relationships existed for Hypothesis 3 and Hypothesis 4. Expanding entrepreneurs were willing to make significant sacrifices in terms of giving up time with their family, incurring more risk and financial burdens, losing recreation and leisure opportunities and working diligently by putting in long hours.

Entrepreneurial motivations were the best predictors showing the highest R^2 (.276, .284 and .449) respectively for the three components of expansion plans. Freedom to do their 'own thing' and personal development opportunity were especially strongly related to expansion plans. To be innovative and develop their idea for a product or service, to network with others of their own choice, as well as being *directly* responsible for the success of their company were also strongly related. Desire for high earnings was not especially strong (although significant), but access to fringe benefits perhaps would allow them to have the security to pursue further expansion plans.

Infrastructure Obstacles (Hypothesis 5) were predicted to be negatively related to expansion plans. However, the opposite proved to be the case. The entrepreneur would pursue expansion plans *in spite* of the obstacles thrown into his path. Perhaps he/she has already developed strategies about *overcoming* those obstacles and in that process has developed the strength, ingenuity and confidence to grow the company. Perhaps the many years that Romanians were confronted with numerous political/economic obstacles has hardened them and also made them flexible enough so that the current obstacles do not become debilitating for them. This counter-intuitive finding thus reflects on the hardiness and perseverance of the Romanian entrepreneur.

Pearson Correlations

Table 7.3   Demographics

	EXPANSION PLANS		
	Market Expansion	Technological Upgrade	Operation/ Production
Age	-.099 *	-.156 **	-.095 *
Education	.082 *	.099 *	.042
Family members/Full Time	.123 *	.188 ***	.182 ***
Family members/Part Time	.052 *	.126 *	.061
Sales next year	.013	.037	.001
Number of employees in five years	.238 ***	.220 ***	.176 ***

* = $p \leq .05$ ** = $p \leq .01$ *** = $p \leq .001$

Table 7.4   Intensity

	EXPANSION PLANS		
	Market Expansion	Technological Upgrade	Operation/ Production
My business most important activity of my life	.111 *		.131 **
I will do whatever it takes	.216 ***	.235 ***	.008
No limit to maximum effort	.07	.256 ***	.164 ***
Willing to make significant sacrifices	.13 **	.249 ***	.104 *
Work else only for time attempt again	.049	.067	.135 ***
'Whatever it takes' philosophy	.071	.102 *	.011
Plan to eventually sell business	-.005	.139 **	.019
Contribution to community	.284 ***	.327 ***	.138 **

* = $p \leq .05$ ** = $p \leq .01$ *** = $p \leq .001$

Table 7.5   **Sacrifice**

| | EXPANSION PLANS | | |
	Market Expansion	Technological Upgrade	Operation/ Production
Conflict with family	.033	.216 ***	.114 *
Loss time with the family	.007	.028	-.011
Use all of my savings	.072	.140 **	.025
Loss time in another profession	.197 ***	.224 ***	.069
Risk of total failure in this business	.108 *	.113 *	.049
The wrath of my family	.135 **	.298 ***	.202 ***
My position in the eyes of my friends	.095	.221 ***	.156 ***
Give up my friends	.127 *	.219 ***	.097 *
Quality time with my children	.044	.063	.064
Mortgage on my house	.078	.221 ***	.094 *
Borrowing on my assets	.064	.213 ***	.076
Willingness to take an additional debt	.103 *	.171 ***	.073
Break up of my marriage	.022	.176 ***	.108 *
Significant recreation time	.108 *	.048	.033
Sixty hours of working per week	.253 ***	.368 ***	.204 ***
Sending kids to better college (school)	.212 ***	.244 ***	.125 **
Watching my favorite TV programs	.173 ***	.151 ***	.097 *
Attending my favorite sporting events	.15 **	.230 ***	.139 **
Attending to undesirable responsibilities	-.044	.006	.029
Willing to take on any task	.14 **	.167 ***	.126 **
Acquire skills at significant personal exp	.182 ***	.280 ***	.217 ***
Contribute to welfare of community	.122 *	.179 ***	.141 **

$* = p \leq .05$ $** = p \leq .01$ $*** = p \leq .001$

Table 7.6   Motivation

	EXPANSION PLANS		
	Market Expansion	Technological Upgrade	Operation/ Production
Freedom to adopt my own approach	.177 ***	.229 ***	.250 ***
To keep learning	.174 ***	.304 ***	.244 ***
Give myself/spouse security	.158 ***	.157 ***	.205 ***
It was the only thing I could do	-.030	.014	-.061
To have variety and adventure in my life	-.042	.186 ***	.127 **
Opportunity to lead rather than be led	.046	.103 *	.102 *
To escape unsafe working conditions	.036	.029	.008
Contribute to the welfare of my relatives	.122 *	.107 *	.123 **
Work in desirable locale for me and my family	.024	.028	.405 *
Make better use of my training/skills	.128 **	.206 ***	.175 ***
Develop idea for a product or business	.128 ***	.254 ***	.145 **
To have fun	-.007	.179 ***	.086 *
Desire to have high earnings	.153 ***	.132 **	.086 *
Continue a family tradition	.101 *	.309 ***	.223 ***
Challenge by affects starting business	.104 *	.314 ***	.214 ***
Achieve and get recognition for it	.016	.076	.153 ***
Achieve sense of accomplishment	.058	.104 *	.121 **
Network with other entrepreneurs	.254 ***	.339 ***	.201 ***
Increase status and prestige of my family	.082 *	.156 ***	.227 ***
Need more money to survive	-.011	.070	.010
Not to work for unreasonable boss	.037	.076	.046
Take advantage opportunity appeared	.118	.188 ***	.081
Higher position for myself in society	.169 ***	.407 ***	.209 ***
Frustrated in previous job	.067	.160 ***	.081
Follow example of a person I admire	-.009	.175 ***	.083 *
Control my own time	.080	.185 ***	.116 **
Able to work with people I choose	.250 ***	.180 ***	.172 ***
Be my own boss, Work for myself	.152 ***	.078	.095 *
Direct contribution to the success of the company	.259 ***	.464 ***	.251 ***
Greater flexibility in my life	.110 *	.184 ***	.250 ***
Be respected by my friends	.026	.196 ***	.164 ***
Be innovated, On forefront of technical development	.202 ***	.456 ***	.322 ***
Contribute to welfare of ethnic group	.133 **	.289 ***	.231 ***
Access to fringe benefits	.174 ***	.295 ***	.169 ***
Have influence in my community	.218 ***	.357 ***	.220 ***
Work with people I like	.132 **	.142 **	.194 ***
Time in my life when it made sense	.096 *	.082 *	.168 ***

   $* = p \leq .05$ $** = p \leq .01$ $*** = p \leq .001$

Table 7.7   Obstacles

	EXPANSION PLANS		
	Market Expansion	Technological Upgrade	Operation/ Production
Lack understanding of entrepreneurship	.078	.170 ***	.034
Negative attitudes toward profit-making	.060	.129 **	.010
Corruption	.101 *	.193 ***	.152 ***
Anti-market attitudes & behavior by govt.	.156 ***	.129 **	.122 **
Govt. assistant agencies	.138 **	.215 ***	.034
Number of competitors	-.080	-.096 *	-.162
Lack of market information	.118 *	.219 ***	.077
Lack of sources of technical assistance	.131 **	.297 ***	.127 **
Lack of managerial services	.173 ***	.282 ***	.137 **
Lack employees trained financial affairs	.201 ***	.334 ***	.162 ***
Lack of employees trained in marketing	.228 ***	.345 ***	.145 **

* = $p \leq .05$ ** = $p \leq .01$ *** = $p \leq .001$

Table 7.8   Regressions (R^2, N = 410)

	EXPANSION PLANS		
Demographics	Market Expansion	Operation/ Production	Technological Upgrade
Age Year of Establishment # Family members (Full Time) # Family members (Part Time) Education Level # of Employees in 5 years	.118	.141	.248
Entrepreneurial Intensity	.123	.073	.258
Entrepreneurial Sacrifices	.172	.143	.321
Motivation	.276	.284	.449
Infrastructure Obstacles	.124	.119	.236

Conclusions and Implications

Romanian entrepreneurs seem to have definite, well-defined expansion plans for the future. These original eighteen items measuring expansion plans seem to reflect the scope and magnitude of their long-term future. Although vestiges of socialism remain, they feel that they are becoming masters of their own destiny by biting off 'chunks of the future' in undertaking and implementing these plans. They have devised the mechanisms by which they plan to control their future and also appear to have the strength and motivation to carry them out.

Similar entrepreneurial motivations seem to come into play both initiating *and* expanding the business. So it is 'more of the same' drive and type of effort which propels the entrepreneur. Future refinements in motivations can be 'teased' out by additional analysis as the entrepreneur continues to 'fine tune' and grow the business.

While this model worked well in the Romanian setting, it should also be tested in other former Soviet Bloc countries as well as in more mature/industrialized economies. Commonalities and differences across different settings should prove useful in expanding the predictive power of the four major variables. Consistency across the factor analytical components of expansion plans would also enhance the predictive power of the model by testing it in a variety of economic and political situations.

References

Amit, R., MacCrimmon, K. and Oesch, J. (1996) *The Decision to Start a New Venture: Values, Beliefs, and Alternatives,* Submitted for presentation at the Babson College-Kauffman Foundation Entrepreneurship Research Conference, University of Washington, Seattle, WA.

Asiedu-Takyi, S. (1993) Some Socio-Cultural Factors Retarding Entrepreneurial Activity in Sub-Saharan Africa. *Journal of Business Venturing,* 8, 91-98.

Begley, T. and Boyd, D. (1986) Psychological Characteristics Associated With Entrepreneurial Performance. *Frontiers of Entrepreneurship Research,* Wellesley, MA, Babson College Center for Entrepreneurial Studies.

Birly, S. and Westhead, P. (1994) A Taxonomy of Business Start-Up Reasons and Their Impact on Firm Growth and Size. *Journal of Business Venturing,* 9, 7-31.

Bohdanowicz, N. (1993) Barriers of growth of small and medium sized enterprises according to the opinion of their owners. *Small and Medium Sized Enterprises and the Role of Private Industry in Poland,* ed. by P. Dominiak, and F. Blawat, Faculty of Management and Economics, Technical University of Gadansk, Poland.

Brunner H. (1993) Entrepreneurship in Eastern Europe: Neither Magic nor Mirage. A Preliminary Investigation. *Journal of Economic Issues,* Vol XXVII No. 2, June.

Carland, J., Hoy, F., Boulton, W., and Carland J.A. (1984) Differentiating entrepreneurs from small business owners: A conceptualization. *Academy of Management Review,* Vol. 9, No. 2 354-359.

Cooper, A. and Gascon (1990) *Entrepreneurs, Processed of Founding, and New Firm Performance.* Institute for Research in the Behavioral, Economic, and Management Sciences, Krannert Graduate School of Management, Purdue University, West Lafayette, Indiana, Unpublished research paper.

Cooper, A. and Gascon (1992) Entrepreneurs, Processed of Founding, and New Firm Performance. *The State of the Art of Entrepreneurship,* ed. by D. Sexton, and J. Kasarda, The Coleman Foundation, PWS-Kent, Boston MA.

Dana, L. (1994) A Marxist Mini-Dragon? Entrepreneurship in Today's Vietnam. *Journal of Small Business Management,* April, 1994.

Davidsson, P. (1991) Continued Entrepreneurship: Ability, Need and Opportunity as Determinants of Small Firm Growth. *Journal of Business Venturing,* 6.

Davidsson, P. (1989) Entrepreneurship-and After? A Study of Growth Willingness in Small Firms. *Journal of Business Venturing,* 4, 211-226.

Davidsson, P. (1995) Determinants of Entrepreneurial Intentions. *RENT IX Conference Proceedings,* Piacenza, Italy.

Dchneider, O. (1990) The Problems of the Development of the Service Sector in Czechoslovakia. *The Geography of Services.*

Dubini, P. (1988) Motivational and Environmental Influences on Business Start Ups: Some Hints for Public Policy. *Frontiers of Entrepreneurship Research*, ed. by B. Kirchhoff, W. Lang, K. Vesper, and W. Wetzel; Wellesley, MA, College Center for Entrepreneurial Studies.

Fombrun, C. and Wally S. (1989) Structuring Small Firms for Rapid Growth. *Journal of Business Venturing*, 4, 107-122.

Gibb, A. and Davies, L. (1990) *Frameworks Aimed at the Development of Possible Growth Models.* Durham Business School, United Kingdom.

Greenberg, D., Barringer, B. and Macy, G. (1996) A Qualitative Study of Managerial Challenges Facing Small Business Geographic Expansion, *Journal of Business Venturing*, 11, 233-256.

Herbeck, T. (1994) *Success, Growth and Failure Among Small Firms: What Do We Know?* Unpublished research paper, European Doctoral Programme in Entrepreneurship and Small Business Management, Universitat Autonoma de Barcelona, Barcelona, Spain.

Hoy, F., McDougall, P. and Dsouza, D. (1993) Strategies and Environments of High-Growth Firms. *The State of the Art of Entrepreneurship*, ed. by D. Sexton, and J. Kasarda, The Coleman Foundation, PWS-Kent, Boston, MA.

Kolvereid, L. (1990) Growth Aspirations Among Norwegian Entrepreneurs. *Journal of Business Venturing*, 209-222.

Krueger, N. and Carsrud, A. (1993) Entrepreneurial intentions: Applying the theory of planned behaviour. *Entrepreneurship & Regional Development*, 5, 315-330.

Osborne, R. (1996) Second Phase Entrepreneurship Breaking Through the Growth Wall. *Business Horizons*, January-February.

Plaschaka, G. (1986) *Characteristics of Successful and Unsuccessful Entrepreneurs. A Theoretically Guided Empirical Investigation of Person-Related and Microsocial Factors.* University of Economics and Business Administration, Department of Small Business, Vienna, Austria, unpublished research paper.

Scott, M. and Bruce, R. (1987) Five Stages of Growth in Small Business. *Long Range Planning*, Vol. 20, No. 3, pp. 45-52, Pergamon Journals Ltd., Great Britain.

Shaver, K. and Scott, L. (1991) Person, Process, Choice: The Psychology of New Venture Creation. *Entrepreneurship Theory and Practice*, Winter, Baylor University, 1991.

Ward, E. (1993) Motivation of Expansion Plans of Entrepreneurs and Small Business Managers. *Journal of Small Business Management*, January.

8 Portfolio Entrepreneurs: Some Empirical Evidence on the Multiple Ownership or Control of SMEs, and its Implication for our Understanding of Start-Up and Growth

Peter J. Rosa and Michael G. Scott

Introduction

Previous work by the authors   (see endnote) has led to a concern that progress in understanding the small firm sector is hampered by elements of the current research paradigm, and specifically by:

1) an over-reliance on the 'firm' as the unit of analysis
2) a neglect of broader processes of ownership and control, and capital accumulation and transference, leading to
3) the depoliticisation of small business research.

This paper builds on earlier work (Scott & Rosa 1996b:81, Scott & Rosa 1996a, Rosa & Scott 1995) to argue that there is the possibility for new insights into both start-up and growth processes when the boundaries of 'small business' are extended to include broader capital ownership and transference decisions of key agents in the business. This paper focuses on the phenomenon of multiple *business* ownership as a subset of the ownership of capital in all its forms, and which is here chosen as the least invisible part of entrepreneurial processes of value extraction and accumulation.

The 'Problem' of Growth

Let us choose as a starting point the large literature on the 'problems' of small firms growth (and more specifically the evidence that small firms typically do not grow. Much of this is conveniently summarised by Storey (1994: 127, 138, 144)). Based partly on this research there has been a plethora of public policy initiatives intended to better equip firms to achieve higher growth levels through enhancing knowledge and management skills.

Yet economic theory assumes that the optimal size of a firm can be uniquely determined and would differ in different industries with different cost structures. Growth is possible only for firms in sub-optimal positions (Davidsson 1989:19). Ecologically, competitive forces tend to optimise the size of firms, so that an efficient optimal size might well be *small*, given the nature of the niche being exploited and sector specific forces in play. The key to growth is diversification (Penrose 1980), but this can take place both within the firm and outside it. How far diversification is managed within a single firm, or is managed through parallel firms, becomes an important *area of choice*.

'Growth potential is thus not the province of *firms*, but of the entrepreneurs who create and run them. A 'firm' is merely a legal unit which can be manipulated by discerning entrepreneurs to maximise their advantage. When an entrepreneur is operating several products, services or in different markets, he or she must decide how to legally 'ring-fence' these activities. When the decision is to ring-fence them in one organisational unit, and performance is strong, it comes to be viewed as a high growth firm. If the decision is to organise the same products or services into more than one legally independent organisational units, the performance would be the same (yet) largely undetectable to conventional analyses where the unit of analysis is focused on the firm rather than the entrepreneur'. (Scott & Rosa 1996a).

If it can be shown that diversification takes place through the agency of ownership manipulations, then quite new analyses of start-up and growth became possible. Firstly, some start-up becomes a part of growth, not an independent process as is so often assumed. Segmentation of new entrants to the economy becomes essential, since we would argue that the start-up firm which is effectively part of an existing ownership 'cluster' is a quite different animal from firms which are not (in terms of access to resources, experience, information and networks for instance) and its potential for success may be considerably above average. Secondly, whilst individual firms in a cluster may not grow (or be deliberately prevented from growing), the cluster as a whole may grow (although this growth would be largely invisible to analyses using only single firms as units of analysis). The more entrepreneurs use ownership diversification to pursue growth, the less evidence there will be of growth in small firms, as long as the single firm is the unit of analysis (Scott & Rosa, 1996a).

Thirdly, we suspect that entrepreneurs may use, *inter alia*, ownership diversification as a means of spreading risk and for the purposes of experimentation. This is all consistent with some current thinking in evolutionary economics which sees an important role for 'competence blocks' or clusters of specialised knowledge in experimentation, innovation, and organisational development. 'When internal parts of the firm do not perform up to preset standards exit, entry, rationalisation or re-organisation processes are initiated that change the boundaries of the financial decision system organised by the owners to serve their wealth accumulation purposes. Since profitability and wealth creation is the ultimate target financial markets are also the ultimate arbiters of that re-organisation process and determine the outer boundaries of the financial decision system that we have called the firm'. (Eliasson, 1996: 135).

Fourthly, processes of damage limitation as part of the experimentation may explain why many 'exits' from business registers simply fade away rather than actively 'fail', providing fresh insights into the failure statistics.

Multiple Ownership

These issues have been initially explored in our earlier papers. The crux of course is the *incidence* of multiple ownership. Previous studies have tended to regard 'serial', 'habitual', or 'portfolio' entrepreneurs as a specialist type, peripheral to any conceptualisation of start-up or growth, a curiosity perhaps. (See for example: Storey, 1982; Macmillan & Lowe, 1986; Storey, Keasey, Watson and Wynarczyk, 1987; Donckels, Dupont and Michel, 1987; Cambridge, 1992; Rosa and Hamilton, 1994; Storey, 1994; Parsons, 1994; Kolvereid and Bullvag, 1993; Birley and Westhead, 1994; Wright, Robbie and Ennew, 1995). Yet there are already tantalising references to the incidence of ownership diversification hidden away in existing studies. For example, the large scale study by Cambridge Small Business Research Centre revealed that 'around 25 per cent of companies do, however, have two or more directors with outside links, and 18.5 per cent of companies have four or more links with other companies arising from the director's outside activities. It is clear therefore that a significant proportion of companies are operating by directors with network links in other businesses'. (Cambridge, 1992: 8,9). Similarly, Keasey, Short and Watson (1994) in a study of director's ownership and small business performance, concluded that 'external shareholdings' by individual directors was an important complication which needed to be addressed in future studies. In our view, showing that perhaps a fifth of business owners are involved in multiple ownerships, or extensive cross holdings of directorships or shareholdings, (i.e. with considerable network linkages) would be sufficient to suggest at the very least that future firm-level analysis to be treated with caution, and that alternative units of analysis be researched as a priority. (We are not suggesting all firm-level analysis be abandoned. To use an analogy, epidemiological studies may help the medical profession to understand disease patterns, but a doctor in treating a patient needs a different 'process' level of knowledge and could not rely on epidemiological data for a patient's prescription).

We do not wish to understate the difficulties of researching multiple ownerships, and our preliminary measures may be weak proxies for what eventually becomes possible, given resources. But the possibilities for a new understanding of the way entrepreneurs *really* operate seems to us worth a leap into the black hole of data absence! This paper charts our 'progress' thus far, and draws on 4 data sets:

    i)   Dun & Bradstreet customised data for new Scottish firms and their directors (7316 incorporations).

    ii)   Primary survey data from a previous gender study (600 matched male and female business owners).

    iii) Registrar of Companies data on a delected sample of Scottish 'role model' growth entrepreneurs (209 cases).

    iv) Data on local business genealogies.

The use of widely differing sources was deliberate, to test if the same phenomenon occurs across measurement instruments.

The Initial Study: Scottish New Incorporations

This continuing study, funded by Scottish Enterprise, was designed to establish the contribution of existing businesses to new firm creation. Our research had few precedents to guide us. We have discovered no systematic assessment of the frequency of multiple business owners in the UK economy, but we now have some clues why this may be so. (Scott & Rosa, 1995). Firstly, existing data bases are firm centred even where ownership is concerned. When we asked Dun and Bradstreet to link the directors of a sample of new firms with all their other ownerships, a special routine had to be written as this analysis had never been asked for. (Nor is this solely a UK phenomenon: an official of the US Small Business Administration has admitted that the data on firms and on individuals 'do not talk with each other'. Because the reporting requirements for US company directors are minimal, data on multiple ownerships there are scarce: if a phenomenon is not measured it is easy to assume it does not exist). Secondly, analyses of interlocking directorships tend to be in the context of the study of business elites, and concern 'corporate governance'. Thirdly, studies of the large firm/small firm interface tend to focus on operational issues rather than ownership and control. Fourthly, many primary data arise from studies which have deliberately set out to sample 'independent' businesses, and exclude any which lie in ownership clusters. Finally in the UK, only limited companies are required by law to register details on company directorships. The external ownership practices of sole traders and partnerships (these include some of our biggest professional practices) have no obligation to formally register ownership or a stake in the ownership and management of other businesses. Without resorting to primary survey work, it becomes almost impossible to obtain any form of estimate on the incidence of multiple business ownership for businesses operating as sole traders or partnerships. Even surveys have their limitations (in addition to obvious problems of obtaining random samples of the diverse small firms sector). Our genealogical case studies have shown that some entrepreneurs do not always declare their full interests, and sometimes do not class certain types of external activities (such as renting property, or farming) as a real 'business', and omit to mention it unprompted.

    We thus had to concentrate firstly on Limited Companies, because ownership data are more readily available, and because the legalities of incorporation are particularly relevant to portfolio building. Our early attempts focused on the FAME data base, following pilot work by one of our students, Parsons (1994). This proved to have problems. It is not designed for searching with a director as a primary focus, and extracting relevant data for each director needs close individual attention, making it very expensive to obtain adequate volumes of data. FAME is ultimately derived from Dun and Bradstreet. We thus went to source, and asked for a customised run on data for directors associated with all companies registered in Scotland in a one year period (1st October 1994 to 30th September 1995), having allowed a sensible period to elapse after the last case to exclude 'business registration agents' effects.

Most analyses of Scottish firms would include these newly formed companies as exemplary 'new' firms. For example they appear as a major item in the 'Scottish New Business Statistics' published by Scottish Enterprise and the Scottish Clearing Banks. Our concern was whether they were linked to existing firms (and therefore in a different category of 'newness').

The 1,498 base companies with one or more multiple directorships were associated via their directors with 14,651 other companies (nearly ten for each base company). These are detailed in two ways in Table 8.1. Firstly frequencies are given for the total number of associated companies for the base company with all directors pooled (the *base company cluster*). Secondly they are given for each individual director (the *director's cluster*). Nearly three quarters of the base companies are associated with at least two other companies, and a fifth with over ten. In the case of individual directors, 41% hold directorships in two to five other companies, and a fifth in at least six. This further confirms that business clustering is a widespread rather than a peripheral phenomenon. It should also be emphasised that the failure rate in the associated companies was extremely low (less than 0.5% were in receivership).

Table 8.1   Number of Associated Companies

| Base | Cluster | | | |
| | Company | | Director's | |
Number	n	%	n	%
One	400	26.7	982	37.4
2 to 5	556	37.1	1065	40.6
6 to 10	237	15.6	328	12.5
11 to 20	160	10.7	115	4.4
21 to 50	83	5.5	91	3.5
51 or more	63	4.2	44	1.7
Total	1499	100	2625	100.0
Mean	9.7	5.6		
Median	3.0	2.0		
Max./Min	1-260	1-136		

The employment data produced by Dun and Bradstreet was far from complete. 79% or 11,463 of the 14,651 associated companies had no data on employment. Those which had valid data are broken down in Table 8.2. The table shows that the phenomenon of multiple directorships is not confined to large companies. A third were associated with very small companies and two thirds were either very small or small. The median was 24 employees. Similar trends were found in the case of average employment in the director's and base company's clusters (Table 8.3).

Table 8.2   **Employment in Associated Companies**

Total employees	n	%
Very small (1-9)	1031	32.3
Small (10-49)	1047	32.8
Medium (50-250)	670	21.0
Large (251-1000)	295	9.3
Very Large (1000+)	145	4.5
Total	3188	100.0
Mean	263.6	
Median	24.0	
Min/Max.	1-41,124	

Table 8.3   **Average Employment for all Associated Companies**

	Cluster			
	Base company		Director's	
Average employees	n	%	n	%
Very small (1-9)	211	27.3	344	26.2
Small (10-49)	291	37.6	474	36.1
Medium (50-250)	188	24.3	334	25.5
Large (251-1000)	64	8.3	123	9.4
Very Large (1000+)	19	2.5	37	2.8
Total	773	100.0	1312	100.0
Mean	170.1		215.1	
Median	26.0		28.0	
Min/Max.	1-8,994		1-23,469	

It could also be argued that if a company has many directors, the chances of multiple ownership or directorships in the base company cluster would be sharply increased. Table 8.4, however, shows that just over half of the base companies are associated with only one director, and that over 90% are associated with 3 or under.

Table 8.4   **Number of Directors Associated with Base Company**

Number	n	%
One	795	53.0
2 to 3	613	40.9
4 to 5	68	4.5
6 to 12	23	1.5
Total	1499	100.0
Mean	1.75	
Median	1	

Finally the results showed that 25% of associated companies were registered in England, confirming that there is a significant interaction between the business owning classes of both countries.

These data seem to show that at least for new company incorporations, the 'new' business is not isolated from the existing business community. Indeed what we may be seeing is the business community re-creating itself. Exactly what role multiple directors play in new businesses has yet to be established, but they are clearly there for a purpose, and in considerable numbers. They are certainly likely to form a 'competence block'. We would argue that their presence is a crucial element in the future performance of these businesses, provided the business is seen as part of ownership clusters not as an isolated entity. Further, we would point to the existence of multiple directorships even in very small firms. Subsidiaries are not merely the province of large companies. Previous research which has sought 'independent' business by excluding the taint of associated or subsidiary companies may have been excluding the very factors which contribute most significantly to performance.

Finally the data on incidence of failure may be significant (but are subject to further enquiry). Whilst it may be very difficult to identify 'winners' at the level of the firm, it may be less so at the level of entrepreneurs. We have private indications that at least one major bank, for example, has evidence that multiple directors have business accounts with significantly above average survival rates.

The Second Study: Gender and Small Business Management Re-Analysed

An important question arises: Is multiple business ownership a phenomenon mostly associated with companies? If not, does the rate differ for other types of business organisation? It is difficult to obtain figures on the incidence of multiple business ownership amongst sole traders or partnerships. However the 1991/2 Stirling gender study (Rosa, Hamilton, Carter and Burns, 1994; Rosa and Hamilton, 1994), based on a quota sample of 600 male and female business owners drawn from three sectors (textile/clothing; business services; and hotel/catering), did ask questions on multiple ownership. Respondents were asked whether they currently owned other businesses, and (separately) whether they possessed other directorships. The results that follow are based on the first question, as there was a high degree of overlap in the answers.

The results revealed that 14% of the sample owned more than one business, but there was a pronounced gender effect. Only 9% of women owned another business, compared to 20% of men. Table 8.5 shows too that in the case of men, nearly half of the multiple owners did not just own one other. 17% owned two others and nearly a third owned more than two.

Table 8.5   Number of Other Current Businesses by Sex of Respondent (of those Owning Others)

	Women %	Men %
One other	83.3	53.6
Two others	12.5	17.9
More than two	4.2	28.6
n=	24	56

Chi square p=0.04

The gender study data also show that the proportion of multiple ownership increases by firm size (Table 8.6) as measured by number of employees. It is uncommon amongst the self-employed, is nearly a fifth in very small male owned businesses (1-9 employees) and rises to almost a third in businesses with 20 or more employees. Table 8.7 also reveals that it is present in all forms of organisation, even though it is much more common in limited companies than in partnerships or sole traders.

Table 8.6   Owning More than One Business by Number of Employees

Number of Employees	Total %	Men %	Women %
none	2.8	0.0	4.1
1-9	11.5	18.2	6.8
10-19	6.3	20.0	11.8
20 or more	27.0	31.5	15.0
Total number	560	280	280

Source: Stirling gender study

Table 8.7   Owning More than One Business by Type of Organisation

Number of Employees	Total %	Men %	Women %
Sole trader	6.4	6.9	6.0
Partnership	14.7	19.6	9.8
Limited company	25.8	36.5	12.1
Total number	554	278	276

Source: Stirling gender study

This re-analysis of earlier primary data suggests that multiple ownership is not restricted to limited companies, but occurs across business types, although appearing to increase as the business becomes more 'serious' (e.g. takes on more workers, or is incorporated).

The Third Study: Scottish 'Local Heroes'

Research commissioned by Scottish Enterprise in the early 1990s appeared to establish that the business birth rate in Scotland lagged significantly behind that of the rest of the UK, particularly the South East of England. 'It is apparent we have a fundamental economic problem. That problem can be traced back to a simple lack of companies in Scotland. We just do not create as many new businesses as other parts of the United Kingdom, let alone our competitor nations' (Crawford Beveridge, Chief Executive Scottish Enterprise, 1994). To remedy this they launched the Scottish Business Birth Rate Campaign, with an aim to significantly increase the number of new businesses started by the year 2000. They were keen to target a pool of at least 600,000 potential entrepreneurs, who appeared to be interested in starting their own businesses. The Local Heroes project was conceived as a source of role models to 'help encourage those starting in Business. It recognises and trumpets the achievements of our Local Heroes - people who have started up and developed successful businesses with determination, courage, perseverance and a willingness to learn from others. They are a lesson for us all.' (Professor Donald MacKay, Chairman of Scottish Enterprise, 1994).

By 1995 there were 209 local heroes in the Scottish Enterprise data base, consisting of case studies of entrepreneurs who have founded new companies or firms of high growth potential, brought to the attention of the project co-ordinators 'from the bottom up', by referrals from the local enterprise network and the business community. Also included are the participants in Scottish Television's 'Business Game'. All are entrepreneurs who have displayed successful and high growth business activity through their entrepreneurial talent over the last ten years. The precise criteria for inclusion in this highly selected data set were:

    1) a green field start-up or 'phoenix' MBO
    2) between 1 and 10 years old
    3) goods or services traded outwith the local area
    4) evidence of growth or growth potential
    5) particular interest if started by women or young people.

It is interesting, and consistent with, the long tradition of firm focused mentality by enterprise development organisations, that the data base is not organised with the entrepreneurial hero in the primary field, but rather indexed according to the firm founded. Firm-level analysis runs deep in the psyche of those researching small business, even when they are overtly dealing with entrepreneurs! The effect of course is to perpetuate a myth of 'one entrepreneur, one firm, one path to growth'.

Scottish Enterprise provided us with the local heroes data base, and invited us to check it for multiple ownership. Essentially we replicated our new incorporation study by checking with Companies House for the multiple directorships of all the companies in the local heroes documentation.

The proportion of multiple directorships was much higher than we had expected. Of the 150 active companies, three quarters had at least one director who was a multiple board member, and half the local heroes themselves were also multiple board members. This appears to show that the local heroes, far from being lone entrepreneurs, tend to be parts of a network of clustered business resources. We do not know yet the precise significance of this. Some may be entrepreneurs who have managed to bring together other portfolio directors to launch the venture. Others may be less entrepreneurial, a managerial 'front' for the entrepreneurial dealings of their more affluent, or busy, or shadowy co-directors. Still others may have become multiple directors following initial success. This is clearly a complex picture that needs further research. But again there is confirmation that multiple linkages are not only common, but in this data set of business 'successes', multiple linkage is overwhelmingly the norm. We would find it unthinkable to carry out any further analysis of these firms without reference, first and foremost, to the characteristics of the ownership or decision-making clusters (or 'competence blocks') of which they are so clearly a part.

Evidence from Case Studies of Local Genealogies

From our research it seems that the number and proportion of multiple business owners is extensive. Key questions, therefore, are why and how entrepreneurs establish second or subsequent businesses, and why and how do they maintain a diversified 'portfolio' of companies? Some studies have tried to address these question. Both Donckels et al. (1987) and Kolveried and Bullrag (1993), for example, have mentioned market incentives to diversification. This can be interpreted in two ways- push and pull.

Firstly there are *push* factors, where opportunities for growth of a single firm are restricted, forcing entrepreneurs to substitute single company growth by starting new ventures. The small business literature on diversification tends to stress that diversification (mostly seen in terms of diversification within firms) is mainly a survivalist strategy (eg. Robson,Gallagher and Daly 1993). There is also a view that small firms tend to operate in small market niches, which can be profitably exploited on a small scale, as it is not worthwhile for larger firms to enter them. If trading in a market niche, a business owner will sooner or later hit the limits of profitable exploitation, and will be forced to try something else if further growth is desired. This may be accelerated in times of severe recession in certain sectors such as construction, where hard pressed larger firms lower their sights and bid for smaller contracts to maintain adequate cash flow. Indeed recession far from acting as a spur to business diversification may lead to retraction, and the concentration of one line of business. Robson and colleagues in fact point out that far more small businesses move back to operating in one line of business than move into an additional line.

Secondly there are *pull* factors, where, as Donckels et al. (1987) point out, diversification through starting and acquiring new businesses may be an important part of an entrepreneur's growth strategy, where market niches may be evaluated, and if found profitable, targeted and exploited. Some ventures may be sustainable for a long while (leading to the growth of parallel businesses), or sold on when it becomes unprofitable, exhausting or complex to manage. In some cases there may be a conscious strategy for looking for profitable opportunities to add to the 'portfolio'. In others this process may be unconscious, resulting from more serendipitous events, where an entrepreneur may stumble by accident on a new opportunity.

Other pull factors may have less to do with economics, and more to do with intrinsic goals. Birley and Westhead (1993) refer to 'habitual' entrepreneurs as having 'role models and heroes', implying, as Parsons (1994:20) points out, that personal materialistic aspirations through the growth of multiple businesses, may go much further than could be deduced when only a single unit of analysis is being studied. Again factors relating to home and family, as Lynn and Reinsch (1990) point out, can also be important. For example an entrepreneur could try and build up several businesses so that each of his sons could start with their own enterprise - not unusual amongst farmers, for instance. Personal motives, we speculate, could also extend to getting a kick out of starting an additional new venture, a hobbyist motive for entrepreneurial diversification.

There is also a group of factors that has been hardly addressed in the literature. This relates to the efficient managing of incoming business. A 'portfolio' approach has several advantages for efficient management. It pools the resources of several firms, and can combine them to improve financial management (the acquisition of loans from banks; optimise taxation advantages). It can also combine other resources (for example administrative) to reduce costs across the units in the cluster. By ring fencing into several units it might make it easier to conceptually manage a complex operation. Finally it might help to enhance personal control of other managers and (possibly) family members through 'divide and rule'.

We have a number of local case studies from Central Scotland that can shed some light on these issues. Some were collected by Parsons (1994), and others as a by product of unpublished ongoing research on family business genealogies by Rosa. We have selected some brief extracts to illustrates some of the key questions just discussed.[1]

A Classic Complex Case: Gould Holdings

James Gould is a 'portfolio' entrepreneur with 12 businesses under one holding company. He currently employs over 150 people throughout the group, with an annual sales turnover of £1-2 million.

There was no clue to his entrepreneurial zeal in his early career in the construction industry. He was forced into self employment at the age of 32 in 1982 when his employer went into liquidation. His first venture as an insulation consultant did not go well, as 'people wanted advice but were unwilling to pay for it, or have work done'. To survive he moved on to a new business as a roof repairer, which grew rapidly after successfully applying for local authority contracts.

Growth Strategy. During interview[2] he emphasised to us that he believed in a strategy of 'creaming' the profits and moving on. It is difficult to establish whether such an attitude is a cause of, or a consequence of 'portfolio' diversification. Whatever the reason, he began to diversify strongly into different products. He acquired an 85 per cent interest in a computing company, which enhanced his ability to control costs

---

[1] All names and localities have been changed to preserve confidentiality.
[2] He would not allow his interview to be taped, and like others, found it difficult to give a clear linear account of his previous business career.

and improve tendering through mastering new IT packages. A building connection brought in business from Hong Kong, which widened his horizons and interest in oriental thinking and doing business. Subsequent years saw the introduction and diversification of stand alone companies in 'quality' and 'computing'. The early 1990s saw further additions in the leisure and food industries, and a joint venture in roofing contracting in India. The recent acquisition of a distressed hotel and leisure business proved less profitable than anticipated, and he is selling it on.

He is a mixture of entrepreneurial opportunism and caution. On the one hand he is always looking out for new profitable business opportunities, and not afraid to tackle them if he thinks they will be 'good for creaming'. Nevertheless he is also cautious, and thrifty. He believes in operating a modest car, and keeping costs down. He is also a pessimist. He predicted that the good days of the 1980s will never return, and that business in general, and his in particular, needs to learn to thrive in 'survivalist' conditions. It is not easy to clearly demarcate survivalist and entrepreneurial motives.

Management Issues. Each company within the group is monitored and costed on a daily and weekly basis with reporting now done via e-mail. He has also centralised accounting and control functions in his holding company, which has enabled him to significantly reduce overheads throughout the group, making individual units more competitive. This has been a planned strategy which he is proud of. This reinforces the notion that 'portfolio' management can be more efficient than managing single units, an area that needs to be further researched.

Future Directions. His sales turnover across the group is expanding, and his businesses are spread over a significant geographical area. He showed no signs of slackening off his desire for future experimentation. He sees his best chance of expansion in developing relationships with businesses in the far East, where much of the future commerce, he believes, will be based. His case is typical of many in showing an interplay of pull and push factors in building his portfolio.

Core and Hobby Businesses

This tendency to suddenly diversify into unrelated lines after years of building a portfolio around a core line of business was observed in several other cases. The founder of local metal engineering group of companies worth several £million, has recently diversified into owning a local newspaper, which arose from a whim following a conversation with a member of the local Rotary Club. He also has a home based business speculating in the American stock exchange. Another local businessman, whose assets are worth close to £5million patiently built up a group of electrical engineering companies based on servicing the shipping industry and oil rigs (including his own dry dock) over twenty years. He has recently bought a distressed hotel for £1.5million, for his disabled son to run. A less illustrious example is a man who has built up a chain of newsagent shops over the last fifteen years. Recently he has diversified into running a tourist bus (a vintage bus dating from the early 1950s). In all these cases the core business has been supplemented by unrelated businesses which have been started because of personal reasons (boredom, to support family, a hobby).

Smaller Multiple Business Groups

The owners of the larger business clusters just outlined have accumulated considerable capital, though they yet appear to be small firms, and have found ways to delegate key management functions across the group. The burden of managing and maintaining a diversified group of firms appears to be much greater amongst smaller businesses of less than £300,000 a year turnover. This is illustrated by a self employed contractor who saw opportunities in home freezers in the Western Highlands. He and his wife noticed that they were much more expensive where he lived than in Glasgow. While his wife sold fabrics, he started to sell freezers in the other half of the shop. Soon he also started to sell frozen food. The business grew fast, and he established four frozen food shops, employing sixteen staff. Additionally he started to deal in property, and bought a grocer's shop. The strain of managing these diversified interests with little delegation led to ill health, and he sold all the shops. He has now retracted to a single business, constructing housing.

In another low turnover case, a couple ran a newsagent and a tool hire business. The strain of managing both has recently led to selling on the newsagency, and to concentrating on the tool hire, which has a greater growth potential.

Summary

These illustrative case studies reveal a diverse and complex picture on the motives for starting, diversifying and maintaining portfolios. Both push and pull factors have been observed, sometimes in the same case study, where diversification has been used in different occasions as a survival strategy and as an expansionist one. In general, proactive entrepreneurialism, though in evidence, appears less common than cautious experimentation and the development of core lines of business. Personal motives also appear strong, especially in second phase diversification from the core businesses. The more capital accumulates, the easier it is for the founders to manage and diversify their portfolios. Many (though by no means all) of the more successful businessmen started either with capital accumulated through property dealing in times of boom, or through taking over a family business.

What is clear is that competencies in setting up and managing portfolios are regularly developed through 'learning by doing'. The existence of such organisation creation competence blocks (cf. Eliasson 1996) is largely ignored in the business formation literature.

One important issue that needs greater development is methodology. The proliferation of linkages in larger family or entrepreneur based clusters are clearly complex, and need considerable resources to research in depth. All of our case studies were restricted to a short interview. The impression was gained in some interviews that much was being left unsaid. Future research would benefit from data based on several interviews and more systematic participant observation over time. Another complication is that owner managers themselves are not logical or clear about the sequence of events in their business genealogies. It is hard work for the researcher in deciphering an ordered sequence of events. These entrepreneurs usually do not think linearly in time or space. That may also be a clue of why they prefer lateral growth through separate ventures rather than to seek to grow a single firm to its hypothetical true growth potential.

Some Initial Conclusions

Our data suggest:

1) The extent of linkages *between* businesses may be substantial and has been overlooked in small business research.
2) Using 'directorships' as a proxy for ownership or decision-making influence, we have indicated that new companies are significantly linked to existing companies , and may be part of 'growth' strategies rather than *de novo* 'start-ups'.
3) Re-analyses of earlier data from a representative sample of small businesses has shown that multiple ownership is present across business types, but its incidence is lower amongst the self employed and sole traders, and higher amongst more substantial businesses and those that are incorporated. There seems also to be a gender dimension.
4) Using a selected sample of business successes (entrepreneurial 'local heroes') we have shown that there are extensive multiple linkages at director level.
5) These findings, although preliminary, are consistent, despite differences in measurement techniques and they are also borne out by local business genealogies.
6) Specialist Know-how in the form of 'competence blocks' may be a crucial element in the creation and re-organisation of firms, and this knowledge may be spread across several firms.

We therefore tentatively suggest:

1) Analysis of ownership *clusters* or *'competence blocks'* is more likely to increase our understanding of start-up and growth processes than studies of individual firms.
2) Entrepreneurial manipulation of firm boundaries requires much more detailed research. (Why are existing businesses so extensively linked to new business?)
3) Entrepreneur-level factors causing the movement of assets between different forms of capital ownership including share ownership in unquoted companies also is worth exploration. (e.g. what are the capital assets of 'local heroes' and what happens to these assets?).
4) It would be helpful if some of the classic firm-level studies of business growth were re-analysed to explore and explain the level of multiple ownership amongst growers and non-growers.

Some Policy Implications

It may be that the main policy implications of the foregoing are 'no policy'. If the business community is effectively re-creating and growing itself through the movement of capital and other resources, then no action is required. However, there are segments of the small business sector which are outside the linkages here described. These are genuine *de novo* entrants, or isolates. The question then is whether policy initiatives can be developed to replicate for these people the competence blocks, the clusters of contacts and resources, from which they are excluded? Traditionally this was the role played by Chambers of Commerce and businessmen's (*sic*) clubs. In the UK, the model of support for business start-up pioneered by one of the first enterprise agencies (Enterprise North) was based on panels of local businessmen who 'took under their wing' potential start-ups, i.e. made available precisely the 'competence block' referred to in this paper. Unfortunately, this model was superseded by quite different organisational forms based on 'Agencies', which in turn have become professionalised, bureaucratised and an integral part of the Governmental support industry, i.e. distanced from the real players in local business communities.

The case studies seemed to imply that by managing a portfolio, companies can produce efficiency gains that could not be implemented within a single unit. However it does also require specialised skills and experience to successfully manage and maintain a successful portfolio of companies. Entrepreneurs with small turnovers often find it difficult to manage their diversified interests. If this is the case, then there is scope for intervention by encouraging management education specialising in 'portfolio' management. To our knowledge no such course or training exists.

The wider policy question is how far to believe firm-level analyses anyway. If even small numbers of entrepreneurs are using ownership of firms as part of their wider capital accumulation and transference activities, then extra-firm factors invisible to current research become crucial. Ownership and control issues are as central to the SME as to the corporate sector, but they have typically only been studied in detail in the latter.

Endnote

In an ESRC funded project on organisational life-cycles (Scott 1990), which followed-up Scottish companies originally interviewed in the early 1970s, it became apparent that the survival and growth of the companies were complex processes that could not be fully explained by firm-focused theories. The ESRC funded gender project (Rosa and Hamilton 1994) also revealed that multiple ownership appeared common. This in particular was difficult to accommodate in firm focused analysis of gender and business performance (Rosa, Hamilton and Carter 1994). The concept of 'entrepreneurial performance' was introduced to accommodate the practice of starting more than one business over time and space, a section running in parallel with more conventional analyses of business performance based on the growth of the firm.

At the time that was written (1994), we supervised a dissertation by Parsons, who established through case studies from firms drawn from the FAME data base that multiple ownership appeared to be common in directors of a sample of medium sized Scottish companies. This introduced the possibility that efficiency of performance over several linked companies may be greater than any of the single constituent companies. These findings were also difficult to reconcile with more conventional approaches to small business growth.

The absence of any systematic empirical evidence for the prevalence of multiple business owners inspired the current research. Preliminary findings were disseminated at RENT IX in 1995, and Babson (1996). Although the more substantive arguments were already developed in these and the ISBJ paper (Scott and Rosa 1996), this paper is the first to present an account of our early empirical findings.

References

Birley, S. and Westhead, P. (1994) A comparison of new businesses established by 'novice' and 'habitual' founders in Great Britain. *International Small Business Journal*, 12(1), 38-60.

Cambridge Small Business Research Centre (1992) *The State of British Enterprise*, Department of Applied Economics, University of Cambridge.

Davidsson, P. (1989) *Continued entrepreneurship and small firm growth*. Stockholm School of Economics.

Donckels, R., Dupont, B. and Michel, P. (1987) Multiple business starters. Who? Why? What? *Journal of Small Business and Entrepreneurship*. 5, 48-63.

Eliasson, G. (1996) Spillovers, integrated production and the theory of the firm. *Journal of Evolutionary Economics* Vol. 6 No 2

Keasey, K., Short, H. and Watson, R. (1994) Director's ownership and the performance of small and medium sized firms in the U.K. *Small Business Economics* 6, 225-236.

Kolvereid, L. and Bullrag, E. (1993) Novices versus habitual entrepreneurs, an exploratory investigation. In Birley, S.; MacMillan, I.C. and Subrammaany, S. (eds.). *Entrepreneurship Research, Global Perspectives*. Amsterdam, Kluwer and Associates.

Lynn, M.L. and Reinsch, N.L. (1990) Diversification patterns among small businesses. *Journal of Small Business Management*, 28, 59-70.

MacMillan, I.C. and Lowe, M.B. (1986) *Techniques of the Habitual Entrepreneur: Team Building*. Snider Entrepreneurial Centre, University of Pennsylvania, Working Paper Series No. 1.

Parsons, J. (1994) Portfolio Entrepreneurs: Growth and Diversification. Dissertation, M.Sc. in Entrepreneurial Studies , Stirling University (supervisor Rosa, P.).

Penrose, E.T. (1980) *The theory of the growth of the firm*. Oxford, Blackwell.

Robson, G., Gallagher, C. and Daly, M. (1993) Diversification strategy and practice in small firms. *International Small Business Journal* , 11, 37-53.

Rosa, P. and Hamilton, D. (1994) Gender and ownership in UK small firms. *Entrepreneurship, Theory and Practice*, 18(3), 11-27.

Rosa, P., Hamilton, D., Carter, S. and Burns, H. (1994) The impact of gender on small business management: preliminary insights from a British Study. *International Small Business Journal*, 12(3), 25-32.

Rosa, P. and Scott, M.G. (1995) Some comments on the Unit of Analysis in Entrepreneurship Research on Growth and Start-up. *Recent Research in Entrepreneurship* (RENT IX), Piacenza, Italy.

Scott, M.G. (1990) 'Entrepreneurial life cycles'. Paper presented to *13th National Small Firms Policy and Research Conference*, Harrogate, November 1990.   Published as: 'Unternehmerkarrieren Und Organisatorische Lebenszyklen' (Entrepreneurial Careers and Organisational Life Cycles). *Internationales Gewerbearchiv* Vol 41 No.4, 1993. pp 223-233.

Scott, M.G. and Rosa, P. (1996a) Existing Businesses as Sources of New Firms: A Missing Topic in Business Formation Research? Babson Conference, *Frontiers of Entrepreneurship Research*, Seattle.

Scott, M.G. and Rosa, P. (1996b) Has firm level analysis reached its limits? Time for a rethink. *International Small Business Journal* Vol. 14, No 4.

Storey, D. (1982) *Entrepreneurship and the New Firm*. London: Croom Helm

Storey, D.J., Keasey, K., Watson, R. and Wynarczyk, P. (1987) *The Performance of Small Firms: Profits, Jobs and Failures*, London:Croom Helm.

Storey, D.J. (1994) *Understanding the Small Business Sector*. London:Routledge.

Wright, M., Robbie, K. and Ennew, C. (1995) Serial entrepreneurs. in Bygrave, W. et al. (eds.) *Frontiers of Entrepreneurship Research*, Babson College, Wellesley, Ma.

Acknowledgements

The study on new incorporations and on 'local heroes' was funded by Scottish Enterprise. The gender study was funded by the UK Economic and Social Research Council. The case studies were conducted an internal research fund from the University of Stirling. We are also grateful for the research assistance of Alison Dawson.

9 The Urban-Rural Dimension of New Firm Formation

Olav R. Spilling

Introduction

The purpose of this paper is to contribute to our understanding of mechanisms in new firm formation, with special emphasis on how new firm formation varies along an urban-rural dimension. The paper adds to a number of studies which have been undertaken during the last years in a number of countries, that have analysed regional variation of new firm formation and developed explanatory models for why some regions perform better than other regions (Reynolds and Storey, 1993; Reynolds, Storey and Westhead, 1994). Comparative analyses between some countries reveal that similar mechanisms are working in different countries. Birth rates are of the same size order, and the ratios between the maximum to minimum values over different regions in different countries are consistent. Furthermore, the models for explaining regional variation of birth rates in different countries to a great extent have the same explanatory variables, like population growth, population density, and proportion of small firms. (Audretsch and Fritsch, 1994; Davidsson, Lindmark and Olofsson, 1994; Fritsch, 1992; Garofoli, 1994; Keeble and Walker, 1994).

In a similar analysis undertaken in Norway, (Isaksen and Spilling, 1996; Spilling, 1996), it is concluded that *the existing industrial structure* provides the main explanation for regional variation of new firm formation. 'High firm density, high proportion of small firms and concentration of industry in the actual sector seem to have a positive influence on the birth rate' (Spilling, 1996). It is said that this confirms both the incubator hypothesis and the role model hypothesis, i.e., in areas with the actual characteristics, many organisations exist where potential entrepreneurs can develop their ideas for new businesses, and there are many people in the local environment that will serve as role models for entrepreneurship.

In the same analysis the importance of the centre periphery-dimension was also tested, but the analysis reveals that this dimension explains just smaller parts of regional variation in start-up when it is applied as the only explanatory variable in the regression analysis. Thus, there are more complicated mechanisms working, and the characteristics referred to above, i.e. the industrial structure, follows a more complex pattern of variation than just the centre-periphery dimension.

However, after observing data on industrial restructuring and development in Norway, there seems to be some very important differences between central and peripheral areas (Isaksen and Spilling, 1996). First, it is clearly seen that manufacturing generally has been through a shift and over the last two decades has had the best development, in relative terms, in rural areas. Second, it can be observed that, within manufacturing, high tech sectors have developed best in central and semi-central areas in Eastern Norway. Third, some of the service sectors, especially producer services, are heavily concentrated to the urban areas. And when analysing data on the individual regions, it may be observed that these patterns to a significant extent are followed by the highest birth rates occurring in the areas of the best general sectoral development, but this only to a lesser extent is identified through our regression analysis.

Thus, there seem to be interesting urban-rural variations of new firm formation which are difficult to identify through the traditional methodological approaches based on regression analysis of macro data. In this paper, new data on new firm formation are presented in order to develop further insight into these variations. Focus is on variation in the structure of new firms and their founders, the processes of start-up and how this is affected by different environments.

Method

The first part of the paper is based on data from Statistics Norway's register of firms and establishments which is based on annual censuses on virtually all private sector firms. The data base contains data on type of firm and establishment, location (municipality), ISIC code, annual employment and turn-over. Further, the register makes it possible to identify start-ups and closures. These data are applied in an introductory analysis of the structure of start-ups in various regions and of the relationship between the start-ups and the existing industrial structure.

The second and major part of the paper is based on survey data obtained from a sample of start-ups which, according to registrations by the register of firms and establishments, occurred during the period 1988-1992. The following procedure of sampling was applied:

1. Six different geographical areas in Southern Norway were chosen in order to represent different urban-rural environments. The areas were chosen along the centre-periphery dimension. One area represents the highest level of centrality (Oslo/Bærum), one represents a semi-central area with two medium sized towns (Horten/Tønsberg), and the four remaining areas represent two rural and two coastal areas.

2. Start-ups were selected within the following industries: manufacturing, wholesale trade and commission trade, producer services and personal services.

3. A total sample of around 1350 start-ups were selected for interviews, with around 200 in each of the geographical areas. In order to avoid too heavy problems with tracking firms that have been closed down, only start-ups recorded during the period 1988-1992 and which, according to the data register, were still existing in 1993, were chosen. Among this group, and within the industries that are mentioned above, 100% of all recorded start-ups in the four rural and coastal areas had to be selected in order to obtain a sufficient number. In the semi-central area 50% of the recorded start-ups were selected, and in the central area 7% of all start-ups were selected.

4. Firm tracking and interviews were undertaken by the interview department of Statistics Norway, and gave a response rate of 68.8%. The reason for no response was that it was not possible to track the firm, which in most cases probably was due to closure of the firms (see Table 9.1). Interviews were obtained with founders or managers of 795 firms, among which 75 turned out to be outside the target group of the survey, thus a remaining sample of 720 firms has been analysed.

Table 9.1   **Total Sample of Firms and Response Rate**

	Number	%
Total sample	1353	100.0
No response due to:		
- not possible to track firm	355	26.2
- not possible to get contact with founder or manager	65	4.8
- not willing to be interviewed	56	4.1
- firm outside target group of survey	64	4.7
- other reasons	18	1.3
Total not responding	558	41.2
Firms interviewed	795	58.8
Interviewed firms outside target group	75	5.5
Sample to be analysed	720	53.2

The Structure of New Firm Formation

Our first step in analysing the relationship between the existing industrial structure and start-ups in the six areas, is to compare the existing industrial structure with the structure of start-ups (see Table 9.2). On average there has been an annual start-up rate of 8.4 start-ups per 100 establishments, and there are small variations between industries and regions. The highest average rates occur in retail, hotel and restaurant (industry no 6) and personal services (no 9), the lowest in transports (no 7). Regional variations seem to be most significant in personal services (no 9), retailing, hotel and restaurants (no 6) and producer services (no 8). Among these industries personal services and retailing, hotel and restaurants have the highest start-up rates in the central areas, while producer services have their highest birth rates in peripheral areas.

Table 9.2   **Annual Start-Up Rates 1988-1992 by Industry for the Investigated Areas**

	Type of region	Total	Annual start-up rate by industry					
			3	5	6	7	8	9
All areas		*8.4*	*7.6*	*8.0*	*10.0*	*5.3*	*7.7*	*9.8*
1. Oslo/Bærum	central	8.6	7.6	8.4	10.4	5.1	7.4	10.8
2. Horten/Tønsberg	semi-central	9.3	8.3	9.0	11.3	5.9	8.2	6.7
3. Kragerø/Risør	coastal	7.2	7.6	6.0	7.9	5.8	10.7	6.4
4. Søre-Sunnhordaland	coastal	7.6	6.2	6.3	8.2	6.9	12.9	9.0
5. Indre Telemark	rural	7.4	8.2	5.9	8.4	4.9	10.4	9.0
6. Gudbrandsdalen	rural	7.6	8.3	8.7	7.3	5.0	11.5	6.1

Start-up rate: Number of new establishments per year and 100 establishments existing by 1987.

Industries: 2 = oil extraction, mining and quarrying   3 = manufacturing
     5 = construction   6 = retailing, hotel and restaurants
     7 = transport   8 = producer services
     9 = private services
     Start-up rates for industry no 2 are not included due to small numbers of start-ups

Source: Statistics Norway, Central Register of Firms and Establishments, own calculations

The general finding here that start-ups are so closely related to the total number of establishments in an area, strongly confirms our basic hypothesis that the existing industrial structure is a very important determining factor for start-ups. This may be illustrated in Table 9.3, where the distribution of start-ups over industries are compared with the distribution of establishments and employment. The data reveal, by simple examination, that there are close similarities between the distributions of establishments and start-ups for the six different areas, while the distributions for employment are quite different. This means that the number of establishments, rather than the total employment, is most important for explaining the structure of start-ups. This may also be interpreted as meaning that smaller firms to a larger extent than bigger firms serve as role models and incubators for new entrepreneurs.

Table 9.3   **Industrial Structure of the Investigated Areas as of 1987 and Number of Recorded Start-Ups (Establishments) 1988-1993**

	Total	Distribution by industry (%)						
		2	3	5	6	7	8	9
All areas								
Establishments	46316	0.2	10.1	14.7	38.0	12.8	17.5	6.8
Employment	267083	0.4	23.1	11.6	31.2	10.2	18.1	5.4
Start-ups	19562	0.2	9.1	13.9	45.1	8.0	15.9	7.9
1. Oslo/Bærum								
Establishments	34832	0.1	8.9	12.2	38.3	13.1	20.8	6.5
Employment	224357	0.3	19.1	11.6	31.8	11.0	20.6	5.6
Start-ups	14996	0.1	7.8	12.0	46.2	7.8	17.9	8.2
2. Horten/Tønsberg								
Establishments	2968	0.1	11.8	15.1	42.0	9.7	12.5	8.8
Employment	15918	0.2	42.2	9.7	29.7	4.8	7.9	5.5
Start-ups	1377	0.1	10.5	14.7	51.3	6.1	11.0	6.4
3. Kragerø/Risør								
Establishments	1781	0.4	16.7	23.2	34.5	12.0	5.9	7.4
Employment	5005	0.6	50.6	10.2	23.9	6.5	3.7	4.5
Start-ups	641	0.0	17.6	19.5	37.9	9.7	8.7	6.6
4. Søre-Sunnhordaland								
Establishments	2368	0.3	15.0	25.5	32.8	12.7	6.8	7.1
Employment	10911	0.2	57.7	14.0	17.5	5.2	3.3	2.1
Start-ups	901	0.0	12.2	21.0	35.5	11.5	11.4	8.3
5. Indre Telemark								
Establishments	2059	0.2	13.6	25.4	34.2	15.2	5.1	6.4
Employment	4759	0.0	34.5	15.0	35.1	7.8	3.0	4.6
Start-ups	766	1.4	15.0	20.1	38.6	10.1	7.0	7.7
6. Gudbrandsdalen								
Establishments	2308	0.8	12.6	24.9	38.9	10.5	4.6	7.8
Employment	6133	5.0	28.4	14.4	39.0	6.7	2.4	4.0
Start-ups	881	0.6	13.6	28.5	37.2	6.9	6.9	6.2

Industries: 2 = oil extraction, mining and quarrying   3 = manufacturing
                    5 = construction   6 = retailing, hotel and restaurants
                    7 = transport   8 = producer services
                    9 = private services

Source: Statistics Norway, Central Register of Firms and Establishments, own calculations

Characteristics of Start-Ups

An overview of the start-ups included in the survey is provided in Table 9.4. Generally, the new firms are very tiny businesses, and among those interviewed, 6% were even closed down or 'sleeping'. This figure, however, most probably represents a significant underestimation of the real number of start-ups that are closed down by the time of interview, as there were considerable problems in tracking many of the firms in the original sample (see Table 9.1), among which probably the majority is closed down. This is also supported by data on survival rates of new firms which indicate rather short life times of new firms (Spilling 1996b, European Observatory for SMEs 1995).

Table 9.4   Distributions of New Firms (%) According to Employment and Turnover by 1996

	Central	Coastal	Rural	All areas	Significant difference*)
Employment					
Not in operation	5.9	5.5	7.3	6.3	
0-1	34.9	49.3	55.6	46.0	****
2-4	36.4	28.8	25.9	30.7	*
5-19	19.7	13.2	8.6	14.2	**
20+	3.0	3.2	2.6	2.9	
Turnover (million NOK):					
Not in operation	5.9	5.5	3.9	5.1	
< 0.1	8.6	15.5	30.6	17.8	****
0.1-1	39.0	50.2	45.7	44.6	*
1-10	38.3	25.1	17.7	27.6	****
10-50	7.8	3.7	1.7	4.6	**
50+	0.4	0.0	0.4	0.3	
Total	100.0	100.0	100.0	100.0	
(N)	(269)	(219)	(232)	(720)	

*) The column indicates if there are significant differences between the areas. Based on chi-square tests. Levels of significance: *: <.05; **: <.01; ***: <.001; ****: <.0001.

Among the firms that were in operation at the time of interview, almost 50% employed one person or less, including the founder or leader of the firm. Thus, many new firms do not even provide full-time employment for the founder, and a significant share of the founders have income from work elsewhere. A similar pattern is revealed by the data on turn-over, where more than 60% of all new firms had less turn-over than NOK 1 million. 14% had even less than NOK 100, which means that the firm provides just a very marginal contribution, if any, to the daily living of the founder.

It follows from this that very few new firms are big. Only 3% of the sample had an employment in excess of 20, and 10% had a turn-over in 1995 of more than NOK 50 million. A very significant part of the new firms are oriented toward local markets, while a rather small share are exporters.

Although the new firms generally are very tiny in all geographical areas, there are some differences between the central and peripheral areas. Generally, the central areas have higher shares of the 'less smaller' firms than the rural and coastal areas. While the peripheral areas have around 50% of all new firms with one man year or less, only 35% of the urban firms are so small. Among the urban new firms, 24% have a turn-over higher than NOK 10 million, in contrast to only around 13-14% of the firms in coastal and rural areas. Thus, there are some significant differences between start-ups in central and peripheral areas.

Data on working hours of founders and their additional income sources point in the same direction. Around two thirds of the urban founders work more than 80% of their working hours in the firm, while the percentage is around 60 and 50 for coastal and rural areas respectively. One third of the urban founders have additional income from work outside the firm, while 50% of the peripheral founders were in the same situation. Also, the share of growing firms is somewhat higher in the urban areas compared to the periphery (Table 9.5).

Table 9.5   Characteristics of the New Firms

	Central	Coastal	Rural	All areas	Significant difference*)
Market orientation:					
Local markets	68.7	81.2	81.4	76.6	*
Exporters	16.3	11.3	11.2	13.8	*
Managers:					
Additional income from other sources	31.8	37.9	47.4	38.8	**
Work more than 80% in the firm	67.2	63.2	50.7	60.7	***
Innovation in the new firm:					
New product or service	17.8	16.0	19.4	17.8	
Improved product or service	49.4	39.3	44.0	44.6	
Improved method of production	23.4	20.5	22.4	22.2	
New method of marketing	14.1	13.2	15.5	14.3	
New market	20.1	21.0	23.3	21.4	
Growth:					
Expected growth of turn-over	64.6	58.4	56.3	60.0	
Expected employment growth	43.0	36.9	31.8	37.5	*

All figures in per cent

*) The column indicates if there are significant differences between the areas. Based on chi-square tests. Levels of significance: *: <.05; **: <.01; ***: <.001; ****: <.0001.

It may also be noted that there are differences between centre and periphery in terms of market orientation, as the share of local market-based firms is somewhat smaller in the central areas than in the coastal and rural areas, and the percentage of exporters in urban areas is somewhat higher.

An important issue related to new firms is to what extent they are innovative. In the interviews it was asked if the new firm represented a new product or service, improved product or service, improved method of production, new method of marketing or new market. To these questions, the highest share of positive responses was obtained on the question regarding improved product or service, to which 45% responded positively. To the other questions, the positive response rates were around 20%. A very important aspect of these results is that there is no significant difference between the various areas, i.e. innovativeness of new firms is independent of geography. This is somewhat surprising, and in contradiction to our hypothesis, that new firms in central areas were expected to represent a higher share of innovative firms than the new firms in peripheral areas.

This conclusion is also maintained if we control for differences in the sectoral composition of new firms in central and peripheral areas. When data are split up for various industries, it turns out that new manufacturing firms to a larger extent than other firms report that they represent a new product or service or a new method of production. Since manufacturing firms are over-represented in rural and coastal areas, this could conceal that there really was a bias towards more innovative firms within the same sectors, in urban areas. But this also turns out not to be the case. When controlling for sector, the data still reveal no significant difference in the share of innovative new firms in central and peripheral areas.

Starters, Motives and Processes of Start-Up

Data on the founders reveal that a significant majority tend to be males, just 20% are females, and 5% are born abroad (i.e. in most cases belong to an ethnic minority). Around 40% have higher education and previous management experience, while 45% have parents who are or have been self-employed. Among these factors, it is especially noteworthy that the high share of starters have self-employed parents. On average, 7.8% of the working population in Norway were self-employed in 1990,[1] thus people with self-employed parents are significantly overrepresented among new starters, and this may support the hypothesis of the importance of role models. Also, the share of founders with previous management experience probably is significantly higher than the average number in the total population.[2]

While some of the background factors are independent of or less dependent on geographical location, like the share of female founders, there is a very strong relationship between higher education and location. The share of urban founders with higher education is almost twice that of the founders in peripheral areas (Table 9.6). And the ethnic minority founder basically starts his or her new business in the urban areas.

Otherwise it may be noted that a higher share of the urban founders has previous management experience compared to the founders in the periphery, while the opposite is the case of founders with self-employed parents, who are most predominant in rural areas, probably due to a large number of founders with parents occupied in agricultural businesses.

Table 9.6   Background and Occupational Status of Founders Before Start-Up

	Central	Coastal	Rural	All areas	Significant difference*)
Background of founder:					
- Female	18.6	22.2	19.4	19.9	
- Born abroad	8.3	2.8	2.6	4.8	**
- Higher education	56.7	32.1	29.9	40.5	****
- Previous management experience	48.1	36.7	38.0	41.3	*
- Self-employed parents	41.3	41.5	52.7	45.1	*
Occupational status before start-up:					
- Employee	63.0	66.7	68.3	65.9	
- Self-employed	20.0	17.4	19.0	18.9	
- Student	7.8	3.6	2.0	4.6	*
- Home-working	2.2	4.1	1.0	2.4	
- Unemployed	6.1	7.7	7.8	7.1	
- Other	0.9	0.5	2.0	1.1	

All figures in per cent

*) The column indicates if there are significant differences between the areas. Based on chi-square tests. Levels of significance: *: <.05; **: <.01; ***: <.001; ****: <.0001.

---

[1] Source: Population Census 1990, Statistics Norway.
[2] Good figures on management experience are not available. According to the Population Census 1990, 5.4% of the working population were in work classified as administration and management of organisations or firms.

Table 9.7   Start-Up Motives of the Founders, Per Cent of Founders Claiming Factors to be Very Important or of Some Importance

	Central	Coastal	Rural	All areas	Significant difference*)
Individual push factors:					
- Economic needs	76.6	72.9	77.5	75.8	
- Unemployed/Insecure work situation	31.5	39.2	41.1	36.9	
- Dissatisfaction with previous work	33.5	33.7	27.3	31.6	
Individual pull factors:					
- Good idea that had to be tried	63.7	60.8	70.8	65.1	
- Self-realisation	88.7	88.4	90.9	89.3	
- Need for independence in work	77.8	82.4	80.9	80.2	
- Good market prospects	85.9	87.9	90.9	88.1	
Environmental factors:					
- Good support from family and friends	58.9	67.8	73.7	66.3	**
- Wants to live in the area	49.6	72.9	76.1	65.1	****
- Need for more activity here	27.0	55.3	52.2	43.6	****
- Good public assistance programs	9.7	24.6	39.7	23.8	****
- Good local support	22.2	28.6	32.5	27.4	*
- Stimulating local business milieu	27.8	35.2	30.6	30.9	

*) The column indicates if there are significant differences between the areas. Based on chi-square tests. Levels of significance: *: <.05; **: <.01; ***: <.001; ****: <.0001.

Table 9.8   Idea Development and Start-Up of New Firms

	Central	Coastal	Rural	All areas
The idea for the firm was developed:				
- by the founder alone	38.3	35.5	36.4	36.8
- together with others	61.7	64.5	63.6	63.2
The new firm was established:				
- by the founder alone	57.2	61.8	58.6	59.1
- together with others	31.6	29.0	30.2	30.4
- by taking over a firm	7.4	7.4	9.9	8.2
- other ways	3.7	1.8	1.3	2.4

All figures in per cent

Most founders had an occupational status as employees before start-up; around two thirds of all founders were in this position, while one fifth were previously self-employed. Just smaller fractions had backgrounds as unemployed, students and home working. There seem to be no regional differences between the founders in these respects, with the exception of students, who have a somewhat higher share among founders in the central areas than in the peripheral areas.

The most important factors motivating people for starting new businesses seem to be a combination of need for self-realisation and self-determinism, good market prospects for the firm and economic needs. Also, some environmental factors like good support from family and friends and interest for living in the areas are of great importance as motivating factors, while unemployment and job dissatisfaction turn out to be of less importance.

When comparing the importance of motivating factors of founders in different locations, it is interesting to observe that among neither the individual push nor the pull factors are there significant differences. On the other hand, differences are significant for almost all environmental factors. The data strongly point to a much more supportive environment for start-ups in peripheral areas than in the central areas. It may also be noted that community related motives, i.e. the recognition of local needs for more economic activity, are much more predominant in coastal and rural areas than in urban areas.

When turning attention to the process of start-up (Table 9.8), the data reveal that two thirds of the founders have developed their business ideas in co-operation with other people, while one third has done it alone. Almost 60% of the new firm were set up by the founder alone, and 30% together with others. This points to the conclusion that starting a new firm is not a lonely business, but often takes place in close collaboration with other people. The fact that so many founders also point to support from family and friends as an important motivational factor, leads to the conclusion that starting up a new business to some extent is a social process, and thus environmental and social structures are of importance.

Environmental Factors

An overview of the importance of different locational factors is provided in Table 9.9. Not very surprisingly, the single most important factor for locating a new business is that of social belonging to the community (see for instance Waagø et al. 1978). Other factors of importance are related to material and economic resources and different environmental aspects.

When analysing these factors and their variation over the different locations, it is revealed that for factors related to economic matters, markets and suppliers, there are small or no differences, while for the environmental factors and assistance program there are very significant differences, as these factors are much more important in coastal and rural areas than in the urban areas. In rural and coastal areas social belonging is more important than in urban areas. Local business environments and quality of residential areas and welfare services are regarded to be of greater importance in these areas than in the urban areas. On the other hand, there are just minor differences related to economic and material resources.

One factor that may be subject to special attention, is the importance of assistance programs. Generally, this factor is not rated to be of great importance. On average, only 20% regard this to be very important or of some importance for deciding where to locate new firms. However, the geographical differences are very significant; while only 13% of the urban founders are in this category, three times as many founders in urban areas regard the factor to be of some or great importance for their choice of locality.

Table 9.9   Locational Factors Claimed to be Very Important or of Some Importance

	Central	Coastal	Rural	All areas	Significant difference*)
Material and economic resources:					
- Good premises/land for the firm	50.4	58.5	56.5	54.8	
- Proximity to the market	69.4	60.0	63.6	64.7	
- Proximity to suppliers	26.2	28.5	25.4	26.6	
- Available competence	36.3	25.5	26.3	29.8	*
- Labour market	27.8	23.0	24.4	25.3	
- Low level of costs	61.7	61.5	70.8	64.5	*
Public assistance programs:					
- Good assistance programs	13.3	17.5	31.1	20.2	****
Social and environmental factors:					
- Social belonging to the community	63.3	85.0	84.7	76.7	****
- Good local business environment	39.1	59.5	65.6	53.7	****
- Good residential area	49.2	70.0	75.6	63.9	****
- Good health-, school, and other services	42.3	54.0	63.2	52.5	****

All figures in per cent

*) The column indicates if there are significant differences between the areas. Based on chi-square tests. Levels of significance: *: <.05; **: <.01; ***: <.001; ****: <.0001.

This picture is supported by the data on to what extent founders take advantage of public support programs (Table 9.10). On average, smaller fractions of founders have been supported, but again the geographical differences are very significant. While the percentages of urban founders who have taken advantage of the programs are almost negligible, quite significant shares of founders in coastal and especially rural areas have been supported. 46% of the rural founders have obtained start-up grants, and 24% have received investment grants, while similar shares in the urban areas are 5% and 2% respectively.

Table 9.10   Use of Public Support Programs, Percentage of Start-Ups that have Taken Advantage of Different Types of Support Programs

	Central	Coastal	Rural	All areas	Significant difference*)
Start-up grant	4.9	31.2	46.1	26.2	****
Investment grant	1.9	14.4	23.7	12.7	****
Loan	11.6	39.1	34.9	27.5	****
Guarantee	2.2	6.5	8.2	5.5	****
Other support	7.5	13.0	12.5	10.8	**

*) The column indicates if there are significant differences between the areas. Based on chi-square tests. Levels of significance: *: <.05; **: <.01; ***: <.001; ****: <.0001.

Growing and Non-Growing Firms

As outlined earlier in this paper, the vast majority of new firms consist of very tiny firms, most of which do not grow significantly. This has been revealed through a number of previous studies

(Storey 1994, Spilling 1996b), and is also confirmed by the data provided for this study (cf. Table 9.4).

However, there are some differences between new firms in terms of size and growth pattern, and it can be of interest to analyse these differences. As proportions of growing and non-growing firms differ in urban and rural areas, differences in the characteristics of these firms may shed some light on patterns of industrial dynamics in urban and rural areas.

The firms in our sample are classified according to their growth pattern in three categories: category 3 are the fastest growing firms which have obtained an employment of at least five man years after a life time of four years; category 1 are the smallest, non-growing firms employing a man year or less after four years, and category 2 is the medium group.[3]

Among the total population of new firms investigated here, 22% may be classified as growth firms according to the criteria introduced above, among which almost 50% are located in urban areas. Thus growing firms are significantly overrepresented in the urban areas as they have just 37% of the total population of the investigated firms.

In Tables 9.10-9.15 growing firms are compared with non-growing firms for the various characteristics. First, it may be observed that there are significant differences between growing and non-growing firms in terms of the human resources upon which they are based (Table 9.11). Growing firms have a higher share of founders with higher education than the non-growing firms (47% vs. 35%), and more founders have previous management experience. For the majority of growth firms the idea of the firm was developed in collaboration with other people, and the start-up of the firm was organised by two or more people together (Table 9.13). In contrast to this, the idea generation and start-up of a non-growing firm are organised by one person alone.

A small minority of 7% of the start-ups are organised by individuals with backgrounds as unemployed, which is about the same level as the national unemployment rate over the years when the investigated firms were started. This supports previous findings from the Scandinavian countries that unemployment is not important for stimulating new firm formation (Johannisson and Bång 1992, Davidsson et al. 1994, Spilling 1996a). It is generally positive motivational factors, i.e. pull factors, that are the main driving forces for starting new ventures. This is particularly true for growing firms where only a very small fraction are started by unemployed people. This tendency is also supported by motivational factors where the threat of unemployment or an insecure working situation were significantly lower for the growing firms compared with the non-growing ones.

Generally, it may be concluded that growing firms have higher quality human resources as a basis for start-up. They have a higher level of competence, and the fact that growth firms often are started as partnerships, i.e. with two or more persons actively involved in the start-up, may also imply a stronger capital basis for the new venture. The growing firms are also better off in economic terms than are the non-growing firms, and they are to a larger extent oriented toward national and export markets.

It may be noticed that female entrepreneurs virtually are absent among the growing firms (Table 9.11). While a total of 20% of all firms have been founded by women, only 10% of the growing firms have been started by women.

---

[3]   The operational definition of growth which has been applied, is as follows: Growth = employment - age of firm + 4 + correction for future employment plans. Future employment plans: expansion = 2; stable development = 0, contraction = -2, closure = (-1) x current employment. Growth categories: 1 = less or equal 1; 2 = 2-4; 3 = greater or equal 5.

Table 9.11   Background and Occupational Status of Founders Before Start-Up

	Growth Category			Total	Significant
	1	2	3		difference*)
Background of founder:					
- Female	25.1	19.7	9.7	20.0	***
- Born abroad	4.2	6.4	4.1	4.8	
- Higher education	35.5	46.2	46.9	41.0	*
- Previous management experience	36.0	41.8	55.0	41.5	**
- Self-employed parents	47.6	45.7	37.6	45.1	
Occupational status before start-up:					
- Employee	65.4	68.5	67.9	66.8	
- Self-employed	18.5	16.8	23.9	19.0	
- Student	4.2	4.9	3.7	4.3	
- Home-working	2.8	1.6	0.0	1.9	
- Unemployed	8.0	7.1	3.7	6.9	
- Other	1.0	1.1	0.9	1.0	

All figures in per cent

*) The column indicates if there are significant differences between the areas. Based on chi-square tests. Levels of significance: *: <.05; **: <.01; ***: <.001; ****: <.0001.

Table 9.12   Start-Up Motives of the Founders, Per Cent of Founders Claiming Factors to be Very Important or of Some Importance

	Growth Category			Total	Significant
	1	2	3		difference*)
Individual push factors:					
- Economic needs	76.3	78.0	66.1	74.7	
- Unemployment/Insecure work situation	41.6	35.5	24.4	36.1	***
- Dissatisfaction with previous work	30.2	33.9	33.1	32.0	
Individual pull factors:					
- Good idea that had to be tried	62.2	71.5	67.7	66.2	
- Self-realisation	91.1	89.8	85.8	89.6	
- Need for independence in work	83.8	81.2	72.4	80.6	*
- Good market prospects	83.5	90.9	93.7	87.9	****
Environmental factors:					
- Good support from family and friends	68.0	71.0	60.6	67.4	
- Wants to live in the area	68.0	71.5	55.1	66.4	*
- Need for more activity here	38.5	47.8	50.4	43.9	*
- Good public assistance programs	20.6	25.3	32.3	24.5	
- Good local support	23.0	31.2	36.2	28.3	
- Stimulating local business milieu	29.9	33.3	32.3	31.5	

*) The column indicates if there are significant differences between the areas. Based on chi-square tests. Levels of significance: *: <.05; **: <.01; ***: <.001; ****: <.0001.

Table 9.13   Idea Development and Start-Up of New Firms

	Growth Category			Total	Significant difference*)
	1	2	3		
The idea for the firm was developed:					
- by the founder alone	73.9	59.5	44.5	63.2	****
- together with others	26.1	40.5	55.5	36.8	****
The new firm was established:					
- by the founder alone	71.8	56.2	31.1	57.9	****
- together with others	19.9	34.0	51.4	31.2	****
- by taking over a firm	6.7	8.4	12.8	8.6	
- other ways	1.6	1.5	4.7	2.3	

All figures in per cent

*) The column indicates if there are significant differences between the areas. Based on chi-square tests. Levels of significance: *: <.05; **: <.01; ***: <.001; ****: <.0001.

Another aspect to be commented upon regarding differences between growing and non-growing firms, are differences in start-up motives and locational factors. Generally, most of the factors turn out to be the same. Starting a new venture is about self-realisation, pursuing interesting ideas and exploiting market opportunities, and the main locational factor is social cohesiveness, i.e. the firm is located in the area where the founder lives and to which he or she belongs. However, there are some differences of interest. On the one hand, the market prospects are more important for the growing firms than for the non-growing, while the factors of need for independence in work and economic needs are most important for the non-growing firms. And as already mentioned, there is a very significant difference in the role of threatening unemployment or insecure work situation. This factor is of importance for more than 40% of the non-growing firms, but just one fourth of the growing firms. On the other hand, social belonging to the area is more important as a locational factor for the non-growing firms, while the labour market, naturally, is significantly more important to the growing firm than the non-growing.

Table 9.14   Location Factors Claimed to be Very Important or of Some Importance

	Growth Category			Total	Significant difference*)
	1	2	3		
Material and economic resources:					
- Good premises/land for the firm	54.6	46.2	69.8	55.3	*
- Proximity to the market	60.8	68.3	69.0	64.9	
- Proximity to suppliers	25.1	23.1	34.9	26.6	
- Available competence	26.8	28.0	42.6	30.5	*
- Labour market	17.2	22.0	51.2	25.9	****
- Low level of costs	68.7	67.2	57.4	65.8	
Public assistance programs:					
- Good assistance programs	19.9	20.4	26.4	21.5	
Social and environmental factors:					
- Social belonging to the community	82.5	76.3	68.2	77.6	*
- Good local business environment	56.0	57.5	46.5	54.5	
- Good residential area	65.3	68.8	59.7	65.2	
- Good health- school and other services	53.6	60.8	44.2	53.8	*

All figures in per cent

*) The column indicates if there are significant differences between the areas. Based on chi-square tests. Levels of significance: *: <.05; **: <.01; ***: <.001; ****: <.0001.

Table 9.15   Use of Public Support Programs, Percentage of Start-Ups that have Taken Advantage of Different Types of Support Programs

	Growth Category			Total	Significant difference*)
	1	2	3		
Start-up grant	25.0	27.6	28.1	26.5	
Investment grant	10.6	13.3	19.2	13.3	*
Loan	24.0	31.5	34.9	28.7	*
Guarantee	4.2	4.4	9.6	5.4	*
Other support	7.7	10.8	17.8	10.9	**

*) The column indicates if there are significant differences between the areas. Based on chi-square tests. Levels of significance: *: <.05; **: <.01; ***: <.001; ****: <.0001.

In a previous section of this paper (Section 6) it has been an important point that environmental factors, i.e. social factors, local business milieu and public support programs, are significantly more important in the coastal and rural settings than in the urban. When these factors are compared for the different firm categories, differences are not revealed in the same way. Social belonging to the community and welfare services are somewhat more important to the non-growing than the growing firm. Among the public support programs, all programs except start-up grants are somewhat more important to the growing than the non-growing firms. But differences are generally small, and for the start-up grants there is no difference at all. This may indicate that public support measures are quite evenly distributed to all kinds of firms without any special targeting towards firms with growth potentials.

However, these tendencies are independent of the urban-rural setting, and one might suspect, based on the previous findings, that there may be significant differences in how various factors affect different firm categories under different geographical settings. This is the background for analysing if there are differences for the various firm categories in the various geographical settings.

Table 9.16 provides an overview of all the previous findings in addition to presenting new data on urban-rural differences when controlled for the different firm categories. The question to be analysed is if the same category of firm is affected differently by the various factors in different geographical settings?

Table 9.16   The Urban-Rural Dimension of Factors Affecting New Firm Formation

	Urban (+) vs. Rural (÷)	Growing (+) vs. non-growing (÷)	Urban (+) vs. Rural (÷) controlled for growing/non-growing		
			Growth categories:		
			1	2	3
The founder:					
Background:					
- Female		+++			
- Born abroad	++			++	
- Higher education	++++	+	+++	++	+
- Previous management experience	+	++	+		
- Self-employed parents	÷				
Occupational status before start-up:					
- Employee					
- Self-employed					
- Student	+				
- Home-working					
- Unemployed					
- Other					
Motivational factors:					
Individual push factors:					
- Economic needs					
- Unemployed/Insecure work situation		+++			
- Dissatisfaction with previous work					
Individual pull factors:					
- Good idea that had to be tried					
- Self-realisation			÷		
- Need for independence in work		÷			
- Good market prospects		++++			
Environmental factors:					
- Good support from family and friends	++		÷		++
- Wants to live in the area	++++	÷	++++	+++	
- Need for more activity here	++++	+	+++	++++	+++
- Good public assistance programs	++++		++++	+	+++
- Good local support	÷				
- Stimulating local business milieu					

	Urban (+) vs. Rural (÷)	Growing (+) vs. non-growing (+)	Urban (+) vs. Rural (÷) controlled for growing/non-growing		
			Growth categories:		
			1	2	3
Strategy for organising the start-up:					
The idea for the firm was developed:					
- By the founder alone		÷÷÷÷			
- Together with others		++++			
The new firm was established:					
- By the founder alone		÷÷÷÷			
- Together with others		++++			
- By taking over a firm					
- Other ways					
Locational factors:					
Material and economic resources:					
- Good premises/land for the firm		+			÷
- Proximity to the market					
- Proximity to suppliers					
- Available competence	+	+			
- Labour market		++++			
- Low level of costs	÷			÷	
Public assistance programs:					
- Good assistance programs	÷÷÷÷		÷÷÷÷		÷÷÷÷
Social and environmental factors:					
- Social belonging to the community	÷÷÷÷	÷	÷	+	÷÷÷
- Good local business environment	÷÷÷÷		÷	÷	÷÷
- Good residential area	÷÷÷÷		÷÷÷	++	÷
- Good health-. school and other services	÷÷÷÷	÷	÷÷÷		
Public support measures:					
- Start-up grant	÷÷÷÷		÷÷÷÷	++++	++
- Investment grant	÷÷÷÷	+	÷÷÷÷	++++	÷÷÷÷
- Loan	÷÷÷÷	+	÷÷÷	++	÷÷÷÷
- Guarantee	÷÷÷÷	+			
- Other support	++	++			

The table indicates all significant relationships based on chi-square tests. +/÷ indicate the direction of the relationships, i.e. if urban is greater than rural or growing greater than non-growing. The number of signs indicate the strength of the relationship, i.e. the level of significance (.05, .01, .001, 0001).

Based on the data in Table 9.16 the following points may be summarised:

1. Among the founder resources, it is mainly the share of founders with higher education that is different in urban and rural areas. This is valid for all categories of firms, i.e. more founders in urban areas have higher education compared with their rural counterparts.

2. Among the motivational factors, most of the environmental factors reveal significant urban-rural differences for virtually all firm categories.
3. The data reveal no significant urban-rural differences regarding patterns of how the idea of the firm was developed and how the firm was established, here the differences follow the growth/non-growth dimension.
4. Among the locational factors, again the most significant differences between urban and rural areas are related to the environmental factors, most of which are significantly more important in rural areas than in urban.
5. The data confirm most of the significant urban-rural differences related to the public support measures. Although there are differences which mean that growing firms to a greater extent take advantage of public support measures than non-growing firms, this difference is of less significance than the difference between the urban and rural areas when it is controlled for firm category. Generally the measures are far more important in rural areas than in urban areas. This may, for instance, be illustrated by the fact that only 7% of the growing new firms in urban areas received start-up grants, while the percentage which received such grants in rural areas was 55 (data not shown in Table 9.16).

The Urban-Rural Dimension of New Firm Formation

On the one side, data presented in this paper contribute to our knowledge about areas in which the urban-rural dimension is quite significant and also reveal differences in start-up patterns. On the other side, also revealed are areas where there are very striking similarities, i.e. the urban-rural dimension is not working. In total, this should provide a more differentiated picture of the importance of the urban-rural dimension of new firm formation.

The first conclusion to be drawn is that the data confirm our general understanding that the existing industrial structure is a main determining factor for the pattern of new firm formation, which basically takes place within this structure and contributes to its reproduction. To the extent there are regional differences in industrial structure, these differences are reproduced in firm formation rates. Thus, there are, for instance, significant urban-rural differences in firm formation in manufacturing and producer services; the urban areas have lower proportions of start-ups in manufacturing and higher ones in producer services. The mechanisms of these reproducing structures are to some extent also supported when data on previous occupational experiences of the founders are examined (data not reported here). There seems to be some connection between the industry in which the new firm is set up, and the industry from which the founder has his or her previous experience. Similarly, in cases where the founders have parents who are or have been self-employed, there is a weak relationship between the industry of the new firm and the industry of the parents' business.

A second conclusion is that, although the vast majority of new firms are very tiny, there are differences in favour of urban areas, which have higher shares of the 'less smaller' and growing firms, while rural areas have higher shares of the very small firms, including the firms that only provide part-time employment. The urban-rural dimension also to some extent affects the market orientation of firms, with the largest shares of firms based on local markets in rural areas, and the largest shares of exporters in urban areas. Although the differences are not very strong, this still points to the conclusion that new firm formation provides more viable businesses in urban areas compared to rural areas. In the long term this may provide a more significant effect than what is revealed by our data.

A third conclusion is that there are some urban-rural differences in the personal resources of the founders. More than 50% of urban founders have higher education, while less than a third of the rural founders have higher education. There is also a difference in favour of urban areas regarding the share of founders with previous management experience. These differences to a certain extent are associated with the growth of firm, and thus can be explained by urban areas having higher shares of growing firms. But even when controlled for firm growth, there is a significant difference between urban and rural areas in the way that the founders of non-growing as well as growing firms to a larger extent have higher education than their rural counterparts.

A fourth conclusion is that there are remarkable similarities between urban and rural areas in a number of factors related to the founders' motives and strategies for starting up new firms. While some of these factors are related to firm growth, there are no significant urban-rural differences. All motivational factors related to individual needs are the same, the firms are established in much the same way, and the importance of economic-based locational factors is much the same over the different types of localities. This points to the conclusion that individual and economic-related processes involved in new firm formation to a large extent are independent of geography.

A fifth conclusion, which represents the most significant difference between urban and rural firm formation, is the importance of social and environmental factors. To some extent firm formation is a social process, but it is much more so in urban than in rural areas. A number of environmental factors are important for new firm formation, but they are significantly more important in rural than in urban areas. And, although public support programs generally seem to play a rather modest role in supporting new start ups, there is significantly more support provided to founders in rural areas than in urban areas.

In particular, the differences related to the importance of public support measures are re-markable. One would expect that the importance of public programs would be more important to growing firms than the non-growing, and to some extent this is confirmed by our data. But the urban-rural differences are much more significant, as just a very small fraction of new firms in urban areas, independent of growth, take advantage of the public support programs, while significant shares do so in rural areas. To a significant extent this is due to regional policies of Norway which are designed for stimulating industrial development in peripheral areas. But the difference is also significant for measures that should not be discriminating between urban and rural areas (start-up grants).

On the one hand, this leads to the conclusion that rural environments generally seem to be much more supportive of new firm formation than urban environments, and rural founders seem to be much more embedded in social structures than their urban counterparts. In this sense our findings can be taken as support for a common view that social cohesiveness is much more important for industrial development in rural areas than in urban areas. Here there seems to be a very significant urban-rural dimension working.

On the other hand, this also raises a paradox: Given the more supportive environment for new firm formation in rural areas, one might expect that this would be an important precondition for viable industrial development. However, our data points quite clearly to the conclusion that the most viable firm formation occurs in urban areas. This raises the question if the supportive environment in rural areas just provides a compensation for lack of embedded economic dynamism, or if the supportive environment provides an embeddedness that actually provides a barrier to more viable economic development. This may be the point of departure for further investigation into the urban-rural differences in firm formation and the role of socio-cultural factors.

References

Audretsch, D. B. and M. Fritsch (1994): The geography of firm births in Germany. *Regional Studies,* 28(4): 359-365.

Davidsson, P., L. Lindmark, Olofsson, C. (1994): New firm formation and regional development in Sweden. *Regional Studies,* 48(4): 395-410.

European Observatory for SMEs (1995), Third Annual Report. EIM, Holland.

Fritsch, M. 1992: Regional differences in new firm formation: Evidence from West Germany. *Regional Studies,* 26(3): 233-241.

Garofoli, G. (1994): New firm formation and Regional Development: The Italian case. *Regional Studies,* 28(4): 381-393.

Isaksen, A. and O.R. Spilling (1996): *Regional utvikling og små bedrifter* . (Regional development and small firms.) Scandinavian University Press, Kristiansand, Norway.

Johannisson, B. and H. Bang (1992). *Nyföretagande och regioner - modeller, fakta, stimulantia..* (New firms and regions - models, facts and stimulation.) Stockholm: Allmänna Förlaget.

Reynolds, P. D. and D. J. Storey (1993): *Local and regional characteristics affecting small business formation: a cross-national comparison.* OECD, Paris.

Reynolds, P., D. J. Storey and P. Westhead (1994): Cross-national comparisons of the variation in new firm formation rates. *Regional Studies,* 28(4): 443-456.

Spilling, O. R. (1996a). Regional variation of new firm formation: the Norwegian case. *Entrepreneurship and Regional Development,* 8(3): 217-243.

Spilling, O. R. (1996b). Do Small Firms Create Jobs? *Journal of Enterprising Culture,* 4(2): 147-161.

Storey, D. J. (1994). *Understanding the Small Business Sector.* London and New York: Routledge.

Waagø, S. J. (1978). *Start og etablering av småforetak.* (Starting and developing small firms.) Institutt for industriell økonomi og organisasjon, NTH, Trondheim.

PART III
GROWTH
AND
INTERNATIONALISATION

10 Entrepreneurial Behaviour in the International Development of Small Firms

Francesco Bifulco

Purposes

The field of studies on small firms has been augmented by analyses aimed at supplanting the traditional model of small firm development based on dimensional growth and processes of internalisation. Within this context the most important interpretative assumptions seem to be:

1) the presumed identity of the concepts of *development* and *growth* . Businesses do not always seek *growth* as an end in itself, since a significant increase in size generates managerial and organisational problems.
2) the *possibility of defining the boundaries*. Size, if referred to a single firm, is a conceptual category which is not ideally suited to understanding the present-day logic of small firm development and, instead, referral should be made to different types of groups.
3) the *different study approaches*. It is hard to find a model which can specify all the variables related to a phenomenology of the small firm and the task of delegating the study of the 'small local firm' to other disciplinary fields seems superficial, merely taking advantage of such work to interpret the role and mechanisms of functioning/behaviour.

In particular, there has been a notable increase in studies concerned with development strategies in the last decade, especially related to inter-company collaboration, even though attention has focused more upon systems of implementation than on entrepreneurial behaviour (Rumelt, 1995; Lipparini and Lorenzoni, 1996).

This paper attempts to explore such behaviour from a processual viewpoint, focusing on the analysis of small industrial firms and paying specific attention to the family context and local risk capital.

The Principal Theoretical Approaches Related to Entrepreneurial Situations

The numerous traditional papers on entrepreneurial models develop differing conceptions of the entrepreneur according to the different cultural context from which they originate.

The psycho-sociological approach, which is partly based on work derived from psychological analysis (Hoselitz, 1951; McClelland, 1961; Kets de Vries, 1977) emphasises certain characteristics of the personality of entrepreneurs (self-realisation, aggressivity, self-defence) and partly on sociological analysis (Stanworth and Curran, 1976; Brockhaus, 1987; Cooper and Dunkelberg, 1987; Watson, 1995). They can be differentiated according to the different importance attributed to determining contextual factors (socio-economic and political conditions, cultural or family models, ideological influence).

The economic approach, on the other hand, develops conceptions of the entrepreneur inspired by an individualised vision of the subject of analysis: the innovative entrepreneur (Moss and Kanter,

1983; Gartner, 1989); the entrepreneur as undertaker and creator of risk (Redlich, 1957); the decision-making entrepreneur (Cole, 1959).

The *company approach*, finally, which can be traced back to traditional approaches and to management and   company strategy theories originating   in the USA. In particular, the concepts developed in Italy are strongly influenced both by functionalism and by the theory of *'diffuse entrepreneurship'* (Zappa, 1957).

The classical work mentioned above tends, in various ways, to use general schemes that could give rise to concepts of abstract entrepreneurs. This risk is accentuated in the reality of small businesses in the case of *'a limited but diffuse entrepreneurship'*.

The entrepreneurial model proposed by Normann, in particular, since it centres on only two general typologies, does not seem particularly useful as a reference to small-scale entrepreneurial situations if measured against the results of various pieces of research at international level (Kroeger, 1974; Scase and Goffee, 1980; Smith and Miner, 1983; Dubini, 1994). Certain elements, however, seem to emerge in all the research; the small decision-making team, the circumscribed competitive environment, the family-business overlap (Cohen and Levinthal, 1990).

Based on the considerations outlined above, even though it does not seem possible to ignore certain fundamental aspects (company size, the business area, age, culture), an attempt has been made to circumscribe the field of study in order to identify several 'universal factors' of small-scale entrepreneurship which could constitute the foundations of an *interpretative framework:*

   1) the perception of the external environment
   2) the propensity to risk
   3) the organisation of resources
   4) the capacity to promote innovation
   5) the attitude towards change.

The Attitude of Theoretical Models of Development Towards Analysing Entrepreneurial Behaviour

In order to avoid a *'speculative'* distinction between small, medium and large firms, a proposal has been put forward in some of the literature to distinguish only between larger and smaller firms. The latter may be considered as an *'intermediate category between the craft firm and the managerial firm'* and can be identified by resorting to qualitative characteristics (the integration between property and decisional power, the participation of owners in management, the refusal to obtain capital on the security market) and quantitative characteristics of statistical type.[1]

Especially regarding the *family firm* it is useful to envisage a firm where there is a very close integration between ownership and directional/entrepreneurial activity, where one or more families condition the strategic choices and are actively involved in the management. Family style entrepreneurship, despite the acknowledged importance of its social and economic role (in Europe 85% of firms are family-run, while in Italy the percentage rises to 99%), is a phenomenon which is still little known and has not yet had its particular characteristics adequately described in research models.

Starting from this defining assumption, studies in the international literature on the strategic problems within the various phases of the small firm's growth cycle seem to be relatively more common. Many models related to this field have been taken from the traditional strand of development theory (Penrose, 1959; Chandler, 1962; Greiner, 1972), seen in terms of the growth of internal organisational structures and their subsequent adaptions. Several models of growth which specifically deal with the

---

[1]   With regard to this, Bolton (1971, pp. 1-2) and Curran and Stanworth (1984, pp. 127-147) use the threshold of 200 employees to distinguish 'small firms' from 'large firms'; Acs and Audretsch (1989, pp. 9-22) have raised this threshold to 500 employees. In the EU the following subdivision has been adopted in recent years: *microfirms (less than 9 employees), small firms (between 10 and 99 employees), medium firms (between 100 and 499 employees), large firms (over 500 employees).*

small firm belong to this approach (Steinmetz, 1969; Barnes and Hershon, 1976; Churchill and Lewis, 1983; Scott and Bruce, 1987).

The most significant problems, which are common to these lines of research, lie in the perspective to adopt for *the interpretation of entrepreneurial behaviour in the strategic processes of development of small firms*, which constitute an entity that is conceptually distinguishable from large firms and present peculiarities due to which each individual firm is distinguishable from every other.

In this regard, research has multiplied in varying forms and content. For this reason it does not seem fruitful to examine further the specific theme of networking strategies and illustrate their theoretical validity, while it would seem to be more useful to proceed to a comparative analysis of the different approaches in order to identify their weaknesses.[2]

Scholars initially outlined two organisational forms of exchange, *'hierarchy'* (internalisation) and the *'market'* (externalisation). Recourse to the latter (Williamson, 1979) depends on the transaction costs which can render the internal production of all the components of a good uneconomic and which are influenced by factors related to human nature (limited rationality and opportunism) and the environment (uncertainty/complexity).

The view was later reached that the market and the hierarchy did not constitute the sole organisational forms, but merely the *'extremes of a continuum'*. Other hybrid forms have been identified within these extremes (Richardson, 1972; Ouchi, 1981; Williamson, 1985), amongst which are the co-operation agreements among firms.

Concepts such as *'network systems'*[3] have thus been defined which generally differ according to the number of units involved, the typology, the degree of co-ordination, the level of relationships (horizontal, vertical, ascendant/descendent), and the maintenance of the system.[4]

Despite disparate intentions, the analysis of theoretical developments thus reveals a widespread conviction that, within the problems of the strategic organisation of the development of the small firm, the search for an adequate answer which hinges on the logic of aggregation becomes all the more significant.

The presence of people who operate on different fronts (supply, sales, planning, designing, etc.), and use different but inter-dependent approaches increases the innovative potential of the individual firms; this allows them to acquire competitive advantages which are difficult for competitors to match (Itami, 1987, p.38).

Only recently has there been a proliferation of work aimed at investigating the possible paths of applicable solutions for development which do not necessarily imply a *'dimensional leap'*. Regarding this point it is extremely interesting to note the focus of the entrepreneur's creative and cultural capacities in determining *'the types of growth which the firm undergoes'*.

Within this context, regarding the intensity of the relationship, differences have emerged in the literature in terms of the behaviour and relations with others in the competitive arena which generate *opportunistic or co-operative attitudes* (Prahalad and Hamel, 1990; Eisenhardt and Schoonhoven, 1996).

---

[2] Fletcher (1994, pp. 27-52) suggests an interesting contribution in this regard.

[3] A *'network firm'* refers to the internal organisation of a firm which is usually large and internalizes the environment through relationships/agreements with external units/subjects (franchising system, sub-contracting agreements). The meaning of *'firm networks'* is instead a system of analogous firms interconnected by certain relationships (Arrow, 1983).

[4] The maintenance of the agreement can be ensured by 'trust among partners', 'reciprocity' of treatment and 'multi-directionality of relational links'. Aldrich and Whetten (1981, pp. 386-387) make a distinction between the *organisation set* (the network of relations which a single firm establishes with external subjects/firms), the *action set* (a group of firms which have reached an agreement which is limited in time, in order to reach a given aim) and *networks* (a group of firms which are interconnected by certain relations). Boari, Grandi and Lorenzoni (1989), develop *three basic concepts* : the *network of external units*, which is constituted by the leader firm and the external firms/organizations with whom it constructs links and relationships; the *network of internal units*, with reference to the organising structure, which is constituted by several business units, juridically regarded as distinct units, and the *network at an interpersonal level* , by which is intended *'social network'*.

Therefore it is believed that the uncritical acceptance of the formulae of collaboration may lead to interpretations which are ill-suited to understanding the reality that small European firms, and especially Italian ones, have to face: the path towards inter-company relations offers opportunities for development only if the pre-conditions and pre-requisites are met; if the opposite is the case, such links can prove unfruitful and counter-productive (Pfeffer and Salancick, 1978; Hannan and Freeman, 1992; Normann and Ramirez, 1993; Nonaka, 1994).

Indeed the type of *'productive decentralisation'* from which aggregation originates, distinguishes between *intentional* behaviour (entrepreneurial choice) and *compulsory* behaviour (obligatory choice). The first expresses vertical aggregations which are sometimes formal and have a single decisional centre (for example the sub-contractors); the second expresses vertical and/or horizontal aggregations which are certainly informal and often have several decisional centres (for example constellations). While aggregations that derive from a desired decentralisation are determined by mainly economic factors, aggregations that stem from forced decentralisation are determined by other factors as well as traditions, localism, innovations (Aldrich and Zimmer, 1986; Larson, 1992; Lorenzoni and Balden Fuller, 1995).

Some Empirical Evidence

With reference to the above discussion, the decision to analyse small industrial firms operating in the so-called traditional sectors[5] has been caused by the need to set up a research plan into the necessary pre-conditions and operational methods which force or should encourage the activation of strategic processes of international development (Herron and Robinson, 1993; Stampacchia, 1993).

The specific aim of this initial empirical examination is to identify the main forms of entrepreneurial behaviour of local firms within the woodworking and furniture sector in the region of Campania. There are two principal questions which the research tried to answer:

1) Does a culture of co-operation exist or, rather, should the firms analysed be regarded simply as territorial aggregates with individualised forms of behaviour ?

2) Can such firms give rise to local productive systems with models of development (traditional or evolved area-systems) comparable to those identified in other parts of Italy or abroad ?

Methodology

The analysis has been carried out by making exclusive reference to a sample of 181 autonomous firms with a number of employees not less than 11 people.

---

5   This approach has been developed starting from the study of Pavitt (1984) which identifies four types of small firms: 'science based' (bio-technologies, electronics, pharmaceutical, left-over materials, etc.); subcontractors of large firms (cars, computers, electric household appliances, telecommunications, etc.); suppliers specialised in equipment (machine tools, wood working machines, textile machines, machines for working plastic materials, systems of production, etc.; 'traditional' (textile, clothing, shoes, wood and furniture, ceramics, food, etc.).

Table 10.1   Sample Characteristics

Factors	Mean Value	AREAS OF BUSINESS							
		A	B	C	D	E	F	G	H
Firms	n°	37	15	14	48	1	5	20	41
Seniority Business	years	20	30	20	20	15	10	20	20
Factory	units	1	2	1	1	1	1	1	1
Turnover max	$ millions	< 10	< 5	< 3	< 10	< 5	< 3	< 3	< 5
Employed max	units	< 15	<35	< 20	< 45	< 25	< 30	< 25	< 25
Production	typology	Large -small series	Large series	Small series	Large series	Large series	Large -small series	Large- small series	Large- small series
Utilisation of Industrial Plants	%	65-75	65-80	65-75	60-70	60-70	60-80	70-80	50-70

A = Interior Design Furniture   E = School Furniture
B = Padded Furniture   F = Air - Naval Furniture
C = Frames and Locks   G = Poles and Frames
D = Kitchens' and Bathrooms' Furniture   H = Various Furniture on Order

The *model of analysis of entrepreneurial behaviour* was based on four areas of reference. It contains the main variables considered along the two axes, the vertical one of innovation and the horizontal one of consolidation.

Figure 10.1   Model of Analysis of Entrepreneurial Behaviour

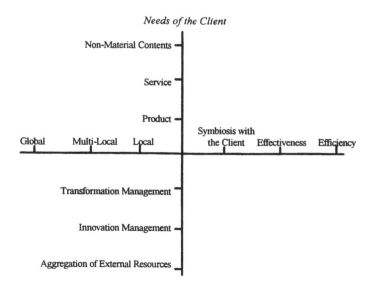

The *innovation* axis is described by several elements which are linked together vertically:
- a) the *needs of the client* (product, service, non-material contents)
- b) *distinctive skills* (transformation management, innovation management, aggregation of external resources).

The *consolidation* axis is described by other elements:
- a) the *field of action of the* local (national/regional) and multi-local *market*
- b) *competitive morphology* (symbiosis with the client, effectiveness and efficiency).

The Entrepreneurial Archetypes that Emerge from Empirical Analysis

Direct observation of the sample under research has enabled the identification of certain critical factors of success, both structural and competitive, that place it within a phase of notable transition. The common strategic planning of many firms emerged during the course of the research, despite the fact that the firms operate in different business fields, with occasionally differing organisational forms and with a history that was shared only in certain aspects.

The most significant results are the following:
- structural 'dwarfism', both in terms of the average number of employees per firm as for the high percentage of firms with one plant
- the widespread presence of family enterprises rooted in the territory undergoing a phase of generational change
- the orientation towards production, with fragmentation and specialisation of production and a satisfying average level of plant use
- mainly national supply and sales markets
- tendency towards international activity and inter-company collaboration.

The majority of entrepreneurs can generally be grouped under the first typology described by Normann, even though not all the firms in the sample, characterised by a lower level of entrepreneurship, can be said to be of limited entrepreneurship and therefore pre-destined to failure if they undertake an activity which is different from the original business idea.

In particular, it was possible to identify the following 'types' of local small firms:
- firms run by a single entrepreneur/owner with a generally traditional cultural background
- firms run by a family group of entrepreneur/owners with a slightly more evolved cultural background.

The firms in the first group generally present a more restricted level of entrepreneurship compared to the second group. The typologies established, when put alongside the strategies adopted, the processes of innovation pursued and the organisational and productive assets, showed a positive correlation between the levels of entrepreneurship and several variables of internal and external context. Indeed all following qualitative/quantitative characteristics co-exist:
- the overlap between ownership and management
- a relative lack of structured organisation in relation to the competitive context of reference
- limited powers of influence with respect to the relevant environment (suppliers, credit institutions, etc.)
- innovative capacity, for the most part restricted to imitation or improving existing processes
- difficulty/impossibility/aversion to gaining finance from the security market.

Potential Paths of Development

If the above resulted from a static reading of the sample, the main strategic models together with the basic reasons of typical entrepreneurial behaviour and, finally, areas of future weakness were all analysed according to a dynamic reading (Johnston and Lawrence, 1988; Gomez and Cassares, 1994).

Table 10.2   Firm Characteristics

BUSINESS STRATEGIC AREA								
Factors	**A**	**B**	**C**	**D**	**E**	**F**	**G**	**H**
Firms	37	15	14	48	1	5	20	41
Foreign Supply Area	Brazil			Canada USA	Russia	UK Germany Sweden USA		
Typology of Supplier	Producers Whole-saler			Producers	Producers Whole-saler	Producers Wholesaler		
Foreign Sales Area	France	Israel Tunisia	Greece	Greece Germany Malta East countries	Greece Germany East countries South Africa	Russia	Germany UK Malta South Africa	Malta
Typology of Customer	Whole-saler	Big delivery	Retailer	Retailer	Whole-saler	Dockyard	Whole-saler	SMEs
Information Sources	Fair	Foreign office Fair	Foreign office	Foreign office Fair Market research	Foreign office Fair Market research	Foreign office	Fair Partnership	Foreign office Agencies
Promotional - Communica-tion Initiative	Direct contact Fair Catalogue	Direct contact Fair Catalogue	Adverti-sing Fair Catalogue	Adverti-sing Fair Catalogue	Adverti-sing Fair Catalogue	Direct contact Fair Catalogue Yearbook Advertising	Direct contact Fair Catalogue Yearbook	Direct contact Fair Catalogue Adverti-sing

A = Interior Design Furniture   E = School Furniture
B = Padded Furniture   F = Air - Naval Furniture
C = Frames and Locks   G = Poles and Frames
D = Kitchens' and Bathrooms' Furniture   H = Various Furniture on Order

The Main Strategic Organisational Models

Only in a few cases are the firms characterised in an integrated way according to a valid technological, commercial and human resource background. The competitive position seems to be precarious: the producer or sub-contractor of products of limited value added, exposed to the contractual power of clients and suppliers, based on flexibility in terms of products/clients and the control of fixed costs, operates over adjoining geographical areas. An entrepreneurial profile can be observed which is characterised by the following: a technical background, a centraliser, oriented towards imitating products and processes, unwilling to undertake dimensional growth, skilful in re-orientating production in a crisis.

The Reasons for Typical Entrepreneurial Behaviour

The *absence of aggregative forms* given the presence of entrepreneurial models which have enabled the achievement of satisfactory equilibriums on restricted dimensional levels, may be explained by three causes:

1) *The competitive characteristics.* The structure of the productive cycle does not favour the genesis and development of decentralising phenomena of specific stages and work; amongst other things several key protagonists of the competitive system (raw material suppliers, plant constructors, clients) often assume a very important role in planning.

2) *The demand situation.* The opportunities for growth offered by the external environment have postponed forms of collaboration after reaching sufficient economic results within the capacity of individual initiative.

3) *The entrepreneurial culture.* The origin of part of the sample can be traced to the dynamics of 'spin-off' which explains why we encounter rival businessmen who, until a few years before, collaborated inside the same firm. A significant cultural resistance exists towards sharing any decisional matter with other people.

The combined action of these phenomena has meant that certain hypotheses of consortium initiatives developed in recent years have never overcome the planning stage. It is precisely the prevalence of a cultural model based on a decisional autonomy and characterised by a mainly conservative learning process which constitutes the main factor of *'inter-firm distance'* and thus the element that has restricted the creation of joint initiatives.

Future Weakness

The level of vulnerability seems to vary specifically in relation to the dimensions of the firms and the areas of business, and originates in four areas:

1) *on the competitive level,* the involvement in one or several market niches leads to the defence of their own areas of dominance. This is a strategic path that, in evolutionary terms, may prove difficult since:

   a) in certain business areas firms compete with international competitors which have far bigger dimensions

   b) the opportunity to abandon the most desired niches in order to break into new market areas may be progressively reduced

   c) the restricted dimension places different firms in a particularly appetising category for those who would like to acquire know-how and market niches by entering firms that are already established.

2) *on the level of innovation,* the need to introduce productive technologies and managerial competencies (technological, logistical and quality control) currently outside the pool of knowledge of the specific business areas which could constitute a critical basis for future development. Until now local firms have obtained their know-how from their own employees, plant producers, suppliers, thus raising their own competitiveness on the level of low innovation costs.

3) *on the level of managing human resources,* the central role of the entrepreneurial figure and his technical-productive competence risk constituting a brake on development. It is necessary to find the motivation to overcome the weak drive that valid resources show in getting involved in firms of modest dimensions.

4) *on the level of improving results,* the competitive and profit-making performances made in the years of development have slowed down the tendency to rationalising operational management. This has frequently provoked a situation where areas of economic improvement or commercial and productive synergies are overlooked.

The Potentially Applicable Forms of Aggregation

The second principal question to which an answer has been sought is the following: Could the development of new forms of co-operation between firms constitute an equal and feasible path for solving the problems raised in areas characterised by a lack of suitability?

Table 10.3   Preferred Forms of Co-operation

	BUSINESS STRATEGIC AREA							
Factors	**A**	**B**	**C**	**D**	**E**	**F**	**G**	**H**
Preferred collaboration	Commercial Production Research & development	Commercial Distribution	Commercial Distribution	Research & development Commercial Distribution	Commercial Distribution	Production Research & development Commercial Distribution	Commercial Distribution Production	Commercial Distribution Production
Ideal partner	Industrial Commercial	Commercial	Commercial	Industrial Commercial	Commercial	Industrial Commercial	Industrial Commercial	Industrial Commercial

A = Interior Design Furniture
B = Padded Furniture
C = Frames and Locks
D = Kitchens' and Bathrooms' Furniture

E = School Furniture
F = Air - Naval Furniture
G = Poles and Frames
H = Various Furniture on Order

Some preliminary points for reflection emerge from the empirical enquiry into the possibility of setting up processes of Cupertino as a potential way of achieving a *'qualitative improvement',* an essential condition for the development of small industrial firms on an international scale.

The possibility of planning and achieving aggregations in firms in such an unsuitable area must follow a path of consolidation which could be sufficient for facing up to the exposed areas of weakness. Apart from specific consolidation work of individual entrepreneurial organisation, it is worthwhile reflecting on the space for rationalisation in the system. We refer to:

1) *research and exploitations of commercial synergies* . Within the local context, firms exist which, although involved in producing different goods or in the same areas of business, insistently aim at the same markets; it is necessary to promote a greater level of co-ordination of commercial work addressed towards new outlets.

2) *economies of scale in the supply stage.* In order to avoid duplicating the product-market combinations under discussion, it is necessary to develop governing mechanisms of the vertical flow of materials. The importance of purchasing raw materials, linked to limited negotiating capacity, encourage the creation of a point of reference for buying operations. The feasibility of such hypotheses depends on the existence of a guiding-role that involves the interested firms within a strategic plan which suits them.

3) *qualification of the labour market* . The firms in the area encounter substantial difficulties in research and employee training in the different functional areas. Joint initiatives aimed at raising professional standards in order to spread and share technological know-how are necessary.

Planning aggregate forms in order to stimulate joint initiatives does not appear to be simple, especially given the interests involved. Entrepreneurial development in a local area clashes at a practical level with a series of obstacles: cultural attitudes; the legitimisation of the figure of entrepreneurial directorship; the identification of areas of rationalisation.

The potential of applying aggregation strategies that can be clearly expressed are the following:

1) *the presence of specific product niches.* Firms might be characterised according to a precise definition of the competitive environment, in terms of product, terminologies employed and market needs. Due to the explicit tendency to operate in international markets, the main market of reference would be Europe. The mode of strategic behaviour could permit a significant number of firms to reach competitive positions of *'best follower'* within the specific section selected, even though possessing restricted dimensions in absolute terms.

2) *the centrality of techno-productive competencies.* A relevant contribution to developing competence in techno-productive areas may be offered by close links with suppliers of raw materials and plants in order to modernise the productive process and reduce costs with a gradual improvement of services given.

3) *flexibility in the development of competitive advantage* . A large number of firms are undergoing a phase of transformation; given structural constraints, entrepreneurs must either accept a reduction in their ambitions or else try to imitate their performance in another market niche using the competitive model used hitherto.

Concluding Remarks

The analysis of theoretical approaches reveals the importance of finding a balance of resources and competencies in order to reach common ends towards the management of discontinuity. However, this awareness is not sufficient for setting up inter-firm processes. Indeed firms, apart from (consciously) tending towards co-operation, must also have the capacity to *'identify the existing opportunities in the environment'*.

Abandoning the constraints and the risks attached to the dependence on the local market is a necessary path to be followed; it is based on the transformation from a logic of the 'natural niche' to a logic of the 'desired niche'. This is a critical transformation which is open to local firms that possess specialised productive knowledge and competencies, acquired by evaluating their local orientation so that they use it as a distinguishing factor which can withstand the international market.

In order to reach these objectives, the evolved system areas should maintain a configuration centred on an atmosphere of trust and cohesion, identify themselves as open systems, guarantee an elevated economic autonomy of the participants; and develop non-random network relations.

In order to appreciate the real diversity of the strategic/organisational planning which characterises the firms involved in aggregation processes compared with that of the firms investigated, it is necessary to compare the attributes described with similar results from several of the most significant pieces of research. The latter feature two principal models of local aggregation to which different behaviour profiles of small firms correspond:

1) local systems which reveal aggregative forms that can be classified under the constellation model; within these, a more or less limited number of small and medium-sized firms converge which, *'while they divide the work, operate with substantial relationships of reciprocal inter-dependence in order to achieve a complex or final product'*.

2) local systems where the small firm assumes a role of fundamental importance. Such contexts normally express both vertical and horizontal aggregations and, due to *'the shared basic strategic orientation*, are characterised by the prevalence of forms of joint entrepreneurship.

The local firms examined express an incomplete competitive physionomy, fed by an unsatisfactorily complete range of competencies, sustained by a modest use of financial resources to create productive and commercial structures.

The situation described has enabled the formulation of entrepreneurial formulae which can adapt but not develop in the absence of aggregative processes. The international competitive arena tends rather to select entrepreneurs who have the ability to manage several functional areas and who know how to identify niches in which it is possible to be competitive even at restricted dimensional levels.

Taking the overall picture, certain concluding considerations emerge that can be summarised in three steps:

1) *A 'universal' role* . Individual small local industrial firms can play a role at an international level. To achieve these results, entrepreneurs should seek to avoid pursuing two paths which are both dangerous: those of *dwarfism* and *macrosomia* . The first suggests keeping the firm the same as in its initial levels for product/market combinations and the human resources involved. The second suggests setting up strategies of rapid dimensional growth without properly weighing up the risks and the transformations. In order to avoid both these paths, several lines of entrepreneurial conduct must be followed: evaluation of the potential evolutionary dynamics in the relevant market; identification of an appropriate dimensional threshold; increase of the firm's dimensions and definition of a collaborative inter-company strategy.

2) *The decisional process as a vector of selective development* . In many of the firms analysed, there are no explicit or conscious processes of strategic management, but there do not seem to be structural obstacles to the diffusion of such processes which must contribute to differentiating the pool of competencies and spreading the *'consciousness'* of the problems to be faced.

c) *The new forms of localism* . The phenomena displayed illustrate the transformation of *localised* firms to *grafted* firms in the productive, institutional and socio-cultural context. From this it is possible to hypothesise:

    a) the existence of a *variety* of company localisms due to the differing intensity of factors which determine it

    b) a *variability* in the forms of localism of the firms caused by the dynamism of factors with which they come into contact over the years

All this, however, should preserve unaltered the typical capacities of small entrepreneurship in order not to risk *creative sclerosis*. Based on this conviction, it appears necessary to carry out further research in other sectors into the issues related to entrepreneurial behaviour which emerge in the strategic processes of development, especially given the strong need for new instruments to analyse the different parameters which are still too restricted by pre-formulated evaluative schemes.

References

Acs Z. and Audretsch D. (1989) *Job creation and firm size in the US and West Germany,* International Small Business Journal, no. 7.

Aldrich H. and Whetten D.A. (1981) *Organization-sets, action-sets and networks: making the most of semplicity,* in Nystrom P.C., Starbuch W.H. (eds.), Handbook of organization design, Oxford University Press, Oxford.

Aldrich H. and Zimmer C. (1986) *Entrepreneurship through social network,* in Sexton D. and Smiler R. (eds.), The art and science of entrepreneurship, Ballinger, NY.

Arrow K. (1983) *Innovation in large and small firms,* in Ronen J. (ed.), Entrepreneurship, Lexington Books, Lexington.

Barnes L.B. and Hershon S.A. (1976) *Trasferring power in the family business,* Harvard Business Review, July-August.

Boari, Grandi and Lorenzoni G. (1989) *Le organizzazioni a rete: tre concetti di base,* Economia e Politica industriale, n. 64.

Bolton J.E. (1971) *Small firms: report of the commission of inquiry on small firms,* HMSO, London.

Brockhaus R.H. (1987) *Entrepreneurial research: are we playing the correct game?*, American Journal of Small Business, Winter.

Chandler A.D. jr. (1962) *Strategy and structure: chapter in the history of the american industrial enterprise*, The MIT Press, Cambridge, Massachussetts, USA.

Churchhill N.C. and Lewis V.L. (1983) *The five stages of small business growth*, Harvard Business Review, n. 3, May-June.

Cohen W.N. and Levinthal D.A. (1990) *The absorptive capacity: a new perspective on learning and innovation*, Administrative Science Quarterly, vol. 35.

Cole A.H. (1959) *Business enterprise in its social setting*, Harvard University Press, Cambridge.

Cooper A.C. and Dunkelberh W.C. (1987) *Entrpreneurial research: old questions, new answer and methodological issues*, American Journal of Small Business, Winter.

Curran J. and Stanworth J. (1984) *Small business research in Britain*, in Levicki C., *Small business: theory and policy*, Croom Helm, Beckenham.

Dubini P. (1994) *The Italian SMES: structural features. Dominant strategies and typical problems*, Economia Aziendale, vol. XIII, 3.

Eisenhardt K.M. and Schoonhoven C.B. (1996) *Resource-based view of strategic alliance formation: Strategic and social effects in entrepreneurial firms*, Organization Science, vo. 7, no. 2, March-April.

Fletcher D. (1994) *Small firm's strategic alliances and value adding networks- A critical review*, Small Business, 2.

Gartner W.B. (1989) W*ho is an entrepreneur? Is the wrong question, entrepreneurship*, Entrepreneurship Theory and Practice, summer.

Gomez L. and Casseres B. (1994) *Group versus group: how alliance network compete*, Harvard Business Review, July-August.

Greiner L.E. (1972) *Evolution and revolution as organization grow*, Harvard Business Review, July-August.

Hannan M. and Freeman J. (1992) *The ecology of organizational founding: American labour unions: 1836,1985*, American Journal of Sociology, 92.

Herron L.A. and Robinson R.B. (1993) *A structural model of the effect of entrepreneurial characteristics on venture performance*, Journal of Business Venturing, no. 8.

Hoselitz B.F. (1951) *The early history of entrepreneurial theory*, Exploration, Spring.

Itami H. (1987) *Mobilizing invisible assets*, Harvard University Press, Boston.

Johnston R. and Lawrence P. (1988) *Beyond vertical integration. The rise of the value adding partnership*, Harvard Business Review, no. 69, July-August.

Kets De Vries M.F.R. (1977) *The entrepreneurial personality: a Parson at the Crossroads*, The Journal of Management Studies, February.

Kroegher V.C. (1974) *Managerial development in the small firm*, California Management Review.

Larson A. (1992) *Network dyads in entrepreneurial settings: a study of the governance of exchange relationship*, Administrative Science Quarterly, 37.

Lipparini A. and Lorenzoni G. (1996) *Le organizzazioni ad alta intensità relazionale*, L'Industria, n. 4.

Lorenzoni G. and Balden Fuller C. (1995) *Creating a strategic center to manage a web of partners*, California Management Review, (37) 3.

McClelland D.C. (1961) *The achieving society*, Van Nostrand, Princeton, N.J.

Moss S. and Kanter R. (1983) *The change masters, innovation and entrepreneurship in the American corporation*, Simon & Shuster, New York.

Nonaka I. (1994) *A dynamic theory of organizational knowledge creation*, Organization Science, 3 (1).

Normann R. and Ramirez R. (1993) *From value chain to value constellation: designing interactive strategy*, Harvard Business Review, July-August.

Ouchi W.G. (1981) *Markets, bureaucracies and clans*, Administrative Science Quarterly, vol. 25.

Pavitt S. (1984) *Sectoral patterns of technical change: towards a taxonomy and theory*, Research Policy, Vol. 13.

Penrose E.T. (1959) *The theory of the growth of the firms*, Blackwell & Mott, Oxford.

Pfeffer J. and Salancick G.R. (1978) *The external control of organizations: a resource dependence perspective*, Harper & Row, New York.

Prahalad C.K. and Hamel G. (1990) *The core competence of the corporation*, Harvard Business Review, May-June.

Redlich F. (1957) *Theory of the risk*, Exploration, vol. 10, no. 1, October.

Richardson G.B. (1972) *The organization of industry*, The Economic Journal, September.

Rumelt R. (1995) *Inertia and transformation*, in MONTGOMERY C.A. (ed.), Resource-based and evolutionary theories of the firm: Towards a synthesis, Kluwer Academic Publishers.

Scase R. and Goffe R. (1980) *The real world of the small business owner*, Cross Helm, London.

Scott M. and Bruce R. (1987) *Five stages of growth in small business*, Long Range Planning , no. 3.

Smith N.R. and Miner J.B. (1983) *Type of firm and managerial motivation: implications for organizational life cycle theory*, Strategic Management Journal.

Stampacchia P. (1993) *Caratteristiche innovative dei processi di globalizzazione*, Proceedings of Conference "L'Azienda di fronte ai processi di internazionalizzazione', Clueb.

Stanworth J.K. and Curran J. (1976) *Growth and small firm. An alternative view*, The Journal of Management Studies, May.

Steinmetz L. (1969) *Critical stages of small business growth: when they occur and how to survive them*, Business Horizon, February.

Watson T.J. (1995) *Entrepreneurship and professional management: a fatal distinction*, International Small Business Journal, no. 13, 2.

Williamson O.E. (1979) *Transaction-cost economics: the governance of contractual relations*, Journal of Law and Economics, vol. 2, April.

Williamson O.E. (1985) *The economics institutions of capitalism: Firms, markets and relational contracting*, Free Press, N.Y.

Zappa G. (1957) *Le produzioni nell'economia delle imprese*, Giuffrè, Milano.

11 The Impact of Size, Industry, and Nation on Internationalisation in Small and Medium-Sized Enterprises

Håkan Boter and Carin Holmquist

Background

Internationalisation is an issue that has come increasingly into focus during the last decades. The processes and effects of internationalisation patterns in large companies are frequently discussed. Today we have a variety of theories and reports on practical experience from this field. To mention but a few we here point to different theories on internationalisation as a gradual process moving over various stages of development (Vernon, 1966; Johanson and Vahlne, 1977), on internationalisation as a strategy process (Welsch and Luostarinen, 1988) or to the process school with a concentration on diversified multinational corporations, balancing between global integration, and local responsiveness (Stopford and Wells, 1972; Bartlett and Ghosal, 1991). Another field closely linked to that of internationalisation is macro-oriented studies that show the effects of the ongoing internationalisation process on competition (Porter, 1990).

In this study the structural aspects of company, such as size, industry, and nation will be analysed in relation to internationalisation in small companies. Ever since Chandler's work (1962) the dualistic relation between structural dimensions and company strategy has been a common approach in studies of strategic management (Miller and Friesen, 1980; Miller, 1987; Mintzberg, 1989). There is a substantial amount of literature in the contingency theory tradition where organisations as open systems must be designed to handle their environments (Lawrence and Lorsch, 1967). In the field of internationalisation this tradition has primarily focused on structural aspects of organisation and in the development and content of management routines in international settings (Stopford and Wells, 1972; Hedlund, 1986; Bartlett and Ghoshal, 1989).

There are only a few studies of the internationalisation process in small and medium-sized enterprises (SMEs). The studies performed have built on knowledge gained in studies of large companies. Some of the approaches mentioned above are also applied to SMEs. While studies of large companies generally seem to be of an investigative nature, that is, seeking explanations for de facto developments, studies of SMEs just as often have a prescriptive ambition that implies the necessity for this type of company to grow. Within the area of SME studies as a whole, the studies of internationalisation processes are often very quantitative (Kirpalani and MacIntosh, 1980; Erramilli, 1991). There are however exceptions to this rule (Kaynak and Kothari, 1984; Roth, 1992). Typical for most studies in this field is their focus on how to become efficient in an international market or what factors are important for success on foreign markets. As a parallel we note that several early studies of a new phenomenon take this comparative stance, as for example those of Woodward (1961).

Previous research has also shown that there are obvious differences between companies of different sizes (Boswell 1972). In this project we have chosen companies with up to 499 employees as representing SMEs and companies with 500 employees or more as large. In the following we will discuss size as a variable more in detail; here we only indicate that there are strong differences between a company with 20,000 employees and a company with 400 or 10 employees. In the long-standing debate on how to measure size of SMEs, most often 200 or 500 employees is used as an upper limit. If we compare the 20,000 and the 10 employee situation it is clear that internationalisation processes will differ from a company viewpoint, i.e. from a strategic viewpoint. These differences are mostly rooted in the resource base of the company in question. At the same time it can be assumed that many features are similar in the large and the small company: internationalisation always implies the commitment and involvement of an individual as a seller or a buyer. We conclude that we may apply the knowledge gained from studies of internationalisation processes in large companies also on SMEs, but with caution. For instance, we need to learn more concerning the initial stages for a company, information which is difficult to find in large companies, except in historical records. The focus on the individual actor is also clearer in SMEs than in large companies.

The Research Question

The aim of this paper is to discuss the theoretical foundations for arguing for the importance of company size, industrial categories, and national origin, when studying internationalisation in SMEs. It also analyses empirical findings concerning the importance of these factors. We will show that there are obvious linkages between the three.

Below it will become clear that there is only slight consistency in research into the effects of important factors on internationalisation processes in companies. There are many approaches with which to operationalise internationalisation, to define small firms, and to design the methodology in the research. Earlier empirical studies in the field of internationalisation processes have their weaknesses: they have been undertaken at one specific time and only involve one region or one nation. Some studies have given rise to replication studies building on the same assumptions as the original study. To replicate an empirical study in terms of the operationalisation of key concepts and other methodological choices is most often an insurmountable task (Kaynak and Kothari, 1984).

This study is conducted within the frame of a comprehensive research project, Interstratos,[1] where research groups from eight European countries during five years (1991 to 1995) study internationalisation in small and medium-sized companies (up to 499 employees). The underlying model for the Interstratos project is that environment affects strategic behaviour, which in turn affects performance, which in turn affects strategic behaviour - all concepts relating to internationalisation. The model is dynamic in that we explicitly study changes in these concepts over the 5-year period. Building on this general model we have selected the following exogenous variables:

- Manager Characteristics (nationality, age, sex, education, experience, use of information)
- Manager Values and Attitudes
- Firm and Structure (industry, region, size, ownership, legal status, degree of independence, type of production)
- Contextual Constraints (changes in competitive conditions, market factors, constraints and inducements for international operations)

As for the endogenous variables of the model, the following represent the dependent ones:

- Corporate Strategy (product, market, and geographic scope, key success factors)
- Business Strategy (export orientation, degree of co-operation).

---

[1]   The international research group known as INTERSTRATOS is composed of: J. Hanns Pichler, Erwin Frölich, and Peter Voithofer (Austria), Rik Donckels and Ria Arts (Belgium), Graham Hall (Great Britain), Antti Haahti and Petri Ahokangas (Finland), Koos van Dijken and Harold Gankema (The Netherlands), Per-Anders Havnes, Arild Saether, and Johanne Sletten (Norway), Håkan Boter and Carin Holmquist (Sweden), Hans Pleitner and Margrit Habersaat (Switzerland).

In this paper we focus on some components of this model to analyse the relations between internationalisation and structural factors as size, industry, and nation.[2] The dependent and endogenous variables are represented by indicators of business performance, for example turnover and export figures. The factors used for stratification of the material are size, industry, and nation. These variables are all viewed as exogenous in the research model, i.e. they are treated as being outside the realm of direct company intervention - at least in the short run. In virtually all SME literature the factors size, industry, and region are considered to be of major importance for SME behaviour; internationalisation issues are no different. The research mission for this paper is to analyse the importance of size, industry, and nation for the internationalisation behaviour in SMEs for a specific year, using the Interstratos database. Before presenting the empirical evidence of the influence of the three variables we will discuss the theoretical arguments for why these factors should, at least hypothetically, be considered relevant.

The following discussion may give the impression that there are three independent factors (size, industry, and nation). This is of course not the case, even if we need to separate the factors for analytical purposes. In reality they are strongly related. We know that there is a clear connection between size and industry, that some industries consist of smaller companies than do other. We also know that different countries have a different mix of industries and company sizes. In this study we control for this through stratification of the material.

Determinants of Internationalisation Behaviour

Company Size

Company size obviously determines SME behaviour - to say the least. If we should not consider size to be important there would be no argument for studying SMEs as a special group differing from large companies. In studies of SMEs we find that the arguments for size as a vital factor are instead overwhelming. Arguments often given for a further differentiation within the category small firms state that one cannot compare a microcompany with only a few employees to companies with 200 employees. The theoretical argument for size as an explanatory factor is that the number of employees (the most usual indicator of size), as well as the level of turnover, capital, and investments, normally gives a distinct behaviour. For example, the market position in terms of market share is directly correlated to size of turnover. The most typical effect of size is found when the focus is on organisational issues. A company with 5 employees functions in organisational terms as a small group, and often we find SMEs that consist of solely one family. The company with 20 employees functions in a more indirect manner, but there is still eye to eye contact. The business strategy is formed differently in companies of different sizes.

Small firm characteristics are often related to limited managerial, financial, and physical resources. A number of studies have shown that an increase in company size also results in a relatively stronger resource base. Some studies also suggest that there are critical points, or transition stages, when a pure entrepreneurial mode change toward more professional management styles (Smith and Miner, 1983; Boswell, 1972). Market size is also connected to company size: a concentration to a geographic area close to the company is the normal situation. When - and if - more distant markets are penetrated, this will be a successive and cautious process (Culpan, 1989).

Results from empirical studies concerning the direct relationship between company size and export intensity are mixed. For example, Bilkey and Tesar (1977) and Czinkota and Johnston (1983) found no such distinct relation while Calof (1993) found a negative association between company size and international sales intensity. Likewise, Kirpalani and MacIntosh (1980) showed

---

[2]   Later in this paper we will add other factors: manager characteristics (education, experience) and firm/ structure (ownership, degree of independence, and cooperation).

that company size has no significant association with export success. According to them, every firm has the same potential for international activities regardless of size.

In contrast to the above Mugler and Miesenbock (1986), Christensen et al. (1987), and Baird et al. (1994) offered evidence for a strong relation between company size and export behaviour. Cavusgil (1984) found that company size is only vaguely related to export activity (company size was a significant factor only for the very small firms) and proposed that firm size must be viewed as a concomitant variable instead of a causative variable. The arguments given for this are that growing company size normally implies a stronger position in terms of physical, administrative, managerial, and market resources. These resources create an advantage for the company when active in international business.

A number of studies have investigated the relationship between company size and attitudes to internationalisation. For example, Ali and Schwiercz (1991) found that the managers of small and medium-sized companies have the same type of attitudes toward exporting. However, the same study, and also Reid (1985), found that the management's attitudes to methods and techniques for exporting are more reserved. The managers of these small companies have a great respect for cultural differences.

Industry

The term industry is frequently used to classify individual companies with a set of common characteristics, related to types of products, production technology, or market attributes. These industries are normally analysed on a rather aggregated level, such as the competitive advantage of nations, including industrial strategies for specific business sectors (Spender, 1989; Porter, 1990). The approach underlines the importance of linking the analysis of the company to the specific sector to which it belongs (Child, 1988). There are also studies that certify that most industrial sectors are nowadays exposed to international competition. Porter (1990) showed that industries nevertheless differ in their ability to create a competitive edge on an international market scene. Industry is something that is not changed easily; from the company's point of view it is something only successively amenable to change. On the internationalisation arena industry sets the rules of the game for the company.

Some industries, such as food production, have a more local touch while others, like electronics, have a more global outlook (Morrison and Roth, 1992). The industry is defined by its markets and its core technology and this determines the internationalisation processes. A concentration on business sectors is found in studies that focus R&D activities and the use of 'high tech' applications. These companies normally have an intensive international network which enable exchange of technological information in a fast-changing sector of the economy. Often 'high tech' companies are small (Klofsten, 1992; Lindqvist, 1991). Finally we have the network theories that focus on industrial systems and the structure and operations within such systems. Small firms are frequently involved in industrial systems with actors from a number of industries or as one member in a co-operating network of small firms only (Johanson and Mattsson, 1988; Sharma, 1991).

The core technology determines the general behaviour of a company since it functions as the knowledge base of the company. High-tech companies depend on the free exchange of new knowledge across borders, i.e. they are dependent on a rapid internationalisation process. Core technology also determines more organisational conditions, such as the level of competence in the company - the professional aspect of the organisation. Furthermore it determines the workflow in the company: the use of routine or preorder production. The markets of an industry also determine organisational conditions. Markets may be local or global, consumer or industrial oriented, etc. The type of market normally follows the industry and hence internationalisation processes are formed by this.

Cavusgil (1984) found that variation in export activity can be related to a number of organisational and management characteristics. For instance, market development and the technological orientation of the firm are clearly related to export. The technological level of the firm can be used as a screening tool when identifying high exporting companies. Baird et al. (1994) sought patterns of international strategies differentiating small firms active in various industries. A number of strategy issues were compared for companies from several industries, both manufacturing and service firms; the results indicated that internationally active companies are larger and belong to manufacturing.

Nation

Region is often considered as an important factor in studies of SME behaviour. Region is viewed as a background factor that hinders or fosters the growth and successful behaviour of SMEs. We find regions that are more SME friendly in all countries, and this discussion has been widened to a comparison between countries. Region - or nation - is used in that context as a proxy for cultural factors. There is ample evidence of differences in business behaviour between countries and between regions. Thus a company is affected not only by its size and the industry it belongs to but also by the conditions that form the climate of the nation or region (Hofstede, 1980; Bartlett and Ghoshal, 1989; Calori and de Woot, 1994).

The impact of nation is also seen in organisational matters. The forming of strategies is heavily dependent upon the values that are held within the company. These values are in turn connected to the value system - or culture - held within the community at large (Deal and Kennedy, 1982; Frost et al., 1985). Nation is also a factor to be considered on a more direct level, since the infrastructure and the legal system may differ between countries.

Cross-country studies involve methodological difficulties due to cultural and institutional differences. Studies across countries are nonetheless valuable because in the long run they make it possible to develop specific company strategies suitable for different markets or nations. Only a few of these studies have compared the internationalisation process for companies in various countries or regions. Some studies compare Canadian and US small firms (Kaynak and Kothari, 1984; Kirpalani and MacIntosh, 1980) and there are also comparative studies between the UK and Canada (Rosson and Ford, 1982; Beamish et al., 1993). Even if there are cross-national similarities in business environments, within countries with comparable economies and industrial infrastructure, there are a number of cultural and infrastructural differences. Understanding and managing differences may be the key to increasing the competitive competence for the individual company (Meyerson and Martin, 1987).

A large number of empirical studies refer to the process school of multinational corporations. Managerial issues in international business are focused. In this field global integration versus local responsiveness perspective is emphasised (Bartlett and Ghoshal, 1989; Doz, 1986). Accordingly, the forces linked to technology, scale factors, knowledge management, etc. enforce the globalisation of markets. This often gives rise to a counterpower, local responsiveness, represented by the need for small scale operations in R&D, other entrepreneurial activities, and a necessary sensitivity for customer preferences. The organisational answer to balance the contradictory forces in this complex situation in the large MNCs is to build a transnational organisation (Bartlett and Ghoshal, 1989) or heterarchy (Hedlund, 1986).

Summing up, we conclude that company size is an important factor to be considered in studies of internationalisation processes since it reflects aspects of the market and the resource base of the company, as well as of organisation. Industry characteristics are important since they reflect technological base. Finally, national belonging is important since it reflects the cultural base for internationalisation. After this discussion of the rationale for using size, industry, and nation as explanatory factors for internationalisation processes we will discuss indicators of internationalisation.

Method

The Sample

The main purpose of the Interstratos study is to analyse the internationalisation process in small firms in Europe. The project is designed so that participating researchers from each country - Austria, Belgium, the Netherlands, Switzerland, Great Britain, Sweden, Finland, and Norway - independently collect and analyse data from the jointly designed questionnaire. The population is small and medium-sized manufacturing firms in five size classes, 1-9, 10-19, 20-49, 50-99, and 100-499 employees, engaged in textiles and clothing, electronics, food and drink, furniture making, and mechanical engineering. The population was accessed through sampling frames (for each nation) consisting of individual firms as sampling units listed in national statistical bureaus or other similar sources where available. The sampling procedure was random sampling stratified by industry and size class with a minimum quota for each cell. The quotas for each cell call for 20 observations per year over a period of five years. To achieve this, the original samples have to be large enough to account for the possible loss of panel members.

Material from seven countries (Great Britain excluded) for the year 1993, was chosen as the empirical base for this study. The total material from 1993 comprises 4,394 companies distributed over five size classes, five industries, and seven countries, as shown in Table 11.1 below.

Table 11.1   The Original Database

Company size	No of cases	%	Industry	No of cases	%	Nation	No of cases	%
1- 9	1,373	32	Textile	727	17	Austria	1,139	26
10- 19	869	20	Electronics	659	16	Belgium	315	7
20- 49	956	22	Food/drink	806	19	Netherlands	1,026	23
50- 99	572	13	Furniture	826	19	Switzerland	434	10
100-499	534	13	Mech. engineering	1,245	29	Norway	349	8
						Sweden	842	19
						Finland	289	7
Total	4,394	100		4,263	100		4,304	100

As can be observed the companies have an uneven distribution over the three main factors for classification. For example: A majority of the companies have less than 20 employees; 29% are mechanical engineering companies but only 16% electronics; 26% of the studied companies come from Austria compared to only 7% from Finland.

The distribution between countries was the most uneven dimension, but also size and industry showed uneven distributions. The criteria for the original sampling was taken as the basis for reorganising the material. At first we considered using weights to compensate for the uneven distributions. But given the large number of cases we also considered random sampling from our original database. We chose sampling,[3] and with the purpose to get a database with an approximate even distribution the companies were stratified by size, industry and nation. Five company size classes and five industries imply 25 possible cells and for each country the same number of companies were selected from each cell (strata). A random sampling of 11 companies from each strata would have resulted in 1,925 companies, a limited number of companies in some groups gave a final database for analysis of 1,758 cases, as shown in Table 11.2 below.

Table 11.2   The Final Database

Company size	No of cases	%	Industry	No of cases	%	Nation	No of cases	%
1- 9	375	21	Textile	353	20	Austria	263	15
10- 19	370	21	Electronics	313	18	Belgium	219	12
20- 49	373	21	Food/drink	368	21	Netherlands	268	15
50- 99	328	19	Furniture	341	19	Switzerland	266	15
100-499	312	18	Mech. engineering	383	22	Norway	242	14
						Sweden	275	16
						Finland	225	13
Total	1,758	100		1,758	100		1,758	100

Measures

Internationalisation is a concept widely used but seldom precisely operationalised. The concept relies mainly on the image of contacts that pass borders between countries. Most often we associate the concept with export, with sales agencies abroad, or manufacturing abroad. Less often the concept is associated with import, immigrant entrepreneurs, and foreign owned units. This is peculiar since, of course, on a global basis all export is also import.

The Interstratos study includes a number of indicators of internationalisation. For this paper we have chosen three types of indicators. The first type consists of quantitative measures such as turnover, export, and export quota. This type of variables is used in a number of studies in order to measure export activity (Tookey, 1964; Bilkey and Tesar, 1977; Czinkota and Johnston, 1983; Cavusgil, 1984; Beamish et al., 1993). The second type classifies the companies as exporters or importers and to what extent these have made investments in distribution and/or manufacturing units abroad. These measures can be compared to classical findings within the area of foreign direct investments (Vernon, 1966) and the process model of internationalisation (Johanson and Vahlne, 1977; Bilkey and Tesar, 1977).

Empirical Findings

The analysis of the empirical data starts with the importance of company size, industry, and national belonging. In a second step the combined influence of the three factors and the measures with regard to internationalisation are studied. In a third step the logistic regression analysis technique is used for further testing. The main conclusions are discussed in a separate section.

---

[3]   By doing this we reduce the number of cases (1,758 instead of 4,394). Given the size of the sampling, this is not a big problem, given that the characteristics of our final database are close to that of the total one (Haahti (ed) forthcoming).

Influence of Size, Industry, and Nation

Company Size. The number of employees is very clearly related to average turnover. These two factors are common measures of company size and the correlation in this material is 0.87. The smallest companies' sales are about 400,000 ECU compared to almost 19 millions for firms with 100 employees or more. The correlation between export sales and company size is 0.62.[4] When studying the export quota, we find that the largest companies sell almost 50% of the turnover on international markets; for the smallest firms this part is approximately 25%.

Table 11.3   Size: Turnover/Exports/Export Quota

Company size	Average turnover 1000 ECU	Average exports 1000 ECU	Average export quota %
1- 9 employees	396	141	26
10- 19 -"-	1,129	386	30
20- 49 -"-	2,758	1,129	36
50- 99 -"-	5,864	2,394	37
100-499 -"-	18,449	8,433	44
Total	5,454	3,139	36
Number of companies	1,339	832	824

On average 75% of the companies have export sales and the relation to size is evident. Slightly more than half of the group with under 10 employees have export activities, compared to 9 out of 10 among companies with 100 employees or more. Import is more common than export sales: over 90% have some degree of import. Even if there is a positive correlation between import and company size the spread between small and large companies is relatively small, with 80% of the smallest firms buying from a foreign country.

Table 11.4   Size: Percentage of Exporters, Importers and Companies with Subsidiaries Abroad for Distribution and Manufacturing

Company size	Exporter to some extent	Importer to some extent	Distribution units abroad	Manufacturing units abroad
1- 9 employees	55	81	5	3
10- 19 -"-	74	92	10	5
20- 49 -"-	79	92	17	8
50- 99 -"-	87	94	26	11
100-499 -"-	93	96	40	21
Total	77	91	19	10
Number of companies	1,663	1,675	1,604	1,608
p-value	0.000	0.000	0.000	0.000

Approximately one company out of five has a subsidiary abroad for distribution purposes, i.e. market, sales, trading, or transport units. The correlation to company size is pronounced here.

---

[4]   The figures for export and export quota only include companies that sell part of the turnover on foreign markets. If companies with no export were included in the calculations, the figures showing average export would be on a lower level. For instance, if the Swedish material included the companies with zero export sales the average export quota would be 20%. Other studies (Christensen et al., 1989; NUTEK, 1993) confirm this figure which can be compared to the 33% reported in this paper.

40% of the largest companies have foreign distribution units compared to only 5% in the smallest size group. To have manufacturing units abroad is less usual: one out of every 10 companies has access to such resources. Only 3% of companies with 1-9 employees and 21% of the largest size group have manufacturing units abroad.

Industry. The five industries have different average levels of turnover. The food/drink and mechanical engineering companies report the highest turnover figures. Furniture is the industry with the lowest turnover; the level is just above 50% of the average turnover for the food and drink industry. The textile and electronics industries also have low turnover. Export shows the same pattern as turnover, i.e. food/drink and mechanical engineering the highest and furniture the lowest averages. The differences are however larger in export: mechanical engineering has more than double average export sales compared to furniture making.

An analysis of the export quota (as per cent of the turnover) breaks the pattern discussed above. The textile industry has an export quota of 42% and the electronics companies are on the same level. The export as part of turnover is approximately 30% for food and drink firms with the furniture industry a little bit lower.

Table 11.5   Industry: Turnover/Exports/Export Quota

Industry	Average turnover ECU	Average exports ECU	Average export quota %
Textile	4,937	2,815	42
Electronics	5,002	3,225	40
Food and drink	6,321	1,922	30
Furniture	4,699	4,210	28
Mechanical engineering	6,370	3,139	38
Total	5,454	832	36
Number of companies	1,339		824

Above we found that 77% of the companies in this study are exporters. An analysis of data covering the five industries shows that food and drink companies are exporters to a much lower degree, only 58%. The share of the furniture making companies with export activities is also lower than average (74%), and the remaining three industries all have over 80% exporters. The most internationalised industry, measured in these terms, is electronics with 87% exporters.

We have previously noted that the percentage of importers is higher than exporters. The industries with the highest shares are the same as for exporting companies: 99% of the electronics companies are importers. The textile and the mechanical engineering firms have an average share of over 90%. The food and drink companies have the lowest percentage of importing firms, 82%.

Table 11.6   Industry: Percentage of Exporters, Importers, and Companies with Subsidiaries Abroad for Distribution and Manufacturing

Industry	Exporter to some extent	Importer to some extent	Distribution units abroad	Manufacturing units abroad
Textile	83	93	20	14
Electronics	87	99	26	10
Food and drink	58	82	16	7
Furniture	74	89	13	5
Mechanical engineering	84	93	21	10
Total	77	91	19	10
Number of companies	1,663	1,675	1,604	1,608
p-value	0.000	0.000	0.000	0.002

More than 25% of the electronics companies have own subsidiaries abroad for distribution purposes. This type of investment is least common in the furniture companies, surprisingly to an even lower extent than firms in the food and drink industry, 13% and 16% respectively. Foreign manufacturing units are most common in the textile industry (14%), followed by the electronics and the mechanical engineering companies (10%).

Nation. The average turnover is 5.5 million ECU. While the business volume for companies in the Netherlands is substantially lower, around 3.5 million, Swiss firms exhibit the highest average sales value. In the study exporting companies were asked to declare the amount of foreign sales. For companies with foreign sales, the average export figure is 3.1 million ECU. Austria, Belgium and Switzerland have the highest figures. Companies in the Netherlands are on a low level. The export in per cent of turnover averages 36% with Austria and Belgium over 40% and the Netherlands and Sweden lowest with only 32% and 33% respectively.

Table 11.7   Nation: Turnover/Exports/Export Quota

Nation	Average turnover ECU	Average exports ECU	Average export quota %
Austria	5,910	4,298	42
Belgium	6,691	4,173	43
Netherlands	3,456	1,858	32
Switzerland	7,290	4,101	39
Norway	5,005	2,509	34
Sweden	5,595	2,989	33
Finland	4,716	2,269	34
Total	5,454	3,139	36
Number of companies	1,339	832	824

Belgium has the highest percentage of companies with some export activity. Over average are also Finland and Sweden. Austrian companies show a much lower level (69%). Swedish firms appear also to be very intensive importers (97%).

Dutch companies have the highest degree of foreign investments in terms of units for sales and distribution purposes, 25%. Swiss and Swedish firms are also above average, 23% and 21% respectively. As we saw above nearly 90% of the Belgian companies are exporters. This situation is however not reflected in the figures for investments in foreign units for distribution or manufacturing. In Belgium 16% have made such investments for distribution; for manufacturing purposes the share is only 6%. Switzerland has the highest percentage of foreign manufacturing units (16%) and is followed by Sweden (12%).

Table 11.8   **Nation: Percentage of Exporters, Importers, and Companies with Subsidiaries Abroad for Distribution and Manufacturing**

Nation	Exporter to some extent	Importer to some extent	Distribution units abroad	Manufacturing units abroad
Austria	69	90	18	6
Belgium	87	93	16	6
Netherlands	74	84	25	10
Switzerland	76	94	23	16
Norway	74	92	13	5
Sweden	81	97	21	12
Finland	82	87	18	10
Total	77	91	19	10
Number of companies	1,663	1,675	1,604	1,608
p-value	0.000	0.000	0.017	0.001

The main conclusion this far is that company size correlates to internationalisation activities. In the smallest company group the export quota, calculated for all companies with foreign sales, is 26%. Among the largest companies this figure is nearly double. For the 77% exporters, there is a wider distribution between small and large companies compared to that for the 91% with some import activity. Investments in units abroad for distribution purposes amount to almost 20% and for manufacturing units to 10%. Of those, 5% of the smallest companies, compared to 39% of the largest, have invested in own facilities abroad for distribution.

Looking at industry, we find that furniture is less international than the other four: the average export figure is much lower, the export quota is about 10% lower, the foreign investment level is relatively low, and finally the manager spends shorter periods abroad. The food and drink industry also seems to be domestically oriented with its export quota of 30% (compared to average 36%) and, 42% of its companies with no export activities at all. These companies also have the lowest percentage of import of all five industries. The textile, the electronics, and the mechanical engineering industries are more international in terms of international trade and investments. Textile companies have the highest export quota, 42%, and they have more intensively invested in foreign units for manufacturing. The high internationalisation level of electronics companies can be observed in its highest share of companies engaged in export and import activities (87% and 99% respectively). Another trait of the electronics companies is that 26% have own distribution units abroad (average percentage is 19). The mechanical engineering companies show no extraordinary characteristics, but do in general exhibit a high level of international activities.

Looking then at nation, Austrian and Belgian companies have the highest, and Dutch and Swedish the lowest, export quota. However, this pattern is not consistent throughout the material. For example, the share of the Austrian companies engaged in export sales is 69%, the lowest among the seven countries. Belgian companies, on the other hand, have the highest percentage followed by the Finnish and Swedish. Swedish companies exhibit an extraordinary high percentage of companies that have some import trade, 97% (against an average of 91%). The Dutch companies have with the lowest export quota but the most developed foreign investments for distribution (25%) followed by Swiss and Swedish firms. Companies in Switzerland also invest relatively extensively in production units abroad.

The Combined Influence of Size, Industry, and Nation

As has been underlined in earlier studies, there are obvious links between size, industry, and nation. In this section we discuss the combined effects that these key factors have on internationalisation. In a univariate analysis export quota as the dependent variable is matched against the three exogenous variables. That export quota is among the most frequently used measures for studying internationalisation is discussed earlier in this paper. Finally, we present a multivariate analysis that uses a set of independent variables to explain internationalisation behaviour in small companies.

An analysis focusing company size (see Table 11.9 below) indicates that percentage of foreign sales for the five industries is relatively close to average figures. However, in the largest size group (100-499 employees), furniture, but also food and drink, companies have a much lower export quota compared to average.

Table 11.9   Size/Industry: Export Quota

Company size - empl.	Industry Textile	Electronics	Food/drink	Furniture	Mech. eng.	Total	N
1- 9	28	32	25	20	26	26	79
10- 19	37	30	34	24	29	30	147
20- 49	36	42	22	33	34	36	184
50- 99	43	46	29	29	37	37	197
100-499	53	49	33	29	48	44	217
Total	42	40	30	28	38	36	
N	207	167	81	174	195		824

Table 11.9 also confirms that companies in the textile industry have the highest export quota of all the five industries. Within the textile and the mechanical engineering industries the largest companies sell much more of their turnover abroad and the smallest companies much less compared to average. Among firms in the electronics industry the size group 10-19 employees has a relatively low export degree, even lower than the smallest companies.

As shown in Table 11.10, in the smallest size groups (1-19 employees), companies from Switzerland have a higher degree of export than average figures for this category. Also Norwegian small companies seem to export over average. These two countries, Switzerland and Norway, are also the only countries where the export quota in the very small companies matches the export share in larger companies. Among companies with 50 up to 500 employees the Belgian are exporting more than average.

We find that Belgium and the Netherlands exhibit the most obvious positive correlation between size and export quota: the Belgian companies in the highest size classes are by far the most exporting; the smallest Dutch companies have a very low export quota.

Table 11.10   Size/Nation: Export Quota

Company size - employees	Austria	Belgium	Nether-lands	NATION Switzer-land	Norway	Sweden	Finland	Total	N
1- 9	32	27	19	42	38	22	23	26	79
10- 19	34	34	29	44	27	28	20	30	147
20- 49	49	35	28	39	28	35	39	36	182
50- 99	40	50	33	35	40	28	35	37	196
100-499	44	58	53	40	40	42	42	44	220
Total	42	43	32	39	34	33	34	36	
N	106	139	145	91	102	134	107		824

In Table 11.11 below a cross analysis of industry and nation shows that the export quota for food and drink companies in Sweden and Finland is extremely low. The food and drink industry in these countries is also dominated by the large companies from the co-operative sector. On the other hand Belgian, but also to some degree Dutch, companies in the food and drink sector are considerably over average. This can be explained with the fact that the industrial structure consists of an even distribution of small, medium-sized, and large companies. The products in the food and drink sector are also perishable goods to a large extent and hence transportation over long distances is not possible. This favours densely populated areas such as that of the Benelux countries.

Exports from electronics companies is much lower than average in the Netherlands and above average in Austria and Belgium. In the textile industry especially Swedish but also Norwegian companies have a lower degree of export than companies from the other countries. During the last 25 years the Scandinavian textile industry has been characterised by substantial closedowns of small units and relocation to countries with lower labour costs. The level of export quota in the mechanical engineering industry is rather high, on approximately the same level for all countries. This industry can also be said to represent the backbone of traditional industry, and as such is still important in most of the industrialised world.

Companies from Austria and Belgium have the highest average export quotas. In Austria, however, the percentage of sales abroad is very unevenly distributed between companies from the five industries with textile and electronics over average and food/drink and furniture below. Sweden and Finland have a low export quota in the food and drink industry compared to national averages for these countries. Swedish firms in the mechanical engineering industry have the highest export quota; this pattern seems to be compatible with the engineering tradition in Sweden.

Table 11.11   Industry/Nation: Export Quota

Industry	Austria	Belgium	Nether-lands	Nation Switzer-land	Norway	Sweden	Finland	Total	N
Textile	57	52	43	48	29	25	36	42	207
Electronics	54	52	23	47	49	37	38	40	167
Food/drink	20	46	36	21	24	7	8	30	81
Furniture	24	33	22	24	23	30	35	28	174
Mech eng	38	39	34	34	36	44	36	38	195
Total	42	43	32	39	34	33	34	36	
N	106	139	145	91	102	134	107		824

Multivariate Analysis

The research question discussed in this study is the importance of size, industry, and nation for internationalisation in SMEs. This implies a multivariate situation as well as interdependence between variables. Of the various statistical methods suitable for such situations the logistic regression analysis was considered here (Everitt & Dunn 1991). This technique does not rely on strict assumptions concerning equal variance-covariance matrices and multivariate normality for categories. Another argument is that the logistic regression analysis can better handle nonmetric data for the independent variables (Menard 1995). As discussed above, the concept internationalisation is measured using three types of indicators. Two of these - quantitative measures of export and classification of the companies with regard to having/not having international activities - have also been analysed in a previous section. The multivariate approach initially will be conducted with the three factors size, industry, and nation in focus.

The approach started with bivariate analysis of dependent variables against size, industry, and nation. The logistic regression technique captures the relative importance of the subcategories within the independent variables. In this way it was possible to test and add to earlier traces of patterns in the material.

Table 11.12 below presents results from logistic regression analysis of internationalisation using the independent variable company size. The odds ratio represents the number by which the odds of the 1-value in the dependent variable should be multiplied for every one-unit increase in the independent variable. That is, a value greater than 1 implies that odds for value 1 for the dependent variable increases when the independent variable increases. On the other hand odds ratios below 1 indicate a decrease in odds for the dependent variable when the independent increases. For all three aspects of internationalisation in Table 11.12 company size exhibits significant odds value, thus indicating that increased company size also implies higher level of international activity.

Table 11.12   Size: Measures for Internationalisation, Bivariate Logistic Regression

Measures for internationalisation versus Company Size	Coefficient	p-value	Odds value
Exporting/Not exporting - Company size	.558	.000	1.746
Importing/Not importing - Company size	.430	.000	1.534
Export 1-29%/Export >29% - Company size	.256	.000	1.292

An analysis of subcategories for the three independent variables shows the importance of these subgroups in relation to the dependent variable. One of the subgroups is taken as the point of reference and the odds values are expressed in relation to this group. Overall, we have chosen the first category as the group of reference. Companies with 1-9 employees, belonging to the textile industry, and of Austrian nationality are the respective reference groups for the variables size, industry and nation.

Table 11.13   Size/Industry/Nation: Exporting/Not Exporting Companies, Bivariate and
Multivariate Logistic Regression, Analysis with Subcategories

Variables	BIVARIATE Exporting/Not exporting			MULTIVARIATE Exporting/Not exporting		
	Coefficient	p-value	Odds value	Coefficient	p-value	Odds value
Company size						
1- 9 empl. (Ref group)		.000	1.000		.000	1.000
10- 19 -"-	.842	.000	2.322	.995	.000	2.705
20- 49 -"-	1.137	.000	3.117	1.347	.000	3.846
50- 99 -"-	1.709	.000	5.527	2.065	.000	7.887
100-499 -"-	2.329	.000	10.271	2.707	.000	14.978
Industry						
Textile (Ref group)		.000	1.000		.000	1.000
Electronics	.284	.203	1.329	.417	.078	1.518
Food and drink	-1.297	.000	.274	-1.628	.000	.196
Furniture	-.548	.005	.578	-.592	.004	.553
Mechanical engineering	.040	.844	1.041	-.048	.826	.953
Nation						
Austria (Ref group)		.000	1.000		.000	1.000
Belgium	1.096	.000	2.993	1.586	.000	4.882
Netherlands	.258	.198	1.295	.379	.092	1.461
Switzerland	.391	.054	1.479	.568	.012	1.765
Norway	.265	.196	1.303	.531	.020	1.700
Sweden	.649	.002	1.913	.846	.000	2.330
Finland	.782	.002	2.024	1.092	.000	2.979

The bivariate analysis shows an association between company size and exporting/not exporting. The odds for the largest company group is over 10 times that of the smallest companies. With a multivariate approach, where all three independent variables are simultaneously run against the dependent variable, this tendency becomes even stronger. The difference between the largest and smallest companies is now nearly 15 times in odds ratio. An all-pervading characteristic of company size is that this variable has statistically significant effects on exporting.

As reported earlier, the textile industry has a relatively high level of internationalisation and the figures from the logistic regression show that companies in electronics are more often exporters - odds value 1.5 in the multivariate approach. Mechanical engineering firms are on the same level as the textile companies, but furniture companies are on a lower level. The companies in the food and drink industry export to a lesser degree (odds value 0.2), compared to textile companies. Austria seems to have the lowest level of small firm export, which is in line with the results reported earlier in this paper. In the multivariate analysis, Belgian, and also the Finnish and Swedish, firms exhibit higher odds values.

As could be expected, an analysis with importing/not importing as the dependent variable shows the same type of patterns as above. In the first descriptive analysis we found that import activities are more frequent than are export, 91% compared to 77%, and this higher level of inward-directed foreign trade has resulted in odds values on a more even level. However, the difference between the five size groups is evident with an odds value for the largest size group of 7.2.

Table 11.14 Size/Industry/Nation: Importing/Not Importing Companies, Bivariate and Multivariate Logistic Regression, Analysis with Subcategories

Variables	BIVARIATE Importing/Not importing			MULTIVARIATE Importing/Not importing		
	Coefficient	p-value	Odds value	Coefficient	p-value	Odds value
Company size						
1- 9 empl. (Ref group)		.000	1.000		.000	1.000
10- 19 -"-	1.023	.000	2.782	1.124	.000	3.076
20- 49 -"-	1.033	.000	2.809	1.148	.000	3.151
50- 99 -"-	1.329	.000	3.779	1.529	.000	4.611
100-499 -"-	1.772	.000	5.884	1.975	.000	7.205
Industry						
Textile (Ref group)		.000	1.000		.000	1.000
Electronics	2.075	.000	7.963	2.198	.000	9.008
Food and drink	-1.045	.000	.352	-1.189	.000	.305
Furniture	- .412	.133	.663	- .424	.139	.655
Mechanical engineering	.028	.924	1.028	- .020	.946	.980
Nation						
Austria (Ref group)		.000	1.000		.000	1.000
Belgium	.408	.234	1.504	.682	.057	1.977
Netherlands	- .514	.064	.598	- .566	.054	.568
Switzerland	.519	.123	1.680	.630	.073	1.878
Norway	.215	.504	1.240	.348	.303	1.417
Sweden	1.118	.005	3.060	1.232	.003	3.430
Finland	- .298	.314	.743	- .173	.581	.841

Among the industries electronics has a pronounced position with a very international profile for both export and import. Especially the import figures are extreme: the odds value for being an importer in the electronics business is 9.0 compared to the textile industry. The Swedish companies seem to be importers more often than the companies in the other countries (odds value 3.4 compared to Austria). Small firms in the Netherlands and Finland have the lowest level in this respect.

So far we have concentrated fully on the three factors size, industry, and nation and the relations to internationalisation. It seems quite clear that size is the dominating factor of the three as predictor for internationalisation. In the next section we will elaborate further on additional factors that might be of importance for internationalisation.

The Importance of Structural and Managerial Factors

Above we found there is no clear-cut relation between industry and nation on one hand and internationalisation on the other. Size is obviously important, but nevertheless we wanted to analyse the influence of some other factors. In the beginning of this paper we described the model for the Interstratos project. This model includes different types of variables, and we will now include some of these: manager characteristics (education and experience) and firm/structure (ownership, degree of independence and co-operation).

There are arguments for including variables linked to the competence level of the small business manager: education efforts and earlier experience in the same type of business sector. Cavusgil (1984), for example, showed that a relationship existed between export activities and managerial aspirations and expectations. The managerial characteristics therefore are interesting to include. Also Buckley (1993) and Calof (1993) speculate that strategies, managerial attitudes, and lack of experience can explain more of the differences among firms in international activities than does company size.

Also variables describing type of company in terms of family business, subcontractor and subsidiary are important. The reason for entering these variables is that the decision making as well as the general outlook on internationalisation is influenced by the degree of autonomy and by the degree of participation in different co-operative endeavours (Contractor and Lorange 1988; Casson 1995).

Consequently, the analysis is expanded and we now include nine independent variables. Besides the three main variables in this study (size, industry, nation) three structural variables (subsidiary, subcontractor and family business), one variable referring to co-operation between companies and two variables linked to managerial competence (education efforts and earlier management experience) were included.

Analysis of exporting/not exporting and one independent variable resulted in separate odds values. From this bivariate approach all variables showed significant values (p-values < 0.05) and were entered into a multivariate analysis where the contribution of each variable depends on all the other variables in the model. Because of the specific characteristics for industry and nation (nominal data), these two were included in the analysis mainly to study what effects they would cause on the other seven variables in the multivariate analysis.

Table 11.15   Nine Independent Variables: Exporting/Not Exporting Companies, Bivariate and Multivariate Logistic Regression

	BIVARIATE Exporting/Not exporting			MULTIVARIATE Exporting/Not exporting		
Variables	Coefficient	p-value	Odds value	Coefficient	p-value	Odds value
Company size	.558	.000	1.746	.568	.000	1.764
Subsidiary	.614	.000	1.847	-.104	.611	.901
Subcontractor	.932	.000	2.540	.844	.000	2.325
Family company	-.356	.007	.700	.054	.766	1.056
Education	.992	.000	2.701	.962	.000	2.616
Co-operation	.538	.000	1.714	.218	.185	1.244
Management exper.	-.022	.000	.978	-.009	.205	.992
Industry						
Textile (Ref group)					.000	1.000
Electronics				.151	.581	1.163
Food and drink				-1.785	.000	.168
Furniture				-.621	.010	.537
Mechanical engineering				-.370	.141	.691
Nation						
Austria (Ref group)					.000	1.000
Belgium				1.733	.000	5.656
Netherlands				.816	.005	2.261
Switzerland				.572	.043	1.772
Norway				.750	.009	2.116
Sweden				1.279	.000	3.594
Finland				1.075	.000	2.929

Among the first seven variables the company size again proved its importance in explaining internationalisation and even proved to be powerful (odds value 1.8) when eight other variables are simultaneously compared. However, management education (2.6) and being a subcontractor (2.3) give even higher odds values.

A bivariate analysis carried out for importing/not importing companies gives significant values for all predictor variables. The odds values are in general lower when compared to the export situation but the same variables show here the highest odds values - company size, subcontractor, and managerial education.

Table 11.16   Nine Independent Variables: Importing/Not Importing Companies, Bivariate and Multivariate Logistic Regression

Variables	BIVARIATE Importing/Not importing			MULTIVARIATE Importing/Not importing		
	Coefficient	p-value	Odds value	Coefficient	p-value	Odds value
Company size	.430	.000	1.534	.393	.000	1.482
Subsidiary	.522	.017	1.686	-.260	.368	.771
Subcontractor	.403	.020	1.496	.351	.103	1.421
Family company	-.513	.011	.599	-.334	.213	.716
Education	.889	.000	2.433	.452	.095	1.572
Co-operation	.608	.002	1.837	.341	.152	1.406
Management exper.	-.018	.014	.982	-.012	.200	.988
Industry						
Textile (Ref group)					.000	1.000
Electronics				2.926	.004	18.655
Food and drink				-1.119	.000	.327
Furniture				- .406	.195	.666
Mechanical engineering				- .006	.987	.994
Nation						
Austria (Ref group)					.000	1.000
Belgium				.440	.302	1.553
Netherlands				- .597	.144	.550
Switzerland				.015	.972	1.015
Norway				.116	.789	1.123
Sweden				1.297	.012	3.658
Finland				- .609	.128	.544

The inclusion of additional variables shows that internationalisation is linked to several factors, especially subcontracting and managers education seem to be important. But size is still an important predictor for internationalisation. We will now discuss our findings from a more general standpoint.

Discussion

The most evident conclusion is that size is a factor that has a strong relation to internationalisation. In the first descriptive analysis company size is strongly correlated to all the measures of internationalisation. In the multivariate approach the independent variable for size dominates the results when including industry and nation, and is also noticeable when nine different variables are inserted.

For all five industries we find differences in internationalisation behaviour: textile and electronics seem to be most international and mechanical engineering to some extent compared to companies in the remaining industries. Furniture and food and drink appear to be industries with a domestic orientation. There are differences between nations, for example very low export quotas for Swedish and Finnish food and drink companies. All three Nordic countries are relatively low in the textile business. Austrian and Belgian companies have the highest export quotas, with extraordinary high levels in textile and electronics.

It seems as though size is the only factor that can easily be used, even if some differences do exist. Within industry, all electronics companies are highly international, and within nation, 'domestic' (business within 50 km) for food and drink in the Benelux region means that international trade takes place. The argument for size may be that it is a quite clear measure (number of employees, turnover in ECU). Industry is not a continuous variable and moreover each group of industry consists of several subgroups, niches. The same arguments apply for nation. Even if nationality accounts for similarities, for instance in attitudes as we have shown in Interstratos (Haahti, 1995), there are within a national large differences in regional characteristics etc.

This study shows the necessity of an operationalisation of measures that mirrors the phenomena covered by the concepts of industry and nation. For industry, we need to break down into categories that capture the aspects that influence internationalisation. In a previous study (Boter and Holmquist, 1996) we found that one of the factors linked to high internationalisation is the novelty of a technology/business idea. While electronics is an industry of rather new technologies, within mechanical engineering can be found subgroups with very old as well as new technology. To adequately study internationalisation perhaps we have to create subgroups of industry/nation or work with different regions of a nation as explanatory factors. For nation, perhaps we should only use nation at an aggregated level and study attitudes in a given context.

Consequently, the next step must be to break down the concepts industry and nation into fruitful, operationalised concepts that cover the essential elements of the wider concept. This is a theoretical task as much as an empirical one.

References

Ali, A. & Swiercz, P.M. (1991) Firm size and Export Behaviour: Lessons from the Midwest. *Journal of Small Business Management*, 29(2): 71-78.

Baird, I.S., Lyles, M.A. & Orris, J.B. (1994) The Choice of International Strategies by Small Businesses. *Journal of Small Business Management*, 32(1): 48-59.

Bartlett, C.A. & Ghoshal, S. (1989) *Managing Across Borders. The Transnational Solution*. Boston: Harvard Business School Press.

Bartlett, G.A. & Ghosal, S. (1991) Global Strategic Management: Impact on the new Frontiers Strategy Research. *Strategic Management Journal*, 12(Special Issue-Summer): 5-16.

Beamish, P.W., Craig, R. & McLellan, K. (1993) The Performance Characteristics of Canadian versus U.K. Exporters in Small and Medium Sized Firms. *Management International Review*, 33(2): 121-137.

Bilkey, W.J. & Tesar, G. (1977) The Export Behaviour of Small-Sized Wisconsin Manufacturing Firms. *Journal of International Business Studies*, 8(Spring/Summer): 93-98.

Boswell, J. (1972) *The Rise and Decline of Small Firms*. London: George Allen & Unwin Ltd.

Boter, H. & Holmquist, C. (1996) Industrial Characteristics and Internationalisation Processes in Small Firms. *Journal of Business Venturing*, 11(6): 471-487.

Buckley, P.J. (1993) The Role of Management in Internationalisation Theory. *Management International Review*, 33(3): 197-207.

Calof, J.L. (1993) The Impact of Size on Internationalisation. *Journal of Small Business Management*, 31(4): 60-69.

Calori, R. & de Woot, P. (1994) *A European Management Model. Beyond Diversity*. London: Prentice-Hall.

Casson, M. (1995) *The Organization of International Business*. Aldershot: Edward Elgar.

Cavusgil, S.T. (1984) Differences Among Exporting Firms Based on Their Degree of Internationalisation. *Journal of Business Research*, 25(3): 195-208.

Cavusgil, S.T. (1984) Organisational Characteristics Associated with Export Activity. *Journal of Management Studies*, 21(1): 3-22.

Chandler, A.D.J. (1962) *Strategy and Structure: Chapters in the History of the American Industrial Enterprise*. Cambridge: MIT Press.

Child, J. (1988) On Organisations in their Sectors. *Organisational Studies*, 9(1): 13-19.

Christensen, C., da Rocha, A. & Gertner, R. (1987) An Empirical Investigation of the Factors Influencing Export Success of Brazilian Firms. *Journal of International Business Studies*, 18(Fall): 61-78.

Christensen, P.R., Eskelinen, H., Forsström, B., Fredriksen, T. and Lindmark, L. (1991) Lokal resursmobilisering för internationell konkurrenskraft - några reflektion kring småföretagsutveckling i ett EG-perspektiv. FE-publ. 1991:122, Umeå: Umeå Business School.

Contractor, F.J. & Lorange, P. (1988) *Co-operative Strategies in International Business*. Lexington: Lexington Books.

Czinkota, M.R. & Johnston, W.J. (1983) Exporting: Does Sales Volume Make a Difference? *Journal of International Business Studies*, 14(Spring/Summer): 147-153.

Deal, T. & Kennedy, A. (1982) *Corporate Culture*. Reading: Addison Wesley.

Doz, Y. (1986) *Strategic Management in Multinational Companies*. Oxford: Pergamon Press.

Everitt, B.S. & Dunn, G. (1991) *Applied Multivariate Data Analysis*. New York: Edward Arnold.

Frost, P.J., Moore, L.F., Louis, M.R., Lundberg, C.C. & Martin, J. (1985) *Organisational Culture*. London: Sage.

Haahti, A.J. (1995) *Interstratos - Internationalisation of Strategic Orientation of European Small and Medium-Sized Enterprises*. Brussels: EIASM report 95-1.

Haahti, A.J. (1997) *Interstratos - Internationalisation of Strategic Orientation of European Small and Medium Sized Enterprises*. Brussels: EIASM report (forthcoming).

Hedlund, G. (1986) The Hypermodern MNC - A Heterarchy? *Human Resource Management*, 25(1): 9-35.

Hofstede, G. (1980) *Culture's Consequences*. London: Sage.

Johanson, J. and Mattsson, L.-G. (1988) Internationalisation in Industrial Systems - A Network Approach. In: Hood, N. and Vahlne, J. (Eds.) *Strategies in Global Competion*, New York: Croom Helm.

Johanson, J. & Vahlne, J.-E. (1977) The Internationalisation Process in the Firm - A Model of Knowledge Development and Increasing Market Commitments. *Journal of International Business Studies*, 8(1): 23-32.

Kaynak, E. & Kothari, V. (1984) Export Behaviour of Small and Medium-Sized Manufacturers: Some Policy Guidelines for International Marketers. *Management International Review*, 2(1): 61-69.

Kirpalani, V.H. & MacIntosh, N.B. (1980) International Marketing Effectiveness of Technology-Oriented Small Firms. *Journal of International Business Studies*, 11(Winter): 81-90.

Klofsten, M. (1992) *Tidiga utvecklingsprocesser i teknikbaserade företag. (Early development stages in technology-intensive firms)*. Linköping: Linköping University (Dissertation).

Lawrence, P.R. & Lorsch, J.W. (1967) *Organization and Environment: Managing Differentiation and Integration*. Cambridge: Harvard University Press.

Lindqvist, M. (1991) *Infant Multinationals - The Internationalisation of Young, Technology-Based Swedish Firms*. Stockholm: Institut of International Business. Stockholm School of Economics (Dissertation).

Martinez, J.I. & Jarillo, J.C. (1989) The Evulotion of Research on Coordination Mechanisms in Multinational Corporations. *Journal of International Business Studies*, 20(3): 489-514.

Menard, S. (1995) *Applied Logistic Regression Analysis*. London: Sage.

Meyerson, D. & Martin, J. (1987) Cultural Change: An Integration of Three Different Views. *Journal of Management Studies*, 24(5): 623-647.

Miller, D. (1987) Strategy Making and Structure: Analysis and Implications for Performance. *Academy of Management Journal*, 30(March): 7-31.

Miller, D. & Friesen, P.H. (1980) Archetypes of Organisational Transition. *Administrative Science Quarterly*, 25(3): 268-299.

Mintzberg, H. (1989) *Mintzberg on Management. Inside Our Strange World of Organisations*. New York: Free Press.

Morrison, A.J. & Roth, K. (1992) A Taxonomy of Business-Level Strategies in Global Industries. *Strategic Management Journal*, 13(6): 399-418.

NUTEK - Swedish National Board for Industrial and Technical Development (1994) *Small Business in Sweden*. Stockholm: Report B 1994:7.

Porter, M.E. (1990) *The Competitive Advantage of Nations*. London: MacMillan.

Rosson, P.J. & Ford, D.I. (1982) Manufacturer-Overseas Distributor Relations and Export Performance. *Journal of International Business Studies*, 13(Fall): 57-72.

Sharma, D. (1991) *International Operations of Professional Firms.* Lund: Studentlitteratur.

Smith, N.R. & Miner, J.B. (1983) Type of Entrepreneur, Type of Firm, and Managerial Motivation: Implications for Organisational Life Cycle Theory. *Academy of Management Review,* 4(3): 325-340.

Spender, J.-C. (1989) *Industry Recipes. An Enquiry into the Nature and Sources of Management Judgement.* Oxford: Basil Blackwell.

Stopford, J.M. & Wells, L.T. (1972) *Managing the Multinational Enterprise.* New York: Basic Books.

Tookey, D. (1964) Factors Associated with Success in Exporting. *Journal of Management Studies,* 1(1): 48-66.

Vernon, R. (1966) International Investment and International Trade in the Product Cycle. *Quarterly Journal of Economics,* 80(3): 190-207.

Welch, L.S. & Luostarinen, R. (1988) Internationalisation: Evolution of a concept. *Journal of General Management,* 14(2): 34-55.

12 The Internationalisation Process of Small and Medium Sized Enterprises: An Evaluation of the Stage Theory

Harold G.J. Gankema, Henoch R. Snuif and Koos A. van Dijken

Introduction

Since January 1995, fifteen (Western) European countries form the European Union in which physical, technical and fiscal trade barriers are fading away. The creation of this free trade zone throughout Europe intensively influences the development of market conditions and competition today as well as in the near future. Due to the establishment of this 'Internal Market' the national and international environment of (small and medium sized) firms in Europe is changing rapidly. It has consequences even for small firms whose sphere of operating is strictly local, providing both opportunities and threats. On the one hand, international trading will meet hardly any trade barriers, thus generating opportunities. On the other hand local competition is getting stronger because foreign competitors now can enter the domestic market without complex formalities. Uniformity in product requirements and less time consuming border controls have lowered the costs of international trade (Leeflang and Pahud de Mortanges, 1992).

In addition to these specific European developments, international trends in manufacturing industry such as globalisation, acceleration of technical progress, shortening of product life cycles, changing relations between main and subcontractors and more international co-operation play a significant role. Manufacturing industries - small as well as large - have to adapt to these trends to cope with this increasing international competition. To realise growth, flexibility and quality improvement, both internationally and locally operating firms will have to broaden their view and reconsider their international marketing strategies based on the relative strengths and weaknesses of the firm and the international market opportunities. Both Porter (1990) and Leeflang and Pahud de Mortanges (1992) indicated that European firms should concentrate on international market expansion: 'European firms should concentrate on their original industry and invest to obtain an international market position in their key-activities' (Porter, 1990).

Background

The process of internationalisation has been the subject of widespread theoretical and empirical research (e.g. Johanson and Wiedersheim-Paul, 1975; Johanson and Vahlne 1977; Bilkey, 1978; Cavusgil, 1980; Turnbull, 1987; Welch and Luostarinen, 1988) and benefits from a general acceptance in literature (Bradley, 1991; Buckley and Ghauri, 1993). This process is described as a gradual development taking place in distinct stages (Melin, 1992). Two significant schools in the field of international business concerning the internationalisation process can be identified: the models initially developed by Johanson and Wiedersheim-Paul (1975) and Johanson and Vahlne (1977), which are referred to as the Uppsala models (U-model), and the Innovation-Related Internationalisation Models (I-model) conceptualised by Cavusgil (1980).

Uppsala Model

Johanson and Wiedersheim-Paul (1975) suggested that the export development process has a sequential nature. They distinguished between four different modes of international market entry:

Stage 1:   No regular export activities
Stage 2:   Export via independent representatives
Stage 3:   Establishment of overseas sales subsidiaries
Stage 4:   Overseas production facilities

Johanson and Vahlne (1977) refined this model and described the process of internationalisation as 'a gradual acquisition, integration and use of knowledge about foreign markets and operations, and a ... successively increasing commitment to foreign markets.' This process is seen as one of organisational learning and focuses on experience (Nordstrom, 1991), however, the model is restricted to one export market (Anderson, 1993). The emphasis in this model is put on export organisational forms that are associated with growing export involvement (Turnbull, 1987). The experience/knowledge based Uppsala-model shows the internationalisation process as a slow process, beginning with local representatives in culturally close markets. After the initial steps abroad proof to be successful, involvement will gradually deepen.

In the early nineties Johanson and Vahlne (1990) came up with a renewed experience/knowledge based model for the process of internationalisation. This model is less deterministic and concentrates on the process of learning/gaining experience from being present at a foreign market. The more experience the firm gains in time, the more it is prepared to commit itself to this market and to launch new activities. The more the current activities are expanded, the higher the market commitment will be. From this higher market commitment the firm will gain experience and market knowledge and so on.

Innovation-Related Internationalisation Models

Bilkey and Tesar (1977), Cavusgil (1980), Reid (1981) and Czinkota (1982) consider internationalisation of a firm to be an adoption process analogous to the stages of product adaptation (Rogers, 1962). These models are based on the product (life) cycle model by Vernon (1966) and consider each next stage as an innovation for the firm. Bilkey and Tesar (1977), Reid (1981) and Czinkota (1982) however limit their models to managing export activities, whereas Cavugil's model includes other entry modes as well. Cavusgil (1980) proposed the following conceptualisation of the internationalisation process:

Stage 1
Domestic Marketing   The firm is only interested in the domestic market and does not export at all. The firm is not interested or willing to experiment with exporting; it is too busy doing other things, or it is just not capable of handling an export order. The export/sales ratio = 0.

Stage 2
Pre-Export Stage   The firms searches for information and evaluates the feasibility of exporting activities. Basic information about costs, exchange risks, distribution etc. is still lacking. The export/sales ratio = 0.

Stage 3
Experimental Involvement Stage

The firm starts exporting on a small basis. Physical and cultural distances are limited. The involvement of an experimental exporter is usually marginal and intermittent. The export/sales ratio varies from 0 - 9% .

Stage 4
Active Involvement Stage

Active involvement is apparent from the systematic effort to increase sales through export. Exporting is to multiple new countries and a suitable organisational structure is applied. The export/sales ratio varies from 10 - 39% .

Stage 5
Committed Involvement Stage

The firm depends heavily on foreign markets. Managers are continuously faced with choices for the allocation of limited resources to either domestic or foreign markets. Many firms will be engaged in licensing arrangements or direct investments. The export/sales ratio is 40% or more.

The characterisation of the various stages of the I-model is commonly operationalised by the export/sales ratio, although other operationalisations are possible (e.g. Reid, 1983).

Stage models have been criticised by various researchers. Hedlund and Kverneland (1984) found that firms sometimes leapfrog stages. They internationalise through acquisitions and joint ventures rather than investments in wholly owned sales and production subsidiaries as described in the U-model. This model furthermore was criticised by Reid (1983), Turnbull (1987) and Rosson (1987). They conclude that the mode of entry is not predetermined by stages but is the result of a strategic choice based on the foreign market conditions, managerial philosophy and firms resources. Turnbull (1987) found that industrial companies used a combination of different organisational approaches for various markets at the same time.

Melin (1992) agrees with this point of view whereas he states that the U-models exclude other strategic options during the process of internationalisation, that the models are too deterministic and limited to the early stages of internationalisation. Bonaccorsi and Dalli (1990) question the application of stage models to SMEs because they found that small exporting firms do not adopt integrated organisational forms. Welch and Luostarinen (1988) however, recognised that although not all firms necessarily follow the pattern, the stage theory is consistent.

Research Objectives

Although the internationalisation process has been topic of a lot of research, most of it has concentrated on large firms (Bonaccorsi and Dalli, 1990). The research methodology usually concerned case studies or cross sectional studies and mostly concentrated on one country of origin (Gankema and Zwart, 1990). The progression in the stage process has been underexposed and little attention has been paid to the time dimension of the process (Anderson, 1993).

In this study we want to gain insight in the internationalisation process of small and medium sized enterprises. A large number of SMEs in various Western European countries have been followed for five subsequent years considering their international strategic orientation. The following research questions have been formulated:

(1) Is Hildebrand's Del analysis an appropriate method of analysis to empirically test Cavusgil's stage theory?
(2) Does the stage theory hold for SMEs, and - if yes -;

(3) What is the appropriate time period to consider?

In both the U-model and the I-models - described in section 'Background' - the central issue concentrates on involvement in foreign markets. The operationalisation of the U-model however, interferes with strategic choices, which are influenced by a lot of other factors as well. We therefore use Cavusgil's model, who operationalised the export involvement by the export/sales ratio. The export/sales ratio is defined as the ratio of export sales to total sales and describes the extent to which a firm is involved in export. This operationalisation of the export stages, referred to as export intensity, was also used among others by e.g. Cavusgil (1980; 1984), Diamantopoulos and Inglis (1988) and Mugler and Miesenbock (1989) .

Research Methodology

Data

The empirical part of this paper draws on data gathered through a mail questionnaire by the INTERSTRATOS group[1] (Haahti et al., 1993) . INTERSTRATOS is a longitudinal research project into the INTERnationalisation of STRATegic Orientation of Small sized European enterprises in manufacturing industries. This project covers an annual survey research in several European countries for a period of five consecutive years - the first year being 1991. Co-operating countries are: Austria, Belgium, Finland, Great Britain, The Netherlands, Norway, Sweden and Switzerland. The sample is stratified by firm size and sector of industry. The following five manufacturing branches are included:

- NACE 43 & 45:   Textile and clothing
- NACE 34:   Electrical engineering
- NACE 41 & 42:   Food, drink and tobacco
- NACE 46:   Wooden and timber products, including furniture
- NACE 31 & 32:   Metal products and mechanical engineering

Each of the above sectors of industry consists to a large extent of small and medium sized enterprises. Also, these sectors show varying degrees of internationalisation, market structure, technological development, scale economies, product life cycle duration and sensitivity for the completion of the internal EU market. The selection procedure is believed to guarantee a representative mix of branches for each participating country. Therefore, the results of this study can be representative for other branches as well. The current study uses the data of those firms that provided the information needed to assess their export involvement for the full five year period. This resulted in a panel of 144 firms. Table 12.1 summarises some background statistics.

---

[1] The international research group known as INTERSTRATOS is formed by: J. Hanns Pichler, Erwin Frölich, Inge Frölich and Peter Voithofer (Austria), Rik Donkels and Ria Aerts (Belgium), Graham Hall (Great Britain), Antti Haahti, Allan Lehtimäki† and Petri Ahokangas (Finland), Koos van Dijken and Harold Gankema (The Netherlands), Per-Anders Havnes, Arild Saether and Johanne Sletten (Norway), Håkan Boter and Carin Holmquist (Sweden), Hans Pleitner and Margit Habersaat (Switzerland)

Table 12.1   **Panel Background in 1991**

Country		Industry		# Employees		Turnover (mln.)		Export ratio	
	Freq.		Freq.		Freq.		Freq.		Freq.
A	12	Textile	26	0-9	15	0-1.5	33	0	15
B	8	Electr.	32	10-49	68	1.5-3	36	0-9	42
CH	17	Food	10	50-99	41	3-7.5	42	10-40	53
N	18	Wood	33	100-199	14	7.5-15	24	>40	34
S	76	Mech.	43	>200	6	15-30	9		
FIN	13								
Total	144		144		144		144		144

Method

Cross-classification analysis on categorical data predominantly consists of chi-square analysis to determine whether there is any relationship between the state of one variable and the state of another. However, a chi-square analysis tests for the significance of the relationship, but offers no possibility for testing a custom-designed, a priori prediction rule. Moreover, no insight is provided into the value of a specific prediction rule, i.e. the proportionate reduction in error (PRE) from applying the rule over not applying it. Both shortcomings are covered by Hildebrand's del analysis (Hildebrand, Laing and Rosenthal, 1977). In addition, the technique is independent of sample size, robust for small samples and its test statistic is distributed normally. Drazin and Kazanjian (1993) introduced this technique to management research and proved it to be extremely suitable for cross-classification analysis with the purpose of testing a priori predictions.

Del analysis of row-by-column tables draws on designating cells as either 'predicted cells' or as 'error cells'. Predicted cells are those in which the researchers expect to find many cases; error cells are expected to be empty. In the most straight-forward application of del analysis, predicted cells are awarded a weight - i.e. a penalty - of 0 and error cells a weight of 1. However, del analysis offers researchers a great amount of flexibility in assigning weights to error cells. Sometimes, theoretical considerations suggest certain cells to be more 'error' than others. In these cases, the researcher can decide to assign a weight less than 1 to the latter.

A perfect prediction rule - i.e. when all cases actually are in predicted cells and error cells are empty - renders the maximum del value of 1. In the worst case - i.e. when all cases occur in error cells - the value of del is minus infinity.[2] A zero or negative value of del indicates a poor prediction rule, whereas a positive and significant del value signals a good predictor. Interpretation of del is analogous to that of the coefficient of determination (R^2). Furthermore, del values of two - rival - prediction rules can be compared in the same way as can be done with correlation coefficients.

Prediction Rules

From the above, it is clear that the crux of the del analysis technique is the specification of the prediction rule. The prediction rule implicit in Cavusgil's (1980) model of the internationalisation process can be formulated as: *over time firms progress through the four stages of*

---

[2]   Formulas for calculating del can be found in Appendix A.

internationalisation. The explicitation of Cavusgil's model elicits the following rules (see Table 12.2):

1. Firms that progress one stage per period behave in line with the prediction rule. These cells ([2,1], [3,2] and [4,3]) are therefore assigned a weight of 0, i.e. these are the predicted cells (no penalty).
2. Firms that do not export in one period do not necessarily have to start exporting in the subsequent period. Thus, cell [1,1] is attributed a weight of 0.
3. Internationalisation is assumed to be an irreversible process. The decline cells ([1,2], [1,3], [1,4], [2,3], [2,4] and [3,4]) therefore receive a full error penalty of 1.
4. Firms can not progress further than stage 4: the committed involvement stage. As a consequence, stagnation in this stage can not be penalised (weight = 0).

Table 12.2   Weighting Scheme

		Second period			
	Stage	1	2	3	4
First period	1	0	0	B	A
	2	1	C	0	B
	3	1	1	C	0
	4	1	1	1	0

A = Hyperprogression penalty
B = Overprogression penalty
C = Stagnation penalty

Furthermore the treatment of 'overprogression' and 'hyperprogression', i.e. firms that move up two or three stages respectively in a single period has to be decided upon. Is this behaviour in line with the stage theory, or contradictory? Table 12.2 indicates that three additional weighting factors have to be determined: the *hyperprogression (a), overprogression (b) and stagnation (c)* penalties.

A. Hyperprogression. Hedlund and Kverneland (1984), McKiernon (1992) and Melin (1992) suggested leap froging of intermediate stages to be quite common. Both over- and hyperprogression will therefore be penalised less than regression. On the other hand, if firms are allowed to skip two or more stage in the internationalisation process, the predictive value of the stage model is greatly reduced. Therefore, we assigned a weight of 0.75 to the hyperprogression cell [4.1].

B. Overprogression. In the case of overprogression - i.e. firms progressing two stages in a subsequent period - it is less clear whether a penalty should be given, and - if yes - of which weight. It is quite imaginable that a firm skips one stage in a certain period, notwithstanding the fact that its internationalisation process does follow Cavusgil's model. Again, however, a model in which 'anything goes' is not predictively useful. For this reason, overprogression has to be penalised. Since the appropriate size of the penalty is not obvious, we decided to apply several weights (.25 and .50) and perform a sensitive analysis.

C. Stagnation. The treatment of stagnation - firms staying in the same stage for two subsequent periods - is the third decision to made. In an application of the del technique to a stages of growth model for technology based new ventures, Kazanjian and Drazin (1989) assigned a weight of 0.50 to stagnating firms. In this paper, analogous to the solution of the overprogression issue, we apply multiple weights in a sensitivity analysis (.25, .50 and .75).

Time Frame

For our purposes, however, this stage model is not specific enough. As has been noted by Melin (1992), the prediction lacks reference to the timing of progression. Does the change from one stage to the next occur every year? Every two years or does it take an even longer period of time? Hard to answer as this question may sound, it has severe repercussions for the weighting scheme that has to be applied in Hildebrand's del analysis. If the change from one stage to the next is expected every year, firms residing in the same stage in two subsequent years should be 'penalised'. If the appropriate time frame - however - is two years, these firms would be predicted to be in the same stage.

The presence of a panel data set provides the opportunity to assess for which time frame the internationalisation stages model performs best. Since we have data from a period of five years, it is possible to compare the Del values of the one-year, two-year, three-year and four-year progression intervals with each other.

Findings

We presented our two main questions as our research objectives: (1) does the stage theory hold for SMEs internationalisation process, and - if yes -, (2) what is the appropriate time period to consider? To answer both questions, we applied the del analysis on the INTERSTRATOS panel data. Since it was not clear beforehand, which penalties should be given to 'stagnation' and 'overprogression', we performed a sensitivity analysis, using alternative weighting schemes.

Progress

To calculate the export/sales ratios and to subsequently assign firms to one of Cavusgil's (1980) internationalisation stages, both yearly total sales volume and yearly export sales volume figures are used. Table 12.2 shows the criteria that have been applied, and the resulting number of firms per stage for each of the five years.

Table 12.3   Stage Assignment Criteria and Firms Per Stage Per Year

Export/sales ratio	Internationalisation stage	Firms per stage				
		1991	*1992*	*1993*	*1994*	*1995*
0%	Domestic marketing /pre-export	15	6	0	0	0
0% - 9%	Experimental involvement	42	43	39	37	35
10% - 39%	Active involvement	53	55	59	57	60
> 40%	Committed involvement	34	40	46	50	49

A quick glance at Table 12.3 suggests that firms indeed tend to progress through the stages. The number of firms in the first two stages decreases over time, whereas more firms are assigned to stages three and four in the last years of the research period.

Table 12.4 shows an example of the various standard cross classification tables, which are the basis of the Hildebrand's Del analysis. This table gives us some insight in the progress of firms through the stages. We can e.g. observe that 59 firms moved up one stage in the two year period from 1991 to 1993.

Table 12.4   Cross Tabulation of 1991 Versus 1993

	Stage	1993				
		1	*2*	*3*	*4*	*Total*
	1	0	6	6	3	15
	2	0	30	11	1	42
1991	3	0	2	40	11	53
	4	0	1	2	31	34
	Total	0	39	59	46	144

Weighting

Table 12.5 contains the results of the del analysis, when a time frame of one year is used. The second and third columns show the penalties given to stagnation and overprogression respectively. For each one year period, a del score and a significance level can be calculated. Significant del scores are printed italic. The last column summarises the del score of the four individual periods into a mean score.

Table 12.5   Del Scores for a One Year Period

Period	Weights		*'91 - '92*	*'92 - '93*	*'93- '94*	*'94 - '95*	*Mean*
	Stag.	*Prog.*					
	1.00	1.00	.058	.110	.034	.067	.068
	.25	.50	*.461*	*.547*	*.473*	*.486*	*.495*
1-year	.50	.25	*.249*	*.302*	*.234*	*.258*	*.263*
	.50	.50	*.273*	*.335*	*.264*	*.288*	*.290*
	.75	.25	.093	*.132*	.066	.098	.090

Stag. = Stagnation penalty
Prog. = Overprogression penalty

The significance of the (mean) Del value heavily depends upon the weighting scheme used. A very strict interpretation of the stage theory - fully penalising both stagnation and overprogression with weights of 1 - renders a del value of 0.068, which is clearly not significant. On the other hand, three out of the five weighting schemes applied produce high and significant del values. The model has the best predictive value when stagnation is not too heavily punished. The del score of 0.495 for the [.25, .50]-weighting scheme means that predicting SMEs internationalisation behaviour according to Cavusgil's stage theory reduces prediction error with almost 50%.

Periodicity

The results suggests that in a not too restricted form, the stage theory does hold for small and medium-sized enterprises. At least, when a one year period is considered. However, the panel data set permits us to investigate whether this -rather arbitrarily chosen - time period is the most appropriate. Since five year panel data are available, we can extend our analysis to two, three and four year periods. Table 12.6 presents the results of this exercition in an aggregate form, i.e. the mean del scores per period for each weighting scheme. A full report of the del values can be found in Appendix B.

Table 12.6   Mean Del Scores

Weights		1-year	2-year	3-year	4-year
Stagnation	Progression				
1.00	1.00	.068	.098	.090	.110
.25	.50	*.495*	*.500*	*.459*	*.413*
.50	.25	*.263*	*.277*	*.255*	*.246*
.50	.50	*.290*	*.305*	*.281*	*.267*
.75	.25	.090	.121	.109	.126

Stag. = Stagnation penalty
Prog. = Overprogression penalty

For longer periods too, the strict model (weights [1.00,1.00]) renders non significant Del values. However, just like in Table 12.5, three of the five weighting schemes produce sizeable and highly significant Del values. For all weighting schemes a period of two years presents the highest reduction in the prediction error. However, only little variation exists for the various lengths of periods.

Discussion

Using categorical variables only, Hildebrand's Del appears to be a suitable analysis to measure progress in stages of involvement in foreign markets. More than Chi-square analysis Hildebrand's Del provides the opportunity to specify the relationship researched. As the technique is independent of sample size, robust for small samples and its test statistic are distributed normally, Del values are easy to interpret and comparable to the well known measurement of R^2.

Specifying the weighting scheme is crucial both from a theoretical point of view, as well to the variation in results. On the one hand the influence of the weighting factors could be seen as a disadvantage of the analysis, on the other hand, specifying the weighting factors contributes to making the stage theory more explicit.

In general we clearly can observe a growing degree of international involvement within SMEs. The variation of this increase in involvement however, is enormously. Some SMEs are rocketing from one of the first stages into one of the last stages. These gazelles leapfrogging several stages can't be said to follow a pattern of gradual acquisition, integration and successively increasing commitment to foreign markets or to 'consider each next stage as an innovation'. These findings are in line with Hedlund & Kverneland (1984) and Melin (1992).

Other SMEs seem to stop the process of internationalisation before they have reached the committed involvement stage. They somehow seem to limit themselves from being to dependent on foreign markets. The results suggest that stagnation is quite a common phenomenon for a substantial group of SMEs. Although the process of internationalisation proved to be irreversible and hardly any decline in stages was found, it isn't found to be a never-ending process to all firms. These finding are in line with Bonaccorsi & Dalli (1990).

It is hard to draw conclusions upon the time frame to consider in the stage theory for SMEs. The results are slightly in favour of a 2-year period, because -independent from the weighting factors- this periodicity has the best predictive value. However as indicated above, the variety in period of time for the next stage to observe is large and a lot of firms take several years to grow into the next stage.

Future Research

As the stage theory seems to hold for SMEs, however within conditions, further investigations should be made upon the question how SMEs internationalisation processes are related to the firm (as e.g. type of industry), the surrounding processes, as e.g. country specific conditions and export market specific conditions. Also attention could be paid to the influence of product adaptations, international competitive strategies, entry strategies and number of export destination countries. Future research has to show how useful an integration of the U-models and the I-models can be in gaining more insight in the internationalisation process of SMEs.

Acknowledgement

The authors thank Bas Vorsteveld of his contribution and assistance in the preparation of the document.

References

Anderson, O. (1993) On the Internationalization Process of Firms: A Critical Analysis, *Journal of International Business Studies*, 24, 1993, 209-231.

Bilkey, W.J. (1978) An Attempted Integration of the Literature on the Export Behaviour of Firms, *Journal of International Business Studies*, Spring/Summer 1987, 33-46.

Bilkey, W.J. and Tesar G. (1977) The Export behaviour of Smaller Sized Wisconsin Manufacturing Firms, *Journal of International Business Studies*, Spring-Summer 1977, 93-98.

Bonaccorsi, A. and Dalli D. (1990) Internationalization Process and Entry Channels: Evidence from Small Italian Exporters, *proceedings 19th Annual Conference of the European Marketing Academy*, May 1990, Innsbruck.

Bradley, F. (1991) *International Marketing Strategy*, Prentice Hall, London.

Buckley, P.J. and Ghauri, P. (1993) *The internationalization of the Firm*, Academic Press, London.

Cavusgil, S.T. (1980) On the Internationalization Process of Firms, *European Research*, Vol. 8, November, 273-281.

Czinkota, M.R. (1982) *Export Development Strategies*, New York, Preager Publishers.

Diamantopoulos, A. and Inglis K. (1988) Identifying Differences between High- and Low-Involvement Exporters, *International Marketing Review*, Summer, 52-60.

Drazin, R. and Kazanjian R.K. (1993), Applying the del technique to the analysis of cross-classification data: a test of CEO succession and top management team development, *Academy of Management Journal*, Vol. 36 (6), 1374 - 1399.

Haahti A.J. et al. (1993), Internationalisation of Strategic Orientations of European Small and Medium Enterprises, *INTERSTRATOS, EIASM,* Brussels.

Hedlund, G. and Kverneland, A. (1984) Investing in Japan- Experience of Swedish Firms, *IBB, Stockholm School of Economics,* Stockholm.

Hildebrand, D., Laing J. and Rosenthal H. (1977). *Prediction analysis of cross classifications.* New York, Wiley.

Johanson, J. and Wiedersheim P.F. (1975) The Internationalization of the Firm: Four Swedish Cases, *The Journal of Management Studies,* Vol.12, October, 306-307.

Johanson, J. and Vahlne J.E. (1977) The Internationalization Process of the Firm: A Model of Knowledge Development and Increasing Foreign Market Commitment, *Journal of International Business Studies,* Vol. 8, Spring/Summer, 35-40.

Kazanjian, R.K. and Drazin R. (1989) An empirical test of a stage of growth progression model, *Management Science,* Vol. 35, 1489 - 1503.

Leeflang, P.S.H. and de Mortanges C.P. (1992) The internal European Market and Strategic Marketing planning: Implications and Expectations, *Journal of International Consumer Marketing.*

Melin, L. (1992) Internationalization as a Strategic Process, *Strategic Management Journal,* 13, 99-118.

Mugler, J. and Miesenbock K.J. (1989) Determinants of Increasing Export of Small Firms, *proceedings 34th World Conference of the International Council for Small Business,* June, Québec.

Nordstrom, K.A. (1991) The internationalization Process of the Firm, searching for new Patterns and Explanations, *dissertation, Stockholm School of Economics, Stockholm.*

Porter, M. (1990) De Doodlopende Weg naar Europa 1992 (Dead End Street Towards Europe 1992), *The Economist,* NRC Handelsblad, 4 juli, supplement ECONOMIE, 4-5.

Reid, S.D. (1981) The decision maker and export entry and expansion, *Journal of International Business Studies,* 12, 101-112.

Reid, S.D. (1983) Managerial and Firm Influences on Exportbehavior, *Journal of Academy of Marketing Science,* Summer, Vol. 11, No. 3, 323-332.

Rogers, E.M. (1962) *Diffusion of Innovations,* New York, Free Press.

Rosson, P.J. (1987) The overseas distribution method: performance and change in a harsh environment, in Rosson, P.J. & Reid, S.D., *Managing Export Entry and Expansion,* Preager, New York.

Tesar, G. (1977) Identification of Planning, Attitudinal, and Operational Differences among Types of Exporters, *American Journal of Small Business,* Vol.11, No 2, 16-21.

Turnbull, P.W. (1987) A Challenge to the Stage Theory of the Internationalization Process, in: Rosson, P.J. and Reid, S.D., *Managing Export Entry and Expansion,* Preager Publishers, New York.

Vernon, R. (1966) International Investment and International Trade in the Product Cycle, *Quarterly Journal of Economics,* 190-207.

Welch, L.S. and Luostarinen R. (1988) Internationalization: evolution of a concept, *Journal of General Management,* 2, 34-55.

Zwart, P.S. and Gankema H.G.J. (1990) Het Exportgedrag van het Midden- en Kleinbedrijf in Noord Nederland, *Research Memorandum no.393 van het Instituut voor Economisch Onderzoek, 1990, University of Groningen,* Groningen.

Appendix A

Formulas used for calculating del (Ñ):

$$\Delta = 1 - \frac{\Sigma_i \Sigma_j (w_{ij} P_{ij})}{\Sigma_i \Sigma_j (w_{ij} P_{i.} P_{.j})}$$

with:

w_{ij} = 1 or less for specified error cells and 0 for predicted cells;

P_{ij} = cell probabilities;

$P_{i.}, P_{.j}$ = marginal probabilities for the ith row and the jth column, respectively.

The hypothesis that del is greater than zero is tested against normal tables using the Z-statistic, defined as:

$$Z = \frac{\Delta}{(V)^{1/2}}$$

with:

V= variance of del, defined as:

$$V = \frac{\Sigma_i \Sigma_j (w_{ij}^2 P_{ij}) - (\Sigma_i \Sigma_j w_{ij} P_{ij}^2)}{n [\Sigma_i \Sigma_j (w_{ij} P_{i.} P_{.j})]^2}$$

with:

n = total sample size.

Appendix B   Del Scores

Period	Weights		'91 - '92	'92 - '93	'93- '94	'94 - '95	Mean
	Stag.	Prog.					
1-year	1.00	1.00	.058	.110	.034	.067	.068
	.25	.50	.461	.547	.473	.486	.495
	.50	.25	.249	.302	.234	.258	.263
	.50	.50	.273	.335	.264	.288	.290
	.75	.25	.093	.132	.066	.098	.090

			'91 - '93	'92 - '94	'93 - '95	Mean
2-years	1.00	1.00	.105	.091	.098	.098
	.25	.50	.519	.493	.478	.500
	.50	.25	.298	.278	.254	.277
	.50	.50	.322	.303	.290	.305
	.75	.25	.135	.123	.106	.121

			'91 - '94	'92 - '95	Mean
3-years	1.00	1.00	.046	.133	.090
	.25	.50	.447	.472	.459
	.50	.25	.230	.279	.255
	.50	.50	.256	.306	.281
	.75	.25	.071	.146	.109

			'91 - '95
4-years	1.00	1.00	.110
	.25	.50	.413
	.50	.25	.246
	.50	.50	.267
	.75	.25	.126

Stag. = Stagnation penalty
Prog. = Overprogression penalty

13 Measuring Growth: Methodological Considerations and Empirical Results

Frédéric Delmar

Introduction

Regardless of their sizes, expanding and growing firms are indeed the creators of new jobs and of a healthy economy (c.f., Storey, 1995). This is also one of the central issues of entrepreneurship research beside innovation and venture creation. Consequently, it is important to examine the determinants of business growth, and the measurement of growth in new ventures and small businesses presents a significant challenge for scholars. Accurate and appropriate measurement of growth is of central importance to entrepreneurship research. In order to accumulate knowledge about the processes and variables that affect business growth, we have to understand how the choice and construct of the dependent variable of growth will affect the resulting model. Without adequate understanding of the importance of the construct of the dependent variable, theory development will be impeded, results will conflict with each other and will have little practical relevance.

This is not an unknown problem, and some work has been done to guide academics in their choice of performance measures in the quest to assess and model entrepreneurship (e.g., Brush & Vanderwerf, 1992; Chandler & Hanks, 1993; Murphy, Trailer, & Hill, 1996). However, the literature has mainly concentrated on the reliability and validity of different performance measures which are available in that literature. The purpose of these papers has been to compare different performance measures and data collection methods, because data gathering related to performance has been seen as a problem. It is acknowledged here that data gathering can be a problem, but this study goes one step further by focusing on the single performance indicator of growth and how its calculation affects model building and theory development. This is an important issue because, as stated above, expanding firms have a crucial economic importance, and the above mentioned studies found growth to be one of the most reliable and valid measures of new venture performance.

My point of view is that the growth literature has put too little emphasis on the measurement of growth and how this affects the results and theoretical development. The purpose of this article is to show that the heterogeneity of different measures is problematic, and that scholars should in the future show more concern for the methodological artifacts that characterise their studies. More specifically, researchers have different concepts of how to measure growth; these differences in measurement affect the relationship among the independent variables and the dependent variable, and consequently the theory development. It is, therefore, important to examine the consequences of different concepts and how they are measured in order to assess recommendations for measuring growth when both the theoretical perspective and data characteristics are taken into account.

This study consists of two parts examining the measurement of business growth: in the first part 55 published research articles using growth as a dependent variable were reviewed and analysed. The articles were sampled from some of the more important entrepreneurship and small business research journals. Each separate article was coded on several relevant parameters. In the second part, data from a sample of small businesses were used to examine the pros and cons of different growth measures. Based on the results from the present study, I will suggest some steps that will hopefully increase our possibility to further develop entrepreneurship research.

The Growth Literature

Sample and Procedure

In this first part, the empirical growth literature was examined for the years 1989 to 1996, with the exception for four articles which can be considered as classics (Begley & Boyd, 1987; Cragg & King, 1988; Miller & Toulouse, 1986; Miller, 1987). A total of 55 articles were surveyed from journals such as: Journal of Business Venturing, Entrepreneurship Theory and Practice, Regional Studies, and Small Business Economics. These four journals accounted for 69.1% of the sampled articles. An article was chosen if: (a) it was an empirical study, (b) it included growth as a dependent variable, and (c) the sample was composed of small businesses and/or new entrepreneurial ventures.

Each article was coded for the study. The articles were coded for the used dimensions of growth and how these measurements were calculated. In order to assess the general state of the research area concerning growth each article was also coded for year of publication, journal, sample, response frequency, used analysis method, research perspective, and explained variance. I will start to describe the characteristics of the sample, because the measurement of growth is dependent on several of the mentioned variables.

Sample Characteristics

The sample could be organised in four broad categories depending on the research perspective: strategy (40%), psychology (29.1%), economics (25.5%), and network (5.5%). Thus, the largest group of articles focused on problems concerning the relationship among the environment, business strategies and growth. The second largest groups focused on the behaviour of the entrepreneur, and especially his or her stable disposition or biographical data. The third group focused on the role of small businesses for the development of the regional or national economy. This research was mainly concerned with the relationship among the growth, the size, the age of the firm, and industry, and how these relationships can be understood and theorised. The smallest group was represented by the network approach, i.e., the importance of social relationships, and comprised more recent articles. The difference in research perspective had an important effect on the choice of research design, where the economic approach stands out as the most homogeneous in problem statement and design compared to the other perspectives. Researchers here depended more on large data bases and on time series than others, but they also concentrated their effort on fewer independent variables.

It is of interest to comment upon three variables characterising the studies, notably the size of the sample used in the analyses, the response frequency for those studies relying on surveys, and the explained variance of the reported models. Table 13.1 shows some statistics for each variable. When a study reported several models, the highest explained variance was coded. It is interesting to note that the correlations among explained variance and sample size, year of publication, and response frequency were insignificant and close to zero, indicating that we have not been able to achieve better estimates over the years. Although perhaps a more reasonable explanation is that many studies did not indicate if adjusted statistics were reported or not. The difference between an adjusted and a not adjusted statistic is more important with small samples and a large number of variables.

Table 13.1   Descriptive Statistics for the 55 Studies

Variable	n	Mean	Median	Standard deviation	Minimum	Maximum
Sample [a]	49	446	175	841	44	4558
Response frequency	38	35.16	33.00	15.42	8.20	74.00
Explained variance	27	30.37	29.00	14.04	8.00	63.00

a) An outlier has been here eliminated, because it had a sample of 219,754 cases. The mean would have been 4,832 with all cases included.

An alarming concern was the bias towards sampling only manufacturing industries. High technology and manufacturing represented 49.1% of all studies. The service sector was underrepresented with only 3.6% of the studies dealing explicitly with service firms. The rest of the studies (47.3%) were based on general samples with no specific perspective. The result is problematic because the sample was based on recent research, and we know how relatively more important the service sector has become during the last decade. This knowledge has apparently not led to a greater research interest in the service sector. In the future, we have to focus more on this apparently forgotten area of entrepreneurship research.

The Measurement of Growth

The growth measure was coded for three different variables that have an effect on the obtained final results. The three variables were: (1) the choice of growth indicator (e.g., employment, market share), (2) the choice of the studied time period (numbers of years studied to determine growth), and (3) the choice of the calculation (as an absolute, relative or logarithmised figure).

The Choice of Growth Indicator. The different growth indicators and their frequencies of use are included in Table 13.2. Five different indicators were identified in this sample; they assessed different theoretical concepts, but cannot, on a theoretical level, be assumed to be totally commensurable. The most used growth indicators were employment and turnover/sales. Probably because they were easily available and because they are seen as non-controversial either from a research point of view or from the respondent's point of view. Furthermore, employment is an important indicator of job creation dynamics. It is an objective measure, as well as sales or assets, compared to indicators such as market share and performance index which are subjective, i.e., the respondent is asked to evaluate the business performance relative to the industry, the closest competitors, or his or her goals. Apparently each indicator is unique in some respects, and we shall therefore examine them separately in more depth.

Table 13.2   **Dimensions of Growth and their Frequencies**

Indicator	Frequency	Percent
Turnover/sales	17	30.9
Employment	16	29.1
Multiple indicators	10	18.2
Performance	7	12.7
Market share	3	5.5
Assets	1	1.8
Not reported	1	1.8
Total	55	100

Subjective satisfaction measures of growth or performance, such as the index proposed by Gupta and Govinrandja (1984), have been severely criticised by Chandler & Hanks (1993), who have, in my opinion, rightfully questioned the validity of such measures. They argue that these satisfaction measures are as much a function of the entrepreneurs' personal expectations, as they are of the objective performance. Therefore, it can be questioned what is really measured. Furthermore, different individuals can differ in their satisfaction of the same level of growth or performance. For example, an entrepreneur can be highly satisfied with a 25% growth, e.g., in market shares, because he or she only expected a 10% growth. On the other hand, another entrepreneur can be dissatisfied with 25% growth in market share, because he or she expected a 100% growth. Finally, subjective relative measures are dependent on the entrepreneurs knowledge and perception of the situation. Without having the possibility to control these factors it is difficult to say anything at all about the actual growth performance of a venture. The only thing that can be stated is that the independent variables found to explain the model probably affect the entrepreneur's cognitive and perceptual structure. This is seldom the purpose in the growth literature.

However, the differences were not only restricted to the objective or subjective nature of the indicators, but were also dependent on whether growth was measured in terms of changes in the number of employees, or in sales volume. In other words, depending on the choice of indicator, different stages of the growth processes will be focused upon. Changes in demands for a product or a service will affect the firms in different phases (e.g., Anderson & Strigel, 1981). That is, in the first phase, the entrepreneurs will perceive some general changes in *demand* or a higher interest in the offered product/ service from the customer. In the second phase, this higher demand will lead to higher *sales*. In the third phase, changes in sales volume will lead to changes in the organisation in order to adapt to a new level of demand, i.e., to hire more *personnel* or sublet some of the production. Thus, demand can be seen as an anticipatory variable whose expected future constellation forms the basis for business plans. Sales can be seen as an intermediate variable, showing the existent trade-off between the demand and supply forces. Finally, changes in the organisation such as hiring more personnel or subletting, can be seen as the final adjustment to changes. It is also the variable with the lowest volatility, i.e., entrepreneurs will wait until they are sure that the new level of demand will be stable. More precisely, they will refrain from hiring or dismissing an employee until they are sure about the changes. Hence, *the amount of employees is an instrumental variable planned by the entrepreneur, and it is often lagged compared to the financial development.* This difference in volatility will affect the model, because different factors will affect changes in sales, and changes in the number of employees. Changes in sales are probably highly correlated with changes of number of employees, but not necessarily. The entrepreneur can choose to meet changes in demands in different ways, through hiring more personnel, sub-contracting, or improving productivity. Thereby, depending on how we assess growth as changes in sales or employees, we assess different phases of the growth process and different responses to external changes.

Changes in assets is not recommended as a growth measure, simply because it is mainly appropriate to use for firms which tend to be capital-intensive. Consequently, it will not be an appropriate measure for the service sector which is relatively less capital-intensive than the manufacturing sector. Another aspect that concerns both changes in assets and in sales is that these are both subjected to changes in inflation. Thereby growth as measured by assets or sales is the effect of real growth plus inflation. On that count, growth in numbers of employees is a better measure if the researcher believes that inflation may play an important role in a given study.

To conclude this section, the empirical literature has used five types of growth indicators. I have argued that subjective measures such as perceived market share and performance satisfaction were not appropriate measures, because they were based on the entrepreneurs' knowledge and expectations. Change in assets is only an appropriate measure for the manufacturing sector, because it is highly dependent on the capital structure. I have also argued that changes in sales and in number of employees assess different processes. First, sales and employees have a different flexibility, with sales changing more rapidly with demands than does the number of employees. Secondly, the entrepreneurs can either hire more people or subcontract. Assuming that growth in broad terms is interesting, then multiple indicators is an option, and also because we can assume that they represent the theoretical concept of growth.

The Choice of the Calculation of the Growth Measure. Organisational growth was mainly measured as the difference between two points in time. This change was either seen as an absolute change or as a relative change. Furthermore, the measure was often logarithmised to adjust for skewness in the sample. These calculations affect the final results of a model; and the purpose of this section was to investigate those difference and how they affected the possibilities of comparing results. The results from Table 13.3 indicates that relative measures were the most frequent, and were followed by absolute measures.

Table 13.3   Calculations of Growth and their Frequencies

Growth measure	Frequency	Percent
Relative	28	50.9
Absolute	16	29.1
Log absolute	6	10.9
Log relative	3	5.5
Not reported	2	3.6
Total	55	100

The problem with relative and absolute measures is fairly obvious. A relative measure will favour growth in small firms, whereas an absolute measure will bias the results in favour of larger firms. For example, if firm A has started with 1 employee and has after three years 6 employees, its growth is 600% or 5 employees; at the same time, firm B has started with 10 employees and has after the same period 15 employees, its growth is 50% or 5 employees. Both will have the same absolute growth but the former will have achieved a substantially higher relative growth (600% compared to 50%). This exemplifies the problem with relative and absolute measures. Consequently, regardless of the used measure, growth will be dependent of the size of the firm. This is a well-known problem which is often reported in the method section, and thereafter is ignored when the results are discussed and compared with results of other studies. An exception is researchers in economics, who have worked extensively with this problem, which becomes especially clear when testing Gibrat's Law, which states that firm growth rate is independent of firm size (c.f., Konings, 1995; Storey, 1989). A possibility to avoid this kind of problems is to work with samples and sub-samples where size is either randomised or preferably controlled for.

Many studies have logarithmised the dependent variable in order to correct a skewed distribution, and thereby fulfilling the assumption of the normal distribution of residuals. Skewness is not a significant problem, because normality is not an important assumption in estimating the most efficient unbiased coefficient, but skewness generates unnecessary outliers. Consequently, skewness compromises the interpretation of the least square fit, because fit is dependent on the distribution around the mean, and the mean is not an appropriate measure for a skewed distribution (Fox, 1991; Tabachnick & Fidell, 1989). Differently stated, whereas the estimates will be correct, we will have a low explained variance. Therefore, the logarithm of the dependent variable is often an option for obtaining both a higher fit and a better use of the data. The problem is the interpretation of the model after a transformation has been made. In other terms, we have to consider how the interpretation of the model is changed by the transformation and how it affects our theoretical conclusions. In a linear (non-transformed) model, the interpretation is pretty straightforward, i.e., when x changes with one unit, then y' changes with β units. In a log-transformed model the relation is also the same (additive), but we assume an exponential growth function. In other words, we should be careful to compare the effect of a variable that is linear, and in another model exponential, as is the case with a logarithmised model. If different studies use different models we cannot compare their fit to data. Furthermore, the coefficients for the variables are not comparable, but we should assume that variables found statistically different in an additive model, thereby having an influence on the dependent variable, are also significant in an exponential model. What affects y should normally also affect log y. It is consequently possible to compare if the same variables are included in different studies, if the only difference is log transformation; and thereby assess the importance of a variable as an predictor. However, an additive and a log-transformed model assume different theoretical explanations. This is something that was seldom acknowledged in the sampled studies when the results from one study was compared with the results from previous studies

In sum, I conclude that most researchers seem to calculate their measures in order to arrange data in such a way that the highest possible explanation can be achieved, warranting little importance to the possibility of comparing results among studies. The simplest way would be to present several models with the dependent variable calculated differently. To summarise, too much emphasis is probably put on achieving a high explained variance and significant variables, when researchers should perhaps concentrate on making studies more easily comparable, and acknowledge the fact that research can evolve only if it is possible to accumulate findings that are easily comparable, e.g., using confidence interval instead of significance. The effect of log transformation will be dealt with more closely in Part 2 of this paper.

The Measurement Period. The third choice to be made is the numbers of years to be included in the measurement period. This choice should be based on the chosen problem of the study, i.e., are we more interested in factors determining changes over a longer period of time or over a shorter period of time? Table 13.4 summarises different time periods chosen and their frequencies.

Table 13.4   **The Measurement Periods in Number of Years and their Frequencies**

Years	Frequency	Percent
5	13	23.6
1	12	21.8
3	9	16.4
2	4	7.3
4	2	3.6
6	1	1.8
7	1	1.8
8	1	1.8
Missing	12	21.8
Total	55	100

The most common time periods are periods of five years, of one year and of three years. When reviewing the studies included in the sample little or no information was given why one time period was favoured over another. However, we can assume that the measurement period does affect the variables included in the final model, because growth is dependent on both short and long term changes.

Another large group was missing value. This group was composed of three sub-groups: studies using subjective measures without stating the time period (n = 5), studies measuring growth as the difference between the birth year and the measuring year (n = 5), and studies where the time period was not found by the author (n = 2).

Little work has been done on the choice of time period and its consequences on the outcome of an analysis. It is probable that the time period has an effect, because, as stated earlier, some changes in the organisation due to a change in demand are lagged. We do not know how these changes are reflected in the choice of time period, and how they affect the resulting model.

The Comparability of Growth Studies. After this review of the growth measures, it is concluded that there was an abundance of different ways of assessing growth in a firm, but were there patterns in growth measurement that allowed comparison of results or were the choice of measures more or less random? A cross-tabulation of the growth indicator based on (a) the chosen indicator, (b) the chosen calculation, and (c) the chosen time period, was performed, yielding an indication on how many researcher have used the same growth indicator, and can therefore be considered to be directly comparable.

The most frequently used combination was relative changes in sales measured over a five-year period. This combination was chosen in six studies. The second most popular combinations were relative changes in number of employees or sales over a three-year period with three studies respectively. In third position, relative changes in numbers of employees, absolute changes in sales over a one-year period, and multiple indicators over a five-year period, were used in two studies respectively. All other combinations scored a maximum of one in each cell.

To conclude, little congruence was found among the used growth measures. This is a somewhat alarming result considering that the differences stemming from working with alternative analytic methods have not even been accounted for. Theses differences can, however, be largely corrected with meta-analytic procedures (Rosenthal, 1991). I am more concerned with how growth measures are apparently chosen in a relatively *ad hoc* manner without any (reported) considerations to the theoretical consequences. The choices that were made, were often based on empirical matters.

Summary of Result of Part 1. This review was based on 55 studies published in some of the major research journals dealing with small business and entrepreneurship. It was concluded that direct comparability among studies was low because a large array of different indicators, time periods, and calculations were used when assessing growth. It was argued that objective measures such as growth in numbers of employees and sales were favourable compared to subjective measures such as perceived performance or market share. Furthermore, the growth indicators were calculated as relative or absolute changes, and some times logarithmised. Most researchers were aware of the problems connected with relative and absolute changes, but the differences between an additive and an exponential model was seldom commented upon. Finally, little attention has been given to the importance of the measured time period. It was argued that different time perspectives might yield different results, because organisational changes are lagged relative to each other. In the next section, I will empirically illustrate some of the points made in this section. More precisely, I will test the relationship among number of employees and sales, relative and absolute changes, and the effect of exponential and additive models.

An Empirical Test of Different Growth Measures

The purpose of Part 2 was to empirically test the effects of different growth measures on analysis outcomes. After a first correlation table, data were analysed from a theoretical as well as an empirical perspective. That is, in the first case (the theoretical perspective) the same set of variables was tested on the different indicators. With this design, changes in explained variance were assessed and explained. In the second case (the empirical model), the best model was chosen on the basis of maximum explained variance. The purpose was to focus on the changes in variables found significant and how these changes affect the final conclusions.

The Sample

The tests in this part were performed on data gathered for my dissertation work on growth in small and medium sized enterprises (Delmar, 1996). Thus, data were not gathered for the prime purpose of testing the use of different growth measures, but they were judged as having a good potential of exemplifying some of the problems related to the specification of the dependent variable of growth.

The sample was taken from Statistics Sweden's register of all Swedish companies. Several restrictions were imposed. First, the sample was restricted to enterprises between 5 to 49 employees. The 1 to 5 employee class was not included because it contains a large part of part time enterprises. The classes above 50 employees were not included either, because the actual effect of the entrepreneur's behaviour on the business was assumed to diminish with an increasing number of employees. Secondly, the sample was restricted to certain industries (high tech, manufacturing, services, and professional services). Thirdly, the sample was restricted to independent firms, i.e., firms that are not subsidiaries of other firms. Finally, the sample was stratified to ensure equal representation from different size classes and industries.

Of the 730 contacted entrepreneurs, 400 (54.8%) completed the phone interview. The purpose of the survey was to capture data, that according to theory and earlier empirical studies, might explain entrepreneurial and business performance. The first reason to use telephone interviews was the greater probability of a high response rate. The second reason was the large number of questions; the interview and the mail questionnaire contained altogether 261 questions. A split was reasonable to keep up the respondent's attention. The third reason was that the telephone interview afforded a possibility to check that the right person was interviewed. The data were collected during October -December of 1994. Only data from the phone interview were used in this article, because it allowed the use of a larger sample.

The Dependent Variables

Growth was measured as changes in either number of employees or sales over a three year period. There was no particular reason why I choose three years as the time period, other than that my thesis advisor previously used the same time period in one of his studies. Now afterwards, I could argue that the reliability of the measure is dependent on the memory of the respondent and that most entrepreneurs can remember with some accuracy the sales figures and the employment rate three years back.

However, these data made it possible to test the difference between absolute and relative calculations; between logarithm transformations and non-logarithm transformation; and among employment, sales, or multiple indicators. This gave twelve possible measures of how to assess growth.

Absolute growth was measured as the difference among year 1 (1991) and year 3 (1994) in numbers of employees or sales; relative growth was measured by dividing the numbers of employees or sales year 3 (1994) by the corresponding figures year 1 (1991); Multiple indicators were measured as the sum of changes in employees and in sales; Log transformed measures were based on the natural log.

Analysis

All analyses were based on multiple regression, where in the first case all variables were entered at the same time, and in the second case, stepwise regression was used. Stepwise regression was used because it was the most popular of the regression techniques in the reviewed sample (47.3% of the sampled articles used regression and the single most popular variation was stepwise regression representing 23% of the sample).

Results

Relationship Among the Growth Indicators. The purpose was to examine if there was a pattern of relationships among the different growth measures. Table 13.5 displays the correlation matrix for the twelve different growth measures. All relationships were significant at $p<0.05$. This does not have any practical meaning in this case, because the significance test would detect a relationship as significant at the $p<0.05$ level at correlation levels of 0.1 or higher given the size of the present sample.

What is observed in the correlation matrix was sets of measures being highly correlated with each other, but not with other groups. The main result was that relative measures were not comparable to absolute measures (i.e., poorly correlated with each other), regardless of the choice sales, multiple indicator or number of employees, or whether it was logarithmised or not.

Sales and employment correlated highly with each other, which suggests that they were comparable from an empirical point of view. Changes in productivity, the suggested lagged effect, or the possibility to sub contract (discussed in part 1) did not have a substantial effect, at least not over the measured three-year period. It is possible that the chosen time period has erased these effects, because a business adapts faster. Nevertheless, it should be noticed that sales explained 80.3% of the variance at best (ln abs sales and ln abs emp), and at worst 37.9% of variance in employees (ln abs sales and rel empl). The variation in magnitude of the relationships among different growth indicators indicates that the outcome of one model cannot be compared with another. These differences were further investigated by testing a set of variables, focusing on how the different growth measures changed the outcomes. Furthermore, I did not control for if the relationship between sales and employees has altered over time.

Table 13.5   Correlation Matrix of the Investigated Twelve Growth Measures (N = 396)

	Abs empl	Abs growth	Abs sales	Rel empl	Rel growth	Rel sales	Ln abs emp	Ln abs growth	Ln abs sales	Ln rel emp	Ln rel growth	Ln rel sales
Abs empl	1.000											
Abs multiple	.970	1.000										
Abs sales	.830	.941	1.000									
Rel empl	.240	.228	.190	1.000								
Rel multiple	.245	.267	.270	.889	1.000							
Rel sales	.203	.250	.291	.615	.908	1.000						
Ln abs emp	.878	.792	.592	.187	.192	.159	1.000					
Ln abs multiple	.725	.653	.488	.124	.140	.127	.935	1.000				
Ln abs sales	.768	.761	.675	.158	.216	.228	.896	.958	1.000			
Ln rel emp	.389	.371	.309	.828	.808	.632	.334	.226	.277	1.000		
Ln rel multiple	.345	.368	.363	.748	.882	.835	.289	.208	.307	.919	1.000	
Ln rel sales	.277	.333	.376	.565	.811	.879	.226	.175	.306	.734	.935	1.000

Test of the Theoretical Model. Here, the purpose was to examine how the same variables differed in their ability to explain variance in the different growth indicators. Six variables were chosen to be included in this theoretical model. They were chosen because they are well known, and often used as control variables. The six variables were: firm size, start-up year (as indication of firm age), industry, mode of entry (two dummy variables, created and bought), and the age of the entrepreneur (birth year). Table 13.6 displays the results from the analysis, and it was concluded that the same model apparently differed substantially in its ability to explain the variance in the dependent variable. Explained variance for the same applied model ranged from 3% to 45%. The difference was even greater if adjusted figures were examined and where even a negative value showed up.

Table 13.6   Explained Variance for Different Growth Measures with the Same Model

Growth measure	Explained variance	Adj. explained variance	N
Abs empl	.029	.014	396
Abs multiple	.009	-.007	393
Abs sales	.032	.017	393
Rel empl	.055	.040	396
Rel multiple	.073	.059	393
Rel sales	.066	.052	393
Ln abs empl	.326	.316	396
Ln abs multiple	.447	.439	393
Ln abs sales	.245	.234	393
Ln rel empl	.090	.076	396
Ln rel multiple	.100	.087	393
Ln rel sales	.098	.084	393

Can we conclude that the model was only significant in some and not in other cases? If we should choose a model based on explained variance and significance of the independent variables alone, we should choose the one with logarithmised absolute growth as the dependent variable. However, how bad were the rest of the models and why? This variation in explained variance was mainly a result of the distribution of the dependent variables. All dependent variables departed from the normal distribution assumption (as measured by skewness and kurtosis), therefore generating these large differences in explained variance.

Consequently, the influence of each variable (the expected direction) was the same in almost every case, as suggested in part 1. The normal distribution assumption, as has been stated earlier, is not necessary (but helpful), to produce the best linear unbiased estimator. Even if explained variance is an important factor to consider, we should also focus on the estimator and its confidence interval, if explanation, and not only prediction, is the research goal.

The Empirical Model. In this section, the best model was chosen on the basis of maximum explained variance. The purpose was to focus on the changes in the variables found statistically significant and on how these changes affect the final conclusions. This was achieved by adding another ten variables to the previous set of variables. They were also chosen on the basis of their attributed importance in the literature. These were: type of customers (businesses or consumers), dependence on most important customers, export, present competitive position, intensity of competition, dependence on suppliers, number of board meetings per year, board composition, attributed importance of the board, and planning. A total of sixteen variables were tested with a forward stepwise selection procedure. Table 13.7 displays the outcomes of these analyses.

Table 13.7 **Results from the Empirical Model with 95% Confidence Interval for B (N = 378)**

Growth measure	Variable	B	Lower bound	Upper Bound	Adj. R^2
Abs emplo	Constant	3.071	.345	5.797	.017
	Size	-.103	-.176	-.030	
Abs multiple	Constant	18.878	2.822	34.933	.005
	Competition	-3.464	-7.491	.562	
Abs sales	Constant	2.733	.761	4.705	.023
	Size	.086	.032	.141	
Rel emplo	Constant	.737	.163	1.311	.105
	Suppliers	.020	.011	.029	
	Birth year of entrepreneur	.016	.007	.026	
	Create	.253	.081	.425	
	Competition	-.115	-.198	-.032	
Rel multiple	Constant	.503	-.348	1.354	.106
	Suppliers	.038	.022	.054	
	Birth year of entrepreneur	.040	.022	.057	
	Create	.457	.140	.775	
Rel sales	Constant	.423	-.063	.909	.066
	Birth year of entrepreneur	.021	.011	.031	
	Suppliers	.017	.008	.027	
ln abs emplo	Constant	5.645	5.633	5.657	.317
	Size	-.002	-.002	-.002	
Ln abs multiple	Constant	5.872	5.847	5.898	.434
	Size	-.003	-.003	-.003	
Ln abs sales	Constant	4.522	4.497	4.548	.230
	Size	-.004	-.004	-.003	
Ln rel emplo	Constant	-.078	-.376	.221	.099
	Birth year of entrepreneur	.009	.004	.014	
	Size	-.002	-.003	-.001	
	Competition	-.071	-.114	-.028	
	Create	.139	.050	.228	
Ln rel multiple	Constant	.499	.210	.788	.088
	Birth year of entrepreneur	.012	.007	.016	
	Create	.136	.049	.222	
	Competition	-.058	-.100	-.016	
Ln rel sales	Constant	-.035	-.682	-.179	.074
	Birth year of entrepreneur	.013	.008	.019	
	Manufacturing	.137	.042	.232	

Two main results were obvious from this session. Firstly, all dependent variables based on absolute figures were dependent on size and nothing else. Consequently, a high explained variance is *per se* not especially interesting. Size was negatively related to all dependent variables except in one model. The interpretation was that small firms grow faster than larger firms when growth was measured as absolute changes, except for growth as absolute changes in sales. For the dependent variables calculated as relative changes, different variables emerged for the different growth variables. However, younger entrepreneurs, that had created their business, had achieved higher levels of growth in their firms than older entrepreneurs. Being in a market were competition was low also led to higher growth rates. Thus, dependent variables calculated as relative changes yielded more complex models than dependent variables calculated as absolute changes. Thereby, the same set of variables gave a totally different picture of the processes underlying firm growth. It was concluded that choice of growth indicator yielded different results even when tested on the same data.

Secondly, the high variation in explained variance persisted, which was expected because of the distribution of the dependent variables (i.e., the growth indicators). The explained variance was on the average lower for these models than in the sample surveyed in part 1 of the present study. The reason is that the explanatory variables were mainly included in the mail questionnaire, and the purpose of the phone survey was to collect control and the dependent variables.

Summary of Result of Part 2. We have seen that there were large differences between growth calculated as absolute changes and growth calculated as relative changes. The correlations between the two were low, ranging from a minimum of .175 to a maximum of .389. We have also witnessed how the same set of variables drastically differed in their ability to measure growth dependent on how the growth was measured. These differences were attributed to the distribution of the dependent variable which had high values of skewness and kurtosis. It was argued that the estimators were BLUE (best linear unbiased estimator) (Wonnacott & Wonnacott, 1979) and that more emphasis should be put on the estimation of the predictors, rather than on seeking to achieve a high explained variance. Furthermore, we have seen that models based on relative measures gave a totally different result than a model based on an absolute measure. The logarithm of a measure did not significantly alter the included independent variables, but the coefficients changed in amplitude.

Conclusions and Discussions

The purpose of this study was to examine the effects due to differences in the measurement and calculation of the dependent variable of growth. It was argued that the heterogeneity of different measures impeded theory development. To this end, I have in a first part reviewed 55 recent growth studies, and in a second part used data from a sample of small businesses to examine the effects of different growth measures.

The major findings were that most previous studies were based on samples from manufacturing industries. Furthermore a large array of different measures were used, making direct comparisons among studies very difficult, if not impossible. The growth measures were broken down into three variables: (a) used indicator, (b) calculation, and (c) time period. Most researchers were aware of the effect of growth calculated as relative or absolute changes. However, little attention was given to the choice of indicator, the chosen time period and the consequences of transformations of the dependent variable. It was argued that different phases of the growth process was measured depending on whether changes were measured as changes in, for instance, sales or numbers of employees. This choice had also direct consequences on the chosen measurement period. In the second part, it was concluded that growth measured as relative or absolute changes differed significantly, consequently yielding different models. In other words, the same model differed greatly in its ability to explain growth dependent on the chosen indicator, and different variables explained relative and absolute changes in organisational growth.

It can be concluded that these results depict a poor image of the research field. Apparently little effort has been done to truly understand the pros and cons of different growth measures. Most of the research done in this field was difficult to compare because of lack in agreement on or interest in how the dependent growth variable should be measured and calculated. This automatically leads to confusion as to whether or not an independent variable is significant, and to the nature of its specific influence on growth. The results also indicated that the use of confidence intervals may be more appropriate to use than simple levels of significance. The reason is that significance tests are poor measures of the influence of a single variable (Schmidt, 1996; Cohen, 1994). It is better to consider each separate study as a contribution to research, were questions about a set variables assumed importance can be resolved by systematically aggregate findings from different studies. Seldom do we find a single study that has the properties needed to generalise and to finally state the influence of a set of variables. This can probably be better done by using meta-analytical methods. If confidence intervals are reported, then even insignificant results may be regarded as valuable, because they can be combined with other studies.

Research findings can be more easily interpret if results were reported for several models, not only the one that yielded the highest explained variance. This procedure would lead to a higher level of direct comparativeness among studies, but also to a higher awareness of the model robustness. Furthermore, if prediction and explanation of organisational growth are the purpose, then multiple indicators should be favoured, rather than of single indicators such as sales, number of employees, or assets. Multiple indicators have the assumed property of representing a theoretical construct, and in that way the researcher avoids the pitfall of whether or not organisational growth can be seen in different phases, and which indicators are possibly the best indicators of the various phases.

The limitations of the present study is that it is concerned dealing with a small sample of the growth literature. Only published articles were reviewed, and other publications were left out of account (such as dissertations and conference proceedings). This may have led to a more negative evaluation of the field, because space limitations in journal may force authors and editors to minimise the method section in favour of other sections. However, it has been shown that more work must be done in justifying how the dependent measures was constructed as reported and why. A qualifiers of this study is that the sample was based on recent articles, and therefore can be assumed to give an accurate description of the state of the art. Furthermore, I have systematised and statistically analysed the results from the review. The limitations of the second part was that data was not primarily gathered to test the validity and reliability of different growth measures. This limitation did not allow me for testing the impact of different time periods, or to compare subjective measures with objective measures. Therefore, only a partial test was actually performed. A qualifier was the possibility to use a large sample with a large set of different variables available. For this study as a whole, the advantage was the combination of a literature review of the field and an empirical investigation, which makes it possible to more deeply penetrate the problems related to the definition and measurement of the dependent variable of growth.

Much more work needs to be done on the consequences of the design of the growth measures. However, I will here focus on what I perceive as the most important features. Apparently, there is little knowledge about the two choices made when designing the growth measure: (1) how does the choice of indicator such as, e.g., numbers of employees or sales, and (2) how does the choice of measurement period affect the final model? I have here presented some arguments that suggest that these two factors may have a higher importance for our models than previously acknowledged. It is therefore important to further investigate the validity of these arguments, because these choices may have a paramount importance for our final models.

To conclude, I truly believe that we will only be able to advance the research frontiers of organisational growth by better systematisation of the dependent variables and of our findings. If we are not able to compare and accumulate knowledge about our results, what is the point of research? It merely becomes an academic discussion where the possibility of consensus is small and practical value even smaller. This cannot be the purpose in such an applied research field as entrepreneurship and organisational growth.

References

Anderson, O., & Strigel, W.H. (1981). Business Surveys and economic research- A review of significant developments. In H. Laumer & M.Ziegler (Eds.), *International Research on Business Cycle Surveys* (pp.25-54). Munich: Springer-Verlag.

Begley, T.M., & Boyd, D.P. (1987). Psychological characteristics associated with performance in entrepreneurial firms and smaller businesses. *Journal of Business Venturing, 2,* 79-93.

Brush, C.G., & Vanderwerf, P.A. (1992). A comparison of methods and sources for obtaining estimates of new venture performance. *Journal of Business Venturing, 7,* 157-170.

Chandler, G.N., & Hanks, S.H. (1993). Measuring the performance of emerging businesses: A validation study. *Journal of Business Venturing, 8,* 391-408.

Cohen, J. (1994). The earth is round (p<.05). *American Psychologist, 49,* 997-1003.

Cragg, P.B., & King, M. (1988). Organizational characteristics and small firms' performance revisited. *Entrepreneurship Theory and Practice, Winter,* 49-64.

Delmar, F. (1996). *Entrepreneurial Behavior and Business Performance.* Doctoral Dissertation, Stockholm School of Economics, Economic Research Institute.

Fox, J. (1991). *Regression Diagnostics.* Newbury Park: Sage Publications, Inc.

Gupta, A.K. & Govinarajan, V. (1984). Business unit strategy, managerial characteristics, and business unit effectiveness at strategy implementation. *Academy of Management Journal, 27,* 25-41.

Konings, J. (1995). Gross job flows and the evolution of size in U.K. establishements. *Small Business Economics, 7,* 213-220.

Miller, D. (1987). Strategy making and structure: Analysis and implications for performance. *Academy of Management Journal, 30,* 7-32.

Miller, D., & Toulouse, J. (1986). Chief executive personality and corporate strategy and structure in small firms. *Management Science, 32,* 1389-1409.

Murphy, G.B., Trailer, J.W., & Hill, R.C. (1996). Measuring Performance in Entrepreneurship. *Journal of Business Research, 36,* 15-23.

Rosenthal, R. (1991). *Meta-Analytic Procedures for Social Research.* Newbury Park, California 91320: Sage Publications, Inc.

Schmidt, F.L. (1996). Statistical significance testing and cumulative knowledge in psychology: Implications for training of researchers. *Psychological Methods, 1,* 115-129.

Storey, D.J. (1995). Symposium on Harrison's "Lean and Mean": A job generation perspective. *Small Business Economics, 7,* 337-340.

Storey, D.J. (1989). Firm performance and size: Explanations from the small firm sectors. *Small Business Economics, 1,* 175-180.

Tabachnick, B.J., & Fidell, L.S. (1989). *Using Multivariate Statistics.* New York: Harper Collins.

Wonnacott, R.J., & Wonnacott, T.H. (1979) *Econometrics* (2nd ed.). New York: John Wiley & Sons.

References Included in the Review

Arbaugh, J.B., & Sexton, D.L. (1996). New firm growth and development: a replication and extension of Reynolds' research. *Journal of Enterprising Culture, 4,* 19-36.

Arrighetti, A. (1994). Entry, growth and survival of manufacturing firms. *Small Business Economics, 6,* 127-137.

Audretsch, D.B. (1995). Innovation, growth and survival. *International Journal of Industrial Organization, 13,* 441-457.

Begley, T.M., & Boyd, D.P. (1987). Psychological characteristics associated with performance in entrepreneurial firms and smaller businesses. *Journal of Business Venturing, 2,* 79-93.

Binks, M.R., & Ennew, C.T. (1996). Growing firms and the credit constraint. *Small Business Economics, 8,* 17-25.

Birley, S., & Westhead, P. (1994). A taxonomy of business start-up reasons and their impact on firm growth and size. *Journal of Business Venturing, 9,* 7-31.

Box, T.M., Watts, L.R., & Hisrich, R.D. (1994). Manufacturing entrepreneurs: An empirical study of the corrolates of employment growth in the Tulsa MSA and Rural East Texas. *Journal of Business Venturing, 9,* 261-270.

Box, T.M., White, M.A., & Barr, S.H. (1993). A contingency model of new manufacturing firm performance. *Entrepreneurship Theory and Practice, 18,* 31-46.

Brooksbank, R., Kirby, D.A., & Wrigth, G. (1992). Marketing and company performance: An examination of medium sized manufacturing firms in Britain. *Small Business Economics, 4,* 221-236.

Chaganti, R., & Schneer, J.A. (1994). A study of the impact of owner's mode of entry on venture performance and management patterns. *Journal of Business Venturing, 9,* 243-260.

Chandler, G.N., & Hanks, S.H. (1994). Market attractiveness, resource-based capabilities, venture strategies, and venture performance. *Journal of Business Venturing, 9,* 331-349.

Chandler, G.N., & Jansen, E. (1992). The founder's self-assessed competence on venture performance. *Journal of Business Venturing, 7,* 223-236.

Cooper, A.C., Gimeno-Gascon, F.J., & Woo, C.Y. (1994). Initial human and financial capital as predictors of new venture performance. *Journal of Business Venturing, 9,* 371-395.

Covin, J.G. (1991). Entrepreneurial versus conservative firms: a comparison of strategies and performance. *Journal of Mangement Studies, 28,* 439-462.

Covin, J.G., & Covin, T.J. (1990). Competitive aggressiveness, environmental context, and small firm performance. *Entrepreneurship Theory and Practice, Summer,* 35-50.

Covin, J.G., & Slevin, D.P. (1990). New venture strategic posture, structure, and performance: An industry life cycle analysis. *Journal of Business Venturing, 5,* 123-135.

Covin, J.G., Slevin, D.P., & Covin, T.J. (1990). Content and performance of growth-seeking strategies. A comparison of small firms in high- and low-technology industries. *Journal of Business Venturing, 5,* 391-412.

Cragg, P.B., & King, M. (1988). Organizational characteristics and small firms' performance revisited. *Entrepreneurship Theory and Practice, Winter,* 49-64.

Cressy, R. (1996). Pre-entrepreneurial income, cash-flow, growth and survival of startup businesses: model and tests on U.K. Data. *Small Business Economics, 8,* 49-58.

Davidsson, P. (1989). Continued Entrepreneurship and Small Firm Growth. Stockholm School of Economics, The Economic Research Institute.

Donckels, R., & Lambrecht, J. (1995). Networks and small business growth: an explanatory. *Small Business Economics, 7,* 273-289.

Doutriaux, J. (1992). Emerging high-tech firms: How durable are their comparative start-up advantages? *Journal of Business Venturing, 7,* 303-322.

Dunne, P., & Hughes, A. (1996). Age, size, growth and survival: UK companies in the 1980s. *Journal of Industrial Economics, XLII,* 115-140.

Dunne, T., Roberts, M.J., & Samuelson, L. (1989). The growth and failure of U.S. manufacturing plants. *The Quartely Journal of economics, November,* 671-698.

Gales, L.M., & Blackburn, R.S. (1990). An analysis of the impact of supplier strategies and relationships on small retailer actions, perceptions, and performance. *Entrepreneurship Theory and Practice, Fall,* 7-21.

Ginn, C.W., & Sexton, D.L. (1990). A comparison of the personality type dimensions of the 1987 Inc. 500 company founders/CEOs with those of slower-growth firms. *Journal of Business Venturing, 5,* 313-326.

Hansen, E.L. (1995). Entrepreneurial network and new organization growth. *Entrepreneurship Theory and Practice,* 7-19.

Kazanjian, R.K., & Drazin, R. (1990). A stage-contingent model of design and growth for technology based new ventures. *Journal of Business Venturing, 5,* 137-150.

Kolvereid, L. (1992). Growth aspirations among Norvegian entrepreneurs. *Journal of Business Venturing, 7,* 209-222.

Kolvereid, L., & Bullvag, E. (1996). Growth intentions and actual growth: The impact of entrepreneurial choice. *Journal of Enterprising Culture, 4,* 1-17.

Mata, J. (1994). Firm growth during infancy. *Small Business Economics, 6,* 27-39.

McCann, J.E. (1991). Patterns of growth, competitive technology, and financial strategies in young ventures. *Journal of Business Venturing,* 189-208.

McGee, J.E., Dowling, M.J., & Megginson, W.L. (1995). Cooperative strategy and new venture performance: The role of business strategy and management experience. *Strategic Management Journal, 16,* 565-580.

Merz, G.R., & Sauber, M.H. (1995). Profiles of manegerial activities in small firms. *Strategic Management Journal, 16,* 551-564.

Miller, D. (1987). Strategy making and structure: Analysis and implications for performance. *Academy of Management Journal, 30,* 7-32.

Miller, D., & Toulouse, J. (1986). Chief executive personality and corporate strategy and structure in small firms. *Management Science, 32,* 1389-1409.

Miner, J.B., Smith, N.R., & Bracker, J.S. (1989). Role of entrepreneurial task motivation in the growth of technologically innovative firms. *Journal of Applied Psychology, 74,* 554-560.

Miner, J.B., Smith, N.R., & Bracker, J.S. (1994). Role of entrepreneurial task motivation in the growth of technologically innovative firms: Interpretations from follow-up data. *Journal of Applied Psychology, 79,* 627-630.

Ming-Hone Tsai, W., MacMillan, I.C., & Low, M.B. (1991). Effects of strategy and environment on corporate venture in industrial markets. *Journal of Business Venturing, 6,* 9-28.

Morris, M.H., & Sexton, D.L. (1996). The concept of entrepreneurial intensity: Implications for company performance. *Journal of Business Research, 36,* 5-13.

O'Farrell, P.N., Hitchens, D.M.W.N., & Moffat, L.A.R. (1992). The competitiveness of business service firms: A matched comparison between Scotland and the South East of England. *Regional Studies, 26,* 519-533.

Ostgaard, T.A., & Birley, S. (1996). New venture growth and personal networks. *Journal of Business Research, 36,* 37-50.

Peters, M.P., & Brush, C.G. (1996). Market information scanning activities and growth in new ventures: A comparison of service and manufacturing businesses. *Journal of Business Research, 36,* 81-89.

Phillips, B.D., & Kirchhoff, B.A. (1989). Formation, growth and survival; small firm dynamics in the U.S. economy. *Small Business Economics, 1,* 65-74.

Siegel, R., Siegel, E., & MacMillan, I.C. (1993). Characteristics distinguishing high-growth ventures. *Journal of Business Venturing, 8,* 169-180.

Storey, D.J. (1994). New firm growth and bank financing. *Small Business Economics, 6,* 139-150.

Stuart, R.W., & Abetti, P.A. (1990). Impact of entrepreneurial and mangement experience on early performance. *Journal of Business Venturing, 5,* 151-162.

Thwaites, A., & Wynarczyk, P. (1996). The economic performance of innovative small firms in the south east region and elsewhere in the UK. *Regional Studies, 30,* 135-149.

Vaessen, P., & Keeble, D. (1995). Growth-oriented SMEs in unfavourable regional environments. *Regional Studies, 29,* 489-505.

Wagner, J. (1992). Firm size, firm growth and persistence of chance. Testing GIBRAT's law with establishment data form lower Saxony, 1978-1989. *Small Business Economics, 4,* 125-131.

Wagner, J. (1994). The post-entry performance of new small firms in German manufacturing industries. *Journal of Industrial Economics, XLII,* 141-154.

Westhead, P. (1995). Source and employment growth contrast between types of owner-managed high-technology firms. *Entrepreneurship Theory and Practice,* 5-27.

Willard, G.E., Krueger, D.A., & Feeser, H.R. (1992). In order to grow, must the founder go: A comparison of performance between founder and non-founder managed high-growth manufacturing firms. *Journal of Business Venturing, 7,* 181-194.

Williams, M.L., Tsai, M., & Day, D. (1991). Intangible assets, entry strategies, and venture success in industrial markets. *Journal of Business Venturing, 6,* 315-333.

Zahra, S.A. (1993). Environment, corporate entrepreneurship, and financial performance: a taxonomic approach. *Journal of Business Venturing, 8,* 319-340.

14 Information Use as Counter-Proof for the Stochastic Growth Theories

Nadine Lybaert

Introduction

In our complex industrial environment, it is more important to 'know' what must be done and when than how to 'do' it. For big companies, the proposition that information can be considered as an increasingly important production factor has been repeatedly supported in the literature. For smaller companies, the evidence is less comprehensive, especially where the Belgian SMEs are concerned (for instance, Bragard et al. 1992). Actually, it is very astounding that in this information age - in which the importance of information for everyone is so accentuated - there are so few profound scientific studies on the role information plays in the SME, and this despite the fact that the potential importance of information processing for success has also been stressed for small companies.

Though it is peculiar for a SME that the strategic position of its owner/manger serves as a 'focal' point around which all business activities are centralised, including those of information search and assimilation. It is precisely this decisive role - not the least in the information process - which is, according to many, the reason why the SMEs are more vulnerable than large companies. Indeed, the SME owner/manager often does not possess the necessary means (knowledge, money and time) to fulfil his need for information (VBO 1990), and perhaps more importantly, to optimally analyse and apply the results from the collected data for use in managing. Many SME owner/managers possess limited knowledge of modern management techniques (Donckels et al. 1987), although this knowledge is a primary requisite for the optimal use of information.

Thus, the central research question we want to answer in this work is whether Belgian SMEs which are better at gathering and analysing information have a competitive advantage over their rivals, or stated differently, do those SME owner/managers who are strongly information oriented, have a better chance of surviving and being successful?

When formulating the hypothesis, we implicitly assume that information does play a definite role for a given level of performance. However, in industrial economies, there is a whole family of stochastic growth theories which state that the growth of a firm is completely random and is only determined by pure chance. Thus, before going into the question of to what extent information has an influence on success, we must show that there really is a role reserved for success factors other than chance. In this study, rejecting the stochastic growth theories does not happen exclusively by referring to former research mentioned in the literature, but also on basis of an empirical sector study. More specifically, we go into the observed growth variability for the various Belgian industrial sectors.

After the stochastic growth theories are rejected on basis of theory and empiricism, we continue with the sector study, and question whether information is one of the many success-determining factors. Once again, so as to obtain an indication of the potential importance of information, we go beyond the literature. By making a connection with certain information-bounded characteristics, we try to prove this finding empirically.

Only after we prove that growth variability is connected with the importance of information, it seems justified to trace whether growth is connected with the use of information. The examination of this relation no longer takes place at the level of the sectors, but at the level of the individual firms. More specifically, the differences in growth finally seem to be the result of the different behaviour at the micro level, since the growth opportunities present in a sector do not necessarily lead to the growth of a firm. Thus, it is the individual actions of the firm which deserve our attention, since they determine the growth of a firm.

As should be clear from this introduction, the paper is organised around three main parts. In the first section we examine whether the stochastic growth theories hold by computing the growth variability in Belgian industrial sectors. If luck is only one of the success factors, we look in the following section for an indication of whether information is a plausible success factor. If the answer is positive, we go in the third and final section into the final question concerning the association between information and success. To link each part, a summary ends every section.

Is Chance the Only Success-Determining Factor?

Gibrat's Law

In industrial economies, there exists a whole family of stochastic growth processes which all have the common feature of making a firm's size in, say, year t+1, proportional, subject to random variation, to its size in year t. According to this theory, the growth of a firm is completely random and chance is more important than any other factor. This process of random growth leading to a lognormal distribution was first described by Gilbrat (1931), and his formulation is termed 'Gilbrat's Law of Proportionate Effect'. The outcome of this stochastic process is a variance that increases steadily over time, leading to an increasing concentration.

To test the hypothesis of the formation of industrial structure over time, two types of information have been investigated. The first is to see how closely the behaviour of firms accords with the assumptions of the theoretical model. The second is to examine how closely the actual size distributions of firms conform with the lognormal distribution.

For the results of these tests, as well as for a more detailed discussion of the theory, we refer to Hay and Morris (1991). Here we can state that the results indicate that the simple formulation of Gibrat's Law does not hold generally. Another overview of some classical and empirical research in which it is traced whether Gibrat's Law holds is given in, for instance, Wagner (1992), where the general impression is also that Gibrat's Law is not valid. Only in very exceptional cases, it was - mostly for a few groups of firms and only for some periods - possible to accept the validity of the Law.

All these results support those people who state that the market structures are, more or less, the determinate result of variables such as technology, the receptiveness of consumers to advertising, the size of the market, the effectiveness of managerial organisation, merger decisions, and government policies. They are of the opinion that we should not expect a model which ignores the underlying cost conditions and market structure to be a good predictor of the market concentration. According to this vision changes in market concentration are the consequence of actions of the individual firms in the first place. However, the stochastical hypothesis is not completely left. Namely the growth equation of a firm is seen as the response on structure determining variables, whereby a substantial stochastic element in the model is allowed.

A First Empirical Counter-Proof for the Validity of Gibrat's Law

Data Collection. We also seek to join the opponents of Gibrat's Law in this study. In our opinion, growth is more than just a random process. Thus, in order to empirically test the validity of Gibrat's Law, we depart from the variability in the sectorial growth performance as an indicator of the uncertainty present in the sector. Stated differently, our dependent variable is the variance of the individual relative growth figures of the firms in the sector.

Next, we must consider how growth should be measured. In Webster's dictionary, growth is defined as 'an increase in size, etc.' This 'etc.' can be a lot of things. A great number of measures are available in the literature (Hay and Morris, 1991). However, in most of the literature, the lack of discussion about the most suitable measure is astounding. Since most Belgian entrepreneurs associate growth with an increase in turnover (Donckels and Hoebeke, 1989), and in view of the popularity of this measure in the literature because of various reasons like availability and compatibility with the goals of the firm (Robinson, 1983), we opt for it. Indeed growth in turnover seems to be the most chosen measure for research concerning entrepreneurship (Crijns et al., 1994).

Thus, as an indication for the growth variability, we compute the variance of the individual relative growth figures for turnover for the firms from the industrial sectors. In order to determine turnover, we use each firm's annual report. Although turnover is key in the business world, only firms with a complete schedule must disclose it.[1]

For the classification in sectors, we use the NACE code, more specifically the three-digit NACE. This brings us to 133 sectors of industry and, in our view, gives a sufficient representation of the data. How many and which firms are considered is explained further in the paper. More specifically, the variability of growth is computed for the sample in Table 14.1, divided over 103 sectors. The results are unskewed since, for instance, firms with a change in turnover of more than 100% are removed from the sample.

Hypothesis and Results. As mentioned, we start from the variability in sectoral growth as a measure of uncertainty in the sectors. According to the stochastic growth theories, it can be assumed that this number differs very little between the sectors since it can be expected that random growth is present in every sector.

The results of 1990 are given in Figure 14.1. The 103 sectors are shown on the horizontal axis in rising sequence of the NACE code. Growth variability is given on the vertical axis. For 1989 and 1988, the same computations are repeated. These results can be found in Figures 14.2 and 14.3.

All together the data indicate that there are very great differences in growth variability for the industrial sectors in Belgium. In 1990, NACE 361 shows a growth variability of 1,584, while it is only 2 for NACE 169. In 1989 these values are between 2,167 (NACE 361) and 1 (NACE 169), and in 1988 between 1,503 (NACE 348) and 18 (NACE 169).

Obviously these results are contrary to the predictions made by the adherents of Gilbrat's Law. The counter-proof is even more convincing by highlighting that it is the same sectors which show a great variability in growth each year and, analogously, the same sectors that show a small variability in growth each year. Given this, we test the following null hypothesis:

H0:   There is no correlation from year to year with respect to the sectoral variability of growth.

To test this hypothesis, we measure the correlation between the three years when the sectors are ranked according to the size of spread, by computing the Spearman Rank Correlation Coefficient. According to these results, the hypothesis of zero correlation in the population between the variable can be rejected at the $p = 0.0001$ level of significance. This strong significant relation holds for 1989-1990, as well as for 1988-1989. The same significance is established when the correlation is measured between the values of the spread, by computing the Pearson Correlation Coefficient.

---

[1]   Firms with an abbreviated schedule may limit themselves to the disclosure of the net added-value (code 7061 + 6071) from the point of view of competition. More specifically, a firm is due to submit an annual report according to the complete schedule from the moment it employs more than 100 people, or it exceeds more than one of the following criteria: turnover ≥ 145 million BEF (excl. VAT), bottom line of business ≥ 70 million BEF and average staff size ≥ 50.

Thus, we conclude that some sectors show a much greater variability in growth than others, and these results are consistent from year to year.

The extent to which the macro-economic situation substantially influences the results is a relevant factor. The three years considered are all situated during an economic boom. So, if there is any influence, it is probably in the same direction every year. Besides, it is our opinion that intersectoral differences are brought about no more, and that the use of cross-sectional data causes no distortion.

Figure 14.1   The Variability of Growth in the Industrial Sectors, 1990

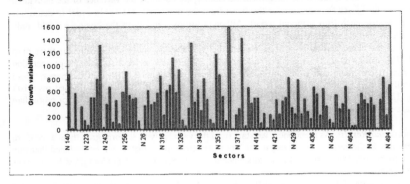

Figure 14.2   The Variability of Growth in the Industrial Sectors, 1989

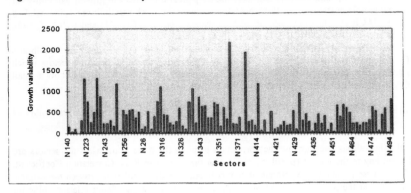

Figure 14.3   The Variability of Growth in the Industrial Sectors, 1988

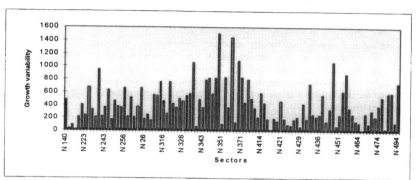

Interpretation as Link to the Plausibility of Information as a Success Factor

Results of our empirical test show that some Belgian industrial sectors show a much greater spread of growth than others and that this phenomenon is consistent. Thus, we have a first indication of the existence of factors other than chance which may determine success. Namely, according to the stochastic growth theories, it can be assumed that there are small differences in the spread between the sectors. Indeed, it is very unlikely that luck plays such a big role in some sectors and is completely absent in other sectors.

Thus, we do not agree with the hypothesis of the stochastic growth theories, stating in its boldest, most radical form, that the market structures observed at any moment in time are the result of pure historical chance. Growth is also determined by other factors, and the industrial structure evolves over time in response to the structure determining variables. Without denying the existence of the innumerable elements with explanatory power for success, we want to emphasise the use of strategic information for growth and to examine whether SMEs which are better at gathering and processing information do gain a competitive advantage over their rivals.[2] To have an indication of the importance of this factor, we trace whether the variability of growth in these sectors is related to certain information-bounded characteristics.

---

[2]   We expect a positive relation between information use and success which is made clear in the doctoral dissertation (Lybaert 1995) starting from the theory of rational expectations. In the more positive approach of this theory it is recognised that information is an economic good for which its use will differ. Because of the cost of information the economic agent will only acquire and process a part of the available information. It is on basis of this partial collection of the relevant information set that the entrepreneur will formulate his expectations. However, when applying such an information set differences will appear between expectation and realisation. The absence of complete information will almost surely lead to misspecifications by the economic agents. Thus, we state that the use of a greater information set by an optimal handling individual will lead to less misspecifications, and therefore, to better expectations. In turn, this will lead to more optimal decisions, and thus to better performance.

Is Information a Plausible Success-Determining Factor?

The Many Success Factors in the Literature

In summarising our findings thus far, we come to two important conclusions. First of all, the random growth hypothesis has considerable appeal. This is completely understandable. Chance plainly does play some role in the company growth: just think about the hiring of key executives or about the choice of an advertising campaign theme. Another reason for its popularity is the fact that firm size distributions observed in the real world often closely correspond to those generated by stochastic process models.

On the other hand, we are also all so thoroughly imbued with the belief that chance favours the well prepared; so much so that it is difficult to accept a model which makes corporate growth the result of mere chance. Those firms which experience a quick rise in their market shares, often seem to be doing 'something' to add value to their products, services, pricing strategies, production processes, and the like. It would be unwise, therefore, to reject more conventional explanations of market structure. Factors such as economies of scale, mergers, and government policies are surely influential, and not merely in a random way. Indeed, the fact that many industries remain atomistically structured despite the concentration-increasing forces associated with stochastic growth suggests that static and dynamic managerial diseconomies of large size and rapid growth must frequently retard the rise of firms to dominance (Scherer 1980).

It is impossible to attribute the success of a firm to one single factor. *The* success factor does not exist and can differ by branch of the firm, by firm and over time. It can even be traced to one group of managers. Many studies have searched for those factors which may explain why some firms - large ones as well as small - are successful, and why some are not. This article does not provide a survey of the sizeable literature. However, most studies about successful and unsuccessful SMEs concentrate on the association between their performances and one or more clear-cut elements. Indeed, possible explanations for differences in performance can be divided into three domains.[3]

So it is important to examine the role of the SME owner/manager in detail because of his strong influence on the firm. Studies of factors such as motivation, personality, education and experience lead to interesting results. Other studies link the success of the SME with firm-specific factors like firm size, location, knowledge of personnel, market research, financial resources, planning process and services. Others are convinced that performance can be attributed to the external environment, and seek possible explanations for differences in performance in the domain of, for instance, the general economic conditions, the structure of industry and legal and fiscal influences.

Given the diversity of the data, there is no one explanation for the success or failure of a company. However, one finding is clear: there is no golden rule or formula to identify future success, however measured. Growth is not a random process but is determined by many other factors, and although we do not claim that the possession of or the correct use of accurate up-to-date information automatically makes the owner/manager successful or rich, we want to further explore the possible relation between information and success.

Information as a Success Factor as Described in the Literature

When discussing the resources necessary for competitive success, the literature almost exclusively is concerned with information based assets, whether these are technological skills, distribution channels, customer knowledge, firm culture, brand names, reputation, managerial skills or entrance to knowledge intensive networks. Over time, the focus of the economy has shifted first from

---

[3]   Naturally, a lot of studies fall into two or three domains.

agriculture to production and distribution, and then to 'information and services'. In this 'information age', machines and equipment are the external proofs, rather than the real core of the 'knowledge revolution' (Garvin and Bermont, 1985). Yet, the electronic revolution makes data available for the firm without precedent in extent and accessibility (Cole, 1985).

Although most discussions are directed towards the intrinsic characteristics of the new information technology (IT), that is, on how they affect the form, extent and depth of information, and pay little attention to how this revolution influences the performance of the firm, it has been demonstrated repeatedly that information and information systems can bring about competitive advantages. Namely, the way information is used leads to a particular type of policymaking, whether intentional or not (Cole, 1985).

Bagwell (1990) demonstrates that the information differentiation of the product can be a barrier to entry. Thus, deterrence comprises not only price, patent policy, product variety, reputation, scale, and capacity (Smiley, 1988), but also information (Fudenberg and Tirole, 1986). Some authors have also proven that information and knowledge are necessary to improve stagnating production levels (Garvin and Bermont, 1985). And although researchers such as, for instance, Strassman (1985) are not equally convinced, this is rather an exception.

Many other studies show that in a hostile environment, a firm's performance is especially improved by introducing changes to the organisational structure, for instance, in the internal administrative structures, the frequency of reporting or the procedures of decisionmaking (for a survey, see Covin and Slevin, 1989). Also, the economic two-period model of Vives (1990) shows that an improvement in the accuracy of information of the firm advances its competitive position as well as its profitability. To understand this result it is important to realise that with an increase in the precision of the information of a firm, the firm will react more on the received signal.

In the industrial world, it repeatedly becomes clear that with the same quality levels of physical inputs some succeed and some do not. A competitive edge can be found in the successful management of the intangible assets (Punset and Sweeney, 1989). Information efficiency also explains why some regions and countries are more developed than others. Until now, conventional economic theories have found no effective explanation for why some regions achieve more, given the same resources.

It is also supposed that Japan's competitive advantage in many sectors can be explained by the active role of the country's decisionmaker played in setting up a system for gathering and spreading information (Cole, 1985). Comparisons between American and Japanese industrial firms highlight that not only administration is important, but also that managers need to use external information, which can lead to important competitive advantages (Lynn, 1982).

Thus, at present it is difficult to underestimate the strategic importance of the IT (IT refers to the flow of information, as well as to the allied technology and applications). Thus, it is very important for a manager to make a competitive analysis in order to establish where IT fits in his firm. This can help the manager to determine the right level of expenses as well as the suited management structure for IT. The right action to be undertaken differs according to the strategy, structure and culture of each firm. Size plays no part. Even the smallest firm can be affected by the progress of computer technology. This also applies, for instance, CAD technology.

Although it is more dangerous than ever to ignore the power of IT, it is more dangerous still to believe that an information system alone can lead to an eduring competitive advantage (Hopper, 1990). The next arena for competitive differentiation revolves around the intensification of analysis, while at the same time new forms of organisation, aimed at the management of the intangible assets, are necessary. A number of authors plead in favour of viewing firms as information processing systems (Applegate et al., 1988; Garvin and Bermont, 1985; Ledin, 1987), although within these companies, the focus must be less on developing stand-alone applications, than on building electronic platforms that can transform their organisational structures and support new ways of making decisions (Hopper, 1990).

An Empirical Indication for the Importance of Information

The Hypothesis. In the section 'A First Empirical Counter-Proof for the Validity of Gilbrat's Law', we showed that there are great differences in the variability of growth of industrial sectors. The question which we now ask is whether the importance of information in the sector explains these differences, as the importance of information differs greatly across sectors.

The industrial classification is linked with the extent of information use because firms in different industrial sectors also generally operate in different factor and product markets. Thus, it can be expected that a manufacturer has other information needs than a retailer. Holmes et al. (1991) showed that a much greater proportion of SMEs from the manufacturing, the wholesale and the finance and services sectors are inclined to draft and use more detailed administrative information, than firms active in the transport, construction and retail sectors. Also, a former study (Holmes and Nicholls, 1989) shows similar conclusions.

Consequently, we want to trace whether the differences in sectoral growth can be linked with the presence of certain structural characteristics that are important for information sensitivity. When we establish a greater variability in growth with a stronger presence of information based strategic variables, we conclude that the importance of strategic planning is a possible explanation. More specifically, firms in sectors with a great variability - or great uncertainty - should also use more information to be successful. This is the most recommended way to reduce or eliminate uncertainty.

Before looking at whether the extent of information use by firms in sectors with a high importance of information explains the extent of growth, we must test the following hypothesis:

> H1: The spread in growth is the same for all sectors, notwithstanding the presence of information related strategic variables.

This hypothesis can be translated as H1: $\beta_i = 0$ for all i. When accepting, two options are possible with respect to the use of information. Or we support the stochastic hypothesis partly, where growth is attributed to luck, and we conclude that information is not important. Or we decide that information is important, although we decide that it does not bring about the differences in growth. Rejecting the hypothesis makes us conclude that the presence of information related strategic variables is systematically related to the growth variance established in the sector.

The Model. As starting point to test the hypothesis, we state that differences appear in the importance of information (II_S) between the sectors. These differences should lead to differences in the degree of uncertainty in those sectors which are measured by the sectoral variation in growth (VG_S). Naturally, the spread in growth is still a function of 1,001 other factors. These influences are jointly given by ε.

$$(1) VG_S = f (II_S) + \varepsilon_1$$

In turn, the importance of information for a given sector (i.e., II_S) is dependent on certain sectoral characteristics which can be presented as X_S.

$$(2) II_S = g (X_S) + \varepsilon_2$$

When we summarise both equations, we find that measurements of VG_S, show differences as a function of X_S.

$$(3) VG_S = h (R\&D_s, INV_s, MAR_s, CON_s, EMP_s) + \varepsilon_4$$

The question that arises here is how we can define X_s, or, which sectoral characteristics should we consider as information-related strategic variables. The sources of uncertainty are numerous and varied. Referring to the theory of Hansen and Wernerfelt (1989), we opt for some characteristics of the industry in which the firm is competing. More specifically, we opt to take into account the sectoral data concerning R&D expenses (R&D), the investment expenses (INV), the marketing expenses (MAR), the degree of concentration (CON), and the share of the white collars (EMP).

(4) $VG_s = h (R\&D_s, INV_s, MAR_s, CON_s, EMP_s) + \varepsilon_4$

In the literature, R&D, INV and MAR are, together with mergers, considered as those ways in which the firm can use accumulated funds to escape the constraints of its existing cost structure and market share (Hay and Morris 1991). In each case the firm acquires and organises new factors of production. The three elements are, as well as CON, also the independent variables which are, without exception, used when regressions are performed for looking at profitability, together with other classic measures such as capital and scale economies. The integration of EMP as fifth variable is self-evident.

For the purpose of our study the integration of the five chosen variables can be justified on basis of some common necessary characteristics: (a) they are strategically important so as to survive and to grow, (b) they need some information orientation, (c) they are relevant for smaller firms as well. Also, problems concerning the gathering of these data are minimal.

Thus, we have five variables that should help to explain or predict the observed variability in the growth of the turnover. To measure the influence of the independent variables, a linear model is used.

(5) $VG_s = \beta_0 + \beta_1 R\&D_s + \beta_2 INV_s + \beta_3 MAR_s + \beta_4 CON_s + \beta_5 EMP_s + \varepsilon_5$

Since not all sectors comprise as many firms, the use of the variables measured in absolute terms is not relevant. Therefore, the independent variables are best measured as relative amounts. With respect to the degree of concentration, there is no problem; although expenses for R&D, investments and marketing are related to the turnover, and the number of white-collar employees to the total staff.

In the literature, many studies have examined the association between two or more variables as, for instance, the association between R&D intensity and advertising with changes in the degree of concentration or between investments and personnel. It is not improbable that a certain multicollinearity exists between the selected variables, although we provisionally treat the variables as separate elements.

We assume that the variability in growth rates differs from industry to industry, and is dependent on the kind of product, the kind of competition, and the like. For the coefficient of the explanatory variables, the following signs are assumed:

R&D: +
INV: +
MAR: +
CON: -
EMP: ?

For instance, with respect to advertising, it can be expected that variability will be very high in industries characterised by quick changes in the product designs, owing to technological innovation, as well as in markets populated by disloyal consumers, who react enthusiastically to a smart advertising campaign. Firms with a good product or promotional idea can make great advances while those who incorrectly predict what the market wants may lose a large part of their market share. Therefore, in advertising-intensive sectors more fluctuations are expected. Thus, the influence of this variable on the variability of growth is supposed to be positive. Analogously, it can be stated that it is important to take advantage of evolutions in R&D, new technologies and the actions of competitors. Thus, strong fluctuations in market shares are also expected in sectors with high R&D expenses, investments and competition.

Only the association with employees is rather doubtful. It seems most logical to assume a positive relation, since the share of white collars gives an indication of the know-how available in a firm. It is this kind of personnel that is charged with acquiring and processing of information (amongst which information about R&D, technological developments, competition and marketing), so that greater differences become possible with a greater representation of this group. On the other hand, it can be assumed that once a certain proportion between workers and employees is exceeded, we are looking at cumbersome, administrative-oriented sectors, or at sectors where elements such as R&D or production renewal are less important, and so do not lead to strong differences in productivity and possibilities for growth. The question here is whether firms with a large share of white-collar employees points to inefficient firms where middle-managers are charged with tasks which are otherwise automated in other firms.

Data Collection. As mentioned, our target group consists of all Belgian industrial firms, belonging to 133 sectors as divided according to the three-digit NACE code. Sectoral data about concentration are collected from the National Institute for Statistics (i.e., a governmental institution which gathers all kinds of Belgian economic data), and sectoral data about marketing expenses from Media Mark (i.e., a private organisation which gathers data on marketing expenses in Belgium).

The other data was drawn from the annual reports submitted according to the complete schedule.[4] Here the necessary data are found under code 8021 (i.e., acquisitions and fixed assets of R&D expenses during the period), under code 8169 (i.e., acquisitions and fixed assets of tangible fixed assets during the period), and under codes 9092, 9093 and 9090 (i.e., employees, management personnel and average number of employed workers). The number of firms available is given in Table 14.1, referred to as target group.

Out necessity, firms that do not mention their turnover for two subsequent years are excluded from the sample, nor do we consider the annual reports of firms that do not mention data about staff, since their annual report is considered as incomplete and inaccurate. The same decision is taken for firms with a relative growth in turnover of more than 100%, since their presence causes a distorted view for the variance of that sector.

We assume that a sector with a greater number of firms gives a more sound picture and is more trustworthy. Therefore, because of the great differences in the number of firms in the various sectors (from 1 to 159), those sectors with 1 and 2 firms are removed, while the others are given weights via the use of 'NUM'. More specifically, sectors with 20 firms or less are given a weight of 1/3. Another new independent variable integrated in the regression is the dummy variable 'TYPE', with an interactive relation with the five other independent variables. This variable makes it possible to make a distinction between the production and consumption sectors since data about marketing expenses are only available for the last ones.[5]

---

[4] Once again we cannot concentrate on firms that submitted an annual report according to the abbreviated schedule, since they do not have to mention data with respect to their turnover, details on intangible fixed assets or the average staff size.

[5] Media Mark compilates figures for marketing expenses in Belgium, from the press, TV and radio, bulletin boards and cinema. Since production sectors have other firms as clients, the organisation does not possess any data about their marketing expenses. For the breakdown between industries of production goods (56 sectors) and industries of consumption goods (47 sectors) we refer to a study by Jacquemin et al. (1978).

Finally, we make one change concerning the dependent variable. Although the variance of the growth in turnover is useful to give an idea about the changes in the variability of growth in the various industrial sectors (cfr. Section 1), this number does not come up to the requirement of normality. Therefore, we apply the standard deviation.

Table 14.1   The Number of Firms in the Final Sample

	1990	1989	1988
NACE 1	42	47	46
NACE 2	487	496	487
NACE 3	771	762	757
NACE 4	1,411	1,494	1,498
NACE 1-4	2,711	2,799	2,788
Target group *	3,488	3,563	3,432

> * i.e., the number of firms in NACE 1-4 with an annual report according
> to the complete schedule, available via the 'Balanscentrale'

The number of firms in the final sample, divided over 103 sectors, is given in Table 14.1. After all the mentioned changes, we arrive to the following model. The subscript s indicates that it concerns sectoral data.

(6) $VG_s = \beta_0 + \beta_1 R\&D_s * TYPE + \beta_2 INV_s * TYPE + \beta_3 MAR_s * TYPE + \beta_4 CON_s * TYPE + \beta_5 EMP_s * TYPE + \varepsilon_6$

Weight = NUM_s

where:

VG_s = the standard deviation of the relative growth in turnover of the sample firms;

$R\&D_s$ = the R&D expenses of all firms with a complete schedule / the turnover of all firms with a complete schedule;

INV_s = the investment expenses of the sample firms / the turnover of the sample firms;

MAR_s = the marketing expenses of the sector / the turnover of all firms with a complete schedule;

CON_s = the Herfindahl(-Hirschman) index of concentration;

EMP_s = the number of employees and board-members of the sample firms / the total staff size of the sample firms;

$TYPE$ = 'product' if it concerns a production sector and 'consume' if it concerns a consumption sector;

NUM_s = 1/3 if the number of studied firms in the sector is less than or equal to 20 and 2/3 if this number is more than 20.

Results. The results of equation (6) are given in Table 14.2. Clearly, an F-value is obtained in two years that allows us to conclude the regression is significant, i.e., that not all β_i's are equal to zero at the $p = 0.05$ level. So we accept the alternative hypothesis that in sectors with a greater variability of growth, a greater presence of information-related strategic variables is established.

Also, the value of R^2 is worth looking at. According to the stochastic growth theories – which view growth as completely stochastic – this quantity should be zero or at least very small. The fact that we come to explain almost one fifth of the variability of growth with only six variables surely is of value. Our model only tries to explain a part of the reality, and we know an innumerable number of other elements exist to remove the remaining percentage. In short, mindful of the theory of Gilbrat and his adherents, these percentages of 15% to 19% are not unimportant numbers and much better than the casualness that explains nothing.

A significant parameter was obtained in only five cases for the significance of the independent variables, be it in the hypothesised direction. Thus, in 1988, there is a significant positive influence of R&D on the dependent variable indicating, as premised, that a greater spread of growth exists in sectors with more R&D. With respect to CON, a significant positive influence is achieved without one exception. Thus, competition influences the company growth to a large extent.

INV is insignificant, but this may be due to the restrictions of the data. First of all, the division in accounting periods is a measure which is artificial in nature. This influence is accentuated by the fact that for each firm the annual report of each financial year is considered separately. For instance, the investments in the examined period can be relatively small, because in a former period important investments were made. Another consideration is that no distinction can be made according to the nature of the investments: expansion or replacement.

Data about MAR were gathered for products and product groups, that we had to divide up within the firms within the NACE code, so as to become usable for our regression. Since data may be incomplete and/or the division of the data incorrect, the absence of any significant results is not that surprising. For EMP it was not obvious to presume a conclusive theoretical and influential direction, as distinct from the other independent variables. No significant influence could be obtained empirically.

Interpretation as Link to the Reality of Information as a Success Factor

Results of our empirical test show that within a sector, the spread of growth is greater according to the stronger presence of certain structural characteristics which are important for information orientation because of the link with growth. Thus, we can conclude that strategic planning is potentially important for growth. More specifically, the strong differences in growth, noticeable in sectors where information is very important, could be due to the mutual differences in information use and strategic planning of the firms. This is the most proper way to eliminate the great uncertainty present in the sector. Since we know the importance of information strongly differs, the next step is to determine whether the use of information explains the mutual differences in growth within the sector.

We can already state that the possibilities for growth present in a sector do not necessarily lead to the growth of a firm. The strong presence of the investigated variables in a sector refers to the existence of possibilities for growth in that sector. However, in such sectors there are all possible forms, ranging from rapid growers to stagnators to rapid shrinkers. The question that arises here is whether the growers are those that make use of the growth possibilities the sector offers, and the shrinkers those who do not make use of them. Since growth is not determined by sector-bounded possibilities, it seems acceptable that the individual actions of the firm itself determine to what group the firm belongs. In other words, growth seems to be attributable to the firm-bounded elements. To test this, we move to the level of the individual firms.

Table 14.2   The Results of the Regression, Presented in Equation (6)

1990:	F-value = 1.90	p-value = 0.0612	$R^2 = 0.1554$

Sector	variable	β-value	T-test (H1: β=0)	p-value
Consume				
	R&D$_s$ * TYPE	- 31.33	- 0.41	0.6794
	INV$_s$ * TYPE	- 5.32	- 0.15	0.8837
	MAR$_s$ * TYPE	18.80	0.82	0.4136
	CON$_s$ * TYPE	- 25.61	- 3.30	*0.0014*
	EMP$_s$ * TYPE	3.92	0.68	0.4976
Product				
	R&D$_s$ * TYPE	124.55	1.33	0.1858
	INV$_s$ * TYPE	- 7.17	- 0.49	0.6222
	CON$_s$ * TYPE	- 4.59	- 0.55	0.5810
	EMP$_s$ * TYPE	3.07	0.41	0.6810

1989:	F-value = 2.03	p-value = *0.0447*	$R^2 = 0.1640$

Sector	variable	β-value	T-test (H1: β=0)	p-value
Consume				
	R&D$_s$ * TYPE	14.11	0.25	0.7995
	INV$_s$ * TYPE	- 49.08	- 1.36	0.1758
	MAR$_s$ * TYPE	27.62	0.77	0.4423
	CON$_s$ * TYPE	- 24.06	- 3.23	*0.0017*
	EMP$_s$ * TYPE	1.55	0.26	0.7936
Product				
	R&D$_s$ * TYPE	100.82	1.45	0.1494
	INV$_s$ * TYPE	15.64	0.79	0.4315
	CON$_s$ * TYPE	- 6.40	- 0.74	0.4589
	EMP$_s$ * TYPE	- 12.25	- 1.75	0.0827

1988:	F-value = 2.42	p-value = *0.0161*	$R^2 = 0.1900$

Sector	variable	β-value	T-test (H1: β=0)	p-value
Consume				
	R&D$_s$ * TYPE	150.95	2.22	**0.0285**
	INV$_s$ * TYPE	- 2.08	- 0.13	0.8967
	MAR$_s$ * TYPE	35.83	1.06	0.2898
	CON$_s$ * TYPE	- 16.40	- 2.46	**0.0159**
	EMP$_s$ * TYPE	- 6.85	- 1.33	0.1872
Product				
	R&D$_s$ * TYPE	138.25	3.02	*0.0032*
	INV$_s$ * TYPE	2.09	0.11	0.9111
	CON$_s$ * TYPE	- 10.90	- 1.48	0.1416
	EMP$_s$ * TYPE	- 2.44	- 0.41	0.6857

p < 0.01   **p < 0.05**

Is Information a Real Success-Determining Factor?

The Hypothesis

From Section 'Information as a Success Factor as Described in the Literature' we can conclude that in this information age, it is hard to overestimate the strategic importance of information. The proposition that having adequate information and a sound information system can bring about competitive advantages has been stated and proved many times in the literature. Also our own empirical results of Section 'An Empirical Indication for the Importance of Information' give a plausible indication of the strategic importance of information.

Given these findings, we look at the firm level in order to trace whether the success of the SME is really explained by its information use. In view of the above results, it is possible to give a limited content to the information variable. More specifically, we restrict the study to the information use concerning the two most significant explanatory strategic variables, that is, competition and R&D. Thus, we formulate the hypothesis as:

> H2: SMEs that are better informed about R&D and their competitors will perform better than average.

So we have no intention here of tracing to what extent the degree of concentration in the sector affects the success of the firm. The individual actions of the firm – that is, the extent to which information about competitors is acquired, processed and interpreted – is what demands our attention. The same approach is presumed for R&D. It is not the importance of these activities in the sector, nor the extent to which the firm performs R&D that is considered, but rather the extent of information use concerning this factor. This approach is especially of importance for the SME because they generally do not invest in R&D themselves, but become informed about what others are doing.

The Methodology: the LISREL-Method

The question we now pose is by which statistical method the causality between both variables needs to be examined. The fact that we are confronted with a connection between two theoretical variables, indicated by a set of indicators, does not leave many alternatives for empirical study. Therefore, the econometric structural equation models (Bollen 1989) are the most suitable. These models allow the researcher to decompose relations among variables and to test causal models that involve both observable (manifest) and unobservable (latent) variables.

Indeed, the two concepts used in the hypothesis are both abstract notions, that must be filled in concretely. Such unobservable, unmeasurable hypothetical constructs are also called latent variables. They can be divided into endogenous (dependent) variables on the one hand (in our study being success), denoted by η, and into exogenous (independent) variables on the other hand (in our study being information use), denoted by ξ.

One of the most relevant approaches which makes it possible to encompass unobservable variables is the general 'LInear Structural RELations' (LISREL) model. Simply described, the LISREL model is a regression methodology for empirical variables which has many advantages. Probably the most important one is its high information content, because it allows the researcher to simultaneously evaluate both the measurement and causal (i.e., structural) components of a system. Other advantages are, for instance, that the LISREL model can easily handle latent factors, measurement errors in both independent and dependent variables, reciprocal causation, simultaneity and interdependence.

The general LISREL model consists of two parts. The second part, that is the structural equation model, looks at whether there are significant relations between the theoretical constructs as formulated in the hypothesis. However, before we concentrate on this, we need to specify the latent variables. Thus, we must collect observable measures. Since the observable variables cannot be taken exclusively from the existing objective data, we used a written survey. It was very important to question the owner/manager himself, since they generally are strongly involved in the management of the SME. His position serves as a strategic focal point, around which all firm activities are centralised, including those of information searcher and assimilator. Thus, he plays a key role in the process of information gathering and processing and is the most important factor that determines the use of information in the SME.[6]

Stated differently, the valid answers of the presidents that were ultimately taken into account had to make it possible to measure and define the two hypothetical constructs and to fulfil the role of observable measures called the manifest variables. They, too, can be divided into the endogenous variables denoted by y and into the exogenous variables denoted by x. In the first part of LISREL, that is the measurement model, it is traced then how well the selected manifest variables measure the latent constructs, both individually and in the group.

The Sample

Choice of the Sectors. From our sector study (cfr. 'An Empirical Indication for the Importance of Information'.), as well as from the literature (Holmes et al., 1991), it appears that not all sectors place an equal importance on information. So it can be expected that in those sectors where information is a very important condition for the strategic success of the firm, the manager will be more inclined to look for adequate information than in those sectors where the possession of these data will not have a similar affect on success. Thus, for the empirical analysis we want the industrial environment as homogeneous as possible and focus upon those sectors where the same information is important, and where the acquiring and processing of this information can contribute to success.

Using the results of our sector study, it concerns those sectors with the greatest spread of growth. As mentioned, this variability is positively related to the presence of various information-related strategic variables, so that the acquiring and processing of information can be considered to be more strategically important for these sectors than for others.

Given our definition of information use, it is also advisable to target industrial sectors with a high variability for growth, not only, but also higher expenses for R&D and a low degree of concentration. In total, the sectors NACE 25 (chemical industry), NACE 31 (production of metal products, excl. machines and means of transport) and NACE 34 (electrical industry) fulfil these three presumed conditions to a large measure. Therefore, firms from these three sectors are selected for further study.

Data Collection. In this section of the study, we concentrate ourselves only on SMEs, whereby a SME is defined as a firm with less than 100 employees, irrespective of the form of the submitted annual report.[7] The use of this maximum is to restrict the study to those firms where the determinant

---

[6] Indirectly, there is a certain amount of control whether or not it really was the president himself who filled in the sent questionnaire. Namely in the research, we also trace for some person- and firm-specific characteristics that have a certain influence on the use of information by the SME owner/manager (for more details concerning this part of the research, see Lybaert 1997a), and these data are necessarily answered by the president.

[7] In the sector studies of Section 1 and 2, the SMEs do not make up the sample, but rather firms that submitted an annual report according to the complete schedule (being the big firms according to some references). This criteria was necessary since the needed data are not given in the abbreviated schedule.

role of the owner/manager still exists. At the same time, a minimum of 20 employees is premised, because smaller firms are often in the start-up phase. By setting this minimum, the smallest firms that offer very personalised services are also excluded. Moreover, research shows that in SMEs with at least 20 employees, technical matters no longer take precedence over managerial matters (Donckels and Mok, 1990), which is to the benefit of this research.

In the three sectors just selected, there are 834 firms with such a staff size which have submitted an annual report in 1991. We reduce the size of this sample by restricting the study to the Dutch speaking presidents. Also, some individuals are the presidents of a number of firms, thus only one firm in the group is approached.

Firms that satisfy these two conditions were asked to fill in the questionnaire. Before sending it, the presidents were first contacted by telephone. The original reason was that the call made it possible to explain the aims of the study to increase the motivation to participate. It also gave us the opportunity for an initial response. Another advantage was that the call made it possible to contact the right person at the right address.

All together, we succeeded in contacting the presidents of 387 firms. Of these, 311 presidents were somewhat prepared to co-operate, i.e., 80%. They received the questionnaire from May to June 1993. After another call and/or sending out a reminder, the survey was finalised in December 1993. The total usable number of questionnaires was 208. This is an average of 67%, when only the number of sent out questionnaires is taken into account.

The Measurement Model

Measurement of the Hypothetical Concepts. As mentioned, a questionnaire is used to gather manifest variables. As to the measurement of information use, a generally accepted scale does not exist. Since the most comprehensive and theory-based method to measure 'environmental scanning' empirically is the typology of Hambrick (1979, 1981), we use it. We selected 20 questions concerning R&D and competition, which contained – according to our view – the most relevant kinds of internal and external information. We asked the respondents how frequently they learn of the stated events and trends (cfr. the 'frequency' method), and to rate the extent to which they make a point of staying abreast of these same domains (cfr. the 'interest' method).[8] For both, the Likert-scale is used.[9]

One might criticise that these questions look at the behaviour of the SME owner/manager in terms of 'scanning' information, but not so much his behaviour concerning the 'use' of information.[10] However, information gathering merely for the sake of collecting information is not

---

Though a closer look at this selected group shows that more than 60% of these firms consists of SMEs, when defined as 'firms that employ less than 100 persons'. So it seems justified to use the results of this sector study when we descend to the micro-level, especially since the exploration of the explaining factors is to justify for the big as well as for the small firms. More specifically, it is decided to lean on the results of the sectoral empirical test for the definition of information use and the selection of the most relevant sectors.

[8] Hambrick uses three methods. Thirdly, there is the 'hours' method, in which the owner/managers are asked what percent of their scanning time is directed at each of the environmental sectors and, in turn, how many total hours they spent scanning in an average week. Though Hambrick, as well as others (Fahr et al., 1984), point out that this third method has some limitations, and because the other two methods are valid and trustworthy, we restrict our study to this limited model.

[9] More specifically, Hambrick proposes seven answer alternatives for the first method, going from 1 = once a year or less to 7 = once a day or more. For the second method, there are five possibilities, going from 1 = I generally do not try to stay abreast of this type of information to 5 = I try to know all there is to know about this type of information.

[10] In the literature scanning is defined as 'the searching in the external environment for those events or elements that can be important for the firm' (Miliken, 1987).

in line with the limited time and means of the SME owner/manager. There must be made a workable tool of it for the operational conduct and for delineating the strategy. Since we target on SMEs with a maximum of 100 employees, it seems justified to make the assumption that the entrepreneur most probably will assimilate and use the information one way or another, once he makes the efforts and the costs to gather the data.

As to the measurement of success, there have been a lot of attempts to define and measure the effectiveness of firms.[11] Although there is no unanimous consent on how success should be measured best, it is clear that it would be wrong to base our work on only one kind of variable of success. Therefore, we chose ten firm measures, taking into account the popularity with researchers as well as with SME owner/managers, and taking care of the possibility for manipulation and existing ideas in financial literature. Because of the unfamiliarity of many SME owner/managers with the precise internal 'hard' figures, as well as the inclination for secrecy, we asked for relative measures which show an evolution over time, rather than for concrete data. In addition, we asked the participants of the study to gauge their expectations for the future concerning these same ten selected measures. Because of the high level of identification between the SME owner/manager and his firm, we also asked for subjective information using four measures. Though the importance of these 'soft' measures may not be overstated. If a SME does not make any profit, it will eventually go bankrupt, and all other reasons for having a firm will be sacrificed.

Choice of the Manifest Variables. In total the questionnaire included 64 questions for the measurement of information use and success.[12] The valid answers on these 64 questions that ultimately would be taken into account had to make it possible to measure and define the endogenous hypothetical constructs.[13] Though not all 64 answers were applied as manifest variables. In order to indicate those variables which would be used for the development of the endogenous latent variables, it was decided to apply an exploratory factor analysis, using the polychoric correlation matrix as input.[14]

Because of the two kinds of questions for each latent variable in the questionnaire (i.e., 'what really happens' versus 'what would ideally have to happen' and 'what has been' versus 'what is expected'), we expect that two factors will result, and not one factor will explain the most of the variance. Results show that our expectations are confirmed. So as to integrate both kinds of questions with the assimilation, we consider both factors in both cases. Thus, we have four latent variables instead of two. In order to limit the number of endogenous manifest variables, we take only those four variables per factor into account which show the highest loading after rotation.

Justification of the Manifest Variables. By rearranging the measurement model, it is possible to trace whether the chosen observed variables measure the latent constructs. For each latent variable, a separate data matrix is set up – making use of the listwise deletion of observations[15] – on which

---

[11]   An overview of these questions is given in Lybaert (1997b).

[12]   A good survey of many of these attempts is, for instance, in Lewin and Minton (1986).

[13]   To minimise mistakes due to interpretation, quotations are always made in the same direction. More specifically, a high score is given when the response points to a high frequency of and great interest in information gathering on the one hand, and to hard and soft proof of good performance on the other hand.

[14]   Since all questions are ordinal variables, the polychoric correlation matrix and not the raw data is used as input. Here, a contingency table is obtained for each two ordinal variables, from which the maximum likelihood estimate of the correlation is computed, whereby an underlying bivariate normal distribution is assumed. For the calculation of this polychoric correlation matrix we have used PRELIS, a 'preprocessor' of LISREL, and according to the manual, the only program available for calculating all possible correlations and other moments of ordinal variables.

[15]   With listwise deletion, all observations with missing values are deleted, such that the data matrix is effectively reduced to a matrix without missing values. This procedure is preferable to the pairwise deletion, though the difference is the (sometimes drastic) loss of observations. In this study, the

the measurement model can be performed. The results obtained this way show a very good fit of the models with the selected empirical indicators. Thus, the models cannot be rejected on basis of our data. However, with respect to the first latent variable for information use, it can be stated that, in spite of the significance of the individual parameters, the indices for the fit of the whole model are a little worse, but acceptable nonetheless. Since this is due mostly to the presence of the manifest variable with the highest loading, we opt for the replacement of this variable by the one with the fifth highest loading. Once this replacement was made, the results of the four measurement models[16] demonstrate very clearly that the selected manifest variables can be applied very well as measurement instruments for the various exogenous and endogenous latent variables.[17]

Now that the manifest variables are definitively selected, the latent variables can be specified. It is obvious that the names 'information use' and 'success' are too broad, and comprise much more than the chosen indicators. Thus, we must define more detailed names for the latent variables on basis of our choices. The names which we opt for are shown in Table 14.3. More specifically, we present in this table those variables which are chosen to fulfil the role of observable variables (x and y), as well as the obtained latent variables (ξ and η).

Table 14.3   The Chosen Manifest and Latent Variables

- Variables with respect to information use

To what degree do you keep up to date concerning:
    $x_1 =$ changes in needs and attitudes of customers concerning the products offered by your firm?
    $x_2 =$ the price level of products offered by your competitors?
    $x_3 =$ the possible consequences of the unified market for your firm?
    $x_4 =$ the knowledge and the capacities of the own personnel?

       $\xi_1 =$ use of information about market and personnel

To what degree would you like to remain up to date concerning:
    $x_5 =$ the price level of products offered by your competitors?
    $x_6 =$ the new products and product assortments offered by the competitors?
    $x_7 =$ the research activities of the other firms in your sector?
    $x_8 =$ the management practices of your competitors?

       $\xi_2 =$ desired use of external information about competitors

---

indication 'missing value' does not always refer to blank answers; it also refers to invalid (that is, when the respondent chose more than one answer when only one was possible) or inconsistent answers.

[16] We opt for the 'maximum likelihood' (ML) method to test the measurement and the latent variable models.

[17] It is also important to us – in addition to performing the measurement model on each latent variable separately – to introduce all selected manifest variables together in one measurement model. From these results, it appears that the observed indicators can be used without a problem as a measurement instrument for the various hypothetical constructs. More specifically, all elements of Λ_x and Λ_y are statistically significant at the 0.001 level.

- Variables with respect to success

What are your expectations for the coming years for:
$y_1 =$ reserves?
$y_2 =$ owners equity?
$y_3 =$ accumulated profits?
$y_4 =$ the bottom line of your business?

$\eta_1 =$ expected performance

What was the evolution of the last 3 financial years of:
$y_5 =$ reserves?
$y_6 =$ the bottom line of your business?
$y_7 =$ owners equity?
$y_8 =$ accumulated profits?

$\eta_2 =$ performance during the last 3 financial years

The Latent Variable Model

Since information use and success are both represented by two different latent variables, we come to four causal relations between both variables, or in other words, to four subhypotheses. All together, we can state a priori:

H2a: ξ_1 influences η_1 (+)
H2b: ξ_2 influences η_1 (+)
H2c: ξ_1 influences η_2 (+)
H2d: ξ_2 influences η_2 (+)

As mentioned, by rearranging the latent variable model, it is possible to determine whether the premised hypotheses must be rejected. For setting up the data matrix for this analysis, we use the listwise deletion of observations as well. As a result, the original sample size of 208 becomes 181 observations without missing values.

Of the obtained values (t-values are between brackets) given in Table 14.4, the use of information about market and personnel has a significant influence on both the expected performance and the performance during the last 3 financial years at the 0.05 level. In addition, both influences are positive, as hypothesised. Thus, according to these results, an efficient use of information is important for good measures of success.

Table 14.4   The Latent Variable Model

Γ	ξ_1	ξ_2
η_1	0.22	-0.30
	(2.17)	(-3.21)
η_2	0.22	0.02
	(2.16)	(0.23)

$p < 0.001$ $p < 0.05$

The desired use of external information about competitors also has a significant influence on the expected performance at the 0.001 level. Strikingly, this relationship is negative, highlighting that entrepreneurs who wish to use less (more) external information about their competitors also premise good (poor) performance. In our opinion, the logical explanation for this can be found by reversing the relation. More specifically, those SME owner/managers who have poorer (better) expectations for the future also wish to gather more (less) information about their competitors.

The results are not analogous for the desired use of external information about competitors on the performance during the last 3 financial years. This value indicates that this influence is not significant. Thus, of the four hypotheses, H2d is rejected.

Conclusions as Link to Practice

Our empirical results show that the more frequently entrepreneurs use information, the better results they made in the past years, and the more optimistic their view for the future. In this study, we demonstrate that there is a relation between success and the use of information concerning competitors and R&D activities, as shown by the importance of both variables to the selected research group. However, we are convinced that the findings are generalisable. We also find that entrepreneurs value the importance of information use for the obtainment of success. Specifically, we find that those SME owner/managers who are pessimistic about the future are also more interested in information. Thus, they want to arm themselves with information as weapon against bad future results.

This insight is important: SMEs must contend with the same problems and decisions as the big enterprises, but without the advantage of expert personnel and with fewer resources. Managers of big companies have competent co-workers who can search, analyse and handle relevant information. They influence the strategic decisions of the top managers with rational arguments. This influence, based on correct information, is decisive for the efficient organisation (Schilit and Paine, 1987). On the contrary, the process of 'scanning-interpretation-action-performance' (Thomas et al., 1993) in a SME is the work of the owner/manager, and possibly with the co-operation of an external consultant (rather than personnel).

Given the important role the SME sector plays in the economic and social life on the one hand and given the high failure rates on the other hand, it is obvious a number of measures should be implemented. Based on this study, one of the measures that should be taken is convincing the owner/managers of SMEs of the importance of information and to help them in their search for information and the development of sound information systems. Although it cannot be denied that certain entrepreneurs and enterprises will be more open to these measures, all SMEs should be selected as target group. Thus, a lot remains to be done, not only for the SME owner/managers, but also for a lot of organisations which work – directly or indirectly – with or for SMEs.

References

Applegate, L.M., Cash, J.I. and Mills, D.Q. (1988) *Information Technology and Tomorrow's Manager*, in: Harvard Business Review, November-December, 128-136.

Bagwell, K. (1990) *Informational Product Differentiation as a Barrier to Entry*, in: International Journal of Industrial Organization, No. 2, 207-223.

Bollen, K.A. (1989) *Structural Equations with Latent Variables*, John Wiley & Sons, New York.

Bragard, L. et al. (1992) *KMO en informatie. Strategische kennis verwerven en gebruiken*, Koning Boudewijnstichting, Brussel.

Cole, R.E. (1985) *Target Information for Competitive Performance*, in: Harvard Business Review, May-June, 100-109.

Covin, J.G. and Slevin, D.P. (1989) *Strategic Management of Small Firms in Hostile and Benign Environments*, in: Strategic Management Journal, January-February, 75-87.

Crijns, H., Ooghe, H. and Cosaert, M. (1994) *Transitions of Medium-Sized Family Companies. Cross-Roads in the Growth-Process of Medium-Sized Family Enterprises*, Paper Presented at the RENT VIII Workshop, Tampere, Finland, 24-25 November.

Donckels, R., Dupont, B. and Van Langenhove, S. (1987) *Succes in je eigen zaak*, Lannoo, Tielt.

Donckels, R. and Hoebeke, K. (1989) *Groeien of niet groeien? De hamvraag voor elke familiale onderneming*, Koning Boudewijnstichting, Brussel.

Donckels, R. and Mok, A.L. (1990) *Innovative Entrepreneurship: The Case of Belgium*, in: Donckels, R. & Miettinen, A. (eds.): New Findings and Perspectives in Entrepreneurship, Avebury, Aldershot, 256-285.

Farh, J.L., Hoffman, R.C. and Hegarty, W.H. (1984) *Assessing Environmental Scanning at the Subunit Level: A Multitrait-Multimethod Analysis*, in: Decision Sciences, No. 2, 197-220.

Fudenberg, D. and Tirole, J. (1986) *A Signal Jamming Theory of Predation*, in: Rand Journal of Economics, No. 3, 366-376.

Garvin, A.P. and Bermont, H. (1985) *How to Win with Information or Lose without It*, Bermont Books, Sarasota.

Gibrat, R. (1931) *Les Inégalités Economiques*, Recueil Sirey, Paris.

Hambrick, D.C. (1979) *Environmental Scanning, Organizational Strategy, and Executives' Roles: A Study in Three Industries*, Unpublished Ph.D.Dissertation, Pennsylvania State University.

Hambrick, D.C. (1981) *Environment, Strategy, and Power within Top Management Teams*, in: Administrative Science Quarterly, June, 253-276.

Hansen, G.S. and Wernerfelt, B. (1989) *Determinants of Firm Performance: The Relative Importance of Economic and Organizational Factors*, in: Strategic Management Journal, September-October, 399-411.

Hay, D.A. and Morris, D.J. (1991) *Industrial Economics and Organization. Theory and Evidence*, Oxford University Press, New York.

Holmes, S. and Nicholls, D. (1989) *Modelling the Accounting Information Requirements of Small Businesses*, in: Accounting and Business Research, Spring, 143-150.

Holmes, S., Kelly, G. and Cunningham, R. (1991) *The Small Firm Information Cycle: A Reappraisal*, in: International Small Business Journal, No. 1, 41-53.

Hopper, M.D. (1990) *Rattling SABRE - New Ways to Compete on Information*, in: Harvard Business Review, May-June, 118-125.

Ledin, H. (1987) *The Future Organization. A Dynamic Intelligent Network*, Paper Presented to Seminar on Management of the MNC at EIASM, 9 June.

Lewin, A.Y. and Minton, J.W. (1986) *Determining Organizational Effectiveness: Another Look, and an Agenda for Research*, in: Management Science, May, 514-538.

Lybaert, N. (1995) *Informatie als determinant voor lange termijn succes in industriële KMO's*, Doctoral Dissertation, Katholieke Universiteit Brussel.

Lybaert, N. (1997a) *Information Use in a SME: Its Importance and Some Elements of Influence*, Small Business Economics, forthcoming.

Lybaert, N. (1997b) *Information as a Determinant of Success in Industrial SMEs*, Entrepreneurship and Regional Development, forthcoming.

Lynn, L. (1982) *How Japan Innovates: A Comparison with the United States in the Case of Oxygen Steelmaking*, Westview Press, Boulder, Colombia.

Miliken, F.J.(1987) *Three Types of Perceived Uncertainty about the Environment: State, Effect and Response Uncertainty*, in: Academy of Management Journal, No. 1, 133-143.

Porter, M.E. and Millar, V.E. (1985) *How Information Gives You Competitive Advantage*, in: Harvard Business Review, July-August, 149-160.

Punset, P. and Sweeney, G. (1989) *Information Resources and Corporate Growth*, Pinter Publishers, New York.

Robinson, R.B. (1983) *Measures of Small Firm Effectiveness for Strategic Planning Research*, in: Journal of Small Business Management, April, 22-29.

Scherer, F.M. (1980) *Industrial Market Structure and Economic Performance*, Houghton Mifflin Company, Boston.

Smiley, R. (1988) *Empirical Evidence on Strategic Entry Deterrence*, in: International Journal of Industrial Organization, Nber 2, 167-180.

Strassman, P. (1985) *Information Payoff: The Transformation of Work in an Electronic Age*, Free Press, New York.

Thomas, J.B., Clark, S.M. and Gioia, D.A. (1993) *Strategic Sensemaking and Organizational Performance: Linkages among Scanning, Interpretation, and Outcomes*, in: Academy of Management Journal, Nber 2, 239-270.

VBO (1990) *Kmo's en communicatie*, in: VBO-Mededelingen, 1-14 January, 42-43.

Vives, X. (1990) *Information and Competitive Advantage*, in: International Journal of Industrial Organization, No. 1, 17-35.

Wagner, J. (1992) *Firm Size, Firm Growth, and Persistence of Chance: Testing GIBRAT's Law with Establishment Data from Lower Saxony, 1978-1989*, in: Small Business Economics, No. 4, 125-131.

For Product Safety Concerns and Information please contact our EU
representative GPSR@taylorandfrancis.com Taylor & Francis Verlag GmbH,
Kaufingerstraße 24, 80331 München, Germany

Printed and bound by CPI Group (UK) Ltd, Croydon, CR0 4YY
08/05/2025
01864362-0005